STUDIES IN CHRISTIAN HISTORY AND THOUGHT

The Flesh and the Feminine

Gender and Theology in the Writings of Caspar Schwenckfeld

STUDIES IN CHRISTIAN HISTORY AND THOUGHT

STUDIES IN CHRISTIAN HISTORY AND THOUGHT

The Flesh and the Feminine

Gender and Theology in the Writings of Caspar Schwenckfeld

Ruth Gouldbourne

Foreword by Peter Erb

PUBLISHERS

Eugene, Oregon

Wipf and Stock Publishers
199 W 8th Ave, Suite 3
Eugene, OR 97401

The Flesh and the Feminine
Gender and Theology in the Writings of Caspar Schwenckfeld
By Gouldbourne, Ruth
Copyright©2006 by Paternoster
ISBN 13: 978-1-55635-128-0
ISBN 10: 1-55635-128-3
Publication date 12/8/2006
Previously published by Paternoster, 2006

This Edition Published by Wipf and Stock Publishers
by arrangement with Paternoster.

Paternoster
9 Holdom Avenue
Bletchley
Milton Keyes, MK1 1QR
PATERNOSTER Great Britain

Series Preface

This series complements the specialist series of *Studies in Evangelical History and Thought* and *Studies in Baptist History and Thought* for which Paternoster is becoming increasingly well known by offering works that cover the wider field of Christian history and thought. It encompasses accounts of Christian witness at various periods, studies of individual Christians and movements, and works which concern the relations of church and society through history, and the history of Christian thought.

The series includes monographs, revised dissertations and theses, and collections of papers by individuals and groups. As well as 'free standing' volumes, works on particular running themes are being commissioned; authors will be engaged for these from around the world and from a variety of Christian traditions.

A high academic standard combined with lively writing will commend the volumes in this series both to scholars and to a wider readership.

For my Father and in memory of my Mother

Contents

Foreword

Although Caspar Schwenckfeld von Ossig is not central figure in Christian history generally nor in the religious upheavals of sixteenth-century Germany specifically, his thought stimulated a number of differing interpretations during his life-time and continued to do so among his immediate followers, those attracted primarily by his published work, and a few later students of Reformation history and theology. Nevertheless, he never gained a large following and he remains relatively ignored in spite of the bulk of his writing. Indeed, he might have been even more widely disregarded had it not been for the committment of a very few Schwenkfelders in the late nineteenth century who set out to establish their founders on the same basis as members of other more dominant religious traditions were doing for their sixteenth-century progenitors.

On September 24, 1884, Chester D. Hartranft, DD, Professor of Biblical and Ecclesiastical History in the Theological Seminary at Hartford, Connecticut and a direct descendant of earlier Schwenkfelders in America suggested to his fellow-believers (then numbering perhaps only 600 families and all resident in south-eastern Pennsylvania) that they initiate a complete critical edition of the works of Schwenckfeld and his sixteenth-century associates on the model of the Kritische Gesammtausgabe of Luther's *Werke*, begun only a year earlier through the Weimar publisher, Hermann Boehlau. It was Hartranft's hope, along with a small coterie of his Schwenkfelder colleagues that by doing so they could mark their own tradition along side those of others who were then continuing the earlier Reformation debates by intensifying the biblical and patristic *ad fontes* directives of that era with an equal emphasis on the great theologians of the sixteenth century. The *Corpus Schwenckfeldianorum* would stand with the Luther Weimar edition, it was hoped, alongside the Reformed *Corpus Reformatorum* of Melancthon (1834-) and of Calvin (1863), the Anglican Parker Society editions (1840-) and *The Library of Anglo-Catholic Theology* (1843-), and the Catholic *Patrologia Cursus Completus*. (*Latine* from 1844 and *Graeca* from 1857).

What distinguished the Schwenkfelder apologetic concern in this respect from the other larger communities however, was their peculiar setting. Somewhat like, but to a greater degree than, the Mennonites and other German-American sectarian Christians, the Schwenkfelders were faced with an increasing anglicisation of their tradition and mounting pressure to assimilate with the culture at large. They had recently lost a significant number of their adherents to Evangelical churches and chaffed under the continuing designation of their tradition as "sectarian" and themselves as "Schwärmer." At the same time their distinctive theological characteristics were fading: there were

movements underway among them to return to the practice of the Lord's
Supper (an ordinance they had abandoned for ecumenical purposes in 1526)
and to designate themselves as "church" against their founder's explicit refusal
to allow this. Moreover, Schwenckfeld's distinctive doctrine of the celestial
flesh of Christ as food on which the believer feeds spiritually appeared not only
eccentric, but opposed to Protestant emphases on forensic justification and
salvation by faith alone (*sola fide*), when it was as Protestants that
Schwenkfelders had most often identified themselves.

However little the projected critical edition met their direct needs, they
remained firm, gathering the precious books and manuscripts in their private
possession into what would become the Schwenkfelder Library and Heritage
Center in Pennsburg, Pa., and raising the monies for further extensive book
purchases and the support of up to fourteen research assistants centered in the
Herzog August Bibliothek at Wolfenbüttel who were copying all
Schwenkfelder-related manuscripts they could find from Amsterdam to
Liegnitz – all without seeing a single volume, the first finally appearing in
1907. As disappointing as that first volume was (it contained only seven short
documents, two of which remained extant only as titles, in 661 pedantic folio
pages), the Schwenkfelders nevertheless, although in ever decreasing numbers,
continued to support the project which was completed a half century later.

That the *Corpus Schwenckfeldianorum: Letters and Treatises of Caspar
Schwenckfeld von Ossig*[1] edition continued and saw the printing of the final
nineteenth volume in 1961 is in large part because of the committment of one
person, Selina Gerhard Schultz (1880-1969). Like Schwenckfeld's many
sixteenth-century women adherents, Schultz was early devoted to his thought
and travelled to Wolfenbüttel in the early twentieth century to help with the
final work on the first volume. Along with her sister and brother-in-law, Elmer
E. S. Johnson, she remained there until after the First World War, taking on
ever-increasing responsibilities for the next volumes and doing the bulk of the
managing editor's work. The editing of the last four volumes, including the
detailed transcription of Schwenckfeld's biblical annotations fell to her alone.
In recognition of her work on the project as a whole she was awarded an
honorary doctorate from the University of Tübingen in 1962. Regretfully, no
full biography of her career has yet appeared.[2]

---

[1] *Corpus Schwenckfeldianorum, Letters and Treatises of Caspar Schwenckfeld von
Ossig.* Ed. by Chester D. Hartranft, Elmer Ellsworth Schultz Johnson, Selina Gerhard
Schultz, et. al. (19 vols.; Leipzig : Breitkopf & Härtel, 1907-1961).

[2] For a fuller, but brief, overview of her work see my "Introduction" to the fourth
editon of her biography, *Caspar Schwenckfeld von Ossig (1489-1561): Spiritual
Interpreter of Christianity, Apostle of the Middle Way, Pioneer in Modern Religious
Thought.* (Pennsburg, Pa., 1977) and note as well her *A Course of Study in the Life and
Teachings of Caspar Schwenckfeld von Ossig (1489-1561) and the History of the
Schwenkfelder Religious Movement (1518-1964)* (Pennsburg, Pa., 1964).

As Schultz was completing the *Corpus* in the post-Second World War period, academic attention was increasingly directed to other Reformation figures, loosely linked with Schwenckfeld and his colleagues as representing "the Left Wing of the Reformation." In 1943 Harold S. Bender read his "The Anabaptist Vision" as his presidential address to the American Society of Church History, re-igniting interest in the roots of the Mennonite tradition and by 1959 the four-volume *Mennonite Encyclopaedia* was completed, offering new directives into what the Harvard historian, George H. Williams, would designate as "The Radical Reformation" in his 1962 publication under that title.[3] Throughout the 1960s and 70s Williams' study stimulated a number of studies in the area. Those concerned with Schwenckfeld were made easier with the ready accessibility of Schultz's *Corpus* work and had as a result begun to appear some time earlier. Thus in 1956 Gottfried Maron completed his thesis on individualism and community in the work of Schwenckfeld,[4] and in the same year Reinhold Pietz completed his on Schwenckfeld's anthropology.[5]

Schultz herself tended to downplay the central theme in Schwenckfeld's mature theology, his christological concern with the celestial flesh of Christ. This topic had been earlier noted in the work of Hans Joachim Schoeps[6] and Emmanuel Hirsch[7] and at the end of the 1950s was given added emphasis among anglophone readers with the publication of a monograph by Paul L. Maier, *Caspar Schwenckfeld on the Persona nd Work of Christ: A Study of Schwenckfeldian Theology at its Core* (Assen, 1959). Schwenckfeld's Christological centre was further explored in Horst Weigelt's groundbreaking 1973 study of Schwenckfeld and the Schwenkfelder movement as it developed in Silesia (in which christological interests shifted to soteriological ones),[8] but served a limited function in R. Emmet McLaughlin's 1986 intellectual biography of the early Schwenkfeld, closing off as the study did in 1540, before the issue was fully developed by the Reformer.[9]

Not unexpectedly, most of this scholarship considered Schwenckfeld's work primarily in relation to that of his Reformation contemporaries,[10] linking his

---

[3] George Huntston Williams, *The Radical Reformation* (Philadelphia: Westminster Press, 1962).

[4] *Individualismus und Gemeinschaft bei Caspar v. Schwenckfeld. Seine Theologie, dargestellt mit besonderer Ausrichtung auf seinen Kirchenbegriff.* (Unpubl. diss., Göttingen, 1956). (published Stuttgart, 1961).

[5] *Der Mesnsch one Christus. Eine Untersuchung zur Anthropologie Caspar Schwenckfelds* (unpubl. diss, Tübingen, 1956).

[6] *Vom himmlischen Fleisch Christi* (Tübingen, 1951).

[7] "Schwenckfeld und Luther," *Lutherstudien* (Gütersloh, 1954).

[8] *Spiritualistische Tradition im Protestantismus: die Geschichte des Schwenckfeldertums in Schlesien.* (Berlin, 1973); translated as *The Schwenkfelders in Silesia* by Peter C. Erb (Pennsburg, 1985).

[9] *Caspar Schwenckfeld: Reluctant Radical: His Life to 1540* (New Haven , 1986).

[10] On the contrary see the emphasis on Schwenckfeld as an Erasmian humanist in

less-Protestant teaching (his christology and his emphasis on growth in holiness, for example) with his patristic reading , downplaying his distinctive sacramental, Marian, and inclusive body rhetoric and their concomitant gender implications, and, while noting the large number of his women adherents, setting the fact to one side and focussing rather on his nobility and his broader impact among the upper and intellectual classes. Nor was his nor the non-married state of many of his closest associates noted as significant. But to miss this (or to set it to one side), the present study points out, is to miss a great deal. In its feminist turn (not all of which some contemporary feminists will find comfortable) Ruth Gouldbourne's study offers another perspective on Schwenckfeld's thought, but the implications of her work are not limited to this alone. Not only do her reflections bind Schwenckfeld more closely to the medieval world that shaped him and help to explain the attraction of his writing for women specifically, but they require additional and different thinking with respect to his "spiritualist" language, particularly as it relates to the Eucharist, and they offer further directions in understanding aspects of his ecumenical ecclesiology, both medieval and modern, neither fully Protestant nor entirely Catholic – how he could find "refuge" in Protestant Strassburg early in his career and among the Franciscans at Esslingen and the Benedictines at Kempten later in his life.

Gouldbourne's study has implications beyond the study of Schwenkfeld alone. Students of the movement as a whole will very quickly apply the insights in this work to their reading of the work of Schwenckfeld's colleague and amanuensis, Adam Reissner (ca. 1496-1582) and his lengthy ruminations on the New Jerusalem.[11] Her method can be applied as well to the work of the Schwenkfelder emblem engraver and poet, Daniel Sudermann,[12] as well as his admirer, the American Fraktur artist, Suzanna Heebner,[13] and a number of the

---

Andre Seguenny, *Homme charnel, Homme spirituel. Etude sur la christologie de Caspar Schwenckfeld (1489-1561)* (Wiesbaden, 1975); translated as *The Christology of Caspar Schwenckfeld: Spirit and Flesh in the Process of Life Transformation* by Peter C. Erb and Simone Nieuwoldt (Lewiston, 1987).

[11] Adam Reissner, *Jerusalem vetustissima illa et celeberrima totius mundi civitas ex sacris literis et adprobatis historicis ad unguem descripta. Una cum orthodoxis figurae ac veritatis explicationibus ... ac quaenam hujus urbis ... mystica sit repraesentatio ... Quae A. Reissner Germanica lingua delineata edidit, nunc autem Latine omnia perscripta ... et in septem libros digesta sunt per J. Heydenum.* (Frankfurt, 1563) and the German edition: *Jerusalem, die alte Haubtstat der Jüden ... mit kurtzer Historia und Erklärung, was Gott von Anfang an disem ort gehandelt,...* (Franckfurt am Mayn, 1563).

[12] For details on his life and work see Monica Pieper, *Daniel Sudermann (1550-ca. 1631) als Vertreter des mystischen Spiritualismus* (Stuttgart, 1985). Among other works see his *Schöne ausserlesene Figuren und hohe Lehren von der begnadeten liebhabenden Seele, nemlich der Christlichen Kirchen und ihre Gemahl Jesu Christo ... in Teutsche Reymen verfaszt ... Durch D.S* (Strassburg,1620).

[13] For details of her life and work see relevant sections in Dennis K. Moyer, *Fraktur*

early Schwenkfelder immigrants to America who blended Schwenckfeld with the Boehmist tradition. It is important as well for what it betokens for interpreting those mystical spiritualists and pietists (particularly radical pietists) of the late seventeenth and eighteenth centuries who took special interest in his work and whose reification of theological concepts such as the Church as the Bride of Christ and use of medieval *Brautmystik* language, for example, take on new significance if read within the context Gouldbourne has delineated,[14] a context that affords readers of contemporary thought the opportunity to reconsider the positive implications of these earlier, limited and at times heretical, attempts to develop a Marian, nuptial theology of the Christian life within the constraints of their day.[15]

Peter C. Erb
Associate Director, Schwenkfelder Library,
Pennsburg, PA,
USA

Writings and Folk Art Drawings of the Schwenkfelder Library Collection (Kutztown,, Pa., 1998) and my unpublished The Garden in Schwenkfelder Fraktur: Marian Memories and Protestant Realities American Folk Art Museum, New York City, March 14, 2003.

[14] Of special interest is the thought of Johann Wilhelm and Johanna Elenora Petersen and the nuptial theories of Nicholas Ludwig, Count von Zinzendorf on whom see Carter Lindberg (ed.), *The Pietist Theologians* (Oxford, 2005) and texts in my *Pietists* (New York, 1983). For a full discussion of such figures see and in particular the sections by Martin Brecht, *Geschichte des Pietismus* (2 vols.; Göttingen 1993, 1995) and in particular the sections by Hans Schneider, "Der radikale Pietismus im 17. Jahrhundert, " 1:391-437, and "Der radikale Pietismus im 18. Jahrhundert," 2: 107-97. For a treatment of *Brautmystik* among some of these individual see my *Pietists, Protestants, and mysticism : the use of late Medieval spiritual texts in the work of Gottfried Arnold (1666-1714)* (Metuchen, N.J.,1989).

[15] For a recent theological system in which some of themes noted by Gouldbourne find a central place note in particular the work of Hans Urs von Balthasar as introduced in *The Cambridge Companion to Hans Urs von Balthasar* edited by Edward T. Oakes and David Moss, (Cambridge, 2004) and Edward T. Oakes, *Pattern of Redemption: The Theology of Hans Urs von Balthasar* (New York, 1994).

Acknowledgements

This is a lightly revised version of my PhD thesis, and in publishing it, I would like to reiterate the thanks I offered in the original – to my supervisor, Lyndal Roper, for suggesting the subject in the first place, and working out how to teach me to do history, and for her continuing encouragement when her formal responsibilities had ended, to the Schwenckfelder community in Pennsylvania for encouragement and books, to Peter Erb for endless patience and critical help, and for going the extra mile in writing the foreword, to Institut für Culturgeschichte in Augsburg for giving me a grant to spend some time at the Augsburg Archives, and to the congregation at Bunyan Meeting Free Church in Bedford, and the College Community at Bristol Baptist College, two communities who lived with me while I was writing the thesis and then editing the book.

I want to thank all those who encouraged me to offer this for publication, and who lived with me through all the doubts of the process, especially Anthony R. Cross, whose prompting has always been of the gentlest kind, and who has gone above and beyond the call of duty in helping with the preparation and technical know-how, and Jeremy Muddit who has been endlessly patient as I worked to prepare this.

Finally, I want to thank friends who believed when I didn't and don't let me off, my father for his encouragement, to acknowledge the memory of my mother, who would, I think, have been pleased with me, and above all Ian, without whom....

Chapter 1

Caspar Schwenckfeld: Community and Questions

Introduction

Caspar Schwenckfeld von Ossig, nobleman of Silesia, courtier to the Duke of Münsterberg-Oels, reformer and influential theologian, has also been recognised by historians of the Reformation as a man whose theology – indeed whose personality – was particularly attractive to women. However, until now, the reasons why women responded to him and to his teaching have never been adequately investigated. The context of his period, and indeed of the late twentieth century, requires that such a careful and detailed examination of his appeal to women and their response to him should be undertaken. It is the intention of this thesis to do so.

To ignore the women, or rather, to fail to investigate the reasons for their response is to lose sight of an important way of understanding the theology and practice of this man who, although largely forgotten now, was recognised as playing a significant role in the Reformation of the sixteenth century.

In the broad schematisation of reformers and theological thinkers in the sixteenth century in Europe, Schwenckfeld is associated with Luther and with what G. H. Williams has called *the Radical Reformation*.[1] Although he was at times a preacher, and although pastoral involvement on a personal level was clearly very important to him, his main ministry was in writing. He wrote pamphlets, short books, papers, and above all letters, and all that can be recovered have been gathered into a nineteen-volume collection, *Corpus Schwenckfeldianorum*,[2] which will form the primary source material for this thesis. The *Corpus* was published as a project to mark the beginning of the twentieth century by members of the Schwenkfelder (sic) church in the USA, a community which has descended from one part of the life work of Caspar

---

[1] G.H. Williams, *The Radical Reformation*, 3rd Edition, Kirksville, Mo.; Sixteenth Century Journal Publishers, 1992. Schwenckfeld is one of the people whom Williams examines in this work, and he identifies him as a significant player in the radical movement.

[2] *Corpus Schwenckfeldianorum*, eds. Chester David Hartranft, Otto Berhardt Schlutter, Elmer Ellsworth Schultz Johnson, Selina Gerhardt Schulz, 19 vols, Pennsburg, Penn; The Board of Publication of the Schwenkfelder Church, 1907-1961. Hereafter *CS*.

Schwenckfeld, and which moved to the USA between 1725 and 1736 in search of religious freedom. In this move, of a community shaped by a distinctive theology, we have confirmed the image of Schwenckfeld as a man with a theology which was not entirely acceptable to nor comfortable with the mainstream theology either of his own period or that of later generations. Schwenckfeld came under pressure from those around him because he did not conform to the theological norms of the magisterial Reformation. His contemporary followers and those who maintained his memory and his teaching were in their own times to face similar disapproval.

The *Corpus Schwenckfeldianorum* is made up of several types of writing: the published works, sermons and the letters. The published works themselves fall into several categories, both pamphlets and more extended works. Indeed, to refer to them all as *published* is slightly misleading, since there are some which were not written originally for publication, but for private circulation among friends and sympathisers. It was, in fact, the publication, without his knowledge, of two such writings which led to his choice of exile in 1529. During the 1530s, he did publish quite a lot, but it was mainly non-polemical and devotional. For example, in 1523 he wrote a letter, which was circulated, to a friend "labouring under spiritual grief", in which he explored ways in which faith could be nurtured and strengthened.[3] In 1538, he published "Christian Solace for the Sick and Afflicted",[4] in which he was concerned to encourage a friend who was very unwell and in which he spoke about illness as suffering in the "vale of tears", and the value of faith as comfort and assurance. In 1533, he published *Christian Warfare and the Knighthood of God*, a discussion of the struggle of the Christian life, and the methods by which it should be lived.[5] His writings in this early period, at least those which were published at this time, were largely devotional, consolatory or encouraging.

In the 1540s and 1550s he began to publish some of the works which he had previously only circulated privately, which put forward more of his distinctive theology, and in which he was more concerned to argue and rebuke. He wrote about most parts of Christian doctrine, but in particular, about the nature of Christ and the meaning of the Eucharist. Most of these writings arose from a situation of having to defend himself from charges of heresy, or attempts to explain his position. Thus, in 1542, he published *Confession*, an attempt at a complete exploration and explanation of his beliefs about Christology, and most particularly about the divine glory of Christ.[6] The ideas contained within it can be seen in much earlier works, but in this long publication he brought them together in something like a systematic form, and he published it, with the intention of vindicating his position, after he came under attack from the clergy

---

[3] *CS*, vol. 1, pp. 49ff.
[4] *CS*, vol. 6, pp. 324-345.
[5] *CS*, vol. 4, pp. 658ff.
[6] *CS*, vol. 7, pp.451-884.

in Ulm. In 1551, he published *A Brief Confession of Christ the Son of God and the Sacraments.*[7] Again this was written in defence, explaining his position, after he had been accused of denying the humanity of Christ and rejecting the sacraments. In the same month, he published *The Self-evident Testimony respecting the Divinity of Christ's Humanity in Glory, as shown by the New Testament.*[8] This again, was an attempt to explain and justify his position as a result of controversy.

He did not cease producing devotional and exhortatory material during this period, but we can assume that it would have been read in a different way by those who were now able to have access to some of his more controversial theological thinking through these polemical writings.

McLaughlin points out another difference that occurred in the way these writings were received in this second period:

> As a result [of this different kind of publication] isolated individual Schwenkfelders crop up more and more in the visitation records. Schwenckfeld books replace Schwenkfelders as the source of contagion. And in fact one starts to find the adjective "Schwenckfeldisch" more than the noun "Schwenkfelder". By the second half of the sixteenth century, Schwenckfeldianism had become a recognised body of beliefs no longer necessarily associated with membership in a body of fellow believers.[9]

While the final statement of this would take us beyond the bounds of this thesis, it is useful to note that, through his published writings, and particularly those on the nature of Christ and on the Sacraments, Schwenckfeld was able to present his ideas in such a way that people could grasp the whole theology, without personal contact or teaching.

The most common classification of Schwenckfeld is that he was a Spiritualist, one who valued spirit over letter, and argued for the primacy of immediate experience rather than propositional assent.[10] And as far as it goes, this is a fair assessment. However, as becomes clear when his writings are examined, Schwenckfeld was not content simply to describe his experiences and leave people to make of them what they would. His writings were concerned to make his positions clear, to defend himself against the charges and attacks which did come his way, and to instruct, persuade and convince any who were willing to give his ideas a fair hearing. He was dismissed, during his

---

[7] *CS*, vol. 12, pp. 558-569.

[8] *CS*, vol. 12, pp. 570-578.

[9] R. Emmet McLaughlin, "Schwenckfeld and the Schwenkfelders of South Germany," *Schwenckfeld and Early Schwenckfeldianism: Papers Presented at the Colloquium on Schwenckfeld and the Schwenkfelders*, Ed. Peter C. Erb, Pennsburg, Penn; Schwenkfelder Library, 1986, pp. 145-180, p. 164.

[10] See for example, Williams, *The Radical Reformation*, p. 210; Euan Cameron, *The European Reformation*, Oxford; Clarendon, 1991, p. 324.

lifetime, by those who were recognised leaders of reform and whose theologies have continued to be considered as important and formative, as well as by more contemporary writers. His influence nevertheless can be traced in both in such significant movements as seventeenth-century pietism, with its subsequent influence on the evangelicalism of the eighteenth and nineteenth centuries, and also in the powerful movement which started around George Fox, and became the Quakers. In all of these movements too, it is apparent that women played significant roles, sometimes unexpectedly. In investigating the reasons why Schwenckfeld attracted women in such numbers, some further insight into these later questions might also be gained.

Such a legacy gives another insight into the theological positions which Schwenckfeld adopted: an emphasis on inner conviction, and outer quietism. He added to this some very distinctive theological convictions, particularly Christological, which, as I have suggested above, provoked others into attacking his orthodoxy. It is these convictions which have provoked most interest among current writers in considering Schwenckfeld's theology and place among the reformers. His writing about the centre of his theology was at times tortured and difficult to pin down; it is not always clear what he meant, and even if he himself knew what he meant! Various ways have been tried to explain his thinking, but nobody as yet has exploited the vital clue which I believe is offered by the number of women who responded to this theology. If women were finding something significant in this thinking, would an analysis using concepts of gender provide a key to the difficult concepts which the writings of Schwenckfeld present?

There is no doubt that this theology is difficult, and at times seems incoherent. However, people, especially women, did respond to it. This writing is an attempt to bring together concepts of gender and the theology of Caspar Schwenckfeld to explore whether they illuminate each other. This is not an exhaustive social history of the Schwenkfelder movement, nor even of the women involved in it. Rather, the emphasis will be on the ideas and the ways in which they took shape in the lives and contexts of those who adopted them.

Caspar Schwenckfeld von Ossig and his Community

Caspar Schwenckfeld von Ossig was born in 1489, in Silesia. He was born into a family of minor nobility, and was educated in the normal way from such a background. Although he matriculated at the University of Frankfurt-an-der-Oder, he does not appear to have taken a degree, which was not unusual at the time, particularly for people of Schwenckfeld's social class and intended occupation.[11] He remarked in his own writings that he attended the University

---

[11] Selina Gerhardt Schulz, *Caspar Schwenckfeld von Ossig,(1489-1561), Spiritual Interpreter of Christianity, Apostle of the Middle Way, Pioneer of Modern Religious*

of Cologne and several other universities, but again, there is no record of a degree, or even any other matriculation.[12] This would have been a normal type of education for somebody of his class; attending lectures to gain knowledge, mixing with students to gain contacts, and developing skills which would serve him in later life as a courtier, which was, in fact, what he became. But his education was also to have a significant effect theologically. He was not, like many of those who were active in reform, trained in theology or philosophy. His training was primarily pragmatic and diplomatic. What mattered was achieving the desired end. This became an central aspect of his theological thinking, and one whose importance should not be underestimated.

His first position was at the court of Münsterberg-Oels, serving Duke Carl I.[13] From there he seems to have gone to Brieg, to the court of Georg II, and then in about 1518, he went to Liegnitz to be a courtier of Duke Friedrich II.[14] From 1523 he more or less retired from court life because of increasing deafness, although he continued to undertake certain duties until he went into exile in 1529.[15]

In 1518 or so, it appears that he had a religious experience, and he recorded that from 1521 he lived in the light of that experience.[16] This encounter with God and the consequences which it had in his life and thinking became the central feature of his identity, and the driving force of his activity. Following his retirement, in accordance with the Lutheran theology which he adopted at this time, he instituted reform in his estate in Ossig. There he developed around himself and several other leaders a significant reformed community. However, by 1529, following a disagreement and a parting of the ways between him and Luther, reform in Silesia was coming under intense political pressure. The excuse for this pressure was the publication, without his consent, of two of Schwenckfeld's writings in which he outlined the theological position which had separated him from the Lutheran Reformation. In order to protect reform in his homeland, and to prevent the pressure from becoming unbearable, in 1529, Schwenckfeld left Silesia and went, firstly to Strassburg.

Although he intended to return home in due course, in fact he was never to do so, and for the rest of his life, he lived in and travelled around southern Germany. He never owned a home of his own again, nor did he ever become fully integrated into the urban communities in which he spent much of the rest of these thirty-two years. He did spend some extended periods of time in certain communities, and clearly developed a regular and established position

---

Thought. Pennsburg, Penn; The Board of Publication of the Schwenkfelder Church, 1977, p. 4.

[12] *CS*, vol. 4, p.489, ll. 22f, vol. 14, p. 876, ll. 21f.

[13] *CS*, vol. 14, p. 47, ll. 28f.

[14] *CS*, vol. 6, pp. 489-90.

[15] *CS*, vol. 6, p. 490, ll. 5f.

[16] *CS*, vol. 5, p. 535, ll. 13f.

within several cities. However, there were also times when he was under some pressure, and felt it necessary to leave a city for a while. These situations arose at the points when his theology and its attractions became too threatening for the communities in which he was currently operating. The areas in which he was considered to be a threat were particularly his rejection of parish and liturgical structures and his theology of the nature of Christ, and the expression of that nature in Christ's physical and continued being. Early in his career, he stopped receiving the elements of bread and wine at communion, a position he adopted on theological grounds and which he referred to as the *Stillstand.* He withdrew from parish worship and suggested to those who followed him that their attendance at the parish church was permissible in the light of his teaching, but unnecessary. Those in authority, both political and ecclesiastical, found him threatening and dangerous, and there were times when he was in hiding, for fear of his life.

Despite this, he lived to be seventy-two years old, and he died in December 1561, in Ulm at the home of the Streichers, a family to whom he was particularly close. The records of his last days are given in the fourteenth volume of the *Corpus Schwenckfeldianorum,* documents 171 and 172. This story, quite apart from all the rest that we read in his writings and find in the comments of others, makes very clear the important place that women played in his life and in the movement which developed around him. The physician to whom he turned for care in his final illness wrote the original of these accounts. The home in which he died, and in the cellar of which he is reputed to have been buried, belonged to the same family, a family who had been at the centre of the circle of his followers in Ulm.[17] Both the physician and the family as a whole were women. Agathe Streicher was known as a physician in Ulm, and during his final illness, Schwenckfeld told those around his bed that he had come to her for care, knowing himself to be so ill. The family, Helena Streicher, a widow, and her three daughters, were close friends of Schwenckfeld. He stayed in their home when he was in Ulm, and their address was known to be the one where he could be contacted when he was travelling, during the time of his exile.

When in exile, amongst the friends whom he made, groups developed who accepted his teaching and identified with his theology. This movement differed from that in Silesia in that it was not centred in parish churches, and indeed, was often at odds with the parochial clergy. However, it was among this network of families and friends, for whom he wrote some of the pamphlets and booklets, and to whom he wrote most of the letters which have been collected,

---

[17] It is not certain that Schwenckfeld was buried in the Streichers' cellar, but this is certainly the story which was propagated. The reason given was to prevent his body being exhumed and destroyed for heresy. It is also possible that there was a question over his "eligibility" to be buried in church ground. The account of the funeral of Elizabeth Hecklin (see below) gives some credibility to this.

that the distinctive elements of the theology which so worried a number of his contemporaries were worked out in greatest detail. Therefore, it is on the material produced during this period, on the whole, that this discussion will concentrate. From what has been said above, it will therefore be clear that I will be drawing both on devotional and polemical publications, and, because of the number which exist, and the means by which they were gathered, many of the letters, especially those to women, will also be considered.

Two major biographies of Schwenckfeld have been written during the last century. The only full-length biography is *Caspar Schwenckfeld von Ossig (1489-1561): Spiritual Interpreter of Christianity, Apostle of the Middle Way, Pioneer in Modern Religious Thought*, written by Selina Gerhardt Schulz.[18] As an account of the life of a founding father, this biography, while giving valuable information as to facts and dates, is in no way a critical account of the man or his theology. There is very little analysis of either the origins or the impact of his theology, and scarcely any attempt to understand him as a man of his time.

The other major biographical discussion is by R. Emmet McLaughlin. Entitled *Caspar Schwenckfeld: Reluctant Radical, His Life to 1540*,[19] this study covers only part of its subject's lifetime. Rather than a biography, this is an attempt to explore the situation in which his theology developed, and the various streams of thought which influenced it. However, the twenty years prior to his death are not covered, despite the fact that he was active and writing at this time. During that period he was regarded as a leader and teacher by many, and he wrote to them to explain and expand his ideas. It is important that this time of his life, the work which he did and the influence which it had on people should also be taken into account in any attempt to understand him.

Both of these writers reflect the fact that there were a significant number of women among Schwenckfeld's followers and friends, but they account for it in different ways. Moreover, I believe that both of the accounts are inadequate. With language like

> The pleasing personality of our nobleman from Silesia, his characteristic and genuine courtesy, polished speech, and kindly manner to all, and his spiritual giftedness, immediately upon his arrival in Strassburg in the spring of 1529, won him new friends to take the place of those he had left behind.[20]

Schulz does little in the way of critical analysis of why people, and especially women, responded so favourably to the man. The nearest she gets is a suggestion that they found him charming, responded to his courtesy and felt an emotional attachment to him.

---

[18] Schulz, *Caspar Schwenckfeld*.

[19] R. Emmet McLaughlin, *Caspar Schwenckfeld: Reluctant Radical, His Life to 1540*, New Haven and London: Yale University Press, 1986.

[20] Schulz, *Caspar Schwenckfeld*, p. 176.

McLaughlin does make more of an attempt to uncover the root of this response. He argues:

> The return of religion to the hearth and the liberation of the laity from the often unpleasant tutelage of a professional male clergy was especially attractive to women, and the Schwenkfelder movement in southern Germany was always marked by strong female leadership. In part this was surely the result of Schwenckfeld's own personality. Alongside his courtliness and nobility was a genuine respect for the women with whom he corresponded: he took them very seriously, a rarity in the age of paternalism. Perhaps what set him apart from many of his clerical opponents was his ability not only to speak well, but to listen carefully to men and women alike.[21]

There are two aspects to McLaughlin's position: firstly, that of Schulz, that the women were charmed by a handsome man, and secondly, the importance of the home in enabling women to take part. In suggesting that religion was *returned* to the hearth, he is identifying the position he holds about why the women responded. In his essay in *The Freedom of the Spirit*, he makes the point even more explicitly:

> Ever since the sixteenth century observers have commented upon the prominent role played by women in the Schwenkfelder movement. Schwenckfeld had many women are friends and correspondents. Schwenckfeld communities in Ulm and Strassburg (also Augsburg, though McLaughlin misses this here) had women as leaders. It has been suggested that this resulted from Schwenckfeld's personal attractiveness as a member of the nobility, blessed with polished manners and the skills of a courtier. While this may have played a role, there were other factors which were more important…In some ways, the Protestant clergy were more firmly in control of lay piety than the later medieval Catholic clergy had ever been. The division between clergy and laity continued, and in that division, all women were relegated to the laity. Schwenckfeld's teaching on the Sacraments and the Stillstand swept away the clerical monopoly of the sacraments. And his teaching on Scripture and the spirit effectively robbed the Protestant clergy of the advantage of their new "indelible character" – their learning or technical expertise in deciphering the Bible…The result of the Schwenkfelder understanding of the role of the sacraments and Scripture was to displace the focus of religious activity from the public arena dominated by the clergy, to the private sphere of the home, where the supper table replaced the pulpit as the focus…And here women could take responsibility for themselves and teach and "minister" to others.[22]

While I would not wish to dismiss the power of a charismatic personality, neither am I convinced by the suggestion that this was the root and sum of the

---

[21] McLaughlin, *Reluctant Radical*, p. 161.

[22] McLaughlin, *The Freedom of the Spirit, Social Privilege and Religious Dissent*, Bibliotheca Dissendentium, Scripta et studia No 6, Baden-Baden: v Koerner, 1996, p. 28.

response which the women made. Nor, as I will show in the discussion which follows, am I convinced that simply to move from church to home is sufficient reason for the numbers of women, and the roles which they played. To consider home as a *private* place, which was divorced from the public world, is inappropriate in considering the early modern period.[23] McLaughlin himself has stated that Schwenckfeld showed a genuine and rare respect for the women around him. However, he has failed to ask what provoked such a position, and whether the reasons and results of the position might be of help in exploring the theology which was at the heart of Schwenckfeld's life.

Thus, while those who have written extensively about the life of the man, and therefore about the lives of the communities of which he was a part have acknowledged the presence and the role of women, there has been little exploration of what that presence means, and the way in which it could be accounted for by, and perhaps makes sense of the theology which was, after all, the reason why people accounted themselves as followers of this reformer rather than one of the others. Not only were the women present, but they appear to have functioned as leaders, insofar as there were leaders. Certainly, any examination of the letters makes it clear that women were amongst his most frequent correspondents, and in two cases at least were the ones who collected the letters for use by the conventicles.

One of the issues which needs to be addressed is the nature of the relationship between Schwenckfeld and his female friends. As far as can be seen, no scandal ever seems to have been attached to him on a sexual level, despite the recognition that he had so many women friends. Husbands do not appear to have objected to his close correspondence with their wives, nor even to the meetings which were at times arranged. Although his theological opponents attacked him on various levels, nobody appears to have made any suggestion of impropriety. That Schwenckfeld was aware of the possibility of such scandal is hinted at in a comment he made in the first letter to Helena Streicher:

---

[23] See Merry Wiesner, "Nuns, Wives and Mothers", *Women in Reformation and Counter-Reformation Europe: Public and Private Worlds*, Ed. Sherrin Marshall, Bloomington: Indiana University Press, 1989, p. 9; Joel F. Harrington, "Hausväter und Landesväter: Paternalism and Marriage Reform in Sixteenth-century Germany", *Central European History*, vol. 25, 1992, p. 58. See also James Grantham Turner, *Sexuality and Gender in Early Modern Europe: Institutions, Texts and Images,* Cambridge: Cambridge University Press, 1993, p. 13; Heide Wunder, '*He is the Sun, She is the Moon*': *Women in Early Modern Germany,* translated Thomas Dunlap, Cambridge, Mass and London: Harvard University of Press, 1998, pp. 63-84, especially p. 68.

You know, my beloved, (yes, my heart's beloved as it should be in all purity and civilised behaviour for Christians, who are one heart and soul in Christ,) you know that as God is our heavenly Father... [24]

The possibility of scandal was made all the more pressing because he himself was unmarried. Marriage at this period in particular was not only a question of companionship, begetting children or economic security. For those involved in Reform, it was also a political and religious statement. There had long been a perceived association between holiness and celibacy, which found expression in the requirement for those in orders, and those who were priests to live lives without active sexual expression. One of the most visible and immediate changes which the reform centred around Luther made in social ordering was the marriage of priests, and the assertion which went with that that holiness and celibacy were not inseparable. It became almost a necessity for a leader of Reform to marry, in order to demonstrate allegiance to the new way of thinking and living. Certainly it is true that most of those who were leaders in Reform were clergy, and the issue of marriage was a particularly visible one in that life. With such a strong tradition and expectation of clerical celibacy, to marry was truly to align oneself with the new teaching. Schwenckfeld was not a clergyman, and so it could be argued that this whole question was not so important to his position.

It is not easy to understand fully Schwenckfeld's personal situation, since most of the letters which have been preserved have been shorn of their personal references. However, it is clear that he was one of a family of at least three, with a brother and sister. Schulz simply notes their existence, [25] while McLaughlin asserts that Caspar was the oldest. [26] What is clear is that he and his brother together inherited the estate. [27] It is also clear that Caspar never married. Schulz simply records this in a straightforward sentence, while McLaughlin does not refer to it. [28] It seems strange, at first sight, that he did not marry, in the light of his social position. Although, as Olwen Hufton has demonstrated, between ten and fifteen per cent of the population did not marry, including priests and those who entered religious orders, still marriage was the normal expectation of both men and women from all social classes, even if that expectation was not fulfilled. [29] However, for those who did not marry, it was often reasons of financial insecurity or family responsibility. Since, as far as we can tell, Schwenckfeld had a conventional upbringing and education, and followed what might be called an expected career plan, as a courtier and caring

---

[24] CS, vol. 5, p. 480, l. 37ff. Unless otherwise noted, translations are writer's own.

[25] Schulz, *Caspar Schwenckfeld*, p. 2.

[26] McLaughlin, *Reluctant Radical*, p. 4.

[27] Schulz, *Caspar Schwenckfeld*, p. 3.

[28] Schulz, *Caspar Schwenckfeld*, p. 3.

[29] Olwen Hufton, *The Prospect Before Her: A History of Women in Western Europe*. vol. 1, 1500-1800, London: HarperCollins, 1995, pp. 59ff.

for his own estate, there is no immediate reason to suppose that he was not expected by his family and community to marry.

It may be that he did not marry because that would have involved the splitting of the patrimony. Hans, his brother, did marry, and had several children. The protection of family property and land, especially if Caspar were the younger son, might have created a situation in which for economic reasons, and for the well-being of the wider family, he did not want (or was not encouraged) to divide the resources.

It may be that Schwenckfeld did not marry because of the peripatetic life he was forced to lead after exile, although there are several objections to such a theory. He did not go into exile until he was thirty-nine or forty. Others who followed a similar peripatetic lifestyle did marry – see for example, Menno Simons.[30] Others, too, married despite unsettled ways of life, even Luther, although he did originally say that he wouldn't marry because of the danger he felt himself to be in. So, it cannot simply be assumed that Schwenckfeld did not marry because of his travelling. There were other leaders on the radical wing of the Reformation who did not marry, such as Thomas Müntzer and Sebastian Franck, people with whom, in some ways, Schwenckfeld shared more of a theology than he did with Luther. It is possible, though unarticulated, that in this radical movement, there was a continuing emphasis on the link between celibacy and holiness. Marion Kobelt-Groch has suggested that Anabaptist (and we might therefore think, other radicals) developed an understanding of marriage that

> may well have been more closely related to the medieval ascetic ideal than to the Reformation's positive stance towards matrimony.[31]

If she is right, then it is possible that in Schwenckfeld's position we see a reflection of the same belief. However, since he never argued for or advocated celibacy as superior, this is not an entirely convincing suggestion. What is clear is that, in the light of his evident capacity for forming deep and warm relationships with women, there is a question about why he did not marry – a question, it is true, which we will not be able to answer. But it is a question which has a bearing on how we assess his understanding of the nature of male and female. Vern Bullough has argued that masculinity was established by

---

[30] In "Reply to Gellius Faber", comparing himself with preachers in the state churches, Simons wrote, "I, with my poor weak wife and children have for eighteen years endured excessive anxiety, oppression, affliction, misery and persecution.... Yes, when the preachers repose on easy beds and soft pillows, we generally have to hide ouselves in out-of-the-way corners", cited in William R. Estep, *The Anabaptist Story; An Introduction to Sixteenth Century Anabaptism*, Third Edition, Mich. and Cambridge: Eerdmans, 1996, p. 168.

[31] Marion Kobelt-Groch, *Aufsässige Töchter Gottes: Frauen im Bauernkrieg und in der Täuferbewegung*, Frankfurt, 1995. p. 79.

three markers: impregnating a woman, protecting dependants (not necessarily family) and providing for a family.[32] These were not roles which Schwenckfeld fulfilled (with the possible exception of the second one, until he went into exile.) If he himself was not socially in the normal male role – that of husband, father and head of the household – did this mean that he approached the question of what was a normal role from a different position? If questions of gender are to be useful in an analysis of his thinking, it is important that his own social and relational position is taken into account.

Most of the evidence which we have of the relationships which were central to Schwenckfeld's life and through which his teaching was disseminated come from the letters which are part of the collection which forms the *Corpus Schwenckfeldianorum*. The first thing that these letters show us about the relationships between Schwenckfeld and the women with whom he corresponded is evident in sheer weight of numbers. Of the six hundred and thirty collected letters which Schwenckfeld sent, three hundred and thirty-four were either to individual women or to groups of women (53%). Some were sent to more than one person, sometimes to groups and have in this analysis been counted separately. Of these three hundred and thirty-four, one hundred and sixty-two (48.8%) were sent to one woman, Sibilla Eisler of Augsburg. Thus, just over a quarter (25.5%) of the total number of letters collected were sent to her. Of the others, there are single letters, or letters in twos and threes to various individuals, and then also fifty-seven were sent to one, other or both of the sisters, Katherina Ebertz and Cecilia von Kirchen, who lived in Isny. There were also twenty-six sent to the Streicher family, as a whole, or to individual members, in particular, Helena senior and Katherina. There is a gap in the letters to the Streichers, which coincides with the time when Schwenckfeld was living in or around Ulm, their home city – and when, presumably, he did not need to write to them.

The letters to the men show a very different pattern. Schwenckfeld wrote to one hundred and thirty-six individuals, as well as to reform leaders, such as Luther, Blaurer, and Bucer. To most of these men he wrote once or twice. The greatest collection of letters to an individual man is a group of nineteen letters to Jacob Held von Tieffenau, seventeen of which written within a short period of time between 1534 and 1535, when Held was in hiding. Held was a close friend of Schwenckfeld's, and after Schwenckfeld's death, Held was his literary executor. These letters (which are printed in volume eighteen of the *Corpus*) show the close relationship, and are amongst the most personal of Schwenckfeld's letters to a man.

Other than this group of letters, there are some individuals who received more just a few letters: Leonhard Hieber in Augsburg, who received thirteen,

---

[32] Vern L. Bullough, "On Being a Male in the Middle Ages", in Clare A. Lees, S.Thelma, Jo Ann McNamara. *Medieval Masculinities: Regarding Men in the Middle Ages*, Minneapolis and London: University of Minnesota Press, 1992, p. 34.

Hans Wilhelm von Laubenberg, discussed below, who received nine, Crautwald, Schwenckfeld's long-term friend in Silesia who received twelve and the von Thumb brothers, also discussed below, who between them received ten. Clearly none of the men to whom Schwenckfeld wrote became correspondents of the same long-term intensity as the women mentioned above. The content of the letters to the men, too, is rather different. There are letters which are significantly different from those written to the women – those to Luther, Bucer, Pilgram Marpeck for example – because they are engaging specifically, and with the intention of being public, with public leaders of reform in a disputatious mode. These letters might best be classed with the published works mentioned above, as part of Schwenckfeld's ongoing debate and defence of his position. Other letters, the majority of those to men, are of an occasional nature, to deal with a specific query, to point out a particular publication, or to encourage during a time of pressure.

They may, like the letters to the women, be written in response to letters sent to Schwenckfeld, but there is little or no evidence of any on-going relationship supported by these letters. It is clear from some of them that they are part of on-going discussions, especially the letters to Crautwald and to Valentine Ickelsamer. But they do not have the continuity evident in the letters to the women, either in number or in the time-period covered. Even those men who receive more than one or two letters tend to receive their letters within a limited period of a few years. In contrast, Schwenckfeld's letters to the sisters in Isny start in 1544 and continue until 1559, his letters to Sibilla Eisler start in 1544, and continue until his death, and his letters to the Streichers, apart from the gap I have mentioned, cover the period from 1536 until his death, which took place in their house. All these letters are clear evidence of significant and developing relationships, and as such, the discussions related in them give indications of the consistency and the development of Schwenckfeld's thinking. They also show that these women at least found something of lasting worth in the teaching which was offered to them by this teaching. Finally, the length of time of these correspondences demonstrate the depth of the relationships which Schwenckfeld sustained with these individuals over the years.

The letters clearly show a developing network of contacts both between Schwenckfeld and those who found his teaching convincing, and amongst that group themselves. Of course, one of the weaknesses of working with such a collection is that we are dependent on what people chose to collect. There are no letters, for example, to Schwenckfeld, only his letters, often in reply. These letters can give us some indirect information about what people were writing to him about, but at best it is only putting together hints and comments. Another point worth commenting on about the collections of letters, in the light of the argument presented here is that it was Sibilla Eisler and the Catherina Ebertz and Cecila von Kirchen in particular who preserved the letters and made them available to others, in particular, to Daniel Suderman, a second generation Schwenkfelder from Strassburg, who lived from 1555-1631. He transcribed and published collections of Schwenckfeld's writings, and produced an important collection of letters, called *The Suderman Codex*. There are one hundred and eighty-five letters in the *Codex*, which are included in the *Corpus*. Of these, one hundred and thirty-five were sent to Sibilla Eisler of Augsburg, and fifty to Eva Honolt, Catherina Ebertz, and Cecilia von Kirchen, to whom Schwenckfeld sometimes wrote individually and sometimes collectively. The place of these women in particular as preservers and transmitters of the tradition is notable when we are considering the particular place of women in this community, and the impact of the teaching on them. In receiving and transmitting these letters, they, arguably, were seeing themselves in a distinctive role in the community, and with a particular type of authority in it.

Another issue in considering the letters as a trustworthy source is that we do not know what letters he sent which were not collected. The figures given above suggest that over half the letters were sent to women, and a high proportion of these to a few individuals. However, more accurately what such figures show is that a high proportion of the letters which were collected and preserved were sent to women. This is presumably a result of the fact that it seems to have been women, most notably Sibilla Eisler, who made contemporary collections. When it comes to assessing the sources, this becomes a question. To what extent can these be taken as representative letters, and what reliance can be placed on them as evidence for a particular position?

It is clear that Schwenckfeld knew that Eisler was collecting his letters, because he commented that he trusted her to deal with them discreetly.[33] Thus it is justifiable to suggest that he would have written material to her in that knowledge, and in the expectation that it would become part of the collection. So, it is appropriate to assume that the discussions in the letters are not aberrant.

It is also clear, when the material addressed to Sibilla is compared to other letters, including those to men, that the arguments and approaches demonstrated are consistent. Thus, the material contained in the letters can be judged to be representative in significant measure.

We are however left with the problem that the material we have is all that we have, and there is no real way of judging how much was lost, and how much some of the points may have been expanded or developed in different ways in other, no longer extant, letters. To counterbalance that, it is important to remember that we have not only the collected letters, but also of printed and published material, mentioned above. The two types of sources appear to co-ordinate well together, and so, again, we find corroboration for the assertion that the letters which we have, although only a partial source, are still dependable for giving a fair picture of Schwenckfeld's thought. We find nothing in the letters which is not also present in the published material. It is

---

[33] "I write to you without much forethought, for you know well how to judge, and therefore it does not overly concern me." *CS*, vol. 13, p. 56, l. 5f.

therefore justifiable to use both publications and letters as sources from which to draw evidence for his theology. The importance of using the letters as well as the publications is that it allows us to see a more personal presentation of the positions for which he was arguing. Because so many of the letters we have are those which were sent to women, we can also see which, if any, of his main points were of particular importance in his conversations with his women followers.

The final comment to make here about the use of this material as a source for considering Schwenckfeld's theology relates to the point made above about his unmarried state. Although there I suggested that his personal position was not something which could be ignored in this discussion, it is clear in several of the letters that personal material has been removed, so that the letter deals only with theological argument and discussion. Thus, although it remains true that his personal position and the attitudes which he adopted and demonstrated in his way of life and conduct of relationships are important, it is also true that much that we might wish to know, and which he may well have told his friends, remains hidden from us. There are some personal comments, and the letters are by no means impersonal theological treatises, but we certainly cannot assume that what we have about his own feelings and reactions was all that there was. As always in historical research, we must work with the material we have, while accepting that the picture we build up in this way will be incomplete. The best that we can hope is that it will not be too seriously distorted, and I believe, for the reasons outlined above, that this is a fair assumption to make on the basis of the material which we have.

Before we go on to consider the some of the individual women who were significant in the South German Schwenkfelder community, it is necessary to examine the social patterns which were evident. In the early days of the movement, when he was in Silesia, the Schwenkfelder movement was parish-based. As a *godly prince* in the Lutheran manner, Schwenckfeld, within his own authority in his estate, instituted reform through the appointment of like-minded clergy to the parish churches, and by encouraging and enabling prayer and study groups within the local community. In this setting, the theology which he taught, and which was at this time very close to Luther's, could be seen simply as the local expression of reform, and involved everybody. With his move to South Germany and exile, this pattern changed considerably. In his article, "Schwenckfeld and the Schwenkfelders of South Germany",[34] McLaughlin has detailed the journeys which Schwenckfeld made and the groups of contacts which he built up. The majority of these contacts were among the elite of the city and rural communities, and the links which Schwenckfeld made were often through family networks or friends of friends. As such, there was a degree of social homogeneity about the movement. In Speyer, for example, Schwenckfeld became friendly with the bishop, and

---

[34] McLaughlin, "Schwenckfeld and the Schwenkfelders".

through him had access to his court and to the elite in Ulm, as well as possibly the courts of the bishop of Strassburg and the archbishop of Cologne.[35] In Esslingen, his friend and patron was Hans Sachs, the mayor.[36] In Augsburg, his friends were drawn from the patricians and bankers, and those who aspired to patrician status, as well as those who were professionals: jurists and physicians.[37] McLaughlin goes on to show that the same pattern was repeated in Memmingen and Mindelheim, Kempten, Strassburg, Justingen and Oepfingen and Württemberg. As a member of the elite, this was the part of any community into which Schwenckfeld had immediate access, through existing friendships and sometimes family relationships. With the increasing separation which was to develop between him and the mainstream churches, so that he was no longer welcome to preach in local parishes, the transmission of his ideas was not, as it had been, to the majority of the community, but within small groups bound together by family and social ties – the kind of people who met at dinner or parties and talked together. Thus, without any apparent planning on his part, the movement which developed in South Germany was significantly different, socially, from that which he had built in Silesia. It was largely elite, literate, articulate and sophisticated. As McLaughlin points out:

> The social composition, recruitment patterns and organization of Schwenckfeld's following are explainable in large measure by the means through which his message was propagated.[38]

This was not wholly true, since it is clear from some of the letters that servants and artisans also found the teaching attractive. But, in the case of servants at least, it appears that most of them were part of households in which the whole family were influenced by this teaching.

What makes this recognition of the people who responded to Schwenckfeld so important is the way in which the profile differs from those who formed the majority of the radical Reformation followers. Claus-Peter Clasen has analysed the evidence relating to those who can be traced who were known to be Anabaptists.[39] This makes it quite clear that the majority of Anabaptists came from the lower parts of society. Indeed, he suggests that as many as 98% of Anabaptists were from the common people.[40] Less than 2% of the known number were from among the nobility and elite – the part of the community from which, so far as we know, Schwenckfeld drew his greatest support. Clasen

---

[35] McLaughlin, "Schwenckfeld and the Schwenkfelders", p. 147.

[36] McLaughlin, "Schwenckfeld and the Schwenkfelders", p. 148.

[37] McLaughlin, "Schwenckfeld and the Schwenkfelders", p. 148.

[38] McLaughlin, "Schwenckfeld and the Schwenkfelders", p. 163.

[39] Claus-Peter Clasen, *Anabaptism: A Social History, 1525-1618. Switzerland, Austria, Moravia, South and Central Germany*, London and Ithaca: Cornell University Press, 1972.

[40] Clasen, *Anabaptism*, p. 323.

also points out that, in this proportion, Anabaptism reflected the make-up of society fairly closely: most people were among the common sort. This does not mean necessarily that they were poor, but it is important in terms of their access to power within the community. Even in the cities, in which there was some sort of representative government, those who had access to it were from a significantly closed group among the inhabitants of the city.

That said, however, one of the other things which Clasen's research shows is that in the earliest phases of the movement, in the mid to late 1520s, a significant proportion of elite and educated members of society were attracted to Anabaptism. In Augsburg, for example, among the first to accept baptism as believers were some who were propertied.[41] Clasen goes on to argue that here:

> If the poor dominated numerically, people with property were nonetheless the backbone of the congregation.[42]

Thus, in its early days, radical religion was not entirely the preserve of the poor or the powerless, nor did it appeal only to the uneducated. In Ulm and Esslingen, as well as Augsburg, in the early days, Anabaptism drew support from members of the community's elite.[43] However, this support did not continue, on the whole, though there were some notable leaders who reflected this part of society, most importantly in our context, Pilgram Marpeck. Clasen suggests a reason for the withdrawal of this section of society:

> The aesthetic culture of the wealthy burghers of Augsburg and Zurich was strongly condemned by the Anabaptists: the elegant houses and fountains, the sculptures and paintings, the fashionable dress, necklaces and rings, the organ music in the churches.[44]

He goes on to point out that for those who were socially responsible for the maintaining of the community's order and social discipline, the ban on taking oaths became an issue of great importance. For those who made up the majority of the later Anabaptist community, the unpropertied and the poor, separation from political office was of no consequence, because they were not eligible for it anyway. Similarly, the rejection of luxury and fashion was not, on the whole, a problem which they faced with the same acuteness. In the same way, the mistrust of education and learning, did not affect most Anabaptists, because they had little chance of significant education in the normal run of things.[45] Radical religion, therefore, as it began to develop, did hold an appeal for some in the elite, and among intellectuals. However, they soon began to find that

---

[41] Clasen, *Anabaptism*, p. 325.

[42] Clasen, *Anabaptism*, p. 326.

[43] Clasen, *Anabaptism,* p. 312.

[44] Clasen, *Anabaptism,* p. 312.

[45] Clasen, *Anabaptism*, p. 327.

many of the attitudes inherent in its theology alienated them. In Schwenckfeld's teaching, on the other hand, people found the possibility of radical reform, without the social and political consequences. McLaughlin says:

To be sure, one of the major attractions of Schwenckfeldianism was its ability to offer religious radicalism while maintaining a conservative social and political outlook..[46]

There is one interesting little scrap of information which suggests that Schwenckfeldianism did provide a home for those who were seeking radical theology, but without the social upheaval which it could provoke. Clasen records the split which occurred in the Augsburg Anabaptist community between the rich and poorer members, and some of the discomfort felt on both sides:

Honester Crafter, a very wealthy widow, openly stated that she and her two daughters had been baptized "in the absence of the mass of the people" and had left the meeting on Easter morning because too many people had been present.[47]

As well as giving evidence of class divides among Augsburg Anabaptists, this story is particularly important in the discussion of Schwenckfeldianism, since one of Honester Craffter's daughters was Sibilla Eisler, as we have seen, one Schwenckfeld's most important correspondents, and the centre of the movement in Augsburg. We can only speculate, but Clasen's account does raise the possibility that, in some measure at least, she was drawn to Schwenckfeld's theology because of its withdrawal from social involvement and the fact that it was so closely limited to people of her own station.

One of the consequences of the social composition of those who formed the various local Schwenkfelder groups was that, on the whole, they were protected from the pressure which was applied to other radical groupings. McLaughlin points out that in Württemberg, the leaders of the Schwenkfelder group included the von Thumb family, who were the local nobility. It is, therefore, difficult to see the exact extent of the group and its penetration into the elite community of the area.[48]

Thus, the concentration of Schwenckfeld's teaching among the elite of the communities with whom he had contact, although it was largely fortuitous rather than planned, had some significant effects. That his theology was so very quietist meant that it was particularly appealing to those for whom the current social order worked well, and who did not want to be associated with the more politically or socially radical implications of other movements. That most of those who were associated with the movement were from the elite and thus, at

---

[46] McLaughlin "Schwenckfeld and the Schwenkfelders", p. 178, n.164.

[47] Clasen, *Anabaptism*, p. 327.

[48] McLaughlin "Schwenckfeld and the Schwenkfelders", p. 156. He also argues that the same is true of the group in Nürnberg. McLaughlin "Schwenckfeld and the Schwenkfelders", p. 163.

least potentially, had access to political power, meant that the group as a whole, and its individual members, even those who were particularly active, were more likely to be protected than attacked by the Councils. Schwenckfeld did not set out actively to recruit from this part of society, but it was his natural milieu. The community amongst whom his theology developed in itself had an effect on the developing of that theology.

It is also interesting to note a gender difference in the analysis of class. Two of the city circles (as distinct from those based in rural or estate communities) centred on women's homes – the Streichers' home in Ulm, and the Sibilla Eisler's home in Augsburg. In the case of the Streichers, Helena Streicher was a widow by the time she became involved in Schwenckfeld's teaching. Sibilla Eisler was, as we have seen, married, but it is clear that her husband was not as involved with the Schwenkfelder circle as his wife. Indeed, there are letters in which Sibilla was asking for clarification on behalf of her husband of Schwenckfeld's teaching, and in particular, the details of his differences from the parish preacher.[49] It is significant that it was to her, and not to him that Schwenckfeld wrote. Both of these families, while clearly among the elite of their communities, were members of the wealthy merchant classes.

The men who appear to be at the centre of Schwenkfelder circles, on the other hand, such as Hans Friedrich and Hans Conrad Thumb, whose support and friendship was, as we have seen, important in protecting the movement in the Würrtemberg area, were land owners and minor nobility. It is clear, from Weber's analysis of the family networks, discussed below, that the women in the families were involved, and indeed, were important in building the links with Schwenkfelder theology.[50] However, they apparently did not have the same leading roles that Helena Streicher or Sibilla Eisler held. It looks, on the basis of this evidence, as if men of the rural elite responded more positively than men of the city elite, and that women of the city elite were more likely to take leading roles than women of the rural elite. On the latter point, we might suggest that women in the city were perhaps less conservative in their general outlook, and therefore more likely to adopt non-traditional positions, both in terms of theology, and in terms of position in a religious community.

Who were the Schwenkfelders?

It will be helpful at this point to look at some of the individuals who were of particular importance in the lives of these various communities. There were

---

[49] See, for example, his fifth letter to her, dated Dec 12, 1544. Stephen Eiselin has been arguing with the preachers about the divinity of Christ, and the nature of the Eucharist, and Schwenckfeld writes to Sibilla with answers to the questions raised. *CS*, vol 9, pp. 178ff.

[50] Franz Michael Weber, *Kaspar Schwenckfeld und seine Anhänger in den freybergischen Herrschaften, Justingen und Öpfingen*, Stuttgart, 1962.

significant families in most of the main centres of Schwenkfelder life. In Ulm, the Streicher family, those friends to whom Schwenckfeld returned in his final illness, was at the centre of the circle, with their home being used for meetings.[51] They appear to have been among those Caspar Schwenckfeld met on his first visit to Ulm, and soon became close friends and followers. A family who were very close, they formed a significant part of the Ulm network, both in providing hospitality and in facing persecution.[52] Helena Streicher senior, who was a widow, was a shopkeeper. Her son, and apparently also Agathe, one of the daughters, were physicians in the town.[53] Thus, they were fairly substantial members of the civic community. Their home was Schwenckfeld's centre in Ulm for some of the time while he stayed there, and was also the place where people knew they could contact him – letters sent there would reach him, after he had moved from Ulm. The devotion to Caspar Schwenckfeld did not come

---

[51] See F. Fritz, *Ulmische Kirchengeschichte vom Interim bis zum dreissigjaehrigen Krieg (1548-1612)*, Ulm, 1934, p. 185. R. Emmet McLaughlin in "*Schwenckfeld and Early Schwenckfeldianism*", also cites Carl Theodor Keim, *Die Reformation in der Reichstadt Ulm*, Stuttgart 1851.

[52] Keim, *Die Reformation in Der Reichstadt Ulm*, p. 310, cited by McLaughlin p.159, n. 131.

[53] An account of her life, and more particularly of her role as a city physician is given by Lore Sporhan-Krempel in *Lebensbilder aus Schwaben und Franken*, Max Müller und Robert Uhland, Stuttgart, 1960, pp. 52-61. In this essay, Sporhan-Krempel points out that for a woman to practice as a recognised physician in a city was difficult because none of the universities would allow her to train. However, Augustus Streicher, Agathe's brother was a recognised physician, and the suggestion is that she started as his assistant, and learned from him. She was clearly well-known, and respected, being called in to treat the brother of the bishop of Mainz in 1574, the Bishop of Speyer in 1580 and Emperor Maximillian II in 1576. The level of recognition which this gave her allowed some protection to what was known as the "Streicherin Sekte", although only for a limited time. A level of persecution did become obvious after 1575. She died in 1581, and the Council archives record that "*Die verstorbene Junckfraw Agathe Streicher soll in der Bahr ohn das ober lid oder brett zur Erden bestattet werden.*" This may have been an honour, so that people could see her face – an equivalent to "laying in state." On the other hand, it may have been a mark of shame. In 1616, there was a council ruling that those who propagated false teaching must be brought to the grave "ohne Sang und Klang", without song and bell, the normal parts of a funeral service. Sporhan-Krempel points out that it is not known if such an order was in force in 1581, but clearly something of the sort affected her funeral. It is reminiscent of the funeral of Elisabeth Hecklin in Strassburg, which Katherina Zell eventually led, because no member of the clergy wanted to be associated with the Schwenkfelder. Agathe Streicher was obviously an unusual woman of her time. Was it her non-conformity which attracted her to Schwenckfeld, or did her allegiance to Schwenckfeld's theology give her the impetus to play such an unorthodox role? See also Heide Wunder, *'He is the Sun, She is the Moon'*, pp. 103-104.

just from the family members, but also included the maid.[54] Helena Streicher senior's sister, Juliana Roggenburger, also became a follower. After Helena Streicher senior's death, Juliana went to live with the daughters and Schwenckfeld was glad, because he hoped she would be a good example.[55] After Schwenckfeld's death, the circle continued and was still centred on the Streicher home. This became so noticeable that the conventicle was referred to in some council documents as the *Streicherin Sekte*.[56]

Schwenckfeld's correspondence makes it clear that there were others in Ulm with whom he was in close contact, and among them were several women apart from the Streichers. Anna Aitinger, who received several letters, was the daughter of Hans Schöfferlingen, who originally came from Esslingen, and settled in Ulm. She married Conrad Aitinger, secretary to the city council. For services to the city, he was awarded an hereditary coat of arms in 1524. Their son was Sebastian Aitinger. In 1526, he became a secretary of the city of Ulm, and then private secretary to five members of the Council. His position as a trusted member of the city's administration continued, with involvement in negotiations to do with the Schmalkaldic League.[57] Once more, it is clear that among those whom Schwenckfeld counted as friends were members of the elite of the city. What is also interesting about the relationship demonstrated by the letters is that he was in touch not only with the men, or the senior members of the family, but with different generations, and with women in their own right as well as the men. This suggests that the relationships which Schwenckfeld developed, and which were maintained through his letters did not necessarily follow expected patterns. He was concerned to deal with individuals in their own person, and not only with people in social groups.

Another demonstration of this is in his correspondence with Barbara Kurenbach. She was the secretary to Bernhard Besserer, the mayor of Ulm. It is clear from letters which he sent that Schwenckfeld was a close friend of Bernhard Besserer, and it appears that he stayed with Besserer in Ulm for about five years in the mid and late 1530s.[58] Bernhard Besserer and his son Georg were significant and powerful actors in the political situation in Ulm, and it was due to their protection and support that Schwenckfeld was able to stay so long in the city despite the opposition of Martin Frecht, the leading minister of the city. In 1544, Frecht wrote to Blaurer about "sister Barbara, who is liberated

---

[54] *Missiven oder Sendbrieffe die er in Zeit seines Lebens vom XXV Jare an bis/ auff das LV geschrieben.* M250, cited by the editors of *CS*, vol. 5, p. 477.

[55] "I am very glad to see that you are together again. Thus, as the ones long-practised in the way of the Lord you can encourage and help the others as the younger towards salvation with your good example" *CS* vol. 11 p. 954 l. 9 ff.

[56] F. Fritz, *Ulmische Kirchengeschichte*, p. 201.

[57] *CS*, vol. 6, p. 549, vol. 7, p. 3.

[58] See *CS* vol. 5, p. 402, ll. 7f: "….however, as soon as the mayor of Ulm, with whom I am now staying, had given me this message…"

from Schwenckfeldian delusions, who is secretary to our Krito, [Bernhard Besserer]".[59] In the *Ulmer Kirchenvisitation* of 1539, Frecht wrote "Otte, Yedelhus, Lochner, Kirnbech and the Streichers all hold false teaching".[60] In volume five of the *Corpus*, a letter is printed which is addressed to "Fraw BK", in Ulm and the editors suggest that she can be identified with Barbara Kurenbach. Again, here is a woman in correspondence with Schwenckfeld, both directly, and as we will see below, through the involvement of friends. She was clearly connected with the centres of power in the city, part of the elite community, and just as clearly was a woman who took her own religious decisions and made her own choices. It does not appear that she was married, so it also seems that she was in an anomalous position, a single woman who had to earn to support herself, and was employed in a powerful position.[61] It is fair to assume that she, like the Streichers, gained some measure of protection for her unorthodox religious position because of her social standing.

Not all of Schwenckfeld's followers in Ulm, or the other centres where he gathered circles, were from the elite of the community. The trials of Schwenkfelder sympathisers in Augsburg feature individuals who were not part of the elite of the city.[62] In a letter to Helena Streicher, he conveyed greetings from Anna Erhardt and her brother to Helena. It appears that later, Anna Erhardt became the maid of Helena Streicher.[63] Perhaps we can speculate that the shared religious sentiments made the relationship a particularly suitable one.

In Augsburg, as the figures presented above show, Schwenckfeld's most

---

[59] *Traugott Schiess, Briefwechsel der Brüder Ambrosius und Thomas Blaurer 1509-1567,* 3 vols, Freiburg, 1908-1912, vol. 2, p. 289, cited in *CS*, vol. 8, p. 619.

[60] "Die Öttin, Yedelhuserin, Lochnerin, Kirnbechin u. Streicherin halten alle irrige Lehren", "*Ulmer Kirchenvistation 1539*", p. 223, cited in *CS*, vol. 8 p. 619. Interestingly, all the names cited in this list are female forms, another indication of the perceived number of women who were recognised as following Schwenckfeld's teaching.

[61] Ozment points out that this was not an easy or a normal position for a women of the elite to be in. Steven Ozment, *When Fathers Ruled: Family Life in Reformation Europe,* Cambridge, Mass and London: Harvard University Press, 1983. p. 13.

[62] See: Staatsarchiv Augsburg, *Reformationsacten Schwenckfeldiana,* 7/8 53, Staatsarchiv Augsburg, *Reformationsacten Schwenckfeldiana II* 21/8 1553, Staatsarchiv Augsburg, *Reformationsacten Schwenckfeldiana IV* OAV 9 1556, Staatsarchiv Augsburg, *Reformationsacten Schwenckfeldiana V:2.* Augsburg, like many cities, was a community where there were a variety of religious opinions, not all of which fitted accepted orthodoxy. In her study of Haug Marschalck, Miriam Chrisman Usher has presented a portrait of another man who looked for a moral improvement as a result of religious renewal, and who mistrusted purely outward practice. Miriam Chrisman Usher, "Haug Marschalck: Lay Supporter of the Reform"; Andrew C. Fix and Susan C. Karant-Nunn *Germania Illustrata: Essays on Early Modern Germany, Presented to Gerard Strauss,* Kirksville, Mo; Sixteenth Century Journal Publishers, 1992,

[63] *CS*, vol. 5, p. 486.

frequent correspondent was Sibilla Eisler. Eisler was the daughter of Lorenz Crafter, a merchant in Augsburg, and his wife Honester, whose own family claimed connections with the royal family of Scotland. Whatever the truth of that, Lorenz Crafter was a significant merchant and public figure in Augsburg, although he did not originate from the city. The social structure in Augsburg, which has been closely studied, shows the presence of four classes of elite.[64] There was the Patriciate, the Mehrer, merchants who married into the Patriciate following 1548, and then the two guild classes, the Kaufleutestube and the Kaufleutezunft. Members of these communities did not, on the whole, interrelate with the classes above them. It was from the two guild classes that the political and administrative leadership of the city community was drawn until the reorganisation in 1548. Lorenz Crafter seems to have been a member of the Kaufleutzunft, though this is difficult to trace. Certainly, his wife's brother was a member of the Kurschnerzunft, the furriers' guild, from 1529-1548.[65] Their oldest son, Alexander, was born in Antwerp, so it is possible that the paternal side of the family came from that region. Sibilla had six sisters and four brothers, and at least two of the sisters and their husbands were also followers of Schwenckfeld. Her brothers were, like her father, significant merchants. Alexander was a member of the furriers' guild until 1548, and of the Kaufleutestube from 1541-1553. Hieronymus was a member of the Kaufleutestube from 1541-1556, Jakob from 1541-1554 and Christoph of the Kaufleutezunft. from 1539-48. The family progressed socially, as Christoph became a Mehrer in 1542, marrying Barbara Ehem. Hieronymus' two sons also became Mehrer, Anton in 1569, when he married Barbara Rem, and Hieronymus II in 1568, when he married Anna Maria Weiß.[66] Since, as Sieh-Burens has shown, networks played a significant part in determining individual families' places in the community, it is significant to note the upward movement of this family.

The place of the family becomes even clearer when we consider the marriage of one of Sibilla's sisters. Her sister Maria married Jakob Herbrot, a man who was possibly a Zwinglian.[67] He was born in 1490, and died in Neuburg in 1564. He was a rich man, and deeply involved with the financial and business life of the city at a time when Augsburg was one of the richest cities in the country. Roth referred to him as "Ein homo novus",[68] who was to

---

[64] See, for example, Katarina Sieh-Burens, *Oligarchie, Konfession und Politik im 16. Jahrhundert: Zur Sozialen Verfluchten der Augsburger Bürgermeister und Stadtpfleger 1518-1618*, Munich;Vogel, 1986.

[65] Wolfgang Reinhard, *Augsburger Eliten des 16 Jahrhunderts: Prosopagraphie wirtschaftlicher und politischer Fuhrungsgruppen 1500-1620*, Berlin, 1996, p. 102.

[66] Reinhard, *Augsburger Eliten des 16 Jahrhunderts* p. 102 ff.

[67] Reinhard, *Augsburger Eliten des 16 Jahrhunderts* p. 265.

[68] Friedrich Roth, *Augsburgs Refomationgeschichte, 1517-1530*, Munich, 1901, vol. III, p. 2.

start with a member of the furriers' guild, as was Alexander Crafter. He also served on the Councils of the city and was mayor in 1545, 1547 and 1552, which is the period when Sibilla was active in the Schwenkfelder movement.[69] Sieh-Burens has shown how he was significant in other ways in the administrative elite of the city.[70] It is also clear that, within that network, he was connected with Sibilla's husband. In fact, his marriage to Maria would have brought him right into the centre of the Craffter-Eiselin network, a network which could form an important base for him. He seems to have arrived from outside the city, and would have needed to be integrated into some sort of network to function at the level he aimed for.

Sibilla's husband, Stephen Eiselin, played an important part in the life of the city. He was a member of the Kaufleutezunft from 1541-1548.[71] She was his second wife, his first being Elisabeth Pleiß, with whom he had several children. He served on the Council of Twelve from 1525-1540, on the Kleiner Rat from 1526-1533, on the Council of Thirteen from 1527-1533, and in various other official positions. Roth has shown how he, along with others, worked to further the cause of reform in the city, though the political administration.[72] He died in 1549, and Schwenckfeld sent Sibilla a letter of condolence. He and Sibilla had no children, which is perhaps one of the practical reasons why Sibilla was free to take such an active part in the life of the Schwenkfelder circle in Augsburg.[73]

Eiselin's son Sixt married Anna Rehlinger, from a family known to be involved in reform, and possibly connected with Schwenckfeld. Certainly, it was a family which was part of the elite of the city. Anna's father was Bernhard Rehlinger III, a patrician.[74] On their marriage, they lived in the Eiselin family house.[75] Herbrot lived next door, in a house which he appears to have wanted to turn into the centre of a dynasty.[76] These houses, and the houses of other members of this family network were in the centre of the city, near the buildings which formed the administrative heart of the community. This physical location is important in the consideration not only of Herbrot's rise to power, and the concentration of a community both of administrative influence and religious commitment, but also in the consideration of the place of women in the Schwenkfelder circle.

It appears that in 1531, Sibilla came to the attention of the city council for

---

[69] Contra the editors of *CS*, Magdalena Kraffter and Maria Kraffter were two separate people.

[70] Sieh-Burens, *Oligarchie, Konfession und Politik*, p. 110.

[71] Reinhard, *Augsburger Eliten des 16 Jahrhunderts*, p. 103.

[72] Roth, *Augsburgs Refomationgeschichte*, vol. I, p. 343, vol. II, p.10.

[73] Reinhard, *Augsburger Eliten des 16 Jahrhunderts*, p. 102.

[74] Reinhard, *Augsburger Eliten des 16 Jahrhunderts*, p. 653.

[75] Sieh-Burens, *Oligarchie, Konfession und Politik*, p. 115.

[76] Sieh-Burens, *Oligarchie, Konfession und Politik*, pp. 115-116.

having Anabaptist sympathies.[77] Schwenckfeld's first letter to her was in January 1544.[78] The letter makes it clear that she had been reading some of Schwenckfeld's writings and it was she who initiated the communication with him, writing with questions. Her position as part of the movement was clearly known to the city authorities and just as clearly disapproved of. The group in Augsburg was centred on her home. In the bibliography to one of her letters, the editors of the *Corpus* have included a quotation from one of the Council documents:

> It has been reported in detail to the honourable Council that you have not only joined the Schwenkfelder sect, and have dared to encourage others to join, but have also permitted some assemblies to take place in your house where foreign people, amongst whom are some suspicious persons of young years, are sheltered and contained, and in addition have sent suspect letters to and fro...But however that may be, the Council herewith truly warns you in a fatherly way to abstain from this and to desist completely from assembling secretly in these same conventicles and in meeting together to shelter unknown people.[79]

Quite apart from the information which such a comment provides us with regarding Sibilla Eisler's role in the Schwenkfelder circle in Augsburg, it also helps to undermine McLaughlin's suggestion that the reason for female leadership like hers was to do with the move into the privacy of the home. Clearly, the Council was not prepared to look on what happened within the "privacy" of the Eisler home as something outside their concern or control. Rather, it was an area in which they obviously believed they had the right to take an interest, and the responsibility to enforce proper behaviour. The home was not private, but a place of political importance. This must have been all the more the case, in the light of the position of the Eisler home, and the relationship with Herbrot. Sieh-Burens has shown the importance of the various networks in the life of the city, and has demonstrated the way in which they were developed by marriage and by business relationships. It is clear that the Herbrot family, the Craffters, the Eiselins and several others formed one of these networks, and were linked politically and matrimonially. Sieh-Burens does comment that they also shared a commitment to reform.[80] However, she has not explored the fact that for many in this group, and particularly for the women, it was not simply "reform" as a generic position which linked them, but a definite commitment to Schwenkfelder thought – a reform position which separated them from others in the community. It is also clear from this that Caspar Schwenckfeld had significant connections with the mercantile and

---

[77] Ms. germ. 898, B, fol 108a, Preussiche Staatsbibliothek, Berlin, cited in *CS*, vol. 8, p. 824.
[78] *CS*, vol. 8, p. 824ff.
[79] *CS*, vol. 13, p. 354-355
[80] Sieh-Burens, *Oligarchie, Konfession und Politik*, p. 137.

administrative heart of the city during the late 1540s, a crucial time in the life of that community.

Another prominent Schwenkfelder in Augsburg and close friend of Schwenckfeld, along with Georg, her husband, was Anna Regel. There was an Anna who married a Georg Regel in 1510. She was the sister of Melchior Manlich, who appears in the city archives as a Catholic. He was a member of the Kaufleutestube from 1541-1576. There were six other brothers and sisters, one of whom was a nun. The family, and the families with whom she became connected through her marriage were part of the flourishing business community of Augsburg.[81]

The link was not only with Anna Regel. Georg clearly communicated with Schwenckfeld in his own right. In a letter to Hans and Anna Zoll, two more followers in Augsburg, Schwenckfeld wrote:

> So Bonifacius [Wolfhart], [Georg] Regel and Welten can always send the letters to me; and Regel has already written over ten times to me since I left you.[82]

Georg Regel was a patrician in the city and known as a philanthropist.[83] It appears that in 1527 both he and Anna were baptised by Hans Hut, but forced to recant by the measures taken against Anabaptists by the Augsburg council. Despite their recantation, they seem to have moved back to Anabaptist ways, and left the city in 1528. In 1531, they had returned, and in 1553, Anna's name appears on a list drawn up by the Council of respectable citizens who were recognised as Schwenkfelders.[84]

In 1548, following the death of Georg, Anna married Jakob Merzky, about whom nothing else is known. That she was within the Eisler circle of influence is clear from Schwenckfeld's letter to Sibilla Eisler about her and her care of him.[85] It is intriguing to notice that she seems to have been known in the town both as a respectable personand as a Schwenkfelder. Her life story so far as we have it gives evidence that the Anabaptists did not simply draw their adherents from among the artisan classes in the urban communities. What is even more interesting is that she and her husband should, on leaving the Anabaptists, join not the respectable mainstream church, but the Schwenkfelders. It is clear that

---

[81] Reinhard, *Augsburger Eliten des 16 Jahrhunderts*, p. 518.

[82] *CS*, vol. 5, p. 165, l. 5.

[83] Roth, *Augsburgs Refomationgeschichte*, vol. I, p. 246. Georg seems to have taken some time to find a spiritual home. Roth refers to him as being: "one after the other, Lutheran, Zwinglian, Anabaptist, Frankish [a follower of Sebastian Frank] and Schwenckfeldian."

[84] *CS*, vol. 8 p. 432. Unfortunately, the editors of the Corpus simply cite the list, and do not give details of any of the others names which appear on it.

[85] "As regards Sister [Anna] Regel, I am glad to hear that she has come home safely to you", Letter to Sibilla Eisler *CS*, vol. 11, p. 583, l. 20. Schwenckfeld had broken his arm, and Anna Regel had been nursing him.

in Augsburg, as in Ulm, the Schwenckfeld circle was allowed a reasonable degree of latitude, but it was still not regarded as the norm. In the archives in Augsburg, there are records of several trials of those who were considered to be outside the religious conformity of the city. The trial of Leonhard Hieber in 1553[86], and the Confessions of Leonhardt Hieber,[87] Bernhardt Unsinn,[88] and Balthasar Marquart,[89] show clear evidence of Schwenckfeldian theology, as they all make the distinction between inner and outer which, as we shall see, was so important in Schwenckfeld's thinking. Each of them also confessed, as Hieber put it:

> On the Supper, I thus hold, that in the supper of the Lord, when it is held according to his will, the servant, the bread and the cup, the Lord distributes outwardly for his remembrance: but eating and drinking of Christ, that is inner, of his holy body and blood to eternal life.[90]

This is the classic formulation of one of the central assertions of Schwenckfeld's theology. In the record of his trial, Hieber made it clear that he had been aware of correspondence between Schwenckfeld and his followers taking place through Sibilla Eisler.[91]

There are, however, no records of Sibilla Eisler being tried or required to make a confession of her faith, though there are instances of the Council addressing admonitions to her. This suggests either that she was in a secure enough position socially not to be in danger from the authorities, or that, as a woman, her religious position was not considered important. However, the trial of Kunigunda Uberlerin, a midwife, who was charged with Anabaptist sympathies suggests that the Council did take the religious position of at least some women seriously.[92]

Clasen has also pointed out how the Anabaptist attitude both towards aesthetic culture and law and order made their community less than congenial to those who were part of the elite after the initial enthusiasm of the late 1520s.[93] His analysis shows that, in Augsburg at least, the Anabaptists came

---

[86] Staatsarchiv Augsburg, *Reformationsacten Schwenckfeldiana*, 7/8 53.

[87] Staatsarchiv Augsburg, *Reformationsacten Schwenckfeldiana* II 21/8 1553

[88] Staatsarchiv Augsburg, *Reformationsacten Schwenckfeldiana* IV OAV 9 1556

[89] Staatsarchiv Augsburg, *Reformationsacten Schwenckfeldiana* V:2

[90] Staatsarchiv Augsburg, *Reformationsacten Schwenckfeldiana* II 21/8 1553

[91] Staatsarchiv Augsburg, *Reformationsacten Schwenckfeldiana* II 13:
"Er hab bey vier oder 5 Jaren her und dan Caspar Schwenckfeld zum ofttermal und allerers an Sontag vershinen geschriben, hab die brieff allmal der frau Eislerin geben, wolches denselben geen Ulm nit won und khamme diser Schwenckfeld annders mit."

[92] Staatsarchive Augsburg, *Reformationsacten, Wiedertaufer und Religionsacten III.* 1562. Of course, as an Anabaptist suspect who functioned as a midwife, Kunigunda was a particular threat to the city.

[93] Clasen, *Anabaptism*, p. 313.

from all classes, though most were poor.[94] He also demonstrates the way in which the movement eventually divided along class lines.[95]Although the Regels seem to be the only ones for whom we have documentation, there are hints that other former Anabaptists joined the Schwenkfelder circles. Given that we have seen many of those who adopted Schwenckfeld's teaching came from the elite of the communities, it is possible that among the reasons for finding this theology welcoming was that it offered a radical alternative to the mainstream without demanding the social, economic and political changes which were part of some Anabaptist thinking. Thus for those for whom the status quo in society was acceptable, this was a theological position which offered a non-threatening alternative.

Strassburg also had a thriving Schwenkfelder circle.[96] Again, there were families involved, in particular the Schär family. Peter Schär von Schwarzenburg senior of Strassburg had four children – Elizabeth, who married Dr Christoph Hecklin: Margareta, married to Nicolaus von Graveneck, a bailiff of Urach and Blaubeuren: Felicitas, married first to Franz Frosch, Stadtadvocat of Strassburg and then to Dr Winter von Andernach: and Peter junior. The whole family was recognised as Schwenkfelder.[97] Once more we see a family with an elite position in the community who were a significant part of the Schwenkfelder circle. Schwenckfeld wrote to all the sisters and their husbands at various times.[98] He wrote first as to an unknown enquirer,[99] and later the letters show a very close relationship. Felicitas appears to have been introduced to Schwenckfeld by Katherina Zell.[100] This relationship between Elizabeth and Katherina continued to be very warm and when Felicitas died Katherina Zell

---

[94] Clasen, *Anabaptism*, p. 325.

[95] Clasen, *Anabaptism*, p. 326-327.

[96] Strassburg is a city which has been studied in particular detail. See for example Thomas Brady Jr, "Ruling Class, Regime and Reformation at Strassburg", *Studies in Medieval and Reformation Thought*, vol. XXII, Leiden, Brill, 1978; Miriam Usher Chrisman, *Lay Culture, Learned Culture: Books and Social Change in Strassburg 1480-1599*, London and New Haven, Yale University Press, 1982; Lorna Jane Abray, *The People's Reformation: Magistrates, Clergy and Commons in Strassburg 1500-1598*, Oxford: Blackwell, 1985; Mark U Edwards, *Printing, Propaganda and Martin Luther*, Berkley and London: University of California Press, 1992; Thomas A Brady, *Communities, Politics and Reformation in Early Modern Europe*, Leiden: Brill 1998.

[97] The biographical information is in the bibliography to the letter to Felicitas Schär, *CS*, vol. 8, p. 621.

[98] For example: to Margaretha von Graveneck; *CS*, vol. 9, p. 112, to Elizabeth Hecklin:*CS*, vol. 12, p. 715, to Felicitas Andernach: *CS*, vol. 14, p. 447.

[99] For example; After this you wish to know how far you should stretch brotherly love To Margaret von Graveneck: *CS*, vol. 9, p. 113, ll. 2f.

[100] After this, Frau N [Katherine Zell] spoke to me of you eagerness and love for the Lord Jesus Christ and his knowledge. Letter to Elizabeth Hecklin. *CS*, vol.12, p. 717, ll. 14f.

preached at her funeral. Three months later, Zell conducted Elizabeth's funeral service, in both cases, rather than allow clergy who disagreed with the women's theological and spiritual position to use the funerals to decry them. It is also possible that more orthodox clergy were actually unwilling to conduct the funeral services of those who had refused to be part of the mainstream theological community.[101] This event demonstrates the depth of relationship which existed amongst those who counted themselves as friends of Schwenckfeld, as well as being suggestive about the place which women undertook in the life of the Circle. However, it also raises the question of the position of Katherina Zell.

Katherina Zell, née Schütz, was the wife of Mattheus Zell, the preacher at Strassburg cathedral. Mattheus Zell was one of those whose preaching was instrumental in bringing reform to Strassburg, and in shaping it. He was also a friend of Schwenckfeld's and on the latter's first arrival in Strassburg, he welcomed him into the Cathedral pulpit. Katherina Zell appears to have understood herself as an active partner in her husband's ministry, and was involved in several of his projects. She set about reforming the city hospital and produced a hymnbook in an attempt to educate the laity in theology.[102] The editors of the *Corpus Schwenckfeldianorum*, Selina Gerhardt Schultz and R. Emmet McLaughlin all presume and claim that she was a keen and active member of the Schwenkfelder circle in the city, as indeed did the Schwenkfelder community in Strassburg.[103] It is certainly true that Schwenckfeld and the Zells were clearly friends. After Capito's wife died in 1532, and it was no longer suitable for him to stay in that home, he lived with the Zells for some time.[104] But it is also clear that neither Mattheus nor Katherina ever separated themselves from the wider and more mainstream parts of the church. Indeed they worked to bring people together, and refused to become isolated from any group, if at all possible.

The position of Katherina in particular helps to demonstrate the blurred edges that there were around any movement as unstructured and self-consciously non-institutional as the Schwenkfelder circles. Her refusal to commit herself explicitly to the group seems to have caused some resentment from them, and from Schwenckfeld himself. In the letter from Schutz Zell to Schwenckfeld which McKee has edited, it is clear that found herself in the position of having to make a defence for her refusal to be tied to anybody's

---

[101] Scheiss BB III 709, 689, cited in *CS*, vol. 8, p. 622. See also McKee, pp. 417-418.

[102] See Elsie Anne Mckee, *Reforming Popular Piety in Sixteenth Century Strassburg: Katherina Schütz Zell and Her Hymnbook*, Studies in Reformed Theology and History, Volume 2, Number 4, Fall 1994; also Elsie Anne McKee, *The Writings of Katherina Schutz Zell*, Leiden: Brill, 1999. See also Roland Bainton, *Women of the Reformation in Germany and Italy*, Minneapolis; Ausburg Publishing House, 1971.

[103] McKee, *The Writings of Katherina Schutz Zell*, p. 155.

[104] McKee, *The Writings of Katherina Schutz Zell*, p. 84.

theological position.[105] In this situation, she was in fact adopting exactly the position which Schwenckfeld himself presented, insisting that no human authority could command an individual's conscience. However, although it was Schwenckfeld's own position, it does not seem to have gone down well either with him, or to an even greater extent, with his followers in the city.

In the case of Margareta von Graveneck, the first recorded contact was a letter written by Katherine Streicher under Schwenckfeld's direction[106] to answer a letter from a preacher to Margareta. Margareta had sent to Schwenckfeld, who was in Ulm at the time, asking for advice. Felicitas and her husband appear to have been introduced to Schwenckfeld's teaching, and encouraged to accept it, through Elizabeth.[107] This is very clear example of the way in which family and marriage networks were important in the growth of the Schwenkfelder movement.

Apart from the collection of letters to Sibilla Eisler, the largest selection of letters are those sent to Catherina Ebertz and Cecilia von Kirchen, the daughters of Albrecht Paumgartner from Isny, where he was *Münzmeister*, city treasurer.[108] Catherina Ebertz remained in Isny when she married, and both her husband and her father appear to have been sympathetic to her religious views. However, her father-in-law was not so supportive, and he managed to cause the imprisonment of another Schwenkfelder in the district, Blasius Honolt. In a letter to Catherina Ebertz in June 1546, following a trip to the spa, Schwenckfeld wrote:

> I learnt for the first time when I was at the baths that your husband's father had been a cause of Honold's imprisonment, that he had written to the Council at Kempten about him, because he led me to you. [109]

This is one of the few cases in which we have evidence that allegiance to Schwenckfeld's theology gave rise to family tension.

Blasius Honolt appears frequently in Schwenckfeld's correspondence, as does his wife, Eva, to whom Schwenckfeld wrote jointly in his first letter to Catherina Ebertz. He wrote to them because Barbara Kurenbach had given him some of their letters to read, and he wanted to make their acquaintance.[110]

Cecilia von Kirchen lived in Lindau after her marriage, but it is clear that

---

[105] McKee, *The Writings of Katherina Schutz Zell,* pp. 155 ff.

[106] *CS,* vol. 9, p. 18. Bibliography to Document 437

[107] "Caspar Schwenckfeld's greetings to Elizabeth Hecklin's sister Felicitas and her husband Dr Andernach are significant at this time. Elizabeth Hecklin was attempting to induce them to accept Caspar Schwenckfeld's doctrine." *CS,* vol. 13, p. 714, Bibliography to Document 886.

[108] Johann Baptiste Haggenmüller, *Geschichte der Stadt und der gefürsteten Grafschaft Kempten,* 3 volumes, Kempten, 1847, vol. 2, p. 76, cited in *CS,* vol. 9, p. 118.

[109] *CS,* vol. 9, p. 1020, ll. 20f.

[110] See *CS,* vol. 9, p. 120.

she remained very close to her sister emotionally and spiritually. It is also clear that she was often with her sister in Isny, especially when their father was ill. When Schwenckfeld wrote, he normally wrote to them jointly, and he also encouraged them to read and write together. They were part of a wider network in the district, and took some initiative within the group. [111] Their family network was obviously part of the whole district grouping. It also appears that Catherina Ebertz's maid was a Schwenkfelder,[112] and so a similar pattern to that of the Streichers and Anna Erhardt mentioned above is evident. This was a movement which found much of its strength not simply in biological families, but in households, communities of people who shared a home and a life.

Outside Ulm, in Justingen and Oepfingen, there was another group closely linked by blood and marriage, that of the von Pappenheim and von Laubenberg families, which was the foundation of the circle. To this can be added the family of von Freyberg, another of the minor nobility of the area. Georg Ludwig von Freyberg married Katherina von Laubenberg, a member of a family known to be sympathetic to Schwenckfeldian views. They had two sons, Michael Ludwig and Ferdinand, in whose education Schwenckfeld was involved while he was staying at the Justingen castle.[113] Michael Ludwig married Felicitas Landschad von Steinach whose mother, Anna Elizabeth was, according to Schulz, a Schwenkfelder.[114] Ferdinand married Veronika von Pappenheim, a Schwenkfelder.[115]

Caspar von Laubenberg married Elizabeth Marschalck von Pappenheim, and the family were close enough to Schwenckfeld that, when Caspar died, Elizabeth wrote to him asking for comfort and help. There were three children of the marriage, Christopher, Georg and Magdalena, and their names often crop up in the correspondence, as Schwenckfeld sends messages to them. Who brought the theology to whom is unclear, but it is obvious that family and marriage relationships were central to the spread of Schwenckfeldian thinking

---

[111] The bibliography to Document 484 gives details of the visit and its organisation. *CS*, vol. 9, p. 306.

[112] "Greet your Sarlen, the good maid", "Grust ewr Sarlen/ dz gute Meidlin", Letter to Catherine Ebertz, *CS*, vol. .12, p. 683, l. 33.

[113] Weber, *Kaspar Schwenckfeld*, p. 24.

[114] Schulz, Caspar Schwenckfeld, p. 358.

[115] For the whole outline of the relationships, see, R Emmet McLaughlin, "Schwenckfeld and the Schwenkfelders of South Germany", in Schwenckfeld and Early Schwenckfeldianism, pp. 145-180. In this discussion, McLaughlin traces the elationships within and among the Schwenkfelder circles in South Germany. He refers to the women in the groups sometimes, though does not mention them all. He does not discuss the role of the women among the community apart from one short reference to Helena Streicher being the leader of the Ulm circle. See also Weber, *Kaspar Schwenckfeld*, pp. 48-49, and the family tree on p. 129.

and also that such thinking may also have brought people together.[116] Weber has also explored in great detail the community of which the von Pappenheims, the von Laubenbergs and the von Freybergs were part, and has shown the various complex family ties which went to make up the Schwenkfelder circle in the *Herrschaft* of Justingen and Oepfingen.[117]

Caspar von Laubenberg's cousin, Anna von Laubenberg of Wageg married Elizabeth's brother Joachim. They too were part of the epistolary circle, as was a nun at the Urspring Benedictine Convent, called Magdalena Marschalck von Pappenheim, who seems to have been either a sister or a cousin of Elizabeth's. Marschalck evidently, like other members of her family, and perhaps through them, had an interest in radical theology, and had expressed a desire to meet Schwenckfeld. However, she was also in touch with Pilgram Marpeck, the Anabaptist leader, and before she and Schwenckfeld met, she had become convinced by Marpeck's thinking. There then followed several exchanges of letters and pamphlets, focusing around the theology expressed in Marpeck's *Vermahnung*, and Schwenckfeld's response to it, *Juditium Über das new Büchlein der Tauffbrüder.*

The Damenkrieg

Over the next few months, the controversy between the Schwenckfeld and Marpeck continued. Part of it was conducted through publications, part through direct letter writing between the two men.[118] However, there was a third means of communication between the two, and that was through letters between Magdalena Marschalck and Helena Streicher of Ulm, who were friends, and clearly had discussed spiritual matters. Both Marpeck and Schwenckfeld appear to have written to both women, with the intention that the letters would be passed on. Some of the letters even appear to be written in the name of the women, though the contents betray the influence of the two men. There is also evidence that each woman was trying to convince the man with whom she disagreed.

This controversy, because of the involvement of the women, has become known as the *Damenkrieg*, a name which, in itself, serves to emphasise the place of women in the two movements, and the oddity which this was

---

[116] From a comment in a letter to Sibilla Eisler about her niece's wedding, it is clear that Schwenckfeld himself was aware of and valued the importance of such networks in bringing people into the community: "As for Regina's Bridegroom, it is just as I hoped with him. He has come so far, that he is reading our literature, and so God will help him further. I hear much more that the women bring the men to their party than the other way around." *CS*, vol. 13, p. 52, l. 9ff.

[117] Weber, *Kaspar Schwenckfeld.*

[118] For a full description of the course of the controversy, see Williams, *The Radical Reformation*, p. 703ff.

perceived to be. It also demonstrates the role of the letters as polemical tools.

The debate which sparked the controversy was to do with the nature of the sacraments, but it is clear that there were differences over the nature of Christ, the being of the church and human anthropology. Marpeck refused to countenance the separation which Schwenckfeld held to be fundamental, between inner and outer, especially in terms of ceremonies. Marpeck insisted that the inner experience was incomplete without the outer ceremony.[119] He also insisted that the church was not a perfection yet to come, which Schwenckfeld suggested, and which was one of the reasons he argued for the *Stillstand.* Instead, Marpeck argued it was the contemporary body of Christ, and membership of it, through baptism, was important. Anthropologically, the differences were over the relationship between soul/spirit and body.[120]

In his analysis of the debate, Williams suggests that both men were afraid of losing wealthy patronesses, which may be the case.[121] However, this still leaves open the question of agency. Why did women in particular find such a place in the theologies? It is beyond the scope of this thesis to consider Pilgram Marpeck. I am concerned with considering why women responded to Schwenckfeld, and in particular to his theology. I suggest that his beliefs about Christ, and his way of expressing these beliefs which played a significant part in the response of so many women. These women responded because of a particular theological position which was expressed in a specific way. Schwenckfeld's understanding of the nature of Christ, and the implications of that for the physical nature of the being of the believer were central to his theology, and therefore, I suggest, central to his followers' response.

The place of women in such a dispute was not limited to the *Damenkrieg.* On several occasions, Schwenckfeld either composed a letter which was sent in a woman's name to a theological opponent, or helped in the composition of such a letter.[122]

As has already been shown *evangelistic* networks worked through the friendship and kinship links. At least part of the contact of the Schär family with Schwenckfeld was through the friendship that existed with Katherine Zell. The Streicher family was also effective in outreach, both within Ulm and through extended networks. The same social pattern as in the other cities and in the rural community is evident in Ulm, where the network centred in the home

---

[119] Baptism and supper "is no sign, but the external work and reality of the Son", cited in Williams, *The Radical Reformation*, p. 718.

[120] Williams suggests that Schwenckfeld separated soul/spirit and body. (p. 719.) As my argument progresses, I will demonstrate that this was not in fact Schwenckfeld's position.

[121] Williams, *The Radical Reformation*, p. 707.

[122] See, for example, *CS*, vol. 8, pp. 582ff, a letter composed by Schwenckfeld and sent by Katherina Zell to Johann Brentz, again dealing with disagreements about the nature of the person of Christ.

of the Streichers. Kurenbach moved from Ulm to Kaufbeuren for some years, where she got to know Eva Honolt and Catherina Ebertz. When she returned to Ulm, they corresponded and she passed the letters on to Schwenckfeld.[123]

Each of these relationships demonstrates just how interlinked and how politically well-connected the Schwenkfelder groups were. Since they did not, on the whole come under the same sort of pressure from city authorities as other theologically radical groups, it is possible that these connections were exploited for protection. This shape of development and growth obviously fits with the pattern of the movement that Schwenckfeldianism became in South Germany, a movement, like many of the radical communities, centred on conventicles and therefore on the home rather than in a parish or organised church. These communities, especially the Schwenkfelder ones with we are concerned here, met not in public space, such as the parish church. Nor were they expected to be open to the whole community. They were small groups, meeting in defiance of the recognised *system*, perceiving themselves as something separate from it. They had little or no recognition from the civic authorities, and were not part of the parish system.

This survey demonstrates the place of women in the centre of the movement, and also something of the number of women. They were present as significant points of contact and outreach, they were often responsible for bringing families into the community, and through the kinship networks which were so important socially to women, they often seem to have introduced others socially and therefore religiously to Schwenckfeld.

This description of Schwenckfeld's community of friends helps to show that men as well as women responded to his teaching. McLaughlin's and Weber's work both demonstrate that the theology which he was discussing over dinner tables[124] was understood by and accepted by men and women with equal enthusiasm. As we will see, the way of life demanded by such a theology was not detrimental to the current social position in which most of his friends were. The requirements it put on them did not undermine their position in the community, and as such, men as well as women could respond without major disruption.[125]

Although the focus of Schwenckfeld's piety was the home, and the emphasis was on the groups of like-minded people who gathered for prayer, discussion

---

[123] "[O]ur sister, Fraw Barbara Keurenbach sent me some of your letters to read", Letter to Eva Honolt and Katherine Ebertz. *CS*, vol. 9, p. 120, ll. 11f.

[124] See for example *CS*, vol. 5, p. 536, ll 7ff; "Whether, then, I speak with good friends over the table or otherwise at appropriate times of our Lord Jesus Christ, his heavenly Kingdom, of the Gospel and soul's salvation, similarly, of the understanding of the word of God and the holy Scriptures, I do it all without any timidity, without damage, shame or harm to anybody."

[125] See the discussion in chapter five, "Men, Women and God".

and mutual encouragement,[126] adopting this teaching did not even require withdrawal from the local parish church, especially if this would prove problematic.[127] As we will see below, in the discussion of Maron's work, Schwenckfeld's understanding of the nature of the church itself is not entirely clear.[128] What is clear is that, although Schwenckfeldian thinking made significant demands on people's theological understanding, and raised issues about personal morality and piety, it was not necessarily a disruptive element in social living.

Women and the Reformation

Such a survey also brings into focus many of the questions which have been of increasing importance in Reformation studies over recent years, with regard to the positions and actions of women. There have been two ways in which women and the Reformation have been examined, both of which are well illustrated in the work done by Roland Bainton.[129] The two patterns might be characterised as the examination of individual women, and the exploration of the context of women and the effects of the Reformation on them. In this area of study, the question of whether the Reformation could be considered beneficial or harmful for women has been of prime importance. The revaluing of marriage and family by Luther and others was certainly experienced as a positive change, as was the emphasis on the mother's role within a family in training and developing the spiritual life of the children.[130] However, as Wiesner and Roper and others have shown, the valorisation of marriage and motherhood brought with it a narrowing of possibilities available to women.[131]

---

[126] Schwenckfeld wrote of the meetings thus, in a document in which he was writing a summary of his teaching and practice in 1561; "When some of us meet together, we pray together, also for our enemies who persecute Christ in us, some perhaps unwittingly, that God convert them, raise up his kingdom, and increase the number of his believers. Furthermore we instruct each other about Christ and the mystery of the divine trinity, and the Kingdom of God." trans Selina Gerhardt Schulz. *CS*, vol. 16, p. 826, ll. 27ff.

[127] McLaughlin, *Reluctant Radical*, p. 139.

[128] Gottfried Maron, *Individualismus und Gemeinschaft bei Caspar von Schwenckfeld: Seine Theologie, dargestellt mit besonderer Ausrichtung auf seinen Kirchenbegriff*, Stuttgart: Evangelisches verlagswerk, 1961.

[129] Bainton, *Women of the Reformation*, vols 1-3.

[130] See for example, Grethe Jacobsen, "Women, Marriage and the Magisterial Reformation", in Kyle C. Sessions and Phillip N. Bebb, *Pietas et Societas: New Trends in Reformation Social History. Essays in Honour of Harold J. Grimm*, Kirksville Mo.; Sixteenth Century Journal Publishers, 1985; p. 57.

[131] See Susan C. Karant-Nunn, "Continuity and Change: Some Effects of the Reformation On the Women of Zwickau", *Sixteenth Century Journal*, vol. 13/2, 1982, pp.17-42; Natalie Zemon Davis, *Society and Culture in Early Modern France*,

It was not simply that the closure of convents also closed the possibility of a specifically religious role for women within the community: that position had now been transferred to the wife and mother. It was also that the reordering of the family, which was a significant feature of the sixteenth century, increased patriarchal power and diminished the areas of self-determination for women. Thomas Brady has argued that

> [Luther] and the other reformers did not cause men to remove their kinswomen from convents so much as they legitimised action based on the burghers' sensibilities about relations between the genders.[132]

As Harrington[133] and Wiltenberg,[134] among others have shown, the reorganisation and ordering of the family was seen as fundamental in enabling society to function properly.[135] The identification, which Harrington has explored[136] of household and civic rule served to link women with children and subjects, excluded from the centres of power both civilly and in the home: indeed, the one implied the other. These changes, together with the limitation of almost the only religious role available according to the thinking of the Reformers for women to that of wife and mother, mean that the ambiguous nature of the Reformation for women is now much more to the fore in discussions. As most areas of Reformation historiography, study of the radicals has been later in developing, and for some time, it was thought that among them, gender relations were challenged and reordered along with so much else. Bainton first argued that there was a greater degree of marital equality among the Anabaptists than other Reformation movements, and Williams and others also argued for this point of view.[137] However, as more

---

Cambridge, Polity, 1987, "City Women and Religious Change", pp. 65-95, "Women on Top", pp. 124 – 150; Thomas A Brady, "You Hate Us Priests: Anticlericalism, Communalism and the Control of Women at Strassburg in the Age of the Reformation", in Peter A. Dykema and Heiko A. Oberman, *Anticlericalism in Late Medieval and Early Modern Europe*, Leiden: Brill, 1993; pp. 167-207; Merry E. Wiesner, *Women and Gender in Early Modern Europe*, Cambridge: Cambridge University Press, 1993; p. 241; Lyndal Roper, *The Holy Household: Women and Morals in Reformation Augsburg*, Oxford: Clarendon, 1989; p. 259; Heide Wunder, *He is the Sun, She is the Moon*.

[132] Brady, "You Hate Us Priests" p. 204. See also p. 186.

[133] Joel F. Harrington, *Reordering Marriage and Society in Reformation Germany*, Cambridge: Cambridge University Press, 1995.

[134] Joy Wiltenberg, *Disorderly Women and Female Power in the Street Literature of Early Modern England and Germany*, Charlottesville and London: University Press of Virginia, 1992.

[135] See also Davis, "Women On Top" p. 126: Merry Wiesner, *Women and Gender*, p. 201.

[136] Harrington, "Hausväter and Landesväter".

[137] Williams, *The Radical Reformation*. However, by the third edition, 1992, he has modified this approach. See also Sherrin Marshall Wyntjes, "Women in the Reformation

investigation was undertaken, questions were raised,[138] and Klassen in his article "Women and the Family Among Dutch Anabaptist Martyrs"[139] argues that:

> [the Anabaptists] accepted the patriarchal views of society in which the male dominated the female and children obeyed.

Lucille Marr and Marion Kobelt-Groch have explored this recognition in some detail, and it has become obvious that the picture among the radicals is as ambiguous as in other parts of reform.[140]

Wes Harrison's article on Hutterite Women in the sixteenth and seventeenth centuries has shown in more detail just how confused the picture is.[141] Although, as some have argued, women did play new roles in the worshipping life of the Anabaptists communities, it is also obvious that, in family life, and in perception, the basic understandings of women, and of relative gender roles had not changed. As Harrison puts it

> Some [historians of the Radical Reformation] had concluded that the unorthodox groups provided women a far greater role in religious expression and even in leadership than found in traditional society. More careful research revealed, however, that such changes in women's roles did not take place even in a limited way until well into the seventeenth century.[142]

There remains work to be done in this area, to investigate further to what extent, if at all, the theology of Anabaptists, and other radical groups led to a different perception of gender, and perhaps of women's roles.

Among those who have undertaken such research, particularly looking at women of the radical Reformation are Arnold Snyder and Linda A. Heubert

---

Era", in Renathe Bridenthal, and Claudia Koonz, *Becoming Visible: Women in European History*, Boston, Mass: Houghton Mifflin, 1977. p. 175.

[138] Joyce Irwin, *Womanhood in Radical Reformation*, 1525-1675, New York, 1979.

[139] John Klassen, "Women and the Family Among Dutch Anabaptist Martyrs", *Mennonite Quarterly Review*, 60, 1986, pp. 548-571.

[140] Lucille M. Marr, "Anabaptist Women in the North: Peers in the Faith, Subordinate in Marriage.", *Mennonite Quarterly Review*, 60, 1986, pp. 347-358; Marion Kobelt-Groch, *Aufsässige Töchter Gottes*. See also her article "Von 'armen frowen' und 'bösen wibern', Frauen Im Bauernkrieg zwischen Anpassung und Auflehnung", *Archiv für Reformationsgeschichte*, vol. 79, 1988, pp. 103-137, in which she argues that because of the confusion of the period, women played an unprecedented role in the social upheaval of the time, and that their participation in this led to a self-consciousness of women as a coherent group.

[141] Wes Harrison, "The Role of Women in Anabaptist Thought and Practice: The Hutterite Experience of the Sixteenth and Seventeenth Centuries", *Sixteenth Century Journal*, vol. 23, Spring 1992, pp. 49-69.

[142] Harrison, "The Role of Women", p. 50.

Hecht, with their work on individual women among sixteenth century Anabaptists.[143] Their work reflects the other strand of historiography, that of looking at individual, and often heroic women. Such work is important in illuminating what it "felt like" to be part of the Reformation. Others have done this by concentrating on specific individuals, and exploring their biographies.[144] It is an older type of women's history, with the concentration of "filling in the gaps", by telling the stories of women which have otherwise been obscured, and it is very useful in helping illuminating the personalities and therefore the issues involved. Another aspect of this has been the exploration of theology using tools of gender. This has involved exploring what can be obscured in the other studies, the issue of female agency and choice – why and women made specific religious choices, sometimes in defiance of fathers or husbands.[145] There has also been some significant work on the reaction of women to specific theologies, and the ways in which the presence of women may or may not have affected some theological thinkers.[146] This work has shown that it is important to understand not only the social and political context of the time, but also to examine the theology in some detail, in order to understand more of what was happening for women, and in terms of gender. It is in this area that this thesis is placed.

Discussions of Schwenckfeld's Theology

In order to do that, it will be necessary to examine the theology of

---

[143] C. Arnold Snyder and Linda A. Huebert Hecht, *Profiles of Anabaptist Women: Sixteenth Century Reforming Pioneers*, Waterloo, Ont: Wilfrid Laurier University Press, 1996.

[144] See especially Peter Matheson, *Argula von Grumbach: A Woman's Voice in the Reformation*, Edinburgh: T&T Clark, 1995; and McKee, *The Writings of Katherina Schutz Zell*.

[145] Sherrin Marshall Wyntjes, "Women and Religious Choice in Sixteenth Century Netherlands", *Archiv für Reformationsgeschichte*, vol. 75, 1984, pp. 276-289, "Women of the Reformation Era"; Bridenthal and Koonz, "Women and Choice: An Examination of the Martyrs' Mirror", *Mennonite Quarterly Review*, 64, April 1990, pp. 135-145; Lyndal Roper,"Sexual Utopianism in the German Reformation*", Journal of Ecclesiastical History* vol. 42, 1991, pp. 394-418.

[146] See for example, Jane Dempsey Douglass, "Christian Freedom: What Calvin Learnt at the School of Women", *Church History*, vol. 53, 1984, pp. 155-173; Jane Dempsey Douglass, *Women, Freedom and Calvin*, Philadelphia, Penn., Westminster Press, 1985; John L. Thompson, *John Calvin and the Daughters of Sarah: Women in Regular and Exceptional Roles in the Exegesis of Calvin, His Predecessors and His Contemporaries*, Geneva: Droz, 1992; Nancy L. Roelker, "The Appeal of Calvinism to French Noblewomen of the Sixteenth-Century", *Journal of Interdisciplinary History*, vol. II, 1972, pp. 391-418; Merry Wiesner, "The Death of the Two Marys", *Disciplines of Faith: Studies in Religion, Politics and Patriarchy*, ed. Jim Obelkevich, Lyndal Roper, Raphael Samuel, London: Routledge and Kegan Paul, 1987, pp. 295-308.

Schwenckfeld in some detail, and such an examination will form the main thrust of this thesis. The attempt to find a way of understanding Schwenckfeld's theology has never been straightforward, in part at least because of the way in which it was written.

As will be explored in more detail in chapter two, Schwenckfeld's theology was deeply pragmatic. Unlike many Reformation leaders, he was not trained as a theologian, but as a courtier and politician, accustomed to getting things done. As such, his concern in theology, although it often appears to take a philosophical form, being concerned with issues of ontology, is especially concerned with the practical implications of any body of belief, or claims about divinity.

This is a theme that appears most clearly in his approach to spirituality – the living out of the relationship – but it is fundamental to all of his theological thinking. Because of this attitude, he wrote very little in the way that was "systematic". Most of his writing was specifically to answer a question, build up a follower's faith, or deal with a particular attack. There are times when he wrote devotionally, and there is some degree of systematisation in such writings. There were also attempts to lay out the bones of his theology in Confessions and Statements of faith, but they often ended up so convoluted that they do not really count as systematic theology. However, he clearly had a theology, and a foundation for his thinking which determined the shape of the rest. Most of those who have written about Schwenckfeld in this century have done so with the intention of understanding his theology, and finding the key which will systematise it.

Reinhold Pietz, writing in 1959 argued that Schwenckfeld could be understood best through his anthropology, and his insistence on the importance of the "New Man" as a proper topic for theological consideration.[147] Edward Furcha also followed this line, with his book *Caspar Schwenckfeld's Concept of the New Man*.[148] Furcha's "key" to Schwenckfeld's thinking is the concept of new birth.[149] However, although he refers to the "almost physical fact"[150] in Schwenckfeld's understanding of this notion, he does not follow up the physical implications of the way the language is used, nor does he ask whether the use of such a strongly gendered image has an effect on the theology or those who respond to it.

---

[147] Reinhold Pietz, *Der Mensch Ohne Christus (Eine Untersuchung zur Anthropologie Schwenckfelds)*, Theolg. Diss, Tübingen, 1956.

[148] Edward J. Furcha, *Caspar Schwenckfeld's Concept of the New Man: A Study in the Anthropology of Caspar Schwenckfeld von Ossig as Set Forth in His Major Writings,* Pennsburg, Penn; Schwenkfelder Library, 1970.

[149] "The most striking aspect of Schwenckfeld's thought is his stress on the necessity of rebirth. It is almost a foregone conclusion." Furcha, *Caspar Schwenckfeld's Concept of the New Man*, p. 42.

[150] Furcha, *Caspar Schwenckfeld's Concept of the New Man*, p. 46.

In 1959, Paul Maier rose to the challenge of perceiving or imposing a system on Schwenckfeld's thinking, and recognised in Schwenckfeld's Christology a way of doing this.[151] Although he recognised at the beginning of the work that Schwenckfeld's writing shows a "lack of system"[152] and that among other thinkers "the Christology is assumed to be confused",[153] still he set himself to "attempt to systematise the unsystematic".[154] He set about doing this by exploring the Christology, the ways in which Schwenckfeld spoke about Christ and the patterns which he claims can be discerned in such writing. However, in the course of the discussion, he has to posit what he calls "the Schwenckfeldian paradox"[155] and his final conclusion, that

Knowledge of Christ

> it was in his concept of the *immediate Erkenntnis Christi*, through a physical-hyper-physical, finally mystical gift of faith that Schwenckfeld exposed the foundation of his thought-world; the dualism between the material and the spiritual.[156]

is based, I believed on a misreading of the meaning of the dualism which is of fundamental importance in Schwenckfeld's thinking. The misreading comes, in part, because, again, Maier fails to take seriously the gender issues raised by the concepts with which Schwenckfeld is working (gender issues which would help to solve the "paradox"), and which are signalled by the number of women who are present in the Schwenkfelder circles. However, his conclusion does point to two of the central features which any consideration of Schwenckfeld's theology must take into account. These are the *Erkenntnis Christi*, and the significant dualism which shaped all of his thought.

Karl Ecke has suggested that much of Schwenckfeld's theology can best be understood if it is seen as an exploration of what the "true" church should be.[157] he is also concerned to show that Schwenckfeld was significantly shaped by his encounter with Luther, and to demonstrate that much of his thinking continued to derive from Luther. The place of women, and the issue of gender is not a question with which he concerns himself. Gottfried Maron, in his book *Individualismus und Gemeinschaft bei Caspar von Schwenckfeld*, has also examined the ecclesiological consequences of Schwenckfeld's theological position, and argued for a significantly individualistic interpretation as the

---

[151] Paul L. Maier, *Caspar Schwenckfeld on the Person and Work of Christ: A Study of Schwenckfeldian Theology at its Core*, Assen: Royal Van Gorcum, 1959.

[152] Maier, *Caspar Schwenckfeld on the Person and Work of Christ*, p. 2.

[153] Maier, *Caspar Schwenckfeld on the Person and Work of Christ*, p. 3.

[154] Maier, *Caspar Schwenckfeld on the Person and Work of Christ*, p. 5.

[155] Maier, *Caspar Schwenckfeld on the Person and Work of Christ*, p. 49.

[156] Maier, *Caspar Schwenckfeld on the Person and Work of Christ*, p. 110.

[157] Karl Ecke, *Kaspar Schwenckfeld, Ungelöste Geistesfragen der Reformationszeit*, Ulm, 1965.

centre of the thinking.[158] As part of this discussion, he spends quite a bit of time discussing the meaning of *Erkenntnis* and its place in Schwenckfeld's thinking, and this is a discussion to which we shall have to return. He also reflects the fact that there was something significant in the theology as far as women were concerned.[159] However, he does little to explore this significance, and so once again, a clue into Schwenckfeld's perception of the world is not perceived as such, and therefore is not followed up.

The other major contemporary work which has been done on Schwenckfeld's Christology is that of Paul Seguenny, which Peter C Erb and Simone Nieuwolt have translated.[160] Seguenny's argument is that Schwenckfeld can best be understood as a humanist, ands that this is the key above all to his Christology. In Schwenckfeld, Seguenny claims, it is possible to find a thinker whose Christology provides a "way of understanding Renaissance contradictions".[161] He links Schwenckfeld's thinking very closely with that of Erasmus, and focuses in particular on his emphasis on morality. In Seguenny's opinion, the differentiation between divine and non-divine is entirely one of moral order.[162] He also points out that, for Schwenckfeld "The human person…is constituted of body and soul and it is only by that means that one can reach God". He goes on to argue that:

> Schwenckfeld, then, does not accept a partial rehabilitation of the human person. If one is to become a son of God, one's flesh must become, at the same time, like that of Christ – a qualitative transformation.[163]

This is a crucial point in understanding Schwenckfeld's Christology, anthropology and soteriology. However, his use of the description *son of God* demonstrates a major gap in the discussion. As we shall see this is not the language which Schwenckfeld himself uses. Nor does Seguenny's discussion take into account anything of the gender considerations which must be part of any consideration of issues regarding the meaning of flesh.

As well as these major works on Schwenckfeld's theology, there have been some shorter essays and monographs. Many of these areas were discussed in papers given at a colloquium in 1984, and later published in *Schwenckfeld and Early Schwenckfeldianism*.[164] The Colloquium was held to mark the centenary

---

[158] Maron, *Individualismus und Gemeinschaft*.

[159] Maron, *Individualismus und Gemeinschaft*, p. 94.

[160] Paul Segennuy, *Homme charnel, Homme spirituel. Etude sur la Christologie de Caspar Schwenckfeld 1489-1561*, Wiesbaden, 1975, translated by Peter C. Erb and Simone Nieuwolt as *The Christology of Caspar Schwenckfeld: Spirit and Flesh in the Process of Life Transformation*, New York: E. Mellen, 1987.

[161] Seguenny, *The Christology of Caspar Schwenckfeld*, p. 24.

[162] Seguenny, *The Christology of Caspar Schwenckfeld*, p. 84.

[163] Seguenny, *The Christology of Caspar Schwenckfeld*, p. 114.

[164] McLaughlin, *Schwenckfeld and Early Schwenckfeldianism*.

of the beginning of the *Corpus Schwenckfeldianorum* project, and the foundation of the Schwenkfelder library. The papers which were given were grouped around four themes: major issues in Schwenckfeld's own thinking, significant events in his life and ministry, other significant characters in the movement and finally links between Schwenckfeld's thought and wider theological reflections. This placing of Schwenckfeld in the wider context has been important in moving Schwenckfeld away from being the man alone with all the truth, and allowing exploration of the themes he was using, and the ways he used them. As well as the essays in *Schwenckfeld and Early Schwenkfeldianism,* R. Emmet McLaughlin has brought together essays published there and in other journals into a collection called *The Freedom of the Spirit, Social Privilege and Religious Dissent.*[165] In this collection of essays, most of which have been published elsewhere, he examines the life and context of Schwenckfeld.[166] Other essays examine Schwenckfeld's understanding of the Eucharist and how his thinking developed,[167] as well as his Christology.[168]

Running through all considerations of Schwenckfeld's theology, as I suggested above, is the theme of dualism, a fundamental division of all that is into two categories. Schwenckfeld himself categorised these as *inner* and *outer* In 1527, he wrote a "General Letter" (which was later to be known as *Anwysung,* "The Instruction") to explain his position on the Eucharist, addressing it to all believers among the four main parties: Roman, Lutheran, Zwinglian, and Anabaptist, the theological parties from which he wanted to distance himself. In it, he included this description of reality:

> Since all things in heaven and on earth are drawn up and divided into two different orders by God, namely into the order of the heavenly, spiritual, invisible and eternal, and the order of the earthly, the physical visible, ephemeral things, therefore all things must also of necessity be understood and apprehended in two ways; the earthly with an earthly, fleshly apprehension which comes from reason, and the heavenly spiritual, with a spiritual apprehension which comes from the Spirit of God through the revelation of Jesus Christ.[169]

---

[165] McLaughlin, *The Freedom of Spirit.*

[166] McLaughlin, *The Freedom of Spirit,* see "Introduction", pp. 9-35, "Spiritualism and the Bible", pp.73-94; "Sebastian Franck and Caspar Schwenckfeld: Two Spiritualist Viae", pp. 53-72; "Schwenckfeld and the Schwenkfelders in South Germany" pp. 199-232, and "The Politics of Dissent: Martin Bucer, Caspar Schwenckfeld and the Schwenkfelders of Strassburg", pp. 233-255.

[167] McLaughlin, *The Freedom of the Spirit,* see "The Genesis of Schwenckfeld's Eucharistic Doctrine", pp. 95-124 and "Schwenckfeld and the South German Eucharistic Debate", pp. 125-152.

[168] McLaughlin, *The Freedom of Spirit,* "The Schwenckfeld-Vadian Debate.", pp. 153-174.

[169] *CS,* vol. 2, p. 454, ll. 11f.

In this passage, we find the notion of dualism, expressed in terms of *inner* and *outer*, and relating to the concept of the *Ordnungen*, the orders.

Later in 1527, Schwenckfeld wrote to an acquaintance, Conrad Cordatus, to explain the position which he was adopting. This letter, *De Cursu Verbi Dei*, again reflects this concern with the duality of reality. The letter lays out the position like this:

> First, justifying faith belongs to the order of spiritual, invisible, inner things; this no one doubts, for it is of God, of divine nature, yea, the work and gift of God. Hence its origin cannot be of physical things, as of the external word, hearing, ministry or letter, but it remains in its order as something higher and greater, issues from the inner Word which is spirit and life, and must, according to its original state, precede all external ministration. For the flesh, or the natural man, receiveth not the things that are of God. Therefore it is essential that he be prepared beforehand by the Word through the grace of God, spiritual and become a vessel, dwelling or house of the Word. Hence, faith and righteousness do not originate from or through external things, but from God through Jesus Christ, whereunto external things may serve, direct or witness.[170]

So, at the very beginning, as he started to explore the consequences of the Eucharistic theology which he and the others had adopted, the idea of *inner* and *outer*, (in German *innere* and *aüßere*), as the characteristics of the *Ordnung* of existence was present and expressed. The language of inner and outer was not exclusive to Schwenckfeld. Metaphorically, the term *innere* was regularly used to refer to that which was spiritual, *geistig*. Sebastian Frank, for example, contrasted "physically, in literalness" with "spiritual and inner in the mind".[171]

Schwenckfeld's Theology

Schwenckfeld was not the only person to make use of these categories, nor the only one to have them as a central theme of his theology. It was a very common type of thought among several of the radical groups and thinkers, and was for them, as for Schwenckfeld, often the root of their disagreements with Luther. This was clearly the case in particular for Thomas Müntzer[172] and Melchior Hoffman,[173] two of the most important thinkers who used these categories. Although Schwenckfeld had various theological categories in common with

---

[170] *CS*, vol. 2, p. 592, ll 10f. Translated by Selina Gerhardt Schulz.

[171] *Fleischlich im Büchstaben geistlich und inner im Sinn*, Fischer, *Schwäbisches Wörterbuch*, "innere", vol. II, columns 808-809.

[172] Hans-Jürgen Goertz, *Thomas Müntzer: Apocalyptic Mystic and Revolutionary*, translated Jocelyn Jaquiery, Edinburgh: T&T Clark, 1993, p. 66.

[173] Klaus Deppermann, *Melchior Hoffman: Social Unrest and Apocalyptic Visions in the Age of Reformation*, translated Malcom Wren, edited Benjamin Drewery, Edinburgh: T&T Clark, 1987.

these two, he differed significantly from them, not least in his expectation of the working out of theology in the world.

Müntzer, who taught a theology similar to Schwenckfeld's of the importance of the encounter between God and the individual soul, developed his theology in such a way that he was one of the leading thinkers and actors in the Peasants' Uprising which came to such a disastrous end at Franckenhausen. His spiritual insight was always linked to a perception that change should not come just to the individual but also to the society. In this, as Norman Cohn has demonstrated,[174] he was at one with a long tradition of millennialism, which understood the duty of believers not only to involve the transformation of their own lives, but also that of society, by violence if necessary. Hoffman, too, expected a social and political reordering and change as a result of the true teaching of the gospel, though not with such violence. His involvement in the iconoclasm at Livonia was just the first in a series of such actions.

For both Hoffman and Müntzer, their separation of inner and outer was linked to a very strong and specific apocalypticism which regarded the Second Coming as imminent and as something for which believers could prepare. As Cohn argues, what was significant about the teaching of Müntzer and others was not the doctrine itself, but the bringing of the Day of Judgement nearer.[175] It was in this that they differed so radically from Schwenckfeld, and this is the reason why Schwenckfeld's theology, for all the importance that *inner* and *outer* had in its shaping, never led to the demands and expectations of radical social change which is seen in other thinkers. Both Hoffman and Müntzer came under considerable pressure because of the direction in which their much more active apocalypticism led them. Indeed, Müntzer was executed and Hoffman imprisoned because of the uprisings which arose as a result of thinking and acting shaped by their theology. Part of the resistance which was to develop towards Schwenckfeld's theology was driven by a perception that, because he shared a language of inner and outer with them, he also shared a desire to overthrow society. However, this was not the case. In part this might be seen as a reflection of his different social status: he was not under the same social and economic pressures with which Müntzer in particular identified. But there were also theological reasons for the difference in emphasis.

It was not that Schwenckfeld did not have a significant eschatology, but simply that it was focused elsewhere. In his article "The Abomination of Desolation, Schwenckfeld's Christological Apocalyptic",[176] Walter Klaassen argues:

---

[174] Norman Cohn, *The Pursuit of the Millennium: Revolutionary Millenarians and Mystical Anarchists of the Middle Ages*, London: Pimlico, 1993, pp. 234ff.

[175] Cohn, *The Pursuit of the Millennium*, p. 202.

[176] Walter Klaassen, "The Abomination of Desolation: Schwenckfeld's Christological Apocalyptic" in *Schwenckfeld and Early Schwenckfeldianism*, pp. 27-46.

One cannot speak of his apocalyptic if we define the word in the sense of a cataclysmic clashing of kingdoms and rival authorities ending with the inbreaking of the power of God to annihilate his enemies...,[but] as the uncovering of mysteries which had hitherto remained hidden.[177]

He goes on to make the case that Schwenckfeld, although he was interested in apocalyptic literature, most notably Revelation and Daniel, approached them both from a primarily theological rather than historical interest. What mattered was not when these events would come to pass, or the people involved in them, but the meaning which they demonstrated. His main interest was glorification of Christ, and his interest in apocalyptic was shaped by that. Thus the order of existence, discussed in terms of outer and inner, was not primarily something which would be brought to an end in historical terms, still less was it something which was to be brought to an end by violent uprising. Rather, it was the given in which theology, spirituality and Christian living were to be worked out. What was significant to Schwenckfeld was not the philosophical theories, but the practical consequences of his understanding of the nature of reality. Since he did not try to identify the times and people involved in the end times, he was not therefore concerned with how the events which were predicted might be worked out. What mattered to him was that these things would come to pass through God's activity, and the important thing was to be living in harmony with God. The emphasis again was on the pragmatic rather than the philosophical, and as such, there was little systematic thought. It must be noted, however, that Schwenckfeld's pragmatism was based on theological conviction about the nature and aim of God's activity. What mattered to him was what God was doing in Christ, and how this was to be appropriated by the believer. The consequences of such appropriation had then to be worked out.

But it is clear that the categories of inner and outer, and therefore of an oppositional way of perceiving reality were of significance in Schwenckfeld's thinking. Maier suggests that his approach to the world:

pesupposes, in his theology, an axiomatic cosmological, ontological, philosophical and psychological dualism which dichotomises the universe into external and internal, the spiritual and material, the divine and the creaturely, inner and outer – food and drink, baptism Word, ministry, faith, justification, righteousness, revelation, birth, children, men, teaching and life.[178]

The basic way which Schwenckfeld had of approaching anything was to classify it as inner or outer, and this dichotomy and duality dominated his sense of reality. Through the discussion of this thesis, I will be exploring just what the nature of this dualism is, since I am not convinced that Maier is right in his suggestion that it separates spiritual and material. To do that would be to deny

---

[177] Klaassen, "The Abomination of Desolation," p. 28.

[178] Maier, *Caspar Schwenckfeld on the Person and Work of Christ*, p. 14.

the body's position in relation to the spirit, and I believe that this was exactly what Schwenckfeld was *not* doing. Part of the argument of this thesis is that far from dismissing physical existence as unimportant, Schwenckfeld gave a particular value to bodies and their meaning. In this, he was doing nothing unusual. The Christian faith which he was exploring, and attempting to explain centres on the belief that in Jesus God became human, and existed in a physical body. Central to the expression of that faith has been the theology and practice of the sacraments, based around physical actions recognised as having spiritual meanings. It has never been possible in Christian thinking simply to ignore physical reality, and in particular the physical reality of the body. For Schwenckfeld, what a human body was, the meaning and nature of embodiment and the relationship between the body and the Divine were questions which haunted him. Therefore, any attempt to understand Schwenckfeld's theology without exploring the meaning he assigned to body will be seriously hampered.

Body and Gender

Recognising the body as something which can be studied historically has been a relatively recent phenomenon, and it has been even more recently that it has been understood that such study must include issues of gender. Mary Fissell has argued:

> The scholarship of Bakhtin, Elias and Foucalt invented "the body" as a topic for historical study, but a desire to emphasize the alien qualities and strangeness of early modern bodies (an emphasis explicable in terms of the need to historicize the previously a-historical human body) created a very general and implicitly male early modern body.[179]

However, the assumption that history acts on and shapes male and female bodies in the same way has now come to be recognised as untenable. Caroline Walker Bynum, for example, has demonstrated how men and women used physical symbols in different ways to speak of God and to speak of the relationship between the soul and God.[180] The use of the language which she discusses is both strongly physical and strongly gendered. The physical experience of men and women was different, and this was reflected in the use of language and the exploration of the religious symbolism and metaphor which people used.

The study of gender as an analytical tool in its own right has been an important area of research in recent years. Work on gender in sociological terms has given us

---

[179] Mary Fissell, "Gender and Generation: Representing Reproduction in Early Modern England," *Gender and History*, vol. 7, No 3, 1995, p. 433.

[180] Carolyn Walker Bynum, *"...And Woman His Humanity", Religion and Gender: On the Complexity of Symbols*, eds. Caroline Walker Bynum, Stevan Harrell and Paula Richman, Boston, Mass: Beacon, 1986, pp. 263-288.

various suggested models of gender construction, from the dichotomies of MacCormack and Strathern in *Nature, Culture and Gender*,[181] through to the radical postmodernism of Judith Butler in *Bodies that Matter: On the Discursive Limits of Sex*.[182] One of the things which appears in the discussion is the assertion that, whatever else may be important in the discussion of gender, it is necessary to take the issue of body and of somatisation seriously. The experience of body, the language used of body and the meaning attached to body are all central to any discussion of the construction of gender in a community. Joan Wallach Scott suggests that there are two distinct categories of approach to the issues raised by exploiting gender as an analytical tool and she characterises these as *essentially descriptive* and *causal*.[183] To use gender *descriptively* is to explore the issues raised by the differences between the positions of men and women in any given society. Such an approach takes seriously the fact that women and men experienced the same historical events differently. One of the results of such a discussion is shown in Kelly's question "Did Women have a Renaissance", the suggestion that the normal periodisation of history cannot be applied without question to women's experience. Part of Wiesner's work has also examined this aspect, particularly in looking at the ways in which women fitted into the various categories of society.[184] It is this kind of question which has driven much of the reflection on women in the Reformation period, and has given rise to the discussion of whether the Reformation was a good or a bad thing for women.

To approach the issue of gender *causally* is, in Scott's terms to "theorize about the nature of phenomena or realities, seeking an understanding of how and why these take the form they do".[185] Such a discussion questions the construction of the social understanding of gender, and examines the ways in which such a construction is developed and propagated. It is also concerned with the symbolic result of such constructions: the ways in which gender patterns are used to explore and embody other relationships and activities.

Thomas Laqueur has suggested that in the early modern period, at least medically, the model of the body which was determinative was of one sex; that is, there was one type of body, rather than two, and in some instances it was more perfect – male – and in some less, – female.[186] The details of his argument will be discussed more thoroughly in *Concepts of Conception*, but it is

---

[181] Carol MacCormack and Marilyn Strathern, eds, *Nature, Culture and Gender*, Cambridge: Cambridge University Press, 1980.

[182] Judith Butler, *Bodies that Matter: On the Discursive Limits of Sex*, London and New York: Routledge, 1993.

[183] Joan Wallach Scott, "Gender: A Useful Category of Historical Analysis", *Feminism and History*, Ed. Joan Wallach Scott, Oxford and New York: Oxford University Press, 1996, pp. 152-180

[184] See also Wunder, '*He is the Sun, She is the Moon*', p. 5.

[185] Scott, "Gender: A Useful Category of Historical Analysis", p. 155.

[186] See Thomas Laqueur, *Making Sex: Body and Gender from the Greeks to Freud*, Cambridge, Mass. and London: Harvard University Press, 1990.

intriguing to note that such a very late twentieth century argument as that advanced by Butler can be shown to have links to one way of reading the early modern material. However, the total separation of gender from bodily reality, and indeed, the suggestion that gender determines the perception and experience of the sexed body is not the only way in which the argument has progressed, or the only way gender has been defined.

Joan Wallach Scott defines gender in this way:

> Gender...means knowledge about sexual difference... Knowledge is a way of ordering the world; as such it is not prior to social organisation, it is inseparable from social organisation... Sexual difference is not, then, the originary cause from which social organisation ultimately can be derived. It is instead a variable social organisation itself which must be explained.[187]

Such a definition, that gender is about the social ordering of a community, insists that gender is not a biological given, something entirely determined by physical, bodily reality.

Wallach Scott's arguments suggest that sexed body and gender are separate questions, held together by the being of the individual concerned. Gender is the way in which a sexed body acts and is acted upon by a society, but the sexing of the body is something separate from the gender patterns a society builds up. Such an approach presupposes that bodily experience is not part of gender identity except insofar as the individual who is living within a certain society, and therefore whose subjectivity is constructed, among other things, by the gendering of that society, experiences life in and through the body. This is to say something radically different from what has normally been assumed. We have worked, on the whole, with a model which suggests that gender – that is, social role and its place in organising society – is dependent on and determined by the physical reality of a body that is either male or female. The reproductive organs determine the body, in its turn. However, once this starts to be questioned – when, for example, such roles and the understanding of them are shown to change across time – then the link between body and gender position becomes problematized.

One of the ways in which gender studies have been developed is by arguing that gender is absolutely a socially constructed reality, which in itself determines how the physical body is then seen and understood. Judith Butler, for example, has argued for:

> the construct of sex [seen] no longer as a bodily given on which the construct of gender is artificially imposed, but as a cultural norm which governs the materialisation of bodies.[188]

---

187 Joan Wallach Scott, *Gender and the Politics of History*, New York, Columbia University Press, 1988, p. 2.
188 Butler, *Bodies that Matter*, p. 3.

She takes her argument to the logical, but absurd conclusion thus:

> If gender is the social construction of sex, and if there is no access to this "sex" except by means of its construction, then it appears not only that sex is absorbed by gender, but that "sex" becomes something like a fiction, perhaps a fantasy, retroactively installed at a prelinguistic site to which there is no direct access.[189]

Butler therefore argues that what is primary is language, which then constructs the way in which the body is understood.

This can look like a particularly extreme form of post-modern rejection of a metanarrative, but it can be shown to have some relationship to the way we are coming to understand gender to have functioned in early modern Europe. In this thesis, I am not concerned only with gender as it has been investigated historically or anthropologically. At the heart of the discussion is a consideration of theology and its shaping in terms of gender. Thus, it is going to be important in the discussion to explore issues of theology and theological understandings of the issues raised by such an analysis. In a book in which she explores the issues of gender as they relate specifically to question of theology, Elaine Graham critiques Wallach Scott's approach thus:

> However, scientific accounts of biology as a discourse shaped by social conventions, and psychoanalytic accounts of subjectivity that refuse to render the body inert in the acquisition of identity, serve to remind us of the extent to which "sex" is already gendered. A supposedly pre-social sex has been given meaning and status (differential between men and women) by a society in which gender relations already operate. A theory which presupposes that bodies are passive objects of gender, and that bodily difference is incidental to gendered identity and experience, thus obscures the way in which bodily difference itself has emerged from culture.[190]

Such an argument might seem to drive us back into the position espoused by Butler, that gender is the given, and sex, bodily difference is the construct. However, Roper, among others, has put forward another form of approach.

She argues in *Oedipus and the Devil*[191] that bodily difference is part of the impetus towards gender construction, and cannot be ignored. She does this by putting forward the importance of the notion of the psyche:

> But the concept of the psyche assumes that body and mind, emotion and history are interrelated, and that sexual identities, while they may have a history, are not mere social constructions. To a far greater extent than divisions of race and class,

---

[189] Butler, *Bodies that Matter*, p. 5.

[190] Elaine Graham, *Making the Difference: Gender, Personhood and Theology*, London: Mowbray, 1995, p. 123.

[191] Lyndal Roper, *Oedipus and the Devil: Witchcraft, Sex and Religion in Early Modern Europe*, London: Routledge, 1994.

sexual differences are ingrained in the body, and difference, if not its meanings, seem to be an irreducible fact of life.[192]

The debate therefore centres on whether gender, an identity within a social group, or sex, the differential experience of bodies, is primary, and which is to be understood in terms of the other. If the primary factor is gender as a social identity, then clearly the centre of investigation will be in the examination of social structuring, and the impact, so far as it can be assessed, on the lives and thinking of individuals and movements. If the differential experience of bodies is understood as the definitive feature, then exploration will centre on the meaning that is attached to body, and the ways in biology and social reality interrelate. Rublack points out that, in her investigation of Early Modern Germany, giving birth carried with it a particular meaning within a community:

> Gestation and parturition thus made sexual difference an ontological category; they gave essentially different meanings to each sex which were rooted in contemporary perceptions of bodily processes.[193]

Identity, and more crucially, meaning, were located in the reproductive role.

It appears to have been quite clear to early modern people both that the body was a significant marker of gender and that it was an unreliable marker of gender. Its unreliability lay in the fact that it was so mutable. The body itself was not a closed category, but could be invaded, and inhabited by an other:

> the line drawn around the self was not firmly closed. One could get inside other people and receive other people within oneself, and not just during sexual intercourse or when a child was in the womb.[194]

The most obvious place where this was true was in the theology of the Eucharist, where the body of Christ was received in the transubstantiated bread, and became part of the body of the believer. It applied in other places too, and later was to become part of the climate of belief that led to the witch crazes; part of the beliefs about witches involved the Devil's ability to function in, on and through the bodies of others.

---

[192] Roper, *Oedipus and the Devil*, p. 48.

[193] Ulinka Rublack, "Pregnancy, Childbirth and the Female Body in Early Modern Germany", *Past and Present*, vol. 150, 1996, p. 86.

[194] Natalie Zemon Davis, "Boundaries and the Sense of Self in Sixteenth-Century France," *Reconstructing Individualism: Autonomy, Individuality and the Self in Western Thought*, Eds. Thomas C. Heller, Morton Sonsa and David E. Wellberg, California: Stanford University Press, 1986, p. 56. See also Ulinka Rublack, "Pregnancy, Childbirth and the Female Body", in which she points out "A body was not a site of predictable processes, but of sudden changes....Boundaries between inside and outside, the individual and the social, the emotional and the physical, were generally experienced as permeable, not firm". p. 109.

The lack of a secure sense of boundary around self was partly a result of the less defined sense of individualism, a category it is all too easy to attempt to import anachronistically. But there was also a medical or scientific pattern of though behind it. As Fletcher points out:

A sense of constant mutation inside themselves [was] accepted by those who lived in the humoral body.[195]

With only one body to choose from, gendering, that foundational principle for ordering, had to depend on other markers and pointers, not just to indicate it, but also to substantiate and define it. Gender was demonstrated by behaviour and position in society: the undermining of that was treated very fiercely. Roper comments:

masculinity, just as much as femininity, concerned the management of the body.[196]

and Fletcher argues:

An individual's sexual temperament, in effect gender, was a question of the balance in the body of the hot and cold, dry and moist qualities. This gender system had nothing whatsoever to do with the sexual orientation of men and women. Nor was the visible genital difference, except insofar as it reflected and symbolised someone's place on the continuum between human strength and weakness, of significance. Sex, in other words, was still a sociological and not an ontological category.[197]

Despite Fletcher's comments that sex was a sociological category, for Schwenckfeld, sex, and/or gender, are best understood as *symbolic* and *functional* categories. The symbolism by which male and female were defined and understood, and the functions which they carried out then became the way of defining what it meant to be a man or a woman. I am not suggesting that he started with a clean sheet, and only came to his understanding of what it meant to exist in his society as a man or a woman though his elucidation of the symbolic ways in which such categories were used. To exercise the capacity to think is to think within the categories of the society within which individual formation has taken place. But the movement of this reflection is not all one way. It is not that body determines gender, first socially and then symbolically, and then the category is applied to theological and spiritual concepts. Rather, Schwenckfeld began to explore the symbolic meanings of gender categories in

---

[195] Anthony Fletcher, *Gender, Sex and Subordination in England 1500-1800*, New Haven and London, Yale University Press, p. 47.

[196] Roper, *Oedipus and the Devil*, p. 108.

[197] Fletcher, *Gender, Sex and Subordination*, p. xvii.

a different way, meanings he had already drawn from the society in which he learned to think. As he did this, he was then free to uncover and offer different models of what it meant to exist both within society and before God as male and female.

In this thesis, I will be discussing Schwenckfeld's theology of Eucharist, of the Incarnation of Christ, the continuing flesh of Christ and the spirituality which such a theology gave rise to. By looking at these central themes, and by questioning them using the tools of gender analysis, I will show that the responses of so many women, and the roles which they played in the movement, especially in South Germany, were not determined by their reaction to a handsome face and courteous manner, nor by the freedom accorded to them as religion was moved into the home. I will argue that the women who chose to adopt this teaching did so because of the challenges it posed to traditional understandings of what it meant to be female, and to act in a feminine way. The women who became Schwenkfelders exercised their own authority of choice, and chose a road which affirmed them in their humanity and femaleness, allowing them to recognise in this their creation in the image of God, and their place in the saving purpose of God.

Such an examination will also take seriously Schwenckfeld's own sense that his insights into the nature of Christ, and the consequences of that nature on the understanding of embodiment and salvation were not peripheral, but central. His beliefs about the flesh of Christ, what it meant to say that God became incarnate, and the entailed meaning for human embodiment can, by this methodology, be examined in the central place which Schwenckfeld accorded them, rather than as odd and negligible aspects of his thinking.

Thus, by examining the theology of Caspar Schwenckfeld in terms of its beliefs about gender we will be able to gain greater insight into the agency of women within the radical Reformation, and to examine the Reformer's theology in a new and fruitful way.

Chapter 2

Sexuality and Sacrament

But now as the above mentioned error, through Satan, who disguises himself as an angel of light, began to win progress, philosophy and human reason became involved too in the place of the Holy Spirit in godly things, and they helped to confirm the matter. For one group had beautified things (because they had no spiritual judgement) so that in their erroneous understanding they had to invent Transubstantiation and say; The bread cannot be at one and the same time the bread and the body of Christ; therefore, only the figure of the bread remains after the transformation, and as all human senses are deceived, one should only believe.

Because therefore the natural body of Christ, which was born from Mary, must be in the bread, or in the figure of the bread according to their understanding of the word 'This is my body', and it follows 'which is given for you' they have, of necessity had to make an outer offering from this, because the word 'offering' or 'sacrifice', as they find in the previous Fathers serves well to confirm their opinion and thinking, since they didn't understand how to use the Fathers' discussion[…].

So thus, in place of communion the feast of Corpus Christi began, and the bread was carried around as the body of Christ, the bread was honoured as God, yes, was held to be God and all divine honour was paid to it.

What and how further errors, superstitions and idolatry take root with passing time around this article (for one error always gives birth to another), would take too long to tell, and it has also come so far that not only on behalf of living and dead souls, but also for temporal needs, so that Mass is even held for unreasoning animals, and the Sacraments are used. See how the Papists stick in such above mentioned error until they are over their ears. May God wish to be merciful to them and free them from it graciously.[1]

This passage comes from a document written in 1527, *A General Epistle; Ground and Cause of the Error and Controversy concerning the Lord's Supper*. In this passage, Schwenckfeld laid out his understanding of how the celebration of the sacrament has descended from the pure form introduced by Christ at the Last Supper to the abuse which Schwenckfeld sees in the contemporary Roman practice. The description also clearly demonstrates the

---

[1] *CS*, vol. 2, p. 459, ll. 5f.

importance Schwenckfeld attached to not giving honour to that which was not God – that is, not taking part in idolatry.

Much of his distress over the practice of the Eucharist was a sense that the way in which the rite and indeed the elements themselves were treated was effectively idolatry, since it was putting something other than God, something which was outer, in the place of the divine. The position and understanding of the nature of Christ's body was central to this whole discussion for him. His basic complaint was that the bread was being treated as the Body. It was being paid the honour due only to God alone and there was the expectation that in receiving the bread, the being of Christ was received. This then led to a theology which linked the receiving of bread with the receiving of forgiveness, and this cut right across Schwenckfeld's understanding that that which was outer – that is, the bread – could not mediate that which was inner – the experience of the presence and the forgiveness of Christ. As I will show as the discussion progresses, he was not simply proposing a rejection of the physical in favour of the spiritual, but was beginning to ask serious questions about the nature of the spiritual, and the relationship between the physical and the spiritual.

In his rejection of the Roman Mass, he was part of the whole Reformation community which, with varying degrees of emphasis, rejected the doctrine of transubstantiation. However, for Caspar Schwenckfeld, the rejection of the Mass proved to be simply the beginning of the development of his theological thinking about the Eucharist. The long quotation at the beginning of this chapter is taken from a major document, one of four *Circular Letters* (*Sendbrieffe*), in which he discussed both the positions he was rejecting and, in great detail, the doctrines he was adopting. They were self-consciously written to justify his position in regard to all the major theological positions of his period.[2] It is not surprising that Eucharistic theology should prove such a potent force in the defining of Schwenckfeld's distinctive position, since it was one of the major fault-lines of the whole reform movement. In this chapter, I will examine the way in which his Eucharistic theology developed, and the form which it took. That will allow an exploration of the way in which his ideas, driven by his separation of inner and outer, differed from the mainstream theology he inherited and which was being developed around him.

Body and Sacrament

Central to the whole discussion was the understanding of the nature of the relationship between the body and blood of Christ and the bread and wine of

---

[2] In the heading of the letter, which Schwenckfeld later prepared for publication, it is made clear that it is written to "all Christian people among the four parties", *CS*, vol. 2, p. 445, ll. 2f. The four parties he identified in the course of the discussion were the Papists, the Lutherans, the Zwinglians and the Anabaptists.

the Communion. Central to the practice was the reception of the bread (and in some periods also the wine) by the body of the believer. Thus in both theology and practice, the concept of body and its relationship to divinity was the defining feature of Christian thinking and practice. Body and bodily existence are not neutral elements in such a faith, but carry a significant part of its meaning.[3]

It is normally part of the meaning of body, and it certainly was in the sixteenth century, that it involves gender. A body is a male body or a female body. Given a definition as one or the other, such a body is then understood in certain ways and expected to act in particular roles. The definition of male or female is partly shaped by the biological reality of the body (most specifically in terms of reproduction), but the classification then also determines how that body is perceived, and what are appropriate actions. There is a sense, then, in which the Christian faith, sacramental theology and in particular, Eucharistic theology cannot be discussed without consideration of the meaning and perception of the body, including issues of gender. This will relate both to the functions and the understandings of the gendered body, and to the body represented by the elements and the receiving body of the believer. Within the context of the discussion of this thesis, and the questions about gender construction and the use of gender in the construction of a world-view, this has a particular importance. The Christian faith is Incarnational – that is, at its heart is the claim that God lived in human flesh, in a human body. As such, the meaning of body is important. The Sacrament of the Eucharist, or as Schwenckfeld preferred, the Lord's Supper, has at its centre something to do with a relationship within a particular ritual between bread and wine and the body and blood of the Incarnate God. This bread and wine are eaten and drunk, received into the bodies of believers. So, to examine this Sacrament is to consider, in a particular way, both body as understood in terms of the Incarnation, and the bodies of believers as they encounter the divine. Since body functions as a significant marker of gender, and since gender is a fundamental determining feature in the understanding of body, a consideration of the Sacrament is particularly susceptible to questioning using the categories of gender.

Caspar Schwenckfeld became involved in serious religious living and theological reflection as a result of Luther's teaching. However it was

---

[3] Roper writes: It is no accident that it should have been the issue of communion which so inflamed passions and divided early modern people. Communion, after all, is far more than a metaphor. Taking communion is a physical process…through which community and the relationship with God are consummated…That is, the question of body and the boundaries between human and divine lay at the very heart of the Reformation. Roper, *Oedipus and the Devil,* pp. 22-23. Schwenckfeld's use of metaphor will be discussed in greater detail below, but it is certainly true that for him, this area was the heart of spiritual and theological reflection.

Schwenckfeld's Eucharistic theology which propelled him into a theology independent of Luther, and it was to remain the driving force of all his theological and spiritual thinking. This appears strange when we reflect that one of the things which was recognised as a distinctive feature of Schwenckfeld's theology was the moratorium on the celebration of the Lord's Supper, the Stillstand. From 1526 onwards, he, and many of is followers withdrew from the reception of bread and wine. In itself, not to receive the elements was not terribly unusual. For most people, actually eating the bread, as opposed to being present when the service was said, was an infrequent occurrence in pre-Reformation practice. Miri Rubin has shown how as early as the thirteenth century a pattern of *spiritual* communion was a matter of discussion and debate.[4] The language which Schwenckfeld used to discuss these questions bears a striking similarity to some of this debate.

Schwenckfeld's Theology of the Eucharist

Schwenckfeld's understanding of reality was that it could be classified very clearly as, in his terms, inner and outer, according to its Ordnung, order. This is a word which appears, for instance, in social codifications, such as Polizeiordnung, or Hochzeitordnung, and a variety of social legislation.[5] It is a word which refers to a conscious decision to bring something into order, and to make it coherent. The concept is about keeping things under control, and avoiding chaos. It draws on the notion that there is a way for things to be when all is well, and such a way should be sought.[6] His understanding of the

---

[4] Miri Rubin, *Corpus Christi: The Eucharist in Late Medieval Culture*, Cambridge: Cambridge University Press, 1991, pp. 63-64.

[5] The Augsburg Chronicles refer to services "Nach der Ordnung der Christenhait", while Sebastian Frank wrote of a plan being "Auss Gottes Ordnung auf Gott Befehl", Fischer *Schwäbisches Wörterbuch*, "ordnung",vol V, columns 683-689.

[6] The keeping of order was a significant issue in the early modern period, and was closely linked with religious acitivity and patterns. See the discussions in R. Po-Chia Hsai, *Social Discipline in the Reformation: Central Europe, 1550-1750*, London: Routledge, 1989, pp. 122 ff; R. Scribner, "Social Control and Urban Reformation" in *Popular Culture and Popular Movements in Reformation Germany,* London: Hambledon, 1987, pp. 175ff; Thomas A. Brady Jr, "In Search of the Godly City: The Domestication of Religion in the German Urban Reformation" in R. Po-Chia Hsia, *The German People and the Reformation*, Ithaca: Cornell University Press, 1988. Gerhardt Oestriech's discussion inhis book, *Neostoicism and the Early Modern State*, translated David McLintock, Cambridge: Cambridge University Press, 1982, draws an interesting parallel religious covenant theology and political contract thinking in the development of early modern political theory and practice. Although Schwenckfeld was clearly a consummate politician and courtier, this theology seems to have played little part in his thinking. However, it is fair to assume that the maintenance of order and social cohesion was important to him.

Eucharist was driven by his insistence on the separation of the orders of inner and outer, and the implication of this insight, that the inner could not be conveyed by the outer. Indeed, he believed that this confusion of categories was of greatest danger to the Reformation.[7] In 1551, in a letter to Catherina Ebertz and Cecilia von Kirchen, he wrote about the ways in which he believed other understandings and theologies were wrong:

> I am pleased and have thanked God for you that you have read with great eagerness the Postill on the gospel of the Lord's Supper and are firmly established in that Christian teaching, that Christ can be sought and found nowhere but at the right hand of his Father, although almost the whole so-called Christianity struggles against that teaching and Christ, despite the word and command of Christ (Matt 24:23, Lk 17,23), seek him here and there in the Sacrament and elsewhere, which idolatry Luther in our time has only confirmed.[8]

As I suggested in the introduction, Schwenckfeld was fundamentally a theological pragmatist. This insight into what he understood to be false came through his empirical observation rather than philosophical abstraction. Because of what he saw happening in the lives of the people with whom he was concerned, he wanted to find a way of explaining it. The separation of inner and outer formed an acceptable explanation, one which would then shape a theology which could answer the questions such behaviour posed. As a courtier, the avoidance of chaos, the preservation of decency and order would have been among the deepest of Schwenckfeld's instincts. It was certainly deeply ingrained in his theological thinking, and is one of the significant features of it: the determination to distinguish the two orders, and to avoid any suggestion that they blended or could be confused. This was part of his pragmatic approach. What mattered about religion was that it made relationship with the divine possible: it was a way of bridging the two orders without succumbing to chaos. Any theology which did not do this was flawed.

His writings and the doctrinal controversies in which he became involved were not for their own sake or the thrill of intellectual discovery, but in order to enable a true life in God to be found and experienced. With no formal training in theology, his interest was not so much in theology for its own sake, but with ontology – what was existence and how could human existence be brought into contact with the divine? Although on the face of it, questions about the nature of existence look anything but practical, for Schwenckfeld this question about the meaning of being human was the basic one. Only by understanding the proper pattern between human and divine, and therefore discovering the right relationship was there any possibility of salvation. In reply to the suggested accusation that he was indulging in idle speculation, he wrote:

---

[7] See Maron, *Individualismus und Gemienschaft*, p. 103.

[8] *CS*, vol. 12, p. 585, ll. 21f.

Although some are not troubled on such points (the majestic state of Christ, and the heavenly being of the human, or the flesh and blood of Christ) and especially those who are not concerned with His Kingdom and the knowledge of Christ, holding them for a wordy quarrel, some think that they are too difficult and high, but it is actually necessary for us and all Christians to know as much foundation of the Christian faith as possible, of which I here now will tell in summary.[9]

This quotation comes from Schwenckfeld's Confession of 1541, in which he laid out his understanding of Christ and his glory, in order to explain his position when he came under attack from the preachers in Ulm. Thus, the language deals with his questions about the nature of Christ and the relationship between Christ's humanity and divinity. He was concerned that some believed these issues to be too difficult to understand, and so would effectively refuse to consider them. His point was that these were not abstruse doctrines, to be reflected on only by those who were particularly capable or concerned, but that they dealt with what he believed to be the very centre of the faith. Thus, such discussion, although it was hard, was not idle speculation, but of prime importance in the discovery of the way of salvation.

He was not concerned with describing God for the sake of describing God, but in order to make it possible for people to be in the proper relationship to such a God. Part of that description included a description of what it meant to be human. This was the way in which the differences between God and humanity could be understood. Only thus was the possibility of overcoming this basic separation real. Such an approach meant that he was often less concerned with exactly what a doctrine entailed in terms of philosophy and theology, and more with its practical implications. This is a theme that appears most clearly in his approach to spirituality – the living out of the relationship – but it is fundamental to all of his theological thinking

As shown in the quotation at the beginning of the chapter, Schwenckfeld believed that the misuse of the Sacrament within Roman and Lutheran theology had led not only to bad theology, that is, wrong beliefs about the nature of the Sacrament itself, but also to dangerous practical results. The nature of the church was under attack, the understanding of forgiveness was wrong, and the position of the believer in relation to the divine was misrepresented. The implication of the argument laid out in that passage is that, when the theology of the Eucharist is faulty, then everything else becomes fragile. The implication therefore is that when the Eucharist is properly taught and practised, the other parts of the picture will also be correctly focused. However, it became both clear and distressing to him that, although as a result of reform, theology and liturgy were now purified, the lives of the people were not showing the evidences of the new life which was the presence of God. He was not the only one to notice this, but he did not find the explanations of others satisfying. While Luther, for example, suggested that it was as much a matter of time as

---

[9] *CS*, vol. 7, p. 523, ll. 4f.

anything – it would require time and teaching for the results of the new theology to take their effects in people's lives, and he also pointed out that there were generations of misunderstandings and bad practice to overcome – Schwenckfeld believed that faulty theology was the cause. He began to explore the possibility that Lutheran Eucharistic theology was as much at fault as Roman theology had been. He reflected on the issue of what the Real Presence would mean if it were true, that is, if everyone who received bread and wine actually fed on the body and blood of Christ. The instance which he concentrated on was that of Judas. In 1556, in a letter in which he looked back on the steps by which he had come to his Eucharistic theology, he wrote this:

> I was as good a Lutheran as one could be, but it pleased my God that he saw me with the eyes of his mercy, and soon helped me. He threw before me the traitor Judas, and caused me to reflect what kind of fellow he was and how the devil came into him after his eating. Jn 13:27.[10]

Schwenckfeld's contention was always that truth was found in the gift of God, not through human reason.[11] Thus, his claim that the reason he considered Judas was because God led him to such a consideration is consistent with his explicit approach. We might also speculate that the reason why reflection on Judas seemed so appropriate was connected with his attitude to those about whose behaviour he was concerned. The people who distressed him were not those who did not claim to be Christians: pagans and heathens. He was not concerned about them in the slightest, so far as we can tell. Rather, those who distressed him were those who did claim to be Christian, but whose lives belied their words. It was they who continued the pattern of Judas: claiming to be in contact with Christ, but not showing the reality of that encounter in their living. His concentration on Judas suggests that he saw in such people a similar betrayal of Christ, although nowhere does he make this explicit.

Schwenckfeld was quite certain that although Judas took bread and wine at the Last Supper, he could not have received the true body and blood of Christ. In 1530, when he produced a Catechetical Confession of the Lord's Supper, in which he outlined his theology, he wrote this of the question of Judas:

> So did Judas eat the body of the Lord together with the other disciples in the Supper to his guilt and did he condemn himself in eating?

Answer

---

[10] *CS*, vol. 14, p. 802, ll. 17f.

[11] He argued "For proper Christian faith is a heavenly gift, and divine strength (Eph 3:16,17) through which we are reborn, enlightened and proved to salvation." *CS*, vol. 3, p. 7, ll. 18 f.

Judas ate what the other disciples ate externally in the Supper, but not internally. He indeed received the visible Sacrament, as is clear in Luke, but not the Body and Blood of Jesus Christ, which Augustine in the Tractate 59 on John clearly distinguishes. The disciples (he says) have eaten the bread of the Lord himself, but Judas has eaten the bread of the Lord against the Lord; these have eaten for life (for the body of Christ is life and those who eat it have eternal life), but the other has eaten to his death.[12]

Here Schwenckfeld distinguished between the visible sacrament and the body and blood. To eat the bread and drink the wine was to participate in the visible ritual of the sacrament, but Schwenckfeld insisted that in itself was not to encounter Christ in a life-giving way. It is this distinction which drives the rest of his theological thinking. All of the other oppositions which become part of his theological framework take their pattern from this one. Physically to receive bread and wine is not necessarily to encounter Christ spiritually. Thus, the pattern was set – physically to be touched by the water of baptism was not a guarantee, far less a means to enable the spiritual baptism which was the marker of new life.[13] Physically to hear the spoken word of the sermon, or to respond in the prayers was not inevitably to encounter God in faith and truth.[14] What is interesting, however, in the way in which he set up the oppositions, and which is illustrated in the example of Judas, is that he did not put the emphasis on the distinction between physical and spiritual in such a way as to suggest that they were an opposition. The other disciples both ate bread and drank wine *and* encountered Christ as life-giver. The one did not preclude the other.

---

[12] *CS*, vol. 3, p. 747, ll. 13f

[13] John the Baptist also held to such a distinction when he said 'I baptise with water for repentance, but the one who comes after me will baptist you with the Holy Spirit and with fire.' For he distinguished the work of the minister from the role of the Lord, and the visible water from the Holy Spirit... Of such a distinction it is also written in 1 Pet 3:21, where St Peter says "Baptism saves us" and immediately sets it out, not the taking off of the impurity of the flesh, but by the appeal or the answer of a good conscience before God through the resurrection of Jesus Christ.
Therefore Peter distinguishes clearly the two waters and washings of Christian baptism, the inner and the outer, and one wets of purifies the body, but the other the conscience, heart and soul; which alone, as Peter says, makes us saved, holy and righteous. *CS*, vol. 11, p. 106, ll. 23f.

[14] Nobody who knows of your foundation, and that you have a better teacher, yes the only master in all godly things in your heart would wonder that you would idly stand the erring preachers' teaching. Who also the living Word of God from the Father himself hears and learns and comes to Christ in his heavenly school will not allow himself to be disturbed by this preacher's literal dead words. *CS*, vol. 12, p. 705, ll. 5f. This passage comes from a letter to Katherina Ebertz, and incidentally, shows something of the importance which Schwenckfeld placed on individual religious experience and conviction, even in the case, or perhaps particularly in the case of the women to whom he was close.

However, such an approach still left him with the problem of what the nature of the true sacrament was. As the quotation above about being a good Lutheran makes clear, he understood that it was God who led him to think in a different way about the whole issue. In the letter of 1556 he continued to describe the process like this:

> Was it possible that such a one could eat the true and real body of Jesus Christ our Lord, king and saviour and drink his blood (which is the blood of the new eternal covenant) as the Lutherans hold until today? With such a point I continued for a while, pregnant in my mind, but not for long, until the Spirit of the Lord came to my help with his teaching in the sixth chapter of John, where he says "Whoever eats my flesh and drinks my blood, he has eternal life" Jn 6: 54. Then the grace of God also helped me, so that I was certain and sure in my heart that the traitor Judas (whom the Lord had also called "devil" Jn 6:70, and in whom Satan had begun the work of betrayal before the Supper) had in no way been fed with the body and blood of Christ, because the body and blood of Christ is never without divine strength, Spirit and life, nor can it be.[15]

From the time when he came to this conclusion, Jn 6: 54-55[16] became the controlling text of his Eucharistic theology.[17] His letter continued by discussing the further steps that he found himself taking, and he made it clear that he understood this in terms of a spiritual rather than an intellectual exploration. Eventually he reached the point where he could say:

> Then I was certain in my heart that Christ may not be eaten, nor his blood drunk by us without faith.[18]

This statement, interpreted in the light of John chapter 6 was to remain determinative of his Eucharistic theology for the rest of his life. In this he was following a similar method of exegesis as the medieval church, although the conclusions he drew from it were radically different. In the debate over whether the cup should or should not be given to the laity, the Roman church looked to John 6 as a chapter which spoke of the spiritual reality of the Eucharist, and pointed out that in that chapter, Jesus spoke of himself only as the living bread,

---

[15] *CS*, vol. 14, p. 802, ll. 21 f. This passage comes from a letter to Dr Marz Zimmermann of Augsburg. It was written (in 1556) at a time when the theology of Eucharist was being debated again, having been raised by Calvin in 1549. Schwenckfeld was still arguing for the views which he had proposed in 1527, and in this letter, he set out why he had rejected his original (Lutheran) position and come to the conclusions he had.

[16] Those who eat my flesh and drink my blood have eternal life, and I will raise them upon the last day; for my flesh is true food and my blood is true drink. John 6: 54-55. *New Revised Standard Version*.

[17] Maier makes it clear that it is not only the eucharistic theology, but all of Schwenckfeld's theology which is profoundly influenced by the Johannine writings. Maier, *Caspar Schwenckfeld on the Person and Work of Christ*, p. 33.

[18] *CS*, vol. 14, p. 803, ll. 9 f.

and fed the crowd only on bread. Thus, ran the argument, to receive the bread was to receive the fullness of Christ. As we have seen above, such a conclusion was not one which Schwenckfeld would draw, but in regarding John 6 as definitive Eucharistic text, he was treading a well-worn path, and one which, as I will show below, Luther rejected wholeheartedly, instead arguing that the chapter dealt with faith.[19]

In order to explain the form his thinking was taking after he came to this conclusion, in 1525 he wrote a document (Twelve Questions), which he sent to Luther. The original text of this document has been lost, but the editors of the *Corpus Schwenckfeldianorum* insist that:

> It is absolutely certain that these twelve questions concerned themselves with the relation of Judas to the Supper. While the original form is lost, there can hardly be a doubt that the tractate published in 1529 and entitled "Ein Christlich bedenken. Ob Judas/ und die ungleubigen falschen Christen/ den leib und das blut Jhesu Christi/ jm Sacrament des Nachtmals etwan empfangen/ oder auch noch heut empfangen und niessen mogen" is a reproduction of this same argument, probably with the expansion of some points together with changes in the verbiage and form here and there.[20]

Whether or not it is really a reproduction of the *Twelve Questions*, in *Ein Christliche bedencken*, Schwenckfeld stated his argument with the assertion that

> The body of Christ which is broken for us, is a food which is not corruptible; it is a spiritual, heavenly, blessed food, which is carried and distributed in the living word of the Father; it feeds for and remains into eternal life [21]

The second assertion is:

> The Lord Christ is eternal life, and through his flesh and blood he shares nothing other than what he himself is, which is to say, eternal life.[22]

He then continued by arguing that only those who were true believers could receive the food which Christ gave. He referred again to the question about Judas, and stating that:

> From this it incontrovertibly follows that Judas and the godless unbelieving people who are limbs of Satan and outside the body of Christ may not be fed with the body of glory and majesty. [23]

---

[19] See Heinrich Bornkamm, *Luther in Mid-Career, 1521-1530*, translated Theodore Backmann, London: Darton, Longmann and Todd, 1983, p. 504.

[20] *CS*, vol. 2, p. 132.

[21] *CS*, vol. 3, p. 499, ll. 5f.

[22] *CS*, vol. 3, p. 499, ll. 24f.

He insisted that anyone who taught otherwise "separated the body of Christ from the eternal word of the Father",[24] and that such a separation was impossible. His argument continued by making points about the need for the believer really to desire Christ, to be drawn to the Father through the Son, that the Supper is the fulfilment of the Old Testament promises and shadows and finally, again, that this must be a purely spiritual experience, only open to those who were spiritually renewed.

Schwenckfeld, having come to his conclusions, and having laid them out, then began to look for linguistic help. Much of the defence of Schwenckfeld's position rested on an unusual way of interpreting the Greek phrase "*Touto estin to soma mou*", This is my body. It was more commonly discussed in the Vulgate version "*Hoc est corpus meum*", and this, or the German "*Das ist mein leib*" was what Schwenckfeld normally referred to.[25] But with the rise of the humanist interest in original languages, more effort had been put into understanding the Greek. Schwenckfeld's education had clearly included Latin, and some of his early letters and treatises were written in Latin, and some in both Latin and German. In later years he almost invariably wrote in German.[26] However, although he clearly understood Greek to a degree, he was not a skilled Greek scholar. His interpretation of the phrase was that it should be read as "My body is this", that is, my body is a food for you in the way that bread is. However, he clearly understood that he needed help in justifying this interpretation, and that his own linguistic ability was not sufficient. Valentine Crautwald, a colleague in Liegnitz was a renowned and skilful linguist, and Schwenckfeld appealed to him. Crautwald at first disagreed with Schwenckfeld, but after a fortnight's study and prayer, he too was convinced,

---

[23] *CS*, vol. 3, p. 502, ll. 29f.

[24] *CS*, vol. 3, p. 502, l. 37.

[25] See Maron, *Individualismus und Gemeinschaft*, pp. 88-89.

[26] The issue of language and communication is an interesting one in the examination of Schwenckfeld's movement. As Mark U. Edwards Jr. has argued, in *Printing, Propaganda and Martin Luther* the choice of Latin or German was driven by which audience the writer was trying to reach. The proportion of the population who could read was faily small, and and a smaller part of that read Latin. Thus, those who wrote in German were making a particular statement about accessibility. Even then, however, literacy was not widespread. Edwards argues that the Reformation was primarily an *oral* event. (p. 37) Schwenckfeld, on the other hand, communicated most frequently through writing, published or private. It remains unclear how much this was a conscious decision to reach only those of his own class, and how much it was happenstance. His activities in Silesia demonstrated a desire to reach widely, and therefore presumably beyond the literate. This is not so clear when he is in exile. It also raises the interesting question of the literacy rates of women at the time. Is it possible that some of those to whom he sent greetings rather than personal letters among those who could not read?

and wrote a treatise defending the position.[27]

Armed with this, Schwenckfeld made a trip to Wittenberg to try and convince Luther, who appeared at first to receive him with tolerance, though not agreeing. In fact, most of the discussion was with Bugenhagen, as Luther was either too busy, or not interested enough in Schwenckfeld's argument to listen.

This is the point where Schwenckfeld's commitment to the duality of reality that I have identified above was exploited and made explicit. The separation of the two orders was the touchstone of his discussion with both Luther and Bugenhagen. It was also the point at which he believed the disagreements were focused. During the time when he was in Wittenberg, Schwenckfeld kept a diary, and used it as the basis for a letter to his uncle, in which he described his reception and the discussions.

> I asked over and again, whether it was in accordance with our faith that Christ should have left his natural body or flesh here for us under the bread as a food. He answered: "Yes, he has left his body or flesh here invisibly." Schwenckfeld: "How then do I eat this invisible bread?" Pomeranus:[28] "I eat the bread externally, and in the bread, the body of Christ." Schwenckfeld: "How do I eat this, physically or spiritually?" Pomeranus: "I eat it spiritually" Schwenckfeld: "I thank you for this, dear preacher" and I shook hands with him. "Now we are at one." Pomeranus: "I still say that the words of Christ are that this is his body. So I follow the Institution of Christ and concern myself no further." Schwenckfeld: "But you must eat either the mortal or the glorified body." Pomeranus: "I eat the body of Christ." Schwenckfeld: "But you have allowed me that you eat the body spiritually." Pomeranus: "Yes, I eat him in the bread, where he is also after the words have been spoken over it according to the Institution of Christ." Schwenckfeld: "But he must be there physically or spiritually." Pomeranus: "I do not need to know this. I know that the body of Christ is there by the content of the words." Schwenckfeld: "By which words does he enter into the bread?" Pomeranus: "I simply hold to the Institution of Christ and let him care." [29]

This is typical of the ground the discussions covered, circling around other issues, but always coming back to this one of the separation between inner and outer in the understanding of the body of Christ.

Luther himself drew a distinction between outer and inner. In a sermon he

---

[27] There is significant discussion about who was the driving the force in the exploration of the new interpretation, Schwenckfeld or Crautwald. While chronologically it is clear that Schwenckfeld started to reinterpret the words and then spoke to Crautwald, there is disagreement over whether Crautwald or Schwenckfeld was the leading *theological* thinker. See Douglas H. Schantz, "The Role of Valentine Crautwald in the Growth of Sixteenth Century Schwenckfeldian Reform: A New Look at the Crautwald-Schwenckfeld Relationship", *Mennonite Quarterly Review*, vol. 65, 1991.

[28] Bugenhagen came from Pomerania and was therefore referred to often, including in this extract from Schwenckfeld's letter, as Pomeranus.

[29] *CS*, vol. 2, p. 254, ll. 1f.

presented his argument saying:

> The first [the outer] is out of the heart, which we hold externally before our eyes, which is to say the Sacrament in itself, about which we believe the bread and wine is truly Christ's body and blood.

> The second [the inner] is within the heart, it cannot come out but it stands therein, as the heart should remain against the outer Sacrament.[30]

However, although they were using the same words, *innerlich* and *eusserlich*, inner and outer, there was clearly a profoundly different connotation. There does not appear to be anywhere in Luther's usage with regard to the Sacrament, anything like Schwenckfeld's denial of a spiritual content to an outer experience. Rather, it seems that Luther argued that the outer experience, that is, the physical existence of the bread and wine, contained within it a spiritual meaning, that is, the body and blood of Christ. He went on later in this sermon for example, to argue that those who used *physical* arguments against the presence of Christ in the Sacrament – that Christ's body was in heaven and therefore cannot be in the bread and wine – were missing the point. It is as if they could be said to be too physical. Luther was quite certain that there was a connection between the outer bread and wine, and the inner encounter with the body and blood of Christ. Thus he could argue:

> But this I know that the word there is 'Take, eat, this is my Body given for you. Do this in remembrance of me', When we speak this over the bread, so he is truly there and yet it is a simple word and voice that one hears. Just as he now comes into our hearts, and does not break a hole, but is grasped only through word and hearing, so he also comes in the bread, though he does not make a hole in it.[31]

Luther did not set out to dismantle the theology of the Mass, but rather, the changes were forced upon him as he worked out other bits of his theology. It was largely in his debate with Zwingli that he made explicit his thinking about the Real Presence. Until challenged by Zwingli and other "memorialists", he appears to have been content to assume a shared belief in the presence of Christ linked to bread and wine, without examining the details too closely.[32] The argument which was important to him, that he set out in "The Babylonian Captivity of the Church", was more to do with the "use" of the sacraments, and the opportunity to receive them, than with the mechanics of the theology. His main attack in this was on the doctrine that the Mass as a sacrifice offered by

---

[30] 1526, *Luthers Werke*, Weimar, 1897, vol 19, p. 482.

[31] Luther "Sermon von dem Sacrament", p. 500.

[32] Bornkamm, *Luther in Mid-Career*, pp. 310-324, Martin Brecht, *Martin Luther: Shaping and Defining the Reformation, 1521-1532*, Minneapolis, Minn: Fortress Press, 1990, pp. 293-340.

the priest on behalf of the people. This he understood to undermine the once and for all nature of Christ's work at Calvary, and to suggest that there was something yet to be completed in the action of salvation. However, he did argue that the words "This is my body" were to be taken at their face value, and that the body and blood and the bread and wine existed in some way together.[33] He based this argument not on the miracle of the consecration brought about by the action of the priest, but on the ubiquity of the glorified body of Christ. The Eucharist was the place where Christ promised to be, and so there was a sacramental reality in the bread and wine which could be identified with the body and blood. As the argument progressed, Luther became aware not only of the different theology of Zwingli, but also of that coming from Silesia, which Luther at first identified with "Valentine", that is Valentine Crautwald.[34] It is clear that for Luther, what we now refer to as the Schwenckfeldian-spiritualist position was basically the same as Zwingli's. This was a mistake on Luther's part, as I will show below. Bornkamm summarises the difference between the two positions, Luther's and Schwenckfeld's thus:

> Facing Luther's biblical realism there was now a spiritual realism: opposite the body of the crucified Lord, the spiritually real heavenly flesh of Christ received by the believer in a spiritual enjoyment of communion by the believer: confronting the justification of the sinner, essentially a transforming rebirth: over against the incarnate humanity of Christ, the Son of God's hypercreaturely corporeality since birth, which draws us into its heavenly being.[35]

This characterisation makes very clear not only the dichotomy which opened up between Schwenckfeld and his previous mentor, but also the fact that the division, while being focused at first on the nature of the Eucharist, was actually driven by a much deeper distinction in the understanding of the nature of reality. However, it is important that we do not assume, from this distinction between them, that in rejecting Luther's commitment to the link between body and bread, wine and blood, Schwenckfeld was refusing any physical reality to the inner experience. For Schwenckfeld, inner was not to be identified with *non-corporeal* nor outer with *corporeal*. The relationships are much subtler than that. It is clear in his language that he did not dismiss the physical as unimportant or without a role. What he did was redefine physical, and this is part of the distinctive position which he adopted.[36]

---

[33] In 1527, he produced a tract the title of which, as Brecht remarks (p. 311) "at once stated his agenda": "That These Words of Christ 'This is my Body' etc, Still Stand Firm Against the Fanatics". Weimar, vol. 23, pp. 38-320.) By this stage, Luther counted Schwenckfeld as one of the "fanatics".

[34] Bornkamm, *Luther in Mid-Career*, p. 513.

[35] Bornkamm, *Luther in Mid-Career*, p. 516.

[36] Edward Muir has pointed out that in the early modern period, it was normal for Christians to think in bodily and physical images. Edward Muir, *Ritual in Early Modern*

Dualism and Spiritual Physicality: Differences with Luther and Zwingli

Although there is a long Christian tradition of dualism, partly shaped by gnosticism, which regarded physical existence as at best a hindrance in the spiritual life and at worst evil per se, this is not a tradition, despite appearances, into which Schwenckfeld can easily be made to fit. His dualism was not of the sort which argued for the inherent superiority of non-corporeality. Rather, as his language and his manipulation of concepts show over and over again, his understanding of being was that it had *physical* existence. However, having said that, it is also clear that *physical* does have to be understood in a very specific way. Instead of accepting the straightforward division of the universe into spiritual and physical, Schwenckfeld worked with a series of concepts which allowed for a *spiritual physicality*, that is, inner: and a type of spirituality which could be rejected and discounted because it was *outer*. Thus, in discussions of the Supper, although he avoided the suggestion that bread and wine played the sort of role which Luther assigned to them, he did write in two distinctive ways. He made a very clear distinction between liturgical practice, that is, an expression of spirituality, and a true *inner* encounter and he continually used language of eating and drinking in a way that insisted these were real experiences.[37] This is true right from the beginning of his writing. Thus, in 1527, in the first of the four *General Epistles* which was titled *The Ground and Cause of the Error and Controversy concerning the Lord's Supper,*[38] in a passage which illustrates both aspects, he wrote this:

> This is what the Lord Christ primarily intended with the institution of the memorial of his supper, so that it is held in his remembrance, and first of all in the work of the breaking of bread, in eating and drinking, and he depicted this carnally for the sake of the disciples, because of the weakness of their flesh and as we heard at the start he gave this secret, according to his custom through a creaturely so that the disciples should learn through the manner and quality of the transient food and temporal bread, the type, nature and identity of the eternal heavenly bread in faith, and thus better be able to understand the greater heavenly matter. But not just that, but the Lord Christ has also by such a meaning or outer sign, as some might call it, the believing disciples were fed inwardly in their souls through the strength of his divine almighty word truly given them to eat and drink of his body and blood, so that the disciples at that time by faith in the word of life, received his body and blood and in the Supper were truly satisfied with

---

Europe, Cambridge: Cambridge University Press, 1997, p. 149. Although as I will discuss below, Schwenckfeld's use of such notions was not only on the level of imagery, still, it is clear that in this insistence on physical reality as a part of meaning, he was working with the accepted notions of his age.

[37] Maron, *Individualismus und Gemeinschafft,* p. 86 suggests that Schwenckfeld's theology looks only to what Maron calls "a spiritual eating". However, this is to ignore the force of the language and the insistence with which it is used.

[38] "Der erste dieser Sendbrieffe. Vom grund und ursache des Irrthumbs und Spans imm Articket vom Sacrament des Herrn Nachtmals." *CS,* vol. 2, pp. 445 ff.

them; with which He still today in the secret of His Supper feeds all Christians believers, gives them drink and satisfies them.[39]

The physical eating of bread and wine has a place. It is connected to memory and to teaching. But the *inner* experience can also be described in the same concrete terms, and with the same linguistic field. The words of *eating* and *drinking* are not to be understood simply as pictures, but as real experiences.

Ein Christliche Bedenken outlines the theology of the Sacrament that was to be fundamental to Schwenckfeld's thinking and practice for the rest of his life. Some of the points were to be elaborated on, and following the Stillstand of 1527, some were to become of especial importance, in particular the suggestion that the physical bread and wine were of little importance. But nothing was to be fundamentally altered. Although he was disappointed that he had not convinced Luther, Schwenckfeld continued to develop and teach his understanding. Luther, in the meantime, identified Schwenckfeld's Eucharistic understanding with that of Zwingli, and so characterised it as very dangerous. However, although Schwenckfeld rejected Luther's understanding because it mixed Creator and Creation, and therefore was in danger of being idolatrous, he rejected Zwingli's memorialism as well. So, in 1542, in a letter to Elizabeth von Laubenberg, in which he responded to her request to give instruction on Confession, baptism and the Supper, he wrote:

> We should also rejoice that we can hold this [Supper] with him daily, not just to remember the sacrifice of his body for us, nor the shedding of his blood for us, but to expect the gift and influence in our heart, through the Spirit of faith...[40]

Memorialism was rejected because it did not acknowledge the true encounter between Christ and the believer. Like Schwenckfeld, Zwingli argued that the Scriptures teach that salvation is through the faith that Christ has died for the believer, not through sacramental eating. Therefore, he maintained, the eating of the bread could not be a salvific action. The bread points to the saving action, but does not *contain* it. Again like Schwenckfeld, Zwingli was concerned with the words of institution, and suggested that they had been misinterpreted, and needed to be read in a wider context, since they could not simply mean what they seemed to say. The bread could not be Christ's body, because, when he said the words, Jesus was standing before his disciples, and his body was separate from the bread. Thus Zwingli argued that *is* in this statement must be understood as *signifies*, and the bread and wine seen as symbolic memorials, prompts to memory and faith. The encounter between the believer and Christ was entirely mediated subjectively, and the use of bread and wine was in response to the command of Christ, not because they had any merit

---

[39] *CS*, vol. 2, p. 539, ll. 5f.
[40] *CS*, vol. 8, p. 228, ll. 15f.

or meaning in themselves. He began writing about this in 1524, at first in Latin, and in 1526 he wrote a German treatise, *Eine klare Unterrichtung vom Nachtmahl Christi*, which outlined this symbolic position.[41] It is easy to see why Luther should have assumed that Schwenckfeld's position was the same as Zwingli's, but it clearly was not. Schwenckfeld insisted that *is* meant *is*. His grammatical innovation was the inversion of the subject and object which Crautwald had helped him to justify. Schwenckfeld and Zwingli also differed in their interpretation of the language of John 6. While Schwenckfeld argued that this was the controlling chapter in understanding the language of the Last Supper stories, Zwingli approached it from a different perspective. Like Schwenckfeld, and indeed many medieval theologians, he recognised the chapter as of critical importance in understanding the Supper.[42] However, insisting that elsewhere it was made clear that sacramental did not save, he argued that the "food" referred to in John 6 should be recognised as faith, and that the reference to Christ's flesh was to do with death, not with eating. He took verse 63 as the centre of the argument.[43] From this basis, he argued that anything physical in the sacrament was not in itself life-giving, and that any sense of a spiritual body was a contradiction in terms.[44] This is the place where Schwenckfeld found he was not in harmony with the Swiss Reformers, although it appeared at one time as if he might find a spiritual home there. That they took him seriously is clear from the enthusiasm that they had to publish his writings. Indeed, it was their enthusiasm to publish his letter *Ein Anwysung das die opinion der leyplichen gegenwertigkeit unsers Herren Jesu Christ im Brote oder unter der gestalt des brots etc. (The Refutation of the Opinion that the Corporeal Presence is in the Elements)*[45] despite his request that it should be kept private, which led to his exile from Silesia.[46]

Schwenckfeld thus reacted to both Luther and Zwingli in a manner coherent with their reactions to each other. Zwingli argued that Luther was continuing the *idolatry* of the traditional belief of transubstantiation. Luther believed Zwingli was emptying the sacrament of any objective reality. Schwenckfeld agreed with both of these characterisations. However, his relationship with the two respective positions is not fully described in such a summary. For as well as rejecting Luther's theology because it was too focused on the created order, too physical, he also questioned him because he was not physical enough. Schwenckfeld

---

[41] Zwingli, "A Clear Briefing About Christ's Supper", *Huldrych Zwingli sämtliche Werke*, Eds Emil Egli et al, Zurich, 1905, vol. IV, pp. 773-862.

[42] Ulrich Gäbler, *Huldrych Zwingli: His Life and Work*, trans Ruth C. L. Gritsch, Philadelphia, Penn., 1986, p. 133.

[43] "It is the spirit which gives life. The flesh is useless. The words I have spoken to you are spirit and life". John 6:63, *New Revised Standard Version*.

[44] For further discussion of Zwingli's eucharistic theology, see W.P. Stephens, *The Theology of Huldrych Zwingli,* Oxford: Clarendon, 1986, pp. 218-259.

[45] *CS.* vol. 3, pp. 1-23.

[46] See Schulz, *Caspar Schwenckfeld*, pp. 152-158.

understood the present reality of the physical being of Christ as the glorified flesh sitting at the right hand of God in heaven. This meant that he could not accept Luther's approach. One of his criticisms of Luther was that there would not be enough of Christ's body to go round, another that if Christ were in heaven, how could he also be said to be in the bread and wine, since no physical body can be in two places at once? In 1529, Schwenckfeld wrote a document called *Warhafftig ursach/ das der leib Christi/ nit jn der Creatur deß brotts/ aber durch wort gotts jm nachtmal und hertzen des glaubigen sey (The true cause: that the body of Christ is not in the creature of bread, but through the word of God, in the supper and in the heart of the believer.)* In this he argued:

> If Christ's body and blood were able to be in its essence in so many places and altars in the Sacrament, then he would not have had a reason to work such miracles.

He went on to raise the case of Stephen:

> Christ sits in heaven and there Stephen has seen him Acts 7:55-56. One should not believe anybody who points to him or seeks him elsewhere. Matt 24:23

and he also argued explicitly about the logical incoherence as he saw it of the Lutheran view:

> If one wants the bread in the Supper physically to be the body of Christ and thus every piece of the bread to be the true body of Christ physically, then the body of Christ will be in many more than one place, physically and really, and so will not be one body, but many.[47]

So, his rejection of Luther's theology was, at least on one level, not because Luther was not spiritual enough, but because he was being too spiritual, and not allowing enough corporeal reality to the physical being of Christ. Here we have a grounding of the category I was defining above: spiritual materiality. Schwenckfeld insisted on the *reality* of Christ's body in such a way that it could not be divided between heaven and the altar as he understood Luther's theology to imply. There was some sense in which, for Schwenckfeld, Christ's body had extension and spatial existence. That it could not be touched or measured or responded to in the way that physically material bodies could be was, at this point in the argument, irrelevant. There was something in the existence of the body of Christ, which could only be put into the category of physical. However, it was never to be understood in the category of *outer* and so there could be no identification of the two sets of categories.

He was also uncertain about Zwingli and the Swiss reformers. In Schwenckfeld's perception Zwingli was questionable because the memorialism

---

[47] *CS*, vol. 3, p. 523, ll. 37f; *CS*, vol. 3, p. 525, l. 10f; *CS*, vol. 3, p. 526, ll. 30f.

which lay at the heart of his Eucharistic theology did not give enough weight to the objective and physical encounter with Christ. This, in Schwenckfeld's understanding, was the centre of Eucharistic worship. In Zwingli's teaching, the Eucharist had become so *spiritualised* – so focused on the action of the faith of the believer – that it was quite removed from anything Schwenckfeld recognised as real. Schwenckfeld was insistent, with his emphasis on *real food and real drink*, that there was an objective reality in the Eucharist:

> ...so that the disciples at that time by faith in the word of life received his body and blood and in the Supper were truly satisfied with them: with which today he still, in the secret of his Supper feeds all Christian believers, gives them drink and satisfies them.

And also

> For the Lord Christ himself first brought down the secret of true heavenly bread, and taught perfectly that his body, flesh and blood and blood were true food and drink for eternal life.[48]

But again, his rejection of Zwingli was not straightforward. There was a sense in which Zwingli was unacceptable because of his insistence on the physicality of the rite. Zwingli stressed that the bread and wine were necessary in order to focus the attention and enable the memorial. For Schwenckfeld, this was to place too much value on the outer elements, possibly at the expense of the inner encounter. He did not totally dismiss the thanksgiving and memorial aspect, and acknowledged the importance of the elements of bread and wine in them. However as far as Schwenckfeld was concerned, this was a very different activity from the feeding which was the essence of the true *Supper of the Lord*.
Thus he could write:

> Now, it is quite clear from this that one can well learn to recognise such spiritual bread or food and know to seek the same in the Word of life and properly learn to distinguish it from the visible Sacramental Bread of the Lord which is eaten because of the remembrance in faith, not one going into the other, the heavenly Bread mixing with the earthly, nor the heavenly bread passed out through the earthly, but according to the type of Sacramental matter the two should be distinguished and always held apart in the appropriate order.[49]

Zwingli's insistence on physical bread and wine became a limiting factor.
Schwenckfeld's discussions in Wittenberg made it clear that he was not going to convince the leaders there of the rightness of his convictions. On his return home, it was obvious that, although he had undertaken to remain quiet until some agreement was reached, the party at Wittenberg were not going to

---

[48] *CS*, vol. 2, p. 539, ll. 18f. and *CS*, vol. 10, p. 540, ll. 10f.
[49] *CS*, vol. 2, p. 540, ll. 9f.

do the same. He found his approach attacked in various forms. It was these attacks which provoked the development of his writing about the Supper. The documents which are of particular interest here fall into two groups. There are those which date from the time of the Eucharistic controversy in the mid 1520s, in which he is first exploring and expressing his theology. These are written largely either to his companions in Liegnitz, or on their behalf to other reformers, in order to outline their position. The first three volumes of the Corpus largely reflect the time before he went into exile, and contain the theology which led him into separation and eventual isolation from the mainstream of reform. In them, there is a significant amount about the understanding of the Supper. In the later volumes, until about 1553, there is little published material dealing with these questions. Much of the material gathered from this period is made up of letters. The question of understanding and practice of the Supper does appear, but the discussion in the letters is mainly focused on explaining the already determined position, and examining its practical working out in the lives and, especially, the controversies of those who identified themselves with Schwenckfeld's teaching.

In the mid-1550s, the controversy emerged again, and there are a few more substantial letters, designed for publication, as well as some tractates which deal specifically with the issues. The theology in these is not significantly different from that arrived at prior to 1526, although some of the emphases are different as Schwenckfeld engaged with another set of questions and questioners.

In 1526, apparently in distress at the continuing controversies, Schwenckfeld withdrew from receiving the elements of the Supper physically, and those who worshipped with him in Liegnitz followed suit. He wrote a defence of this position, giving nine reasons why he no longer participated. The first of these was:

> I know that I am unworthy that I should hold this Supper with the heavenly King Christ, or sit at table, and will content myself in the meantime with his word.[50]

The sixth reason he gave was:

> I know that a person is satisfied in their soul by the Lord's Supper, and is filled full of heavenly grace, for whoever eats the flesh of Christ and drinks his blood, he remains in Christ and Christ in him.[51]

He then went on to point out that Paul had said if we partook of one bread we were one body, and since this was not the case, it would be better not to partake. Thus the Stillstand became an ongoing part of the spiritual experience of Schwenckfeld and those who followed him – and it was largely out of this

---

[50] *CS*, vol. 3, p. 383, ll. 3f.
[51] *CS*, vol. 3, p. 384, ll. 9f.

that the themes which were already present in his thinking, of inner and outer, the relationship of spiritual and physical, eating and drinking as spiritual realities, became such important issues. Removing himself from the debate about the way in which Christ could be present in bread and wine, Schwenckfeld opened up for himself and his followers a whole new area for exploration and meditation – that of the spiritual meaning of the Sacrament, and how it could have significance apart from its physical anchor.

So, the Eucharistic theology of Schwenckfeld is dependent on his understanding of inner and outer. This has its own theological dynamic. His use of outer to define inner, and the physical to describe and delimit the spiritual, suggest that Schwenckfeld was unable to conceive of a world which did not have as a fundamental part of its being a physical reality. It is out of this tension that the new understanding of inner as something which is spiritual, but is not non-corporeal, gains its impetus. In the context of a consideration of the sacraments, the place of the physical body is thus both central and marginal, and this incoherence was to provide the tension from which Schwenckfeld's most imaginative and creative theology was to spring. Any discussion therefore about Eucharistic theology must pick up questions about the understanding of body which is implied by the concepts used.

Sacrament, Spirit and Body

The most common way in which the link between human and divine has always been understood in Christian theology is through some form of physical encounter. This is the thinking which is at the heart of any Eucharistic theology. It is thinking that is shaped by the centrality of the notion of Incarnation: that God has become "enfleshed". However, by separating himself from a theology of physical sacraments, Schwenckfeld was loosing his hold on the most obvious and accepted link between the physical and the divine. But, as his dispute with Luther shows, he did not follow the path which led to the assumption that the body itself was unimportant and had no spiritual role. Rather, he invested the body with a spiritual meaning, and in the process, by implication, redefined how *body* was to be understood.

The traditional understanding of body is that is distinct from spirit. Since God is defined as Spirit, there is an ontological separation between God and embodied humanity. For both Luther and Zwingli, this was the point from which they began their Eucharistic theology. The question they had to answer was how that ontological divide was to be bridged. The traditional explanation argues that part of the human encounter with God involves the physical body. Because God is Spirit, this encounter can only take place if God takes into the divine being a physical expression. This was, after all, the basis of a doctrine of Incarnation – that, in order to save fallen humanity, God became enfleshed; adopted a physical expression that was not inherent in the divine nature. God does not have to have physical expression to be God. The doctrine of

Transubstantiation can be seen as an extension of this type of thinking – the transformation of the bread in its essence into the physical body of Christ is necessary so that embodied followers can encounter God.[52] The distinction between God and humanity is expressed as a distinction between spirit and embodiment. Communication is only possible between the two if an ontological journey is made, and in this theology, God must make the journey. Embodied humanity cannot meet God unless God comes to humanity in a body. Luther's doctrine of the Real Presence, although it drew the lines in different places, was reflecting the same approach. Bodies are separate from divinity, and it is God who crosses the divide.

Zwingli chose another approach, and suggested that bodies and divinity did not meet at all (except in the Incarnation). The encounter between humanity and divinity was understood as entirely non-corporeal, thus relegating the body to an arena outside the spiritual realm. It simply was not part of religious experience, nor related to divinity in any way.

Schwenckfeld was faced with the same question, made all the sharper by his doctrine of the two orders. He chose a third approach. Driven by the belief that nothing outer can mediate the inner, he was unable to locate the body of Christ in the bread, even in as undefined a way as Luther. However, rather than adopting an approach like Zwingli's, and removing the whole encounter from the bodily, he chose instead to define the body as part of the spiritual or inner. This was to become even more explicit when he began to explore the nature of Christ's incarnate body, but it has its origins in this theology. Unable to conceive of an existence which did not physical expression, he found himself in the position of having to define the body not as the realm to which God journeyed, taking on that which was alien, but as the location in which God was present and to be encountered. Thus, for Schwenckfeld, the Incarnation was not contingent, but necessary. As will become clear in the next chapter, for Schwenckfeld it is the Incarnation which is at the heart of God's action of salvation. The Cross is a consequence of or a stage in the Incarnation, rather than, as in most theologies, being the prime purpose of the Incarnation.

This insistence that the body was not something alien taken up by divinity, nor something to be left behind by the believer, but the place of encounter allowed Schwenckfeld to live without the elements of bread and wine. Not only can nothing of the outer order mediate the inner, it is not necessary for anything to do so. The divine does not need to be mediated to the body, because body is not opposed to but included within the divine nature.

Such an understanding transformed the understanding of body. No longer

---

[52] While it is true that, philosophically, a distinction was drawn between accident and substance, in popular understanding such a distinction was irrelevant, and the bread was understood as body. The various visions of bread turning into bleeding flesh at the moment of consecration, or ingestion are evidence of this. See Rubin, *Corpus Christi*, pp. 135ff.

that which alienates from God, it becomes the means by which God is encountered. Thus, bodily existence can be perceived in a very different way, and assumptions about the roles of various bodies can be safely questioned. It is important to notice that, despite Schwenckfeld's pragmatic approach to issues, it was not pragmatism (such as what was considered possible in a home and impossible in a church) but a theological conviction which shaped his understanding of body.

Having looked at the way in which Schwenckfeld reached the main points of his Eucharistic theology and begun to map out some of its consequences, we need now to examine the wider debates, and in particular, the part which the understanding of *body* played in the shaping of sacramental theology.

Approaches to Eucharistic Theology

The Eucharist was one of the biggest areas of contention in the sixteenth century. Not only was it one of the biggest divisions between Reform and the traditional theology, as the Mass with its theology and philosophy of transubstantiation was rejected, it gave rise to some of the bitterest disagreements among the Reformers.

The insistence on physicality strained the language of all who wrote about it. Schwenckfeld in particular put a great deal of effort into expressing and exploring his position. His language, never straightforward at the best of times, became especially opaque in this discussion. From this, it is fair to make the judgement I have outlined above that body held a particular importance for him. This is the clue to placing him in the Eucharistic debate. Reformation historiography has viewed the movement between the two poles represented by Luther and Zwingli as the defining pattern of Eucharistic theology, and everybody else is understood as taking a place somewhere on the continuum between them. However, once the Eucharistic theology of Schwenckfeld is considered not, as it often is, as a by-product of Zwinglianism,[53] but as a third strand of Eucharistic thinking,[54] then the pattern shifts considerably. It is true that Schwenckfeld had some theological agreement with Zwingli, more than he shared with Luther. Like Zwingli, he took the verse "The letter kills, the spirit gives life" as central to Eucharistic understanding. However, as I have shown above, he did not adopt a Zwinglian view and then modify it, nor did he work with a similar understanding of the nature of the body, either the body of the believer, or the Body of Christ. Not only that, but seen from the stance of Schwenckfeld, the received understandings of and relationship between the other two also shifts. No longer are they polar opposites, and the final

---

[53] Horst Weigelt, *The Schwenckfelders in Silesia*, Pennsburg, Penn: Schwenckfelder Library, 1985, p. 28.

[54] McLaughlin, "Schwenckfeld and the South German Eucharistic Controversy, 1526-1529," *Schwenckfeld and Early Schwenckfeldianism*. Erb, p. 196.

parameters of any discussion. Instead they can be seen clearly to be positioned according to the understanding which they adopted of body, and the meaning they gave to it. It also becomes clear that they are in fact more closely related to each other than either is to Schwenckfeld. For both Luther and Zwingli, the central question in Eucharistic theology was the meaning of the bread and its relation to the Body of Christ – that is, the physical reality or otherwise of the presence. For Schwenckfeld, on the other hand, the question centred on the meaning of physical reality itself, and therefore the meaning of body.

Caroline Walker Bynum argues that between the twelfth and fourteenth centuries there was a significantly increased valorisation of the body.[55] She puts forward two reasons for this: firstly that a positive recognition of the body in Christian theology was a way of counteracting the dualistic and body-denying heresies of the time, and, secondly, by focusing devotion on the Host and the miracle of transubstantiation, clerical control was increased. It was also a useful defence against heretical developments.[56] However, she goes on to argue that the issue of the meaning of body goes much deeper than countering heresy. She suggests that:

> *all* the religiosity of the period was animated in deep ways by the need to take account of (rather than merely to deny) matter, body and sensual response.[57]

She points out too that:

> One of the most important philosophical formulations of the thirteenth century, Thomas Aquinas's statement of the hylomorphic composition of the human person was a new attempt to come to terms with matter. The doctrine says that what a person *is*, the existing substance *man*, is form and matter, soul and body. To Aquinas, the person *is* his body, not just a soul using a body...[58]

If Schwenckfeld were in fact working in this third approach, then he would be working in a context deeply shaped by Aquinas. Schwenckfeld certainly evinced this medieval understanding of the body that there was an identity between body and person. Thus it was difficult, if not impossible, for him to conceive of an existence which was not in some way embodied. To be was to be embodied. The soul could not be detached from the body, being could not be conceived of without physical expression. Indeed, although he says little directly about heaven, and eternal life, as we will see in considering his understanding of salvation, he even seemed to perceive the heavenly state as, in

---

[55] Caroline Walker Bynum, *Holy Feast and Holy Fast: The Religious Significance of Food to Medieval Women,* Berkeley and London, University of California Press, 1987.
[56] See also Charles Zika, "Hosts, Processions and Pilgrimage: Controlling the Sacred in Fifteenth Century Germany," *Past and Present*, 1988, pp. 25-64.
[57] Bynum, *Holy Feast and Holy Fast*, p. 253.
[58] Bynum, *Holy Feast and Holy Fast*, p. 254.

some way, physical.

However, the separation of orders meant that the outer could not communicate the inner. Therefore, the body which Schwenckfeld understood to be an integral part of Christ's existence, and the means of the salvific encounter, had to be understood in a particular way. It is this thinking about what he calls the "glorified flesh" which I will explore in "Incarnation and Embodiment", but it is important here because of the similarity of the language which he used. In discussing the flesh which was Christ's following the Incarnation, he regularly used the term "wahr", "true". This signified the real and human reality of the flesh that Christ received from his mother.[59] See for example, the major publication *Vom Ursrpung des Fleisches Christi*, written in 1555 to counteract the accusations that he believed the Hoffmanite doctrine of heavenly flesh. (*CS*, vol. 14, p. 307ff). Here he used the terms several times, for example:

> But because she did not become pregnant by herself and has not given the origin to this child, Jesus Christ, but God the Father through his Spirit in a bearing manner has brought about the origin of this new person and his new flesh, indeeed, the whole secret of the birth of Christ in the power of his Spirit, so it is easy to judge that God is the true Father of this child Jesus, just as Mary is his true Mother...Therefore the flesh of Christ is to be recognised in two respects; firstly, that it was a true human flesh, from Mary the blessed virgin, secondly that it was conceived of the Holy Spirit and therefore was holy, new, without sin and full of grace.

The same word is used in the description of the body and blood. They are "true" food and drink. He regularly uses these terms to reinforce his point about the nature of that which he is discussing.

> From this [false teaching] it would follow that the one, single Christ did not always remain the same, single Christ, and his body, flesh and blood was not always a true food and drink, nor a life-giving flesh and blood...[60]

---

[59] The German is given here and in the following notes, because the issue of the language itself is so important. Weil sie aber nit von ir selbst ist schwanger worden noch disem kinde Jesu Christo den ursprung hat gegeben/ sonder Got der vater durch seinen geist geberender weise den ursprung dises newen menschens und seines newen fleisches/ ja das gantzen geheimnüs der geburt Christi in verwaltung seines geists gewirckt hat/ so ist leicht außzurechnen/ das Gott dises kindes Jesu warer vater ist/ wie auch Maria seine ware mütter ist...Drumb so wil das fleisch Christi zwene Respect oder gemerckt zü seinem erkhantnüs haben/ Einen/ das es ein war menschlich fleisch auß Mariam der begnadeten Jungkfrawen war/ Den andern/ das es vom h. geiste empfangen unnd deßhalben heilig/ New/ one sünd und vol gnad war. *CS*, vol. 14, p. 323, ll. 5f.

[60] Denn Es wurde drauß volgenn/ das der Ainige ainfaltige Christus nicht allweg eben derselbige einige Christus pleibe/ unnd sein Leib/ flaisch unnd plut nich allweg ain ware

But of the true living bread and of the heavenly food of this supper the Lord Jesus Christ has clearly and fully taught in Jn 6:48-56 the use and action of such food; namely, that he is the living bread of God and his flesh is truly a food for our souls.[61]

So then by this my confession is clear and obvious, that I like them [the Lutheran preachers] do not hold that the Supper of the Lord Christ is only a ceremony or a sign, and shut out from it the true, real food and drink of the body and blood of Christ.[62]

This identity of language suggests that there is an equivalence of thought. Just as the flesh and bones of Christ were known to be "true" because they were in some way "physical", so this food and drink had a "physicality" about them,

---

speiß unnd tranckh/ noch ein Lebendigmachendes flaische und blut wer/ *CS*, vol. 9, p. 44, ll. 15f.

[61] Aber vom waren lebendigen brote/ und von der himlischen speyse dises abentmals/ was auch solche speise nutzet und wircket/ het der herr Jesus Christus Johan 6: 48-56. klärlich wol und vil geleeret/ das nemlich Er das lebendige brot Gottes/ und sein flaisch warhafftig ain speise (unserer seelen) sey/. *CS*, vol. 10, p. 377, ll. 32f.

[62] Zü dem so wirt auß jetzt gemeltem meinem bekantnis klar und offenbar/ das ich auch mit denen nicht halte/ die deß Herren Christi Nachtmall allein für ein Ceremoni oder zeichen hallte/ und die ware wesentliche Speise und Tranck des leibs und blüts Christi darvon außschliessenn/. *CS*, vol. 11, p. 116, ll. 12f.

Others examples include: He[Jesus] wanted to teach them through that, I say, that his body given for us is the true food, nourishment, life and eternal preservation of our souls and his blood shed for us a true drink, quickener and cleanser of our hearts". Er hat sie/ sprich ich/ dadurch wöllen lehren/ daß sein Leib/ für uns gegeben/ die ware speise/ narung/ leben unnd ewige erhaltung unserer seelen/ und sein Blüt/ so für uns vergossen/ ein warer tranck/ labsal/ erquickung und reinigung unsers hertzens sey/. *CS*, vol. 12, p. 746, ll. 3f.

...and that his flesh, body and blood which he [the believer] eats in the supper are true food, drink and nourishment, yes true, life-giving bread and drink for all true, believing children of God. ... und das sein fleisch leib und blutt/ damitt er in seinem nachtmahl speisset/ die wahr speis tranck und narung/ ia das wahre lebendigmachende brott und tranck aller wahren gleubigen aller knder gottes seÿ/ *CS*, vol. 13, p. 615, ll. 37f.

...and his blood shed for us is a true drink ...und sein Blüt für uns vergossen/ ein warer trank sey. *CS*, vol. 14, p. 804, l. 28.

And one should further believe that the body of Christ which is given for us and his blood which is shed for the forgiveness of sins are true food, drink and nourishment, yes, a true, life-giving bread and drink. Unnd weitter soll man glauben/ das der leib Christi welcher für uns gegeben/ und sein blüt so zür vergebung der sünden ist vergossen/ die ware speiß/ tranck und narung/ jha ein wares lebendigmachendes brot und tranck ist/. *CS*, vol. 15, p. 380, ll. 21f.

Aber vom waren lebendigen brote/ und von der himlischen speyse dises abentmals/ was auch solche speise nutzet und wircket/ het der herr Jesus Christus Johan 6: 48-56. klärlich wol und vil geleeret/ das nemlich Er das lebendige brot Gottes/ und sein flaisch warhafftig ain speise (unserer seelen) sey/. *CS*, vol. 10, p. 377, ll. 32f.

which were an important part of their meaning. Unless they were "true" that is, expressed in some sort of physical way, they were not real and no meaningful nourishment or encounter could take place. There are many examples of the way in which he used the language to reinforce this basic conviction. For example;If the whole thing was spiritualised away from any sense of physicality, then there was no content to it.

Body and Physicality in Christian Thinking

The human body has always been an ambiguous area for Christian theological thinking. Starting with the assertion that God made the body and physical reality, it is not possible for orthodox Christian thinkers to follow the Gnostics in their assertion that matter is intrinsically evil, and to be abhorred in all its manifestations. However, the impact of Gnostic thinking, together with what Peter Brown has shown to have been the predominant Greco-Roman climate did combine to produce a profoundly ascetic culture which continued to inform the development of Christian thinking.[63] The body, particularly but not only in sexual terms, was understood as the site of sinfulness. Thus, not only celibacy, but severe fasting, lack of sleep and refusal to meet basic needs like warm clothing or washing became practices which were adopted by those who aspired to holiness.[64] Flesh had the meaning of sinfulness and, possibly more importantly, the entry-point of sinfulness. This had religious implications for everybody. However, for women, these implications had social consequences as well. The experience of motherhood is central to the definition of female in all cultures. As Clarissa Atkinson suggests, the patterns of asceticism which developed in early and medieval Christianity were specifically focused on denying this aspect of female existence – in particular by causing a suppression of menstruation.[65] Thus, a particular strand of ascetic thinking, which was important in the shaping of Christian approaches to the body, was one which at the same time denied one of the basic female physical realities.[66] Added to this was the symbolic and powerful link between female and corporeality. The Aristotelian understanding of female as the provider of matter to the male's

---

[63] Peter Brown, *The Body and Society, Men, Women and Sexual Renunciation in Early Christianity*, London: Faber, 1989.

[64] See Jocelyn Wogan-Browne, "Chaste Bodies: Frames and Experiences" in *Framing Medieval Bodies*, Ed. Sarah Kay and Miri Rubin, Manchester: Manchester University Press, 1994, p. 24.

[65] Clarissa W. Atkinson, *The Oldest Vocation: Christian Motherhood in the Middle Ages*, Ithaca and London: Cornell University Press, 1991, p. 44

[66] Jocelyn Wogan-Browne, "Chaste Bodies", p. 30. Joan Cadden also discusses menstruation, and its meaning in *Meanings of Sex Difference in the Middle Ages: Medicine, Science and Culture*, Cambridge: Cambridge University Press, 1993. See especially pp. 173-177, in which she points that menstruation was "no sin", but the "mark of a natural falling away from perfection", p. 174.

form made this not only a philosophical or symbolic link, but a scientific one.[67] Aristotelian science taught that in conception the element which gave life, being, as it were to the new individual was the male sperm. The mother provided simply the material which this sperm imprinted with life, rather as wax is imprinted with a seal. There was no value, meaning or significant reality about the material unless it was so imprinted. Such an understanding then reinforced and gave another aspect to the prevailing notion of women's inferiority.[68]

These two aspects have meant that while Christian attitudes to body in general have been ambiguous, Christian attitudes to the female body have, on the whole, been negative. The famous anti-women quotations from various early fathers are often produced to suggest that women were expected to feel guilty simply by virtue of being female.[69] It must be pointed out that such an extreme position was by no means universally accepted. However, it had its influence, especially when added to the social issues about the acceptability of the female body which I will examine in more detail in the next chapter. While Caroline Walker Bynum has produced evidence that there was an aspect of medieval spirituality which was strongly affirming of female physicality, this was by no means the most widely accepted position. On the whole, it appears that the attitude to women's bodily existence was not one which would enable women to celebrate their embodiment. By making the body a positive element in spirituality, a place of encounter and of exploration of the divine, Schwenckfeld was creating another set of symbols.

The symbolic universe that begins to emerge from his Eucharistic theology is one which provides a spiritual affirmation of physical reality. In the light of the identification of female and body, this must also have affirmed the physical existence of women, not simply as people, but specifically as women. Here are

---

[67] See Maryanne Cline Horowitz, "The 'Science' of Embryology Before the Discovery of the Ovum", *Connecting Spheres: Women in the Western World 1500 to the Present*, ed. Marilyn J Boxer and Jean H. Quaetart, Oxford and New York: Oxford University Press, 1987, p. 87; Caroline Walker Bynum, *Fragmentation and Redemption: Essays on Gender and the Human Body in Medieval Religion*, New York: Zone Books, 1991, pp. 98-101.

[68] Aristotle's teaching was not the only one, but it was the most prevalent. There was also Galen's theory of a two-seed conception which was beginning to gain ground in the early sixteenth century. However, it had not yet become the accepted understanding, partly, I suggest, because it did not fit the prevailing perception of women's inferiority.

[69] For example, Tertullian's famous opening to his book "On The Apparel of Women": "And do you not know that you are (each) an Eve? The sentence of God on this sex of yours lives in this age: the guilt must of necessity live too. You are the devil's gateway: you are the unsealer of that (forbidden) tree: you are the first deserter of the divine law: you are she who persuaded him whom the devil was not valiant enough to attack. You destroyed so easily God's image, man. On account of your desert – that is, death – even the Son of God had to die." *Ante-Nicene Fathers*, Vol. IV, trans. Rev. S. Thelwell. nd.

the first hints of a theological reason why women were so responsive to this theology. That it should emerge in the theology of the Eucharist is not surprising. It was not simply that this was such a central area in the development of Schwenckfeld's own thinking. Eucharistic theology, and sacramental theology in general shapes the heart of Christian thinking about physical reality, and also reflects the assumptions that Christian thinkers make about physical being.

From its earliest existence, the life of the church has been marked by the practice of the Sacraments – rituals that have been held to carry and pass on the reality of God's grace. These rituals, normally involving physical elements – bread, wine, water, oil – and/or bodily actions – eating, drinking, anointing, bathing, speaking, hearing – served, among other things, to mark both the passing of time and rites of passage. In the late medieval church, out of which the first generation of reformers, including Schwenckfeld, came, there was the sacrament for the beginning of life – baptism: the sacrament for reception into the church, recognition as a full human – confirmation: the sacrament for adulthood – marriage, or orders: and the sacrament for the end of life – extreme unction. As well as these *one-off* events, there were the repeated sacraments, though they were possibly not repeated very often – penance and communion. Each of these was linked directly to the relationship between the believer and the church, the purveyor of salvation. It was the church which defined the sins that had to be confessed, the church which determined the nature of penitence and the church which performed the miracle of the Eucharist. Of course the other sacraments were all part of the life of the church as well, but there was a difference. Baptism marked the entry into the life of the church, but in so doing, also marked the entry into the life of the whole community. Marriage, although regarded as a sacrament, was in late medieval times not always performed in a church building or by a priest, and was certainly more to do with life in the community than the strictly religious. It is indeed true to say that the church's role in marriage was as much legal and administrative as spiritual. It was the church authorities that made the decisions on the degrees within which people could marry, what made a marriage legal, and under what circumstances it could be dissolved. Ordination, while clearly a religious ceremony, was again an issue to do with an individual's place in society while extreme unction was as much about the assertion of the proper place of living and dead as it was about the religious issues of life after death.

Each of these ceremonies contained its physical element. Indeed, they might be described as the physical encounter with the grace of God as provided and dispensed by the church, and one of the marks of the church in the late middle ages was the energy with which it defended its right to be the only purveyor of sacramental grace.[70] There was also a correspondingly great increase in the

---

[70] Zika, "Hosts, Processions and Pilgrimages", pp. 225-264. Zika argues that many recent studies have shown how fundamental shifts in religious practice also constitute

perception of the physical power of the sacramental elements – bread, wine, water and oil came to be perceived as containing within them power and presence which could be both worshipped and manipulated. Thus, there was the development of the Corpus Christi festival, when the host was paraded through the streets and adored, quite separately from the surrounding ritual of prayers and actions of the Eucharistic liturgy – the power was inherent in the physical bread, and the issues became focused on more than simple religious worship.[71] Following the same pattern, although with a different end, there was the use of sacramental elements in magic ritual – for planting, for example, or to ward off evil.[72]

There was also what can be referred to as the secondary layer -what were called sacramentals.[73] These could include blessed candles or water or even cloth, provided by the church for specific purposes, such as healing, protecting or even love charms. What all of these go to show is the way in which spiritual power and presence – the encounter between the human and the divine – was in the late medieval mind often mediated through a tangible element. And this, far from being at odds with the historic thinking of the church was actually largely determined by it. People were taught that God came to them physically in, for example, bread and wine, and so extended this lesson to cover other things too. But at the heart of experience was this reality of the presence of God in the bread and the wine – though received by the laity only in the bread, since the practice had developed of reserving the cup for the priest alone. Whatever else the bread and wine were, they were literally the body and blood of Christ in its full physicality.[74]

The doctrine of transubstantiation was not fully defined as dogma until 1215, by the Fourth Lateran Council, but it was among the accepted theologies

---

shifts in religious perceptions and needs and in the structures of power and authority through which these perceptions and needs are expressed, promoted and reproduced. p. 225.

[71] See Rubin, *Corpus Christi*, p. 247. She also shows, pp. 338f, how the Host could be used in magical and medicinal rituals, separate from the church's sanction. See also Muir, *Ritual in Early Modern Europe*, p. 156.

[73]Rubin, *Corpus Christi*, pp. 340-341, Keith Thomas, *Religion and the Decline of Magic*, London: Wiedenfeld and Nicholson, 1991, p. 37.

[73] In R.W. Scribner, "Ritual and Popular Belief in Catholic Germany at the Time of the Reformation," in *Popular Culture*, pp. 17-47, Scribner discusses the whole use of *sacramentals* as protections against evil. He cites the use of candles blessed at Candlemas to protect against bad weather or aid in childbirth, while palms from Palm Sunday were also used to protect against evil forces, pp. 62ff. See also "Sorcery, Superstition and Society: The Witch of Urach", pp. 257-275 in the same volume.

[74] Miri Rubin, "The Person in the Form: medieval challenges to bodily order", *Framing Medieval Bodies*, Ed. Sarah Kay and Miri Rubin, p. 111.

of the church probably from at least the second century.[75] At the Council of Trent, it was described as the change of the whole substance of the bread into the body of Christ and the whole substance of the wine into the blood of Christ, while the species of bread and wine remained unchanged. Such a theology draws on a particular philosophy of matter and reality, which was first expounded by Pater Cantor in the twelfth century, in which he distinguished *form*, the sum of the essential properties, from *substance*, the hypostasis or subject – that which is the inner meaning, but can only be accessed through the *form*. The change of "inner meaning" happened at the words of consecration and the congregation received the body and blood of Jesus. This change was held to happen *ex opere operando* – it did not depend in any way on the piety, purity or holiness of either priest or recipient. This, at least, was the official view. That it was not entirely accepted by the people, nor, at a deep level by the theologians, is evidenced by the restrictions that were put on priests, and it is here that we begin to come across explicitly the connection between sexuality and sacrament.

The celibacy of the priesthood was only enforced fully (or as fully as ever it was) as a requirement from the eleventh century reforms. Part of the reason was the desire to prevent church money and power from falling into family hands, and livings being treated as heirlooms, for family links and networks were the basis of social structures and hierarchies. But there was also the reason of purity. The priest, who was the one entrusted with the duty of conducting the miracles of all the sacraments, but especially that of the Eucharist, was not to be like other men. Part of this unlikeness was that he was not involved in physical sexuality. A significant element in the cry for reform *in head and members* which is the background to the sixteenth century Reformation was focused on this issue of celibacy. The desire of laity was not that their priests should be married, but that they should be truly celibate. In general, congregations did not want their priest to be like them, married and involved in family life.[76] Instead, the perception was that the priest, if he was to function

---

[75] For example, Irenaeus, writing against docetic heretics, and incidentally, insisting on the physicality of the sacrament wrote: "And because we are his members and are nourished by what is created, he...provides us with a created thing when he declares the cup taken from created things...to be his blood, and the bread taken from created things...he affirms to be his body. Therefore when the wine mixed with water and the baked bread receive the Word of God and eucharist becomes that body of Christ...how can they deny our flesh is capable of receiving the gift of God, which is eternal life." Irenaeus *Against the Heretics* V. 2. 2, 3 c. 185.

[76] John Yost has pointed out in his article "The Reformation Defense of Clerical Marriage in the Reigns of Henry VIII and Edward VI", *Church History*, vol 50, 1981, that "...the deeply rooted conviction of the laity that it [clerical marriage] was morally and religiously improper continued to trouble the consciences of married priests". p. 165. See also Susan Karant-Nunn: "Did Lutheran preachers...hold forth so vehemently on the desirability of marriage in part to justify their own abandonment of celibacy to a

properly, should be different in precisely this way.

Much of the anti-clerical literature of the period focuses not on the dangers to church property of a priest with a woman (indeed, much of it focused on the inappropriate wealth of the church), but on the supposedly rampant sexuality of priests and monks, and the danger that this posed to pure wives and daughters.[77] Partly what was at issue was the protection of property, and the family network, but there is also the sense that a priest who is *indulging* his sexual nature cannot function properly as a priest – that sexuality and sacraments are incompatible.[78]

The identification of a link between sexuality and sacrament is one that has been very strong at various points in the tradition. There are roots in the Old Testament understandings of purity and uncleanness. Leviticus 15:18 makes it clear that, following intercourse, both the man and the woman are unclean, and cannot approach the holy community until the next day. This seems to have been both an expression and a reinforcement of the notion that body and divinity had to be kept separate. The perception of "bodiliness" applied in all sorts of other categories as well in Leviticus and elsewhere. But the physical reality of the body as experienced and expressed in intercourse seems to be sensed as much stronger. One of the times when the body is most fully bodily is in sexual intercourse. Brundage has pointed out that the pleasurableness of sex reinforced the sense that it was evil: to take pleasure in the body was to be orientated away from God.[79]

The whole complex was further reinforced by the laws which the church attempted to enforce on sexual relations between husbands and wives – not just at times of penitence and fasting, such as Lent and Advent, when such abstinence might be regarded as *proper* self-denial and in keeping with the season, but also on Saturday nights before the celebration of the Mass.[80] Again, the proximity of sexuality and sacrament was perceived as inappropriate.

It is beyond the scope of this argument to trace the development in Christian tradition of the links between sexuality and sacrament. What is important here

---

public that was not entirely convinced that a godly cleric *should* indulge his sexual appetites?" "Kinder, Küche, Kirche: Social Ideology in the Sermons of Johannes Mattheius." *Germania Illustrata*, p. 137.

[77] Miriam U. Chrisman, "Women and the Reformation in Strassburg, 1490-1530," *Archiv für Reformationsgeschichte*, vol 63-64, 1972-1973, p. 144; Sherrin Marshall Wyntjes, "Women in the Reformation Era," *Becoming Visible*, R. Bridenthal and C. Koonz, p. 172; James A. Brundage, *Law, Sex and Christian Society in Medieval Europe*, Chicago: University of Chicago Press, 1987, p. 536; James Grantham Turner, *Sexuality and Gender in Early Modern Europe*, p. 22.

[78] Brundage, *Law, Sex and Christian Society*, p. 538.

[79] Brundage, *Law, Sex and Christian Society*, p. 549.

[80] In his discussions of medieval penitential literature, James Brundage has shown the way in which liturgical seasons were determinants in the appropriateness or otherwise of marital intercourse. See James A. Brundage, *Sex, Law and Marriage in the Middle Ages*, Aldershot: Variorum, 1993, pp. 10, 198ff, 382, and the statistical tables.

is that one of the impetuses to Reformation was this desire for a celibate priesthood, and one of the markers of Reformation was the marrying of clergy. The marriage of clergy was not simply a sociological phenomenon which asserted that the clergy were not a caste apart but part of the whole community. It was also a statement about the place of sexuality in the life of the sacramental community. Luther made this quite explicit when he presented marriage as necessary because of sexual desire, and insisted that celibacy was a gift given to very few men – and even fewer women.[81] His discussions about marriage, and particularly marriage for those who were sacramental celebrants did not primarily deal with the change this would bring in social perception, but with the personal reality of a legitimate sexual partner.[82] It is also clear that, socially, the role of a reformed priest's wife was not always easy, and the accusations which were made about such women were clearly sexual.[83]

The question about what underlies all this discomfort is one far outside the competence of this discussion, but where it does bear on my argument is that Schwenckfeld effectively side-stepped the debate, and therefore immediately defused it. He made the point in essence that no priest was necessary for the celebration of the Eucharist, but only the believer. Since he did not insist that his followers should be celibate he did not link the Supper, in his theology, with the sexual purity or otherwise of the body.[84] Part of the shift in Schwenckfeld's

---

[81] In 1522 he wrote: "But these [those who are called to celibacy] are rare; not one in a thousand can do it: it is one of God's special miracles." A year later, it was even rarer – he had raised it to one in a hundred thousand.

[82] See for example *Luthers Werke, Briefwechsel*, 3.635, 22-28: a letter to a friend, Spalatin, who was getting married: "When you sleep with your Catherine and embrace her, you should think "This child of man, this wonderful creature of God, has been given to me by my Christ. May he be praised and glorified." Heiko A. Oberman suggests: "Luther's marriage was the genuine and far more offensive form of iconoclasm. It directed itself against the fiction of false saintliness in the hearts of the living and not against the depiction of dead saints. For him, 'saintly' meant to be near his 'dear housewife', as he wrote to her in none too veiled terms : 'I would like to be your lover now.' " Heiko A. Oberman, *Luther: Man between God and the Devil*, translated Eileen Walliser-Schwarzbart, New Haven: Yale University Press, 1993, p. 282.

[83] See Mary Prior, "Reviled and crucified marriages: the position of Tudor bishops' wives", *Women in English Society, 1500-1800*, ed. Mary Prior, London: Methuen, 1986. But see too Grethe Jacobsen's essay "Women, Marriage and the Magisterial Reformation: The Case of Malmø, Denmark". *Pietas et Societas*, Eds. Kyle C. Sessions and Philip N. Bebb. In this she shows both that "To be the lawful wedded wife of a clergyman with a recognised social function was clearly an improvement in status and security [for a concubine]", but also, "In Denmark, the first generation of priests' wives were exposed to the wrath of relatives…referred to as whores.", (pp. 63, 65, 66) There was evidently an ambiguity here as in the rest of the effect of the Reformation changes for women.

[84] On the question of Schwenckfeld's attitude to celibacy, see the discussion in chapter 5, "Men, Women and God."

theology of the Eucharist was to de-sexualise it. Both the medieval tradition and the new patterns introduced by Luther and by Zwingli with their teaching on marriage could be argued to make the issue of the sexuality of the celebrant central. Their emphasis was on the social and spiritual identity between the clergyman and the congregation. This identity was enhanced by the common experience of marriage and family life. The clergy family was also expected to act as a model of Christian living, and that was now presumed to include sexual activity. By having no celebrant, Schwenckfeld removed the whole issue. The only bodies which were involved in the encounter were the bodies of Christ and of the believer. There was no need for a *special* body – that of a celibate priest, or a recognised reformed clergyman – to officiate at the encounter. Thus any question about the body, and bodily integrity of such a person simply was not there. As we will see, this is of a piece with Schwenckfeld's whole theology. He came up with different answers to some of the problematic questions of his age not because he set out to be different, or to challenge the status quo, but because, in the light of his theology, some of the questions others were asking simply did not exist for him.

As well as the development of such strong beliefs about the physical nature of God's presence in the elements, the medieval period saw the growth of a powerful mystical tradition which focused on the Eucharist. In some cases, this developed a very strong erotic imagery.[85] Bynum also shows that, especially in late medieval thinking, there was a close link between women and Eucharist, especially in this mystical aspect.[86] Late medieval mysticism, and especially Eucharistic mysticism was strongly female, and strongly charismatic: that is, outside the normal structures of the church.[87] It is suggested by some that the sixteenth century was a period when the roles of women were becoming more delineated and their presence in society, especially the worshipping society, was becoming more restricted.[88] If that was the case, then a theology which bypassed the structures which were imposing such restrictions can clearly be

---

[85] In *Holy Feast and Holy Fast* Bynum argues that this was a particularly female form of piety. Thus she can say: "The humanity of Christ, understood as including his full participation in bodiliness [and signalled in the Eucharist] was a central and characteristic theme in the religiosity of late medieval women. Often it had erotic or sexual overtones". p. 246. The mystics of the time, for example, Margery Kempe, were often fanatically devoted to the Sacrament, demanding to receive it much more often than was normal, and finding in the contemplation of the elements a focus for their intense devotion to Christ.

[86] Bynum, *Holy Feast and Holy Fast*, pp. 233ff.

[87] If, as I have suggested above, Schwenckfeld's eucharistic theology is shaped significantly by a tradition which was as much late medieval as it was Lutheran, then here again there is part of an account of why women found it so acceptable.

[88] See for example, Joel F. Harrington, "Hausväter and Landesväter": pp. 53, 56 and also Susan Karant-Nunn, *The Reformation of Ritual: An Interpretation of Early Modern Germany*, London: Routledge, 1997.

seen to have its attractions. That this theology drew on a tradition which was already recognised as a female one reinforces the persuasiveness of the argument.

Thus, there was in the late medieval church a very complex and powerful sacramental system through which people encountered the grace of God, and by which the presence of God in various parts of life was asserted. God's presence was encountered in a physical way, through taste (bread and wine) and touch (water and oil). However, there was an unease about any proximity between such an experience – and the provision of such an experience through the ministry of the priest – and the expression of sexuality. Sacramental theology was central to the identity of the church, and to the spiritual experience of the community, and it was also a centre of debate and identity. Miri Rubin describes it thus:

> A site where some (but not only) divergent concepts were articulated, the Eucharist possessed enormous importance; its correct understanding bespoke a host of attitudes and endowed identities. The Eucharist, thus, could never simply be reformed; attempts to do so in the fifteenth century failed to produce sharp and apt new formulations in the language of sacramental religion. If the Eucharist were to change, it had to be a dramatic change, it could either be wholly espoused – Christ, miracle, well-being – or negated and rejected. And as the world of the sixteenth century came both to realise this necessity and to undertake the new design, the Eucharist became identified as a controversial object, a militant emblem of a struggle unto death.[89]

With its assumptions about the meaning and importance of body, the theological issues around the Eucharist also had implications for the understanding of what it meant to exist as a body in the world. As part of her discussion of the meaning of body, Caroline Walker Bynum argues:

> The sense of *imitatio* as *becoming* or *being* (not merely feeling or understanding) lay in the background of Eucharistic devotion. The Eucharist was an especially appropriate vehicle for the effort to become Christ because the Eucharist *is* Christ. The doctrine of transubstantiation was crucial. One *became* Christ's crucified body in *eating* Christ's crucified Body.[90]

She goes on to argue that, within the strand of Catholic mysticism which she is discussing, one of the ways in which this showed was the stigmata, the physical experience of the wounds of Christ. This is a very literal understanding of the believer's body as the place where the encounter with the divine takes place. The body of the believer thus becomes, in its way, a sacramental site, the place where the encounter between what is divine and what is not divine takes place.

---

[89] Miri Rubin, *Corpus Christi*, p. 347.
[90] Bynum, *Holy Feast and Holy Fast*, p. 256.

The Body as the Eucharistic Encounter

It is precisely this type of thinking that Schwenckfeld exemplified. The believer, through receiving the true body and blood, embodies the life which is the eternal life of God. This life, if it is real, must show itself in the actual physical living of the believer. There must be visible, moral regeneration. This was present from the earliest stage of his theology – it is the thinking which underlies his rejection of Lutheranism in the first place. People's lives were not matching the model of Christ, and therefore, there was no physical reality to or demonstration of the claimed spiritual encounter. A consequence of his belief that life without physical expression was not real, he believed that if people were not *living* the life of Christ; that is, expressing it in and through their physical bodies, then it had not substance. At the heart of being is embodiment. The believer's body, as a consequence of the encounter with the divine body of Christ in the sacramental encounter, began to live as and in the expression of that divine body and life.

Together with his rejection of the current practice of the Eucharist, Schwenckfeld also rejected the need for the bread and wine. He centred the experience entirely on the spiritual eating and drinking which was so important for him. However, as we have seen in his disagreement with Zwingli, he was not prepared to give up completely on some form of physical reality. The notion of the Eucharist as entirely memorial or subjective was unacceptable. The spiritual physicality of the body of Christ had still to be recognised and taken into account. The consequence of the encounter with this body of Christ was a physical one. There was a change in the physical life of the believer, as the individual lived a life of moral improvement. It was in that life that the proof of the reality of the encounter could be seen.

Thus, the focus moved from the physical elements to the believer's body and way of life. The believer, him or herself, became the physical representation of the presence of God – the outward and visible sign of the inner and invisible grace. A life that was Christ-like showed that there had been an encounter with Christ, indeed, that Christ was present. The meaning of this for the life of the individual will be further explored in "Men, Women and God". Here it is important because of what it says about the physical existence of the believer's body in the world, and in particular for this study, about what it means to live in or as a female body. Schwenckfeld insisted on the place in the inner order of the physical body, in the first instance of the physical body of Christ, but by extension also the physical body of the believer, as it existed in and through the encounter which he characterised as eating and drinking. I will look in more detail at his theology of divinisation in "Men, Women and God", but here I want to re-emphasise the point that far from distrusting the body as many in the medieval tradition had done, or focusing on sexuality and child-bearing as the other reformers did, Schwenckfeld gave a theological meaning to the body, because of its capability of being the site, when part of the inner order, of the presence of God.

Sacrament and Power

Sacramental theology was also of importance because of the issues that it raised concerning power. The origins of the Eucharist within the tradition of Passover, a gathering around a family meal table, were not quickly forgotten in the Christian pattern. One of the meanings which the Eucharist had had from the very beginning was as a communal event. However, as Miri Rubin has shown, other notions also come to be part of the understanding, particularly the perception of a much more individualistic theology which focused on adoration rather than participation.[91] Nevertheless, in both Lutheran and traditional theology, the provision of bread and wine was firmly and only in the hands of the priests. They were also the ones who determined and judged appropriate standards of behaviour for those who were to receive the sacrament. R. Po-chia Hsia has argued that this gave them a significant amount of power not only in the spiritual realm, but also in the physical and social.[92] In Brady's happy phrase,

> this was the hard lesson the Lutherans taught; if Christians had no community of ritual, they must form a community through doctrine, or they could have no community at all.[93]

The enforcement of doctrine, and the practices which supported it, was in the hands of the clergy, and carried with it social meaning, since the cohesion of a social community was perceived to depend on its religious conformity.

Therefore, the element of community was never entirely lost, as was shown by the continuation of the practice of excommunication which resulted not only in not receiving the bread, but also in social exclusion. This was an element which was retained very insistently by Luther, and as Susan Karant-Nunn has shown, acted as a form of social control in Lutheran communities.[94]

The Eucharist therefore could become an area of control and definition for a community, both spiritually and physically. Explicitly in the early stages of his reforming, and in other ways later, Luther very clearly linked confession and

---

[91] Rubin, *Corpus Christi*, p. 63 ff.

[92] Hsia, *The German People and the Reformation*, p. 68. See also Rubin, *Corpus Christi*, p 13, 35.

[93] Thomas A. Brady Jr., "Architect of Persecution: Jacob Sturm and the Fall of the Sects at Strassburg", *Archiv für Reformationsgeschichte*, vol 79, 1988, p. 279.

[94] Karant-Nunn, *The Reformation of Ritual*, p. 120, where she cites the example of urban churches in North Germany in the early 1530s and p 130, where she discusses the case of Pfalz-Neuburg and Leipzig. See also Muir, *Ritual in Early Modern Europe*, pp. 161-162.

the participation in the Eucharist.[95] David Sabean, who has examined authority relationships in early modern Germany using the analytical concept of Herrschaft, claims that the use of the sacrament as a means of social control and a way of exercising power was inherent in the type of theology which grew up around Lutheran practice.[96] If this is so, then the celebration of the Eucharist was not only a *religious* event, but was also important in shaping and defining *social* reality. Part of that social reality had to do with the defining of the community of the saved. This was an important area for Schwenckfeld. He was distressed at those who did not appear to be of this community receiving the elements. This lay behind his call for the ban and then his decision to suspend the celebration.[97]

However, the suspension of the celebration shifted the power focus. The community now had to be defined in other ways. With the removal of the normal boundaries, the communities that gathered together around Schwenckfeld's teaching could exploit other forms of relationship, most notably kinship links, as shown in chapter one. It could also grow under other forms of leadership, some of which were clearly female ones. The communities were bound in the first instance by friendship and relationship, and by loyalty to Schwenckfeld himself. As Merry Wiesner has pointed out, women did not fit into the socially determining groups of a community, marked, for example, by

---

[95] Karant-Nunn, *The Reformation of Ritual*, pp. 100f.

[96] David Warren Sabean, *Power in the Blood: Popular Culture and Village Discourse in Early Modern Germany*, Cambridge, Cambridge University Press, 1984, pp. 23f, pp. 37-60.

[97] The question of the ban, the exclusion of an individual from the Table as an exercise of discipline was one of the areas where Schwenckfeld had most in common with the Anabaptists. The Schleitheim Confession of 1527 has as its second article the statement

We agree as follows on the ban: The ban shall be employed with all those who have given themselves to the Lord, to walk in His commandments, and with all those who have been baptised into one body of Christ and who are called brethren and sisters, and yet who slip sometimes and fall into error and sin, being inadvertently overtaken. The same shall be admonished twice in secret and the third time openly disciplined or banned according to the command of Christ. Mt 18. But this shall be done according to the regulation of the Spirit (Mt 5) before the breaking of bread, with one mind and in one love, and may drink of one cup. (Lumpkin, *Baptist Confessions of Faith*, pp. 22-31.) It is a topic which does not take up a great deal of Schwenckfeld's attention in comparison to other issues, but it does appear, in particular when he was discussing the nature of the church. Thus, in a letter to his Bishop in 1527, for example, he wrote

So we know too by the gospel that there is no Christian congregation except of the type, form and way in which the holy apostles Peter and Paul, and the former Fathers of the first Christian church wrote of it, that the believers should be of one heart, mind and though; Acts 2 and 4. Therefore, if no Christian ban nor brotherly love is in existence, nobodylooks to see how this could be set up; without which in the communal Christian life little fruit or improvement may be detected.

CS, vol. 2, p. 641, ll. 22f.

processions of membership.[98] What they did have were family networks, and the rituals around these. Thus, a form of community which focused on these connections was likely to be one in which women had a particular place. Karant-Nunn has argued that with an increase in what she calls *hierarchization* there was a move from the communal body to individual *bodies*.[99] Such a shift would be one which would mean that women had even less place in the body public. They would therefore increasingly have to look to other forms of community for belonging and affirmation. Whether Schwenckfeld intended his movement to adopt this pattern we cannot now determine. That his theology lent itself to such a development is clear. Thus, again, we have a theological as well as a social reason for the response of those women who followed him. Socially, by moving away from previous structures of authority and control, there was more room for women to take part. Theologically, the reasons why women were traditionally excluded from leadership roles were no longer valid. Again, it was not so much a result of a reasoned argument which disproved a previously held position, as a new theological trajectory which meant that previous questions and issues ceased to have any meaning.

The question of power around the sacrament also focuses in the right and authority to *create* or enable the sacrament to happen. Only those who were ordained within the orders of the church could consecrate the elements, and therefore mediate the encounter with the divine which flowed through the elements. As in all outer (in the non-technical sense) ceremonies of the Church, Schwenckfeld has little to say about the practice and conduct of the Supper. Here he appears to have shared the assumptions of those around him, that the proper conduct of the sacrament was such as was normal within church life – the celebrant was to be a recognised and ordained person. So, like the majority of the Church, it never appears to have occurred to Schwenckfeld that the celebrant could be anything other than male. The male body was still the assumed locus of sacramental power. Historically, part of the insistence on the maleness of the priesthood has been that the priest at the altar is an icon of Christ.[100] It is also possible that the representative of Christ, the King of the World, had to be socially and culturally a person of power and worth. It is certainly true that priests, as we have seen, functioned in powerful roles. In the pattern of the culture, such a position was not readily accessible to women. The issue was not simply one of social power, but of the perception of where proper power lay. Thus, although there might be individual women who were powerful, they were anomalous. Women, as women, were not holders of

---

[98] Wiesner, *Women and Gender in Early Modern Europe*, p. 83

[99] Karant-Nunn, *The Reformation of Ritual*, p. 135.

[100] See, for example, Cyprian: "If Christ Jesus, our Lord and God, is himself the high priest of God the Father, and first offered himself as a sacrifice to the Father and commanded this to be done in rememberance of himself, then assuredly the priest acts truly in Christ's place when he reproduces what Christ did." *Epistles*, LXIII.14.

power. Thus, although Katherine Zell preached, it was not a *normal* thing, it was an occurrence requiring rebuke or justification. Of course, most men were also not holders of power, but the lack of power for individual men lay not, as with women, in their physical being, and its social meaning, but in the circumstances in which their lives were lived – their social class or financial position. Thus, the priest as a power figure had to be male.

However, in Schwenckfeld's theology of *inner feeding*, there was no place for a celebrant of any sort. The reception of the body and blood of Christ, the true food and drink, was understood to be directly from Christ himself "So the Son promised to give his flesh as bread or food".[101] This altered the whole concept of the body which *enabled* the sacrament, and therefore notions of purity and power. Here there might be seen to be some weight to the argument which McLaughlin puts forward that the move from formal church to informal home allowed women to play a more active role. However, the change did not come because women were more likely to be active within the home but because of this shift in the understanding of the body. Schwenckfeld had effectively decoupled the true (by which he meant *inner*) celebration of the sacrament from the presence of anybody other than the believer. Thus, there did not need to be a particular body, representing sanctifying power, present to enable the encounter to take place. Therefore, the social meaning of the gendered body, male or female, was no longer relevant in this context. The difference, then, between male and female bodies, in terms of the Eucharistic encounter, simply did not exist. McLaughlin's suggestion that women could play a part because of the different location, the home, is to miss this shift in the perception of the bodily difference between men and women.

The Eucharist as Food

The terms in which Schwenckfeld spoke of receiving the body and blood fall into two patterns. As well as the language of receiving eternal life, which will be discussed in the next chapter, he also used the language of feeding, satisfaction and nourishment. So, for example he described the experience this way:

> So the teaching of Christ does not speak about eating and drinking according to the order of earthly things and food, but according to the order of the heavenly food, nourishment and quickening of the soul and the hungry conscience, which food and nourishment is in his knowledge, according to the Holy Spirit.[102]

---

[101] *CS*, vol. 2, p. 573, ll. 16f.

[102] Again, the German is retained, because it is important: So doch die leere Christi icht vom essen oder trincken redet nach ordnung der leiblichen dinger/ und speise/ sonder nach ordnung der himmlischen speise/ narung und erquickung der seelen und

Again, he used this kind of language in the *Confession*:

> And it is truly a bread says the Lord; (Jn 6:51,55): not figuratively, not signifying, but truly; also not physically, nor fleshly but according to the truth of the being in God, so that it is spiritual, godly and heavenly feeding and nourishing to eternal life.[103]

What is important here is the notion of gender in the *placing* of the meal. Schwenckfeld was quite clear in his language and teaching that, however it happened, and whatever he meant by it, the encounter between the soul and the divine which was the essence of the Eucharist was to do with a meal. His preferred term is *Supper*, and his constant reiteration of the language of eating, drinking, feeding, satisfaction all draw on normal meal-table descriptions. However, with his rejection of the physical elements of bread and wine, and the communal experience of eating, he was jettisoning the two central features of meals.

Food preparation was normally understood to be a woman's role, as was the wider provisioning of a household.[104] To prepare food was to take a certain place in the community; it functioned as a gender marker. The sharing of food has always been seen as an act of community, and this was part of the early meanings of the Eucharist. As Susan Karant-Nunn, for one, has shown, celebrations were marked by feasts.[105] Outside of the Eucharistic meaning, food was a marker of belonging, and of family, and of position. It also had this function within the religious community to some extent. It is surely not without meaning that exclusion from the religious community was marked by excommunication – the denial of access to the Eucharistic meal. To be barred from the sacrament was a marker that the transgressor no longer belonged, was not part of the family and had no position in the sacramental community.

Neither of these features, of preparation or of communal activity, is present in Schwenckfeld's teaching or, as far as we can see, practice. With the rejection of the first, the preparation, we see again the sidestepping of one of the central gender issues of his time. He did not suggest any social change, or put forward any notion that women should not be identified with food as preparers. But he

---

hungerigen gewissens/ welche speise und narung stehet an seinem Erkantnus/ dz nach dem heilige Geist ist/ *CS*, vol. 2, p. 554, ll. 6f.

[103] Und warhafftig ists ain broth spricht der Herre (Jo 6:51,55)/ nicht figürlich noch bedeütlich/ sonder warhafftig/ auch nicht leiplich noch flaischlich/ sonder nach der warhait des wesens inn Gott/ drumb es auch gaistlich/ göttlich und himmlisch speiset und nehret/ zum ewigen leben. *CS*, vol. 7, p. 575, ll. 9f.

[104] See Bynum, *Holy Feast and Holy Fast*, pp. 113 ff. Roper also points out that this was not simply a practical task for a woman, but also a religious one. By controlling the type and amount of food prepared for the household, she took part in the religious rituals of the day, and shaped the family life around them.

[105] Karant-Nunn, *The Reformation of Ritual*, pp. 80f.

did raise to a central position a meal which required no preparation except that of the individual believer's heart – and that was a preparation to be carried out irrespective of gender. Again, one of the defining features of being female in the society simply had no place in his theological thinking or expectation.

The second aspect links back to the discussion above about the nature of the believing community to which Schwenckfeld's theology led. It was no longer a community centred around the liturgy of the Eucharist. The social effects of that liturgy, especially in respect of power and gender therefore did not shape it. It was a community, instead, which developed another pattern of existence, and that was a pattern which was much more female centred. And, focusing as it did on homes, it had a place for the role of the provider and preparer of meals which was a very positive one. The provision of meals, although having nothing to do with the *sacramental* meal, was still an important part of creating a community. With no official sacrament to link them together, the meetings in homes, the studying and the discussing must have played that communal role. In that pattern, men and women were able to play the same parts, and so women found and were put into significant leadership roles.

The other link between food and women is in the basic issue of lactation. Through breast-feeding, a woman's body was identified as food in and of itself. The belief that breast-milk was a refined form of blood, blood which was otherwise lost at menstruation, demonstrates just how close an identification was made. Bynum has demonstrated how powerful the link between the female body and food was seen to be.[106] Schwenckfeld's language clearly demonstrates his understanding that body of Christ was a food, and such food was necessary for the life of the believer. To feed on Christ was to be nourished for eternal life. In the *Liegnitz Catechism*, which dates from 1525, he wrote

> Any person who becomes a newborn child of God and has thus been washed or baptised, is also fed with the body and given to drink of the blood of Christ.[107]

In the *Confession* of 1541, as part of his discussion about the eternal nature of Christ, he wrote:

> He is the life-giving heavenly bread, the absolutely essential bread for which the children of God ask for daily in the "Our Father"; yes, the true food of eternal life, not according to one nature only, nor divided, but according to both natures, complete and full.[108]

The close parallel of the image of children with the life-giving food suggests that in some measure at least, Schwenckfeld's understanding of the body and blood is that which feeds Christians for their nourishment and growth. We will

---

[106] Bynum, *Fragmentation and Redemption*, pp. 103f.

[107] *CS*, vol. 18, p. 10, ll. 5f.

[108] *CS*, vol. 7, p. 574, ll. 22f.

look at this in more detail in the chapter on spirituality and Christian development. In this context it is particularly important because of the light it sheds on his understanding of the Eucharist, and the Christ encountered in the feeding. By invoking the position of the believer as child, Schwenckfeld reinforced the notion of dependency. However, he also set up echoes of the way in which a child is fed: from the body of the mother. Thus, the link between the maternal body and the body of Christ – both providing necessary nourishment for the dependent infant – can at least be read here as part of the whole complex. It is unclear whether he did this intentionally, but it is clear that the language he used makes the echoes so obvious that this in itself must have had an effect. So, in this most central of Christian experiences, Christ is present to the believer in a feminine role.

It is not that Schwenckfeld anywhere suggests that Christ is physically female. However, the body which is Christ's is the one on which the believer feeds to live and grow. Bynum has shown that there did exist a tradition in which the wounds of Christ were thought of as the breasts of a nursing mother, and also pictorial images which illustrate the body of Christ being transformed into food.[109] However, on the whole such imaginative concepts were not integrated into a theological system which then examined or questioned the accustomed meaning of the body, male or female. What makes Schwenckfeld's use of such imagery intriguing is that, when it is put together with the number of women who responded, and the roles which they played we are left with at least the possibility that in this theological shift, he had actually changed not only the Eucharistic images, but the effect of those images in the self-perception of those who internalised the teaching. It is possible that the reason why the *maternal* imaging of the Eucharistic Christ did not significantly alter the perception and position of women in previous generations was that such images were not linked with any change in the practice of the Eucharist.

Since Schwenckfeld's language of feeding with its hints of nursing and mothering come together with his abandonment of the normal, patriarchal pattern of celebration, there arose the possibility of a much closer integration between images and perception, between words and practice. But we must still say very strongly that this shift had at root a theological impetus. It was for theological reasons that Schwenckfeld made the changes to the normal pattern which separated him from others. It was for self-confessed theological reasons that women and men adopted his teaching. The consequences of the changes and the adoption might have been further reinforced by the social realities within which such changes took place. But if we account for the revolutionary nature of the Schwenckfeldian communities in gender practices only in social terms, we are doing less than justice either to the women who responded, or to the theology which Schwenckfeld explored and presented.

For Schwenckfeld, it was the theology of the Eucharist which was the clue

---

[109] Bynum, *Holy Feast and Holy Fast*, pp. 68, 172ff.

to making sense of his theological universe. When he began to explore his differences from Luther, and then to distance himself from Zwingli as well, it was not with the intention of developing a new world of gender symbolism. However, evidence of such a new approach is there, and it helps us to construct the beginnings of a new account of why the women responded enthusiastically, and why they played the roles they did.

Chapter 3

Concepts of Conception

In Schwenckfeld's universe, as I have suggested, to be human was to be flesh and blood. In referring to Christ's humanity, what is important is his physicality – Schwenckfeld regularly parallels *fleisch*, flesh, with *mensch*, person. Thus, in a pamphlet called *The Origin of Christ's Flesh*,[1] in which he specifically set out to defend his understanding of the origin of Christ's flesh, he laid out his initial reasons for defending himself this way:

> Secondly, the aforementioned preacher so blasphemes my books and teaching, and in the same way me, because I witness through the Scriptures divinisation or becoming like God, of Christ's flesh through primogeniture and the first birth from the dead, when God the Father raised him through his almighty word from the dead and has begotten him into his eternal divine life, kingdom and being.[2]

Later on in his argument, we find the sentence:

> Which Christian wants to or can deny that such is not of the human Christ, of the fruit of Mary, of the flesh and blood of Christ, yes, of his complete human nature united with the word, which in and through the flesh or humanity of Mary has come to be, and should be properly understood to be so.[3]

The almost casual way in which the phrases are linked make it clear that for Schwenckfeld they were parallel concepts, and that one could be used to stand for or to illustrate the other. Thus we know that Christ is human because he is flesh and bone. Schwenckfeld's concern was not with issues of rationality or personality, but with the physical implications of a body. Consequently, any exploration of Schwenckfeld's theology cannot avoid a consideration of how he understood the body of Christ to have come into being, and the nature of its existence. In this chapter, I am going to examine his understanding of the origin of Christ's flesh by looking at what he taught about the conception of Christ. This will also allow a consideration of the nature of bodies which conceive.

To be human is to be physical, to have a body and to exist in the sensible world. This is what it means for us, and therefore, in the Incarnation, this is

---

[1] *Vom Ursprung des Fleisches Christi.*
[2] *CS*, vol. 14, p. 311, ll. 18f.
[3] *CS*, vol. 14, p. 315, ll. 36f.

what it meant for Christ. Although there is a distinction between the inner and the outer, we have seen above that it is not a simple split between physical and non-physical. That would imply that to be spiritual, all that was necessary was for the physical to be ignored. A consequence of this would be that the Incarnation was a theological impossibility. In all his writings and teachings, Schwenckfeld was concerned to insist that he was committed to the fact of the Incarnation. One of the attacks that was regularly levelled at him was that he denied the true humanity of Christ – for this reason, much of his writing was taken up with defending himself and explaining how he understood Christ's humanity.[4] This involved a great deal of discussion about the nature of Mary's conception of Christ. By getting involved in such a debate, Schwenckfeld found himself in the position of having to deal with issues of sexuality and reproduction, and therefore with the nature of women. In this chapter, I will examine notions and expressions that are involved and also look at the way in which the understanding inherent in Schwenckfeld's approach worked its way out in his attitudes.

It has long been recognised that Schwenckfeld's dualism was not of a type which separated body from spirit. However, there has been very little exploration of the implications of the way he worked his dualism out for his understanding of reproduction, women and sexuality.

There are two main thrusts to his argument, repeated in different ways and at various times. Firstly, he insisted that Christ is fully human, in that his flesh, with which humanity is identified, and by which his humanity is identified, is drawn from Mary. Thus Mary is the guarantor of the humanity of Christ. Secondly, he insisted that the generative activity in Christ's birth is entirely divine. So far, he was entirely in accord with traditional doctrine. Thus the virgin birth is the guarantor of Christ's divinity. It is in fact better to speak of the virgin conception rather than virgin birth, since the issue of Mary's virginity during and after the birth is not a question Schwenckfeld considered at all. The question of Mary's physical virginity will be discussed again when we come to discuss Schwenckfeld's attitude to sexuality. Here, the question is of the generative activity.

Christ's Flesh is Mary's Flesh

Schwenckfeld was accused by one set of opponents of teaching the Hoffmanite theology of the pre-existent flesh of Christ, brought with him from heaven.[5]

---

[4] For further discussion of the controversies he was part of, especially those with Martin Frecht of Ulm, see Schulz, *Caspar Schwenckfeld*, pp. 242- 265, McLaughlin, *Reluctant Radical,* pp. 200-224.

[5] This is a misunderstanding of Schwenckfeld's position which has continued. Timothy George repeats it in a book published in 1988. Timothy George, *Theology of the Reformers*, Nashville, Tenn; Broadman, 1998, p. 281. He suggests that Schwenckfeld

Hoffman and his followers spoke of Christ "passing through Mary like sunlight through glass" – a very beautiful image, but theologically suspect in a faith which argues that salvation depends on an identity between Saviour and saved. Schwenckfeld was most insistent that Mary was the true physical mother of Jesus:

> Therefore, God the Father did not have to bring flesh for the birth of his son Christ from heaven, but he found it in Mary as well as he had conceived and born it holily in and from her flesh by the Holy Spirit.[6]

and again: " ...this is *a true human flesh*, [emphasis mine] which has the flesh and blood of Mary."[7] Indeed, so keen was he to insist that Mary's place in the Incarnation should not be discounted, that there are places where he seems to come very close to the Greek mythological notion of intercourse between gods and human women: "God the father and Mary the mother have a natural son in Christ."[8]

However, his insistence was always on the physical part that Mary played – it was a physical contribution that she made: "...the Holy Spirit took, built and exuded the Temple of the Word of God from the material of her flesh."[9] and again: "In Mary, so to speak, he had found the green wood and the costly material with which to build the pure holy flesh born from God."[10]

And the language makes it clear that this was a physical rather than a personal contribution – she contributed *stuff* rather than anything of herself as an individual. In his insistence that Jesus took on true human flesh (although as we will see below even this was not without its qualifications), he made it clear that all that Mary contributed was the flesh.

Hoffmanite Christology

Here it will be helpful to consider Schwenckfeld's relationship with Melchior Hoffman and the effect they had on each other. McLaughlin has shown how Schwenckfeld developed his theology partly through controversies with other people, and one of those other people was Melchior Hoffman, a radical and eventually an Anabaptist, who was resident in Strassburg for some of the same period as Schwenckfeld. The two shared a common theology of the Eucharist, and like Schwenckfeld, Hoffman's Christology was driven by his Eucharistic

---

"claimed to have introduced this doctrine to the Reformation." George misrepresents Schwenckfeld's position.

[6] *CS*, vol. 14, p. 322, ll. 4f.

[7] "...das ist/ *ein wares menschlichs Fleisch* / des Fleisches und geblüts Maria gehabt." *CS*, vol.7, p. 330, ll. 11f. Emphasis mine.

[8] *CS*, vol. 7, p. 330, ll. 19f.

[9] *CS*, vol. 7, p. 320, ll. 19f.

[10] *CS*, vol. 7, p. 321, ll. 32f.

theology. When they first met, they found that the areas of their agreement – particularly those places where they disagreed with others – were very marked, and they made common cause. However, it came to be clear that while they agreed on a spiritualist understanding of the Eucharist, they did not share completely in their understanding of the body of Christ which individually they extrapolated from the Eucharistic theology. And the area of their disagreement was to do with the passing on of sin, and therefore the presence of sin in the body.

Hoffman, influenced by Karlstadt, as Deppermann has shown,[11] was a *maculist*. That is, he believed that Mary's flesh was, like all other human flesh, sinful (not immaculate), and that, if Christ had taken his flesh from her, he too would be spotted by sin. If that were the case, he would not be able to save sinful humanity. Deppermann states Hoffman's position like this:

> No man who was stained by original sin could have been offered as a ransom to the devil. The devil would have been deceived if Christ took flesh from Mary, a sinful daughter of Adam, because in that case God would have paid Satan in his own coin, with something which already belonged to him.[12]

So, Hoffman had to insist that Christ received nothing from Mary, and, bringing his flesh from heaven, he passed through her body like water through a pipe. This language also makes it clear that he understood *flesh* as an arena particularly susceptible to the presence and action of the Devil, and in fact as belonging to the Devil. In this Hoffman was continuing a long tradition in Christian understanding of bodily existence, that there is some physical reality to the presence of sin in the body, a tradition we will see reflected in the discussion below on baptism. Schwenckfeld, on the other hand, clearly found this approach and implications impossible to consider. It is clear that he did not accept the suggestion that Christ had *passed through* Mary. By extension, he therefore avoided the implication that flesh or bodily existence was in any inherent way particularly the domain of evil. Over and over again he repeated

---

[11] Deppermann, *Melchior Hoffman*, pp. 214ff.

[12] Deppermann, *Melchior Hoffman*, p. 225. He continues by quoting from a writing by Hoffman: *Van der waren hochprachligen eynigen magestadt gottes,* of 1532 B3b-B4a, which says: "For it is certain that the whole of Adam's seed was cursed and damned and belonged to death and Satan. If redemption emerged and took effect from the same seed of Adam it would logically follow that sinners were redeemed by sin...that filthy people were cleansed and purified by filth...If redemption had been achieved by Mary's flesh and blood God would have wronged Satan, which can never happen, because God is a just God who gives everybody that which he deserves, no matter whether he is good or wicked."

the idea that Mary was a true mother (*eine ware mutter*) to Jesus,[13] and that his flesh was from her flesh:

> Therefore, God the Father did not have to bring any flesh from heaven for the birth of his son, Christ, but he found it in Mary. Just as he had already produced and brought it to birth in her and from her flesh in a holy way, by the Holy Spirit through his almighty word.[14]

He was most emphatic that the flesh of Christ did not exist before the conception within Mary:

> The Holy Spirit comes from above into Mary. He masters and builds in her holy virginal body. Mary conceives. What does she conceive? What the Holy Spirit took from the material of her flesh and constructed and produced and separated to be the Temple of the Word of God. Yes she conceives the constructed Temple of God, Jesus Christ.[15]

Thus, although he shared with Hoffman a commitment to the separation of the two *Ordnungen*, he could not carry it through in the same way. There was something about the physical reality of the flesh of Christ, its identity in the material world which was of crucial importance to Schwenckfeld. This identity was so fundamental that he was unable to allow it to be diluted, even if that meant he had to run the risk of being misunderstood and accused of heresy.

But before we consider that, we need to look at the implications for the understanding of gender that arise from this controversy over the place of Mary.

Hoffman appears to have been unwilling to allow Mary any part in Christ's physical being because, as a human – and not necessarily as a woman – she was marked by the physical reality of sin. This was a reality which could not be accepted by God, and was not a worthy offering to God. Schwenckfeld on the other hand was clearly able to conceive of Mary's flesh as being free from this spiritual handicap, such that it could provide a fitting material from which the flesh of Christ could be constructed.[16] What is evident here, in fact, is Schwenckfeld's adoption of what is more or less a doctrine of the Immaculate

---

[13] See for example, "For we are not of their [the Hoffmannites] party, and cannot in any way be, because we do not deny (as they do) that Mary was a true mother of Christ". *CS*, vol. 7, p. 304, ll.3f.

[14] *CS*, vol. 14, p. 322, ll. 4f.

[15] *CS*, vol. 7, p. 320, ll. 17f.

[16] In a discussion on the interpretation of Gen 3:15, written in 1551, after discussing what the writer meant in speaking about enmity between the Serpent and the descendent of Eve, he went on: "Then there must be a new woman, with a new material and a renewed flesh, by nature she is like other women, but in her holiness completely unlike; she can have no sinful flesh in her, nor be subject to sin like other women, but through God before all other women be blessed". *CS*, vol. 12, p. 603, ll. 1f.

Conception of Mary: that is, that she was without the physical reality of sin in her body. This is not because of any inherent quality in Mary (that is, she does not become the mother of Christ because she is pure), but must be logically deduced from the fact that she is the mother of Christ. So, in the pamphlet *The Flesh of Christ*, from 1540, he wrote:

> But if one properly understands such and thinks about it well, one would freely complain about the human in Christ, or that his flesh might be subject to sin (as little in Mary as in Christ himself), but one would soon find a fast new divine beginning through which all flesh shall be helped.[17]

He did not greatly concern himself with the details of Mary's own conception. The issues were unimportant to him, since the only thing that mattered about Mary was that she gave birth to Christ. But, for that birth to be what it was, Mary's own flesh had to be of this sort: without being subject to or damaged by sin. This was essentially the position which led to the development of the doctrine of the Immaculate Conception of Mary.

The Immaculate Conception of Mary

Although belief in the Immaculate Conception was only promulgated as dogma in 1857, commitment to it as part of belief originated, in the Eastern Church, commitment to it as part of orthodox belief started very early, and for the same reasons as Schwenckfeld adopted it.

In the early debates of the church, the relationship between divinity and humanity was central to the discussion about the nature of Christ. Although this was formally settled with the acceptance of the Chalcedonian Definition in 381, the arguments did continue, and involved consideration of the nature of Mary and her flesh. Since his birth from Mary was the guarantor of the humanity of Christ, it could not be ignored. However, as the Catholic Encyclopedia presents it

> There is an incongruity in the supposition that the flesh, from which the flesh of the Son of God was to be formed, should ever have belonged to one who was a slave of that arch-enemy, whose power He came on earth to destroy...It was [therefore] becoming that the Mother of the Redeemer should have been from from the power of sin, and from the first moment of her existence; God could give her this privilege therefore He gave it to her.[18]

Such a belief, later formulated as the Doctrine of the Immaculate Conception also led to language describing Mary as Theotokos, God-bearer. The term

---

[17] *CS*, vol. 7, p. 323, ll. 4f.

[18] Charles Herbermann, et al, *Catholic Encyclopedia*, London: Caxton Printing Co. 1907-1922.

emerged before the Council of Chalcedon, and although for many years it was controversial, it was in the end accepted as orthodox theology. Mary must be Theotokos, since the fullness of God and humanity must both be present in her.

Such a theology therefore raised the issue of Mary's relationship to the Godhead and her place in the scheme of salvation.[19] Ambrose was the thinker in the Western church who really established Mariology as a central part of doctrine there.[20]

The issue again became controversial in the writings of Duns Scotus, a Franciscan, and William of Ware, a Dominican. Ware attacked belief in the Immaculate Conception, because it would put her in a different category from the rest of humanity – that is, unaffected by original sin. Scotus, arguing from the sinless flesh of Christ to the flesh of Mary, insisted that she had to be free from original sin from her conception in order that Christ would truly be sinless. This controversy began in about 1387, and in fact continued until the promulgation of the doctrine in 1857. At the centre was not so much the understanding of Mary, as the beliefs about sin, and redemption. Stratton points out that it was with Augustine's teaching on the link between sexual conception and original sin that the question about Mary's status becomes important. Before that, the understanding that God cleansed her from sin before birth was sufficient.[21] Scotus argued that sin was an absence of good, rather than a physical taint. He also argued that the prevention of original sin was a greater perfection than the removal of it. Thus, he reasoned, since Christ was the perfect Redeemer, it was fitting that he should carry out the most perfect redemption at least once, and that there should be one soul preserved from original sin.

Ware insisted that God had *preserved* Mary from the taint of original sin, although she was born in it. The preservation was through the grace of Christ in his saving role, and therefore she was dependent on him, just as all others were, for salvation.[22] The issue was all the more confused, because of the continuing uncertainty about the status of menstruation, and its link with sin. As Cadden has shown, although menstruation was regarded as *stain* rather than *sin*, still there was some difficulty in understanding the reality of Mary's physiological status. Dominican writers insisted that, as a descendant of Eve, she must have menstruated, while Franciscans argued that it was only in solidarity with Eve that she condescended to do so. Cadden continues:

---

[19] Hilda Graef, *Mary: A History of Doctrine and Devotion*, London: London and New York, 1965, pp. 105ff.

[20] Graef, *Mary*, p. 88.

[21] Suzanne L. Stratton, *The Immaculate Conception in Spanish Art*, Cambridge: Cambridge University Press, 1994.

[22] For further discussion of this debate, and the way in which it developed, see Graef, *Mary*, pp. 300-304.

That Mary's menstruation posed such a problem demonstrates the extent to which the Fall and the stain of womanhood haunted that physiological process.[23]

Although salvation was part of the central Reformation debate, this part of the question was not of such crucial importance to the Reformation thinkers.[24]

The Immaculate Conception and the Nature of the Body

The centre of the debate may well be the understanding of the nature of Christ and of salvation, but it does demonstrate something significant about the understanding of sin and its relationship to and place in the physical body. As discussed previously, the Christian understanding of *body* has always been marked by a certain sense of ambiguity. This ambiguity has certainly played its part in the questioning of Mary's physical being.

As well as the wider philosophical context of the Greco-Roman desire for control, and the Gnostic ideas which emphasised a profound dualism, there are texts and assumptions evident within the biblical writings which serve to support such a mistrust of physical existence. Gen 4:1 was read to mean that sexual intercourse only took place after the Fall – and interpreted to suggest that it was a result of the Fall.[25] For the Prophets, the disobedience of Israel in idolatry was spoken of in terms of unchastity and prostitution.[26] For Paul, in his directions to Christians in the new churches about how to live as believers, the word *sarx*, (flesh) summed up the nature to be rejected. However, it is clear when he lists the things which come under the umbrella term of *sarx*, that he is not dealing simply with *body*.[27] This did not stop some of his later commentators and interpreters from translating this word very strongly with *body* and with physical existence. This reinforced the tendency already described to view the body with mistrust, sometimes fear, and almost always with the expectation that true Christian life would entail a rejection of bodily existence. It was this thinking that drove much of early and medieval monastic practice: the sense that an evil body had to be punished and brought under

---

[23] Cadden, *Meanings of Sex Difference in the Middle Ages*, p. 174.

[24] Timothy George argues that the Reformers in general: generally held that the Holy Spirit miraculously cleansed the corrupt seed of Adam so that Jesus was free from original sin despite the fact that he inherited a fully human nature. George, *Theology of the Reformers*, p. 282.

[25] Now the man knew his wife Eve, and she conceived and bore Cain, saying, "I have produced a man with the help of the Lord." Gen 4:1, *New Revised Standard Version*.

[26] See for example, Is 1:21, Jer 3:1-2, Hosea, where the entire book is structured around Hosea's relationship with Gomer, his wife who turns to prostitution, and the parallels he draws with Israel's behaviour.

[27] For example Galatians 4:20-21 lists as *works of the flesh*: Idolatry, sorcery, enmities, strife, jealousy, anger, quarrels, dissensions, factions, envy, drunkeness, carousing and the like.

control in order to prevent it from drawing the believing soul away from God.

As I will show in the discussion below about baptism, the issue was not simply that through the body it was possible to sin, but that the body was, in some way and to some extent, a site of evil, at least until it was redeemed through baptism.

That it should be of such importance in the consideration of a woman is not surprising. If, as we have seen, women were more closely identified, scientifically, philosophically and theologically with body than men, then any thinking which applied to body would apply with especial force to female bodies. There was a continuing tradition that the body, by reason of its physical existence, was a site of evil and temptation. Old Testament and traditional models of interpretation located this particularly in sexual activity. This whole complex of ideas, while applying to humanity as a whole, applied particularly to women, the ones who were most fully identified with body.

Schwenckfeld's Understanding of Mary's Flesh

A belief in the Incarnation requires some position to be taken about the reality and meaning of the flesh of Christ: that in its turn raises issues about Mary's position. The linking of body, sexuality and sin is so deep, that it is not surprising some took the way out suggested by the theology of the Immaculate Conception. Hoffman, however, appears to have been unwilling to subscribe to such an understanding of the nature of Mary. Schwenckfeld, on the other hand, quite clearly had a sense that there was a particular purity about the flesh which Mary possessed and from which Christ took his. Thus for example, he used language about Mary's body like: *virginal and holy*[28] and a *new, marvellous and holy creature.*[29] In writing to Johann Spreng, a teacher in Augsburg who had written to him with some questions about the nature of Christ's flesh and its origins, he referred back to Mary as part of the argument:

> And now for the question about the origin and flesh of Christ, what Christ received as flesh, whether it is previous, true creaturely though reborn flesh from Mary or not is high and difficult to work out. But if we want to reflect on what is said in the booklet "The Origin"... it is that Mary was a holy, chosen, highly-blessed, spiritual virgin, the Lord was with her, she was full of grace, and blessed among women, even before she had conceived the Son of God for birth, and before the Word became flesh in her: so we may the more easily recognize God's new, initial work in her, as in a holy workshop, and what sort of flesh it was that Christ received from her. It must have been holy, pure and without spot. Thereby faith can soon discover that it was a newborn flesh or humanity, produced and made through the Holy Spirit of God the Father, in and from Mary the holy Virgin, and must be full of grace and truth, never disturbed by sin. Human reason,

---

[28] For example "Jungkfrewlichen heiligen Fleische" *CS*, vol. 7, p. 300, l. 15.

[29] "ein new herrliche heilige Creatur" *CS*, vol. 14, p. 327, l. 4.

which cannot grasp such a secret must give way to faith and see in Mary God's new, wonderful and supernatural work.[30]

The flesh which becomes Jesus' is the flesh which is Mary's and therefore, because of what is known about Jesus' flesh, Schwenckfeld appears to be arguing, certain things can be discovered about Mary's flesh. It is sinless, pure, holy and blessed by God. The reasons and the means for this were not important to him. In line with the pattern mentioned earlier, his interest was not in theological dispute for the sake of the dispute, but in the practical – that is moral and transformational – results of any position which he adopted. What mattered about Mary was not that she was a virgin at the time of Christ's conception, but that that her physical being was the guarantor of Christ's humanity. And the important thing in the discussion was not the theological point of the virgin conception. He did not become involved in discussions about the nature of salvation and the way in which it applied to Mary. What mattered was the physical, but at the same time spiritual (inner) reality of Christ's flesh, because it was this which had transforming power, and meant that salvation was a possibility. Thus, when he does speak about Mary's conception, it is in this context. For example, in a letter to Sibilla Eisler of 1549, he was answering her questions about the nature of the Incarnation. In that context he wrote one of the only extended explorations of his understanding of the nature of Mary's conception. It is such a significant discussion that it must be quoted in full:

> Now about the flesh of Christ, that should have a much higher origin in the flesh for the salvation of all other flesh and a new foundation of birth and identity from the birth of all the children of God, because it was conceived from the Holy Spirit. But it does not follow therefore that it was above in heaven before it was conceived and born; it follows as little as if one says Mary in her first birth is, like everybody else, a daughter of Adam and therefore under a curse. Therefore, should what is born from her after she is reborn hallowed and cleansed also be from Adam and under a curse? Such, I say does not follow at all, for Mary gains quite another standing before God, in that she was prepared for such a high, supernatural work as the bearing of the Son of God, despite the fact that she has come from her parents and from Adam. You should reflect on this and consider Mary in two ways, as well as Abraham her father, about which Helena has sent you a note to which a prayer and the light of faith belong.

> More should you also think, that Mary was elected to this holy work from the beginning. Was God the Lord then not capable of having worked it so that it was possible that his Son, Jesus Christ to take a holy flesh that was without sin for ever and ever from her, if it was his will? who was to resist him, and could he not also protect the holy Virgin from youth up?

---

[30] *CS*, vol. 14, p. 843, ll. 11f.

Therefore we must not see Mary as other people, for she has become a mother of Christ, yes God's mother. But in that she, according to the grace of God, the eternal grace has found in which she has found, as said above and elect from all eternity, as God also knows all his works from eternity.

The monks had, as you without doubt know, disputed about this; whether Mary the mother of Christ was conceived in original sin or not. Therefore there arose many squabbles, envies and hatreds between the black preaching monks and the grey barefoot monks about this. The women are at enmity with the black monks over this, because they have said that the holy virgin Mary was conceived in original sin.

Thus disputes also the master of the high mind, and Adam Reisner can say to you, and all the Creaturists, and the Papists also hold this, that the flesh of Christ, before in Mary was subject to sin, before it is conceived of the Holy Spirit, which is a blasphemy against Christ and his flesh, which has been marked by no blemish of sin, just as the Angel said to Mary; "The holy thing which is born in you shall be called the Son of God."

We also do not want to say that Mary before she conceived Christ was like other people under a curse; that we do not want to hold. But her gracious election and that she in the grace which she found was always before God; the same we should also think of as God's counsel in this matter.[31]

Schwenckfeld was clearly aware that Mary's position in regard to original sin was a matter of dispute, and in this passage, we find some hints about his position. Like William of Ware, he suggested that God would have preserved Mary from sin, by a special act of grace, rather than making her sinless ontologically. He also used the term *God bearer*, and it is further evidence of the fact that he was deeply influenced by the patristic writings, and in particular, the eastern fathers. His understanding of the being of Christ, as his understanding of the final destination of the saved new person, as we will see in chapter five, show close links to the eastern theology of deification.

However he also made it clear that, for him, despite his position in the debate, the question was not about Mary in herself, but what must be the case for the flesh of Christ to be what he believed it must be. The status of Mary's flesh was only important insofar as it had bearing on the understanding of the nature of Christ's flesh.

It is interesting to note in passing that there was at least some perception that women took a position on this matter because they felt it important to believe certain things about Mary. This suggests, as I have proposed above, that

---

[31]*CS*, vol. 11, p. 767, ll. 11f.

although the centre of the debate was, as Schwenckfeld identified, about the nature of Christ, it was also used to illustrate and reinforce certain beliefs about the nature of body and especially of female bodies. By re-emphasising his rejection of that position, Schwenckfeld was again giving a theological position which undermined contemporary assumptions about the meaning of gender.

The Divine Origin of Christ

The second of his main thrusts also focuses on who plays which role, but this time the emphasis is on the action of God as the guarantor of Christ's divinity. Throughout his writings he is very clear that conception takes place at the instigation of God through the action of the Holy Spirit. One of his most frequent biblical citations is from Matt 1:20: *That which is born in her, said the Angel to Joseph, that is from the Holy Spirit.*[32] Even when not using direct quotation, he uses the same terms, speaking of the *overshadowing* of the Spirit.[33]

At times he deliberately emphasises Mary's passivity in the whole event:

> But we only speak of a new origin, in which Mary became pregnant, which is to say, not through herself, naturally through her own powers, but supernaturally by the power of God the father...[34]

If Christ is not to be understood as some sort of super-human, or half-man, half-God figure, then it is important for Schwenckfeld to establish God's role in the conception and birth as being beyond question. This was a normal use of the doctrine of the virginal conception – by its uniqueness, and the space left for divine intervention, it put Christ's divinity beyond question. However, as we shall see below, although Schwenckfeld put a great deal of emphasis on the divine activity, and conception by means of the Holy Spirit, and although this was important to him in demonstrating the divinity of Christ, in fact, the issue

---

[32] *CS*, vol. 7, p. 290, ll. 10f.

[33] See for example, the language in "The Flesh of Christ": It is also the strength of the highest which has overshadowed the holy Virgin…
Er ist auch die krafft des Höchsten/ welche die heilige Junckfraw hat umbschetiget…, *CS*, vol. 7, p. 321, ll. 13f.

[34] *CS*, vol. 14, p. 322, ll. 34f.
It is worth noting, in this discussion of Mary's role in her own pregnancy, Bynum's comment on the argument of Giles of Rome: "Moreover, Giles of Rome in the thirteenth century, who rejected the Galenic theory as mediated by Avicenna and turned to Aristotle, argued against Galen that if a woman provided both menstrual matter and the seed, then she might impregnate herself and the male would have no role at all. *Such an argument shows not only the tendency to associate matter with woman, but also a fear that this threatens the importance of the male contribution to life.*" Bynum, *Fragmentation and Redemption*, p. 214. Emphasis mine.

of Mary's virginity in itself was of little importance here. He did not use it as the proof of Jesus' divinity. Rather, he spoke of Mary normally in terms of the humanity, and the embodiment that it was so important for him to demonstrate. For Schwenckfeld, the concentration had to fall where he believed it to be most appropriate – the generative activity, that is the power determining the nature of the offspring, being male, came from God, while the physical form in terms of embodiment, which involved the identification as human, was supplied by the mother, Mary. [35]

It is in this discussion that the ontological difference between inner and outer becomes clear. The issue is not of spiritual and physical, material and non-material, but a question of origins: that which has its origin in God's *creative* activity is outer, that which has its origins in God's generative (or in Schwenckfeld's own terms "fatherly", *vatterlich*) activity is inner. So, Schwenckfeld's rejection of the outer as a means of the divine was not a moral but an ontological consideration. That which is outer cannot mediate the divine because it is separated from the divine primarily in terms of origin, not simply because of some sin or evil. The inner shares an identity with the divine because of being generated by God. This meant that the question of generation, and therefore of conception, was of central importance to Schwenckfeld's theology. As we will see in the discussion in the fifth chapter, the question of origin was at the heart of the understanding of salvation. Schwenckfeld's understanding of origin, both of Christ and of the believer was shaped by his perception of the mechanics of conception, and therefore his understanding of gender roles had a significant part to play in his notion of the salvific process.

Scientific Understandings of Conception

The two most influential authorities on the subject of conception, whose teachings carried most weight in the sixteenth century, were Aristotle and Galen. At the time we are discussing, Aristotle's views, on the whole, held sway, although a significant number of people were inclining to Galen. It was in part because of this division that the whole issue was so contentious. By the end of the century and the beginning of the seventeenth century, Galen's views

---

[35] In his discussion of Schwenckfeld's understanding of the nature of Christ's conception, Maier points out that Schwenckfeld was "probably assuming that God in the Holy Spirit was the efficient cause of Jesus' conception". However, he goes on to argue from this insight that Schwenckfeld was demonstrating "crypto-docetic tendencies": exactly the position which Schwenckfeld was at such pains to defend himself against. I suggest that Maier finds himself with this conclusion, because he has not taken seriously the biological and and gender realities of the posdition which Schwenckfeld adopted, and therefore he is unable to see the coherence in the position, determined by gender role. Maier, *Caspar Schwenckfeld on the Person and Work of Christ*, p. 55.

were to predominate in popular knowledge.[36]

There was a common understanding between the two views that conception occurred through the expulsion of seed during intercourse. The womb then received this and the foetus developed. The difference in teaching focused on the origin of the seed. Aristotle taught that the seed was entirely from the man, and that woman was simply the field which he ploughed and sowed, and in which the child grew. The woman provided the material out of which the child's body was formed, but its character, soul and humanity depended on the man's seed.[37] Galen's teaching on the other hand, was that there was male and female seed and that conception depended on the conjunction of the two. He argued that the male seed was the dominant and therefore the determinative constituent, but nevertheless, the female seed was a necessary part of the equation.[38]

Maclean argues that these two approaches allow a contrasting view of the determining of the sexes at conception, which view demonstrates a fundamental distinction in the attitude to the relationship between male and female.[39] By showing that Aristotle believed sex to be determined by the male semen alone, while Galen believed it to be dependent on the relative position and heat of the male and female, he argues that this demonstrates within Aristotelian thinking a fundamental discontinuity on an ontological level between male and female. Since Galen's model is to do with balance and relative contributions, it also involves the notion of a continuity, and at least in principle allows for the possibility of intermediate beings. This distinction, if it does exist, would prove important for the perception of the relative roles of male and female. Laqueur has argued that: "sexuality is not just to do with the female, but with the space between the sexes."[40] If this space is an unbridgeable gap, then the relationship between male and female is perceived in terms of irreconcilable differences. If the prevailing vision is of continuity, then the perception will be of an identical basic humanity, expressed in different ways. Joan Cadden argued in a similar

---

[36] Ian Maclean, *The Renaissance Notion of Women*, Cambridge: Cambridge University Press, 1981; Horowitz, "The 'Science' of Embryology"; Laqueur, *Making Sex.*

[37] The contribution which the female makes to generation is the *matter* used therein: and is to be found in the substance constituting the menstrual fluid...The male provides the "form" and the "principle of movement," the female provides the body, in other words, the material. Aristotle: *Generation of Animals*, trans A.L.Peck, Harvard, 1943, Bk 1, p. 101.

[38] From a single principle wisely imagined by the Creator - that whereby the female is less perfect than the male - follow all the conditions useful for the generation of the animal...an imperfect sperm... In the male instead, everything is the reverse...an abundance of this same thick sperm. Galen, *Oeuvres de Galen*, ed. Dr Ch Darembourg 2 vols, Paris, 1854, Vol II, p. 101.

[39] Maclean, *The Renaissance Notion of Women*, p. 37.

[40] Laqueur, *Making Sex* p. 13.

way, pointing out that:

> Since being feminine or masculine entailed, not as incidental effects but as
> definite characteristics, dimensions of disposition, character and habit, the
> variations had to do not only with the complexion and appearance, but also with
> behaviour, including sexual conduct.[41]

Thus, the way in which individuals behaved was as important as the
physiological reality in constructing the social identity and gender. This will
prove crucial in the perception of what it means to be human, and in
understanding the relationship between human and God.

Behind these two approaches lay a theory of *humours* and a notion of *hot*
and *cold* which was related to the perception of perfection. Each body was
believed to be made up of a balance of humorous fluids. The exact nature of
this balance determined the position of the body on the continua hot-cold and
dry-moist. The hotter and drier a body was, the more it tended towards
perfection, and the cooler and moister, the more imperfect. This then had
implications for the way in which sexual differences between bodies could be
viewed.[42] The creation of seed was a function of heat. The hotter the body, the
more effective the seed. To be male was to be able to create generative seed. To
be female, and therefore by definition to be cooler and moister was to be
unable, in Aristotle's view,[43] or less able, in Galen's,[44] to create generative
seed.

Implications of Aristotle and Galen for Gender

It is clear that, although the surface argument is about the differing roles of
women and men in the production of the foetus there is a deeper discussion
contained within this debate about the relative natures of men and women and
their relationship within the social and physical world. Since women's bodies
were not perceived as being as perfect as men's, there was as we have seen, the
possibility of coming to the conclusion that in fact the female body was a lesser
form of creation, or even a malformed creation, and this was indeed the
conclusion that Aquinas found himself drawing.[45] Thus a notion of conception,

---

[41] Cadden, *Meanings of Sex Difference*, p. 202.

[42] The female is more imperfect than the male. The first reason is that she is colder...The
male's testicles are all the stronger because he is warmer. Galen *Oeuvres,* p. 101.

[43] ...the female, in fact, is female on account of an inability of a sort, viz, it lacks the
power to concoct semen out of the final state of nourishment. Aristotle, *Gestation* , p.
103.

[44] see n. 40

[45] As regards the individual nature, woman is defective and misbegotten, for the active
force in the male seed tends to the production of a perfect likeness in the masculine sex;
while the production of a woman comes from a defect in the active force or from some

which was based on the idea that women were inferior to men was also used to support the idea that women were inferior to men.[46]

Together with this macho science approach went the link that was made between semen and thought. This drew on the notion that rationality, as a male attribute, could be paralleled with the production of semen. Just as the male seed gave rise to new life, so thought gave rise to new ideas and understandings. This had become part of Christian thinking about the nature of being human via Augustine, who drew on Aristotle's theories, and shaped the assumption that women were not only deficien*t* in physical nature, but also in mental faculties. This link between semen and mind has two major implications. Firstly, there is the notion that the expenditure of semen is somehow damaging to a man if it is too extreme – and therefore the sense that the expression of sexuality was to be restrained not only for moral but also for health reasons. Entailed in this is the assumption that a woman, already suspect morally for her ability to seduce a man, is also damaging to him physically.

Implications for Christology

Secondly, in Christian terms, this connection of mind and seed has particular resonances in the area of Logos and the nature of Christ. The Logos of God as the being of Christ was a link which was made by early theologians writing of Christian thinking in terms of Greek philosophy, drawing in particular on the Prologue to John's gospel. James D.G. Dunn points out that for the early Christian writers, the Greek term Logos "embraces both *thought, reason* and *speech, utterance*,"[47] and therefore could be used to explain the relationship between Christ and God. The link between seed and thought fitted well with the biblical language of father and son, and provided a philosophical basis for discussion. The emphasis on rationality and communication was one that was to prove decisive in the continuing development of the understanding of the Incarnation in Christian thought. The understanding of Christ as replicating or being part of the fundamental being of God was explored and expressed by this language, language which in both its usage and derivation was symbolically male. The conviction that women, by reason of biology, were deficient in rationality was a pattern of thought which effectively excluded women from close identification with a God who was known through the Logos, the expression of rationality.[48] Part of the debate about whether women could truly

---

material indisposition, or even from some external influence... Aquinas *Summa Theologica* IV. Pt I. Quest XCII. art 1.

[46] Horowitz, "The 'Science' of Embryology", p. 87.

[47] James D.G. Dunn, *Christology in the Making: An Inquiry into the Origins of the Doctrine of the Incarnation*, London: SCM, 1989, p. 223.

[48] See Rosemary Radford Ruether, *Sexism and God-Talk: Towards a Feminist Theology*, London: SCM, 1983, pp. 122ff.

be said to be made in the image of God centred on this point. The understanding of *the image of God* was shaped by the Logos theology of Christ, and so drew heavily on ideas of rationality. Part of the sense of hierarchy which gave order to the world was the expectation, on the basis of this, that rationality was above irrationality, and therefore men were superior to women.[49]

However, although, as Dunn has shown, Logos theology was a way of exploring Christ in and through the Incarnation when it was first developed, it soon became a method for accounting for the pre-existence of Christ. As trinitarian theology became more developed, the being of the Second Person of the Trinity in essence, before the Incarnation, became of importance. Language of pre-existence fitted well with Logos thinking, since concepts of Word could be traced in the Old Testament, and an identification between the two could be made. Since Logos bore so much male symbolism, the essential nature of the Second Person of the Trinity therefore became understood as being male, and therefore the male nature of the Incarnate Christ was understood not to be accidental or contingent, but inherent.

Modern feminist theologians have explored ideas of *Sophia*, Wisdom, as expressive of the essential nature of the Second Person. This is language which is also found in the Old Testament, used of the self-expression of God, and which is grammatically and, to some extent, symbolically female.[50] However, the fact that they are finding the need to explore this in contemporary discussions is witness to the fact that the predominant tradition has been shaped by the Logos pattern. Certainly, in his christological language, Schwenckfeld shows evidence of taking this theology for granted. He frequently referred to Christ as *the Word*: that seems to have been his chosen description of the essence of the Second Person.[51] Just as his Eucharistic thinking was dependent

---

[49] The irrationality of women was an assumption which was never questioned. It was used, for example, in religious propaganda in order to demonstrate the weakness of an opponent's position, as Natalie Zemon Davis has shown. both Catholic and Protestant writers used the appeal of their opponents religion to women to demonstrate that therefore it must be irrational and heretical. Davis, "City Women and Religious Change", *Society and Culture in Early Modern France*, p. 65.

[50] See, for example, Elisabeth Schüssler Fiorenza, *Jesus: Miriam's Child, Sophia's Prophet: Critical Issues in Feminist Theology*, London: SCM, 1995. Such theologies draw particularly on Apocryphal books, in particular The Wisdom of Solomon and Ecclesiasticus. The language which is used of Wisdom as an entity in these books can be seen to be parallel to the languiage which is used of the the Word, and then of Jesus in the New Testament.

[51] See for example, his discussion in the letter to Sibilla Eisler in February 1545, when he wrote: But the two persons, of which I have written before, I say therefore that the Son of God, is born in the nature of the father from the father in eternity and is with him alike in one being and one omnipotence. So much now of the word, and the word has become flesh, yes, God and human, word and flesh, come together in one person, one Son of God and one Christ.*CS*, vol. 9, p. 296, ll. 6ff.

on the theology of the gospel of John, so he used the first chapter of that gospel to speak of the Incarnation, especially the phrase "the Word became flesh." This became a crucial phrase for Schwenckfeld in his dispute with Hoffman. His determination to reject the understanding that Christ brought his flesh with him from heaven, as Hoffman taught, led him to emphasis the word *became* in this verse. There was, as translations of the Bible into the vernacular became available, debate about exactly how this verse should be translated. Luther translated the phrase as "*Und das Wort ward Fleisch und wohnte unter uns, und wir sahen seine Herrlichkeit, eine Herrlichkeit als des eingeborenen Sohnes vom Vater, voller Gnade und Wahrheit.*" This was the translation which Schwenckfeld followed. However, the debate was over the meaning of *werden* – Hoffman argued that it simply meant *turned into*, while Schwenckfeld used language which suggests that he developed an understanding which was closer to *took to himself*. Clearly, this has very different implications for understanding just what the Incarnation meant, as well as how it happened.

For Schwenckfeld, it meant that central to his Christology he was trying to hold together an understanding of the essential nature of Christ which was inherently male as shown by the logos thinking, and that part of being human, the physical, which was most closely identified symbolically with the female. Schwenckfeld's language for Christ was strongly marked by logos thinking. However, as we have seen, he emphasised the flesh of Christ as the agent of salvation. This meant that the implications with regard to the maleness of the immanent nature of the Second Person of the Trinity were less certain than the language might suggest.

The other side of this connection between seed and thought is the link that was made between woman and body – if to be male is to be intellectual, to be female is to be physical. This identification of female and fleshly runs very deep, and will occur at various points throughout this discussion. Since, according to the Aristotelian view it was the woman who was perceived to provide the *raw material* for the growing infant -and to provide only that – then her link with *stuff* was indisputable. Theologically, scientifically and in common perception, the identification of women with body, lust, weakness and irrationality was very strong.[52] The physical realities of a woman's life, dominated as it was by menstruation, pregnancy and lactation, all of which whatever else they are, and whatever other meanings they carry, are bodily, simply went to prove and demonstrate that *female* and *physical* were co-determinative categories. The model of humours was believed to have moral implications too. As Maclean has pointed out, certain virtues and vices were associated with certain humours, and their degree was thereby determined.[53]

---

[52] Davis, *Society and Culture;* Atkinson, *The Oldest Vocation.*

[53] A man would be thought a coward if he had no more courage than a courageous woman, and a woman would be thought loquacious if she imposed no more restraint on

Since physical sex and the understanding of gender were believed to be determined by humoral balance, women's humours predisposed them to certain virtues and vices.

Therefore, although, as said above, the surface debate was on the nature of conception, the ideas that were invoked and the ways in which they were used show that much more was involved in this discussion than physical mechanics. So, when Schwenckfeld spends as much time and energy as he does on explaining the importance and the method of the Incarnation, and specifically the conception of Christ, and of Mary's place within it, what he has to say and the conclusions that he comes to reflect not only on his theology of the Incarnation, but also on his understanding of the role and place of women both socially and physically.

Christology and Anthropology

However, the doctrine of the Incarnation, focusing on the conception and birth of Jesus, is not a doctrine that stands alone and without reference to other understandings. The way in which the Incarnation is understood shapes the rest of theology. This includes the resultant anthropology: the way that humanity is understood to exist before God. Doctrine, and the way in which it is expressed, is part of the context which determines attitudes and expectations about the nature of being, and of society. Therefore, any examination of Schwenckfeld's understanding of the nature of the Incarnation will bring with it implications for the understanding of the rest of his theology and for the world-view with which he operated. In particular it shaped his perceptions of *female*. It is to these that I will now turn.

In any consideration of women in terms of faith, a simple place to start is with Mary, mother of Jesus. The relationship of determination is not easy to define -was the understanding of Mary determined by or determinative of the understanding of *woman*? The doctrine of the virgin birth has been important in Christian understanding as the guarantee of Christ's humanity. It has also acquired great significance in shaping the understanding of women. Although the primary focus of the doctrine was the nature of Christ, as it was developed, its significance changed. The understanding of Mary came to be as important in the theological understanding of the nature of women as it was in explaining the Incarnation. Mariology never became separated from the issue of Christ's humanity, and indeed as devotion to that increased during the middle ages, so did devotion to Mary. However other implications and perceptions also began to come to the fore.

While Mary's virginity was important in earlier thinking because of what it meant for the nature of Christ, it gradually came to be influential in its own

---

her conversation than a good man. Aristotle. *Politics* III:4, quoted by Maclean *Renaissance Notion,* p. 54

right. In connection with the ambiguous nature of Christianity's understanding of sexuality, this elevation of Mary's physical state both reflected and helped to determine the Church's attitude to celibacy. For example, during the eleventh-century reforms, when the celibacy of the priesthood was an issue, the virginity of Mary was one of the reasons that were adduced for the virginity of the priest.[54]

The virginity of Mary served both to emphasise virginity as female perfection and was a reflection of that existing perception. As Atkinson states, as devotion to Mary became heightened, so did the perception of her physical *purity*:

> To medieval Christians, it became increasingly obvious that Mary was always a virgin – during and after, as well as before the birth of Christ. Sexual activity was unthinkable for her, as was a ruptured hymen; perfection was incompatible with loss of bodily integrity...[55]

There were, by the late Middle Ages, two predominant representations of Mary, both of which viewed her as mediatrix. She was Queen of Heaven, a view that had developed in the early period, in parallel to Jesus as King. This approach drew on the tradition of courtly love propagated by the troubadours, many of whose songs spoke of the desired woman in terms of unattainablity, but as one who might provide mercy and grace for the humble suppliant. This image allowed the believer to approach the Lady, Mary, as supplicant, in the trust that she would persuade the Lord to grant the request. The other view was of Mary as mother – firstly of Christ, and therefore in the position to persuade or cajole him onto granting her requests, but also of the believer, and therefore as the one who could be easily approached, as a child approaches a mother.[56] This perception of Mary was especially strong amongst monks, and there was a great deal of writing about the power and authority of mothers, as seen in the power and authority of Mary. However, since such writing was mainly by and for celibate men, rather than to and about families, it is unclear just how much influence such a veneration for motherhood and such an assumption of motherly authority had on the lives of actual women.

Both of these representations of her persona, the unattainable Queen who was powerful and the Mother who could persuade her son and was approachable, were deeply marked by the high emotional value which was placed on Mary's virginity, which ran through both these representations and which had implications for the perceptions of other women. The incompatibility of virginity and motherhood, a physical impossibility, and the

---

[54] By whom then, I ask you, does he want his body handled now, except also by virgins. Peter Damian: *Opuscula 173: opera omnia Petri Damiana*, cited by Clarissa Atkinson in *The Oldest Vocation* p. 17

[55] Atkinson, *The Oldest Vocation*, p. 112.

[56] See for example Anselm, *Oratio 7*, "The mother of God is our mother."

unusual combination of perfect femininity and power, a social anomaly, which these images provoked do not seem to have been an issue for those who wrote about and who venerated Mary. However, we can surmise that such a confused presentation of and ideal image would have had its effect in making the personal experience of women uncertain. To which of these models, if either, were they to aspire, and how was it to be achieved, given the inherent contradictions? To raise this as an issue is not to suggest that women were consciously alienated from the mainstream religious tradition because of these tensions. However, when we are considering theological reasons why some women should have responded to a certain theology, and why within it they should have found power and position, it is worth while reflecting on some of the difficult areas which may have been present in other theologies.

In general, the Reformers rejected any special veneration of Mary, believing that in that they saw the imposition of another mediator in the place that by rights was Christ's. At the root of Reformation thinking, although expressed in various ways, was the belief that the only basis of salvation was the work of Christ, and the fundamental relationship of the believer was with him – this was to move away from the notion of *priest* as previously understood, and as a consequence, also removed any mediating role from Mary. Bossy puts it thus:

> For a social historian the striking character of the new doctrine of the Atonement is its rejection of the event from the field of social relationships...It became less urgent to prove, at least in the way that it had hitherto seemed necessary, the absolute humanity of Christ. It has generally been held that Reformation theologians saw Christ as redeeming more by virtue of his godhead than his manhood .... Devotion to Christ's mother as the locus of universal reconciliation would be taken as an idolatrous detraction from the single-handed victory of her Son.[57]

Thus, for the Reformers, what was important about Mary was not anything in herself, but her relationship with her Son – again, both determining and reflective of the attitude to women. A woman was to be understood, not as a person of self-definition, but in relation to the (powerful) men around her – father, son and so on. There was a definite move to limit the perception of Mary's authority. Erasmus, for example, has a discussion in which Mary is represented as complaining about the way in which she is treated, since it implied that her son was always a baby. In *A Pilgrimage for Religion's Sake*, published in 1526 he wrote, in the voice of Mary:

> Up to this time I was all but exhausted by the shameful entreaties of mortals. They demanded everything from me alone, as if my son were always a baby (because he is carved and painted as such at my bosom), still needing his mother's consent

---

[57] John Bossy, *Christianity in the West 1400-1700*, Oxford: Oxford University Press, 1985. pp. 94-95.

and not daring to deny a person's prayer; fearful, that is, that if he did deny a petitioner something, I for my part would refuse him the breast when he was thirsty.[58]

What mattered about Mary, in this approach, was not her power, nor her virginity, but her relationship with a particular man, who happened to be also the Son of God. This was the approach which seems to have informed Schwenckfeld's position. In examining the meanings of virginity, and the perception of sexuality, such a shift in perception is important. If Mary is to be regarded as an exemplar, which would be to continue part of the tradition of her role, then the example she is setting becomes very different. Previously, her example of feminine perfection had been judged in terms of her physicality – and it was an impossible one in terms of emulation. Here, there is the beginning of a move to *woman* as a relational category, albeit one of subjection. Marc Lienhard points out that one of the conceptual shifts which Luther both shares and shapes was to understand people less as self-contained individuals bearing a certain number of properties, but rather as persons in relation to God and Christ. As a result, his language was "more existential than ontological."[59] I have argued previously that Schwenckfeld was a pragmatic rather than a philosophical theologian; he was concerned with what it meant to exist as a lived experience far more than with discussions about the nature of existence in the abstract. Thus, like Luther, in considering the nature of being human, Schwenckfeld was less concerned with the *qualities* pertaining to humanness philosophically, and more concerned to explore the relational aspect. In the discussion on the implications of logos Christology above, I referred to the argument about the place of women in terms of the *image of God*, the image being understood as reflected in particular qualities of rationality and reason.

To focus on an understanding of being human that was less concerned with such qualitative categories and more centred on the relations between individuals and, by extension, between God and the individual, raises the possibility of discussing what it means to exist as a particular *type* of human – female – in a new way. It is noticeable that Schwenckfeld did not become involved in discussions about the essential nature of being human, being male or being female. He was concerned all the time to look at concrete examples, himself, the individuals he was writing to or, as in this discussion, Mary. These were not discussed as representing or even necessarily as being part of a class or group, but as individuals existing before God in their own place. In this way, Schwenckfeld was doing something rather different from most others in his

---

[58] Erasmus, "The Religious Pilgramage" (sic), *Twenty Select Colloquies of Erasmus*, trans. Sir Roger L'Estrange, 1680, London, n.d. p. 18.

[59] Marc Leinhardt "Luther and the Beginnings of the Reformation",in Jill Raitt, Bernard McGinn and John Meyendorff, eds. *Christian Spirituality, Vol II. High Middle Ages and Reformation.*

discussion of Mary. It is also suggestive to realise, as was demonstrated in the first chapter, just how important family and household relationships were in the spread and strength of the Schwenkfelder community. This at least raises the possibility that a perception of the importance of relationships, with all that that means about space for women to operate, was part of the theological formation of these communities.

However, even a slightly different way of thinking still had to deal with the reality of the biological perceptions that were current, and their effect on the notion of *woman*. It is clear that Schwenckfeld did not see in Mary the exemplar of what it meant to be female. There is nothing in his published writings nor in the instructions and discussions he sends in the personal letters to his followers to suggest that Mary is presented in terms of humility, piety or purity as a model to be followed or as an ideal. When Mary is discussed, it is in terms of her role in the conception and birth of Christ, and as the provider of that which is human in the Incarnation. Her virginity is relevant only insofar as it is part of the whole doctrine of the virginal conception – it has no importance in and of itself, as a physical condition. This, as part of the change in attitude to sexuality around at the time of the Reformation referred to above, is an important change in the thinking about what it means to be a woman – and by extension, a man.

Original Sin

The perception that sexuality, in and of itself, was sinful implied that the sexual activity of a body was an occasion of sin. The connection of sin and sexuality goes back to the early days of the Church, and, as we saw earlier, Paul's use of the term *sarx* for that which was not of God. In the writings of the Fathers, and in particular the writings of Augustine, the link was made between original sin, caused by the eating of the forbidden fruit, and sexual acts and was made explicit – and the passing on of the taint of original sin was also explicitly linked to the lust, inseparably associated in fallen humans with the act of intercourse and conception. The writings of Paul make it clear that a sense of sin as a pervasive factor in human experience has been part of Christian thinking since its formative period.[60] Amongst the early Fathers there was a diversity of opinion about the meaning of sin; Gregory of Nazianzus and Gregory of Nyssa both argued that babies were born without sin, and it was through the exercise of their own will, and their choice of sinful deeds that they became sinners. Augustine, on the other hand, argued that sinfulness was the natural state of fallen being, and also that the guilt of such sin was present in an individual from the very beginning.[61] By this he was not referring to a sense of guilt, a psychological or emotional state, but an objective fact before God; that

---

[60] See for example, Rom 3:23 "since all have sinned and fall short of the glory of God".

[61] See, for example, Augustine, *Confessions*, VII, 11.

in the sight of God, each human who exists is guilty of sin, even at an age where independent action and will is not possible, and when understanding of such a position cannot yet be grasped. He argued, unlike the Greek Fathers, and against Pelagius, that people have no control over their sinfulness. It is not a matter of will, but of being. Because people are sinners, they will sin. Pelagius, a contemporary of Augustine, with whom he had a fierce disagreement, which provoked the working out of this theology, argued that the pattern worked the other way round; that people chose to sin, and in so doing weakened the will, and made the likelihood of further sinning higher. Thus, sinning made people sinners. For Augustine, original sin had a physical expression. It became part of a person at conception: thus it was passed on during, or through intercourse. This reinforced the link between sexuality and sin, and suggested that, on this basis, virginity was the purest state.

Luther's sense of sin, which reflected much of his personal struggle, was overpowering.[62] His theological development was driven by a sense of helplessness in the face of the reality of sin, and the need for God to undertake all that was necessary for redemption. Although his theology of salvation was to differ from Augustine, his sense of sin and of its pervasiveness was very Augustinian. GH Williams has suggested that Schwenckfeld's doctrine of original sin was the same as that of Luther's with this emphasis on helplessness and salvation by faith alone.[63] However, Williams goes on to point out that although formally Schwenckfeld was close to Luther in his understanding on the pervasiveness and helplessness of sin, he did change Luther's emphasis because of his commitment to what Williams calls "the sanctifying, indeed almost deificatory, presence of the glorified Christ".[64] This is an aspect of Schwenckfeld's theology which will be further discussed in "Men, Women and God". Here, however, I am concerned to examine Schwenckfeld's understanding of sin, and the ways in which it resembled or differed from that of others. Like Luther, he did have a sense of despair at sin, and the understanding that resistance in human strength was unavailing. *In Von Dreyerlai Leben der Menschen* he wrote:

> Chapter 4: Every thing in man, without Christ, His grace and Spirit, is sin before God In the natural man there is an original inbred depravity, or that sinful disposition which manifests itself in selfishness, in self love, and all the carnal propensities of the human heart and in a complete perversion of the whole nature. This is a sad state; yea, so lamentable are the disorders of the unrenewed heart, that in the sight of God every thought, affection and word, or whatever he may do, is an offense to God, because polluted by sin, neither can he do any thing that will be acceptable to heaven, as long as he is destitute of faith, or while he lives

---

[62] Thus he could write: "If anyone would feel the greatness of sin, he would not be able to go on living another moment, so great is the power of sin".

[63] Williams, *The Radical Reformation*, p. 1214.

[64] Williams, *The Radical Reformation*, p. 1215.

without Christ and His Spirit. The natural man, being without faith, orders every thing in which he proposes to serve God, with reference to his own benefit. He does nothing out of pure love for God's will, but much more in obedience to the will of his own flesh. His own advantage, praise, or honor, constitute the ruling motive, in attempting to do those things which God has commanded. Concerning this we have an example mirrored in (Luke 18) the Pharisee in the temple. In regard to this character the prophet Isaiah also speaks "We are all as an unclean thing, and our righteousnesses are as filthy rags." Isa. 4:6. In short, where the Spirit of God does not sanctify and Jesus Christ does not forgive and bless, there is sin, condemnation and hell. God only, and Jesus Christ His Son, are our sanctification. Without Him, man is nothing. And although God permits His chosen before the time of their visitation to lead a somewhat honorable life, to fear Him, and to bring forth virtuous works, still in His sight they are not yet holy and good. After they have been blessed through Jesus, forgiven, born again, and received the Holy Ghost, God accounts the efforts of their faith for righteousness, and every thing will be made to contribute to their happiness. Therefore no one is just before God, neither can any one become righteous by his own power or works, (the tree must be made good before it can bear good fruit,) Matt. 12. However it may seem to the world, all men became corrupt in Adam's fall, unholy and helpless, and there is none that doeth good, (that is, which is good in God's sight,) no, not one. Rom. 3:10-12: Ps.14:1[65]

This kind of language makes it very clear, as Williams suggests, that Schwenckfeld shared Luther's sense of helplessness and his understanding of sin as a basic condition which led to sinful acts rather than a consequence of these acts. What is also clear in his language is that he made no distinction between people in the basic sinfulness. It was a condition which applied to all, and which, as this description makes clear, was traced to Adam – that is the representative of all humanity, rather than Eve, the archetypal female figure.

In Christian theology, the connection of sin with women was traced back to the Eden story, since it was Eve who first ate the fruit. This link is made explicit again in the Patristic writings, where there are warnings to believing men to keep away from women, since they are inherently sinful in a way that men are not, and instructions to women that their lives must be spent in penitence for the sinfulness of their sex.[66] This link was given as the reason why women were subject to men. Developed from the verses which follow the immediate account of the Fall, and in which God gives the punishment, there is an explicit identification of women's subjection with her punishment.[67] This is a motif which Schwenckfeld dealt with in another of the passages in which he concentrated on original sin, its cause and effect. In a letter written in 1550 to Katherina Ebertz and Cecilia von Kirchen, he wrote:

CS, vol. 9, p. 836, ll. 16f. (Translation, J.S. Anspach)

[66]See, for example, "A Sermon on Concubines" in Pseudo-Basil, and Jerome: "Adversus Jovinianum".

[67] Gen 3:16b "yet your desire will be for your husband and he shall rule over you".

On Eve, you know yourself what to think, how the poor weak woman was tempted by that old serpent, Satan, and introduced transgression. Therefore also she received a heavy judgement and punishment from God, and that her husband should be her lord, as also Sarah was obedient to Abraham, and called him Lord. But many women now want to rule themselves, and that men should follow them in everything, which attitude or manner they have inherited from Eve, for it is against the order and command of God. But those who have become Christians will set their hope on God, and conduct themselves according to his word and will, being obedient to their husbands in all things that are with God and not against God and the Lord Christ, where obedience and love should also be above that to father and mother according to Lk 14:26. The Lord Christ himself has taught it. But in that which pertains to the soul's salvation, there is no difference between people; here there is neither man nor woman says Paul. For you are now all one in Christ Jesus. Gal 3:28. The woman is also joint heir of the grace of life, but as to how women should behave towards men and also men towards women it is written in Eph 5:22-25 and 1 Peter 4:1,7. God the almighty has also honoured the female sex further, in that he was born as human from a woman's body, and just as the evil spirit brought Eve to evil, so God has brought good again from the image of woman in the Virgin Mary. For our Saviour has come into the world through her. Also, the Lord, after his resurrection, appeared without cause firstly to Mary Magdalene (Jn 20:14-18) to comfort the poor women by casting away her transgression and forgiving it in those who are faithful. Yes, just as in the garden Eve served Satan (Gen 3) and came to grief, distress and accursedness – so by contrast, in the garden where she served the Lord Christ, she was called from grief to joy. But in short, be it man or woman, whoever does the will of God will be saved.[68]

In the context of a discussion of original sin, there are several interesting features in this passage which bear closely on the argument. Firstly, it is clear that Schwenckfeld, although arguing that women's subjection is part of the order *after* the Fall, and not part of the Creation ordinance, still regarded the subjection of a woman to her husband as a given of the faith. He did not argue here or elsewhere for a reconstitution of the social pattern of his world. His conservatism in marriage was of a piece with his conservatism regarding the wider community. He was not part of the radical Reformation politically, understanding the gospel message as having a bearing on the reordering of society. Thus, whatever may have been the reasons for women's adoption of his teaching, it was clearly not to do with a radical redefinition of women's role in marriage or society. His concern was not with women's rights as a concept, (indeed, an anachronistic concept), and he did not argue for greater freedom for or participation by women. The altered roles which women undertook in his communities were a result of the implications of his theology, not any overt desire to change the nature of society.

Secondly, however, he did argue for something of a redefinition of what

---

[68] *CS*, vol. 12, p. 92, ll. 35f.

female was. His emphasis on the role of women in salvation history – not just Mary, but also the Magdalene – suggests an attitude towards women which was not simply limited to women as wives and mothers. Whatever role Mary Magdalene played, and that in itself is an area for discussion, she was not the role model of the wife and mother, nor the virginal *handmaid* which Mary the mother of Jesus was. It is significant that the parallel which he drew for Eve was Mary Magdalene rather than the Virgin Mary. This, while not unknown, was much less usual. Susan Haskins has shown how it did happen amongst some of the Fathers, most notably, she argues, Cyril of Alexandra and Augustine.[69] Haskins has also shown that the predominant understanding of Mary Magdalene was explicitly sexual – the fallen and sinful, and then penitent woman.

However, it is not as a penitent that Schwenckfeld presented her in this discussion, but as a recipient of grace and salvation because of her devotion to Christ. Thirdly, he was quite explicit that the salvation of men and women did not differ. There is no suggestion of separate categories of salvation, of different types of response or of any advantage to one or the other. In this he was speaking in the same language as the other reformers, and making a strong comment about the nature of sinfulness. It is quite clear in his analysis that sin is not linked to sexuality or body specifically, but to obedience or disobedience. His whole discussion of Eve and the two Marys in this passage demonstrates once again that his understanding of salvation, of the life in Christ was centred on obedience, on the *bodying* of this life in the life of the believer, and that this is a duty and a possibility for men and women in the same way.

However, he was still working in a context which did put a particular emphasis on sin as sexual. In all of this discourse about the connections between sexuality and sin, it is the category *female* which bears the marker of body and sexuality – that which is physical and sexual is defined by the presence of the female. That which is male is held, when it is in isolation, to be without sex or gender.[70] It is this connection which brands the sexuality of women as particularly to be feared and avoided, as being especially tainted. It is also often a marker of particular sinfulness, both because of the Eve motif, and the link with physicality. Women in the reality of their physical existence were signs of sin and were sinful in a more particular way.

What it Means to be Female

The assumption that Schwenckfeld made therefore can be seen to be distinctive. Although he did not spell it out, the importance he attached to Mary's virginity was relevant only in terms of the necessity for God to be the

---

[69] Susan Haskins, *Mary Magdalene, Myth and Metaphor*, London, 1993, pp. 94-97.

[70] This is part of the outworking of the comment above that the male is the paradigm body.

Father of Jesus. It had no importance either in her own relationship to God, or in terms of modelling what it was to be female. This is not to say that he did not place importance on the *purity* which he perceived in Mary's flesh. This had its implications in the nature of the flesh which Christ inhabited. But the issue here is the meaning of Mary's virginity in terms of her own being, and as a way of understanding what it was to be born female and be within the plan of God. On that matter he had nothing to say. Mary's virginity was an irrelevance as far as the life of other Christian women as women was concerned. Its only theological significance was in what it meant for the being of Christ. In that context it was of critical importance, but in that context it was of importance to both men and women in the same way.

Since he did not hold up the virginity of Mary per se as a good to be emulated or a model for true womanhood, it can be assumed that Schwenckfeld was not working with the earlier models I mentioned above, that to be female was to be sinful physically and that this could only be redeemed through virginity. In this, he was on ground familiar to the other Reformers. With his emphasis on the vocation of woman to marriage and motherhood, Luther was also denying the virginity of Mary its exemplary power, and the changes in emphasis in the understanding of marriage that became the stock teaching of the Reformers also undermined this motif.[71] However, the emphasis on the vocation to marriage, which carried with it the corollary of motherhood still worked with the assumption that to be female was to be defined in terms of body, and specifically, in terms of the role in reproduction. In line with the broader Christian humanist position, all of the leading reformers argued the marriage was the proper state for all, and especially for women, because it preserved the proper roles of creation.[72] In her examination of the preaching of Johannes Mathesius, Susan Karant-Nunn has explored some of the ways in which Luther's teaching was expressed.[73] Her analysis makes it clear that:

> Women's chief specific duty is the production and rearing of children. This is women's truest vocation, one they must not avoid. Wifehood, motherhood, and housewifery are inseparable points towards which every female should orient herself.[74]

While she suggests that Mathesius may have gone further than Luther in his insistence on the proper place of women, still it is clear that he was not saying anything which was regarded as outrageous or extreme. Marriage, both as a social and as a biological experience was the position for women, and no other

---

[71] For further discussion of Luther's attitude to Mary, and its impact on the perception of what it meant to be female, see Wiesner, "Luther and Women", Obelkevich, Roper, and Samuel, *Disciplines of Faith*.

[72] See, for example, Wiesner, "Nuns, Wives and Mothers", pp. 12-13.

[73] Susan Karant-Nunn, "Kinder, Küche, Kirche".

[74] Karant-Nunn, "Kinder, Küche, Kirche", p. 130.

was to be considered, if at all possible.[75] Virginity, from having been the ideal state had become a state of waiting for proper fulfilment.[76]

Schwenckfeld on the other hand appears not to have been interested in virginity, marriage, either socially or biologically, or the appropriate calling for women as distinct from men to any extent at all. He relegated the virginal conception to a matter of the mechanics of the Incarnation, without any theological significance outside of that doctrine. The assumptions therefore, which this involved him in about the nature of the female body must be examined, especially when this is put together with his doctrine of the *inner* and *outer*. Given the prevalent associations, it might be expected that he would identify the body and therefore sexuality with *outer*, that is, that which can neither know nor mediate the divine. However, he does not appear to make such a link explicitly anywhere, nor to condemn sexuality in itself. His concern is to express the way in which that which is divine, that is the Word, or the Son can become human or flesh, and to insist that this is central to his teaching, over against those who accuse him of teaching docetism. Virginity is not a concept that carried with it a theological meaning of its own, and nowhere does he hold out the virginity of Mary as an example or model of what it means to be a Christian believer. But what does this mean for the way in which he views the women who are his followers, and what he has to say about their sexuality – and by extension, what he has to say about male sexuality?

Firstly, he has little or nothing to say directly about sexuality, or even marriage. He speaks about marriage on a few occasions, but it is more in terms of the social implications of the union, and the contemporary understanding of the power relationships of the union, than of any sexual or procreative issue.[77] However, simply because he says nothing directly, this does not mean that the issue was unimportant, or that his attitudes did not inform how he thought or what he wrote about other issues. There are two main areas in the discussion of Christ's flesh in which the reality of Mary's virginity is of prime importance in Schwenckfeld's teaching. Firstly, it appears that it is the purity of Mary's flesh that in itself guarantees the purity, and therefore sinlessness of Jesus' humanity, as discussed above.

---

[75]Karant-Nunn suggests that, with the emphasis on "chastity, obedience and stability[...]" Lutheranism liberates men from monastic vows, but women must live as semi-nuns", Karant-Nunn, "Kinder, Küche, Kirche", p. 136. See also Angelicka Nowicki-Pastuschka, *Frauen In Der Reformation: Untersuchungen zum Verhalten von Frauen in den Reichstädten Augsburg und Nürnberg zur reformatorischen Bewegung zwischen 1517 and 1537*, Bamberg, 1990, p. 88; Wunder, *'He is the Sun, She is the Moon'*, p. 46.

[76] Wunder, *'He is the Sun, She is the Moon'*, p. 45.

[77] The quotation above which examines Eve's role in original sin is one of the few places in which he made any mention of the "appropriate" pattern for the marriage relationship.

Christ's Descent

The other area is that of Jesus' descent from his forefathers, and the fulfilment of prophecy. In this part of the argument, we meet again the interrelationship between biology and social norms. Since the generative power in the conception of new life comes from the father, the child is counted as descending from the father's line. This was part of the horror of female infidelity -the blurring of family lines, and the possibility that the inheritance could pass out of the pure blood. This notion gained its strength from the belief that the mother contributed nothing to the essential nature of the child – thus all that was the true *being* of the infant came from the father, whoever that might be. With the great emphasis that was put on inheritance, and the preservation of the family property, especially in the elite community, any suggestion that a child was not the offspring of the reputed father was very disruptive.

Having no human father, there is the problem of how Jesus could be fitted into human society. Schwenckfeld deals with this by tracing Jesus' family tree through Mary to *her* male ancestors, and thus connecting him with the people of God. Thus, Jesus' mother could not just have been any woman, but had to be this one, not primarily because of her purity or virginity, but because of her place in the bloodlines of Israel. She was a descendent of Abraham and David, and so it became possible to speak of Jesus as being the son of Abraham and David, the child of the promise and the fulfilment of the prophecy. This was to become an important theme in Schwenckfeld's defence of his position. He wrote at length about Jesus as the child of the promise, the descendent of the Patriarchs and of David – but always *nicht nach dem gemeinem Fleischgange.*[78] To suggest that these men were in any way physical fathers of Jesus would be to cut across his central premise that Christ is the true Son of God. Part – a large part – of Mary's significance lies in her human, family descent, which makes it possible to identify Jesus with a particular set of human relationships. However, he is particularly insistent that this should not be seen as normal descent, *Fleischgange.* He regularly says that Abraham and the other Patriarchs are not *fleischvättern*, (fathers of the flesh) and expands it by saying: "For he did not come according to the desire of the flesh."[79]

He rarely mentions Joseph in any discussion of Jesus' birth, but when he does, it is usually to deny his role in Jesus' birth: "His flesh was not from Joseph's family descent."[80] This appears to be borne out in the further discussion about the physical descent of Christ. In an involved argument, he insisted that while Jesus could be called the son of Abraham and David, this was in terms of promise or faith only. Thus he could argue: "...that Abraham was not a fleshly father of Christ, but a father according to faith."[81] He

---

[78] "not according to the common way of the flesh..." *CS*, vol. 7, p. 295, l. 24.
[79] *CS*, vol. 7, p. 315, l. 9.
[80] *CS*, vol. 7, p. 335, l. 16.
[81] *CS*, vol. 7, p. 295, ll. 27f.

contrasted this with Abraham's role in Isaac's birth:

> In the same way, Abraham was not a physical father of the human Christ as he was Isaac's physical father, but he was his grandfather, because Mary was Abraham's daughter.[82]

Schwenckfeld does allow for a connection with Abraham, but insists on it being at one remove. Thus, as the quotation states, Abraham was Christ's grandfather because he was Mary's father – except of course, he was not Mary's direct father, but removed by several generations. The issue of not one of the number of generations, but rather the place of the link.

In a similar way he argued that David did not exercise a physical fatherly role over Christ, except indirectly, through his descendent, Mary. David's direct connection with the being of Christ was as a father of promise or faith. Part of the argument produced as to why David cannot be called Christ's physical Father is that David in Psalm 110 refers to Jesus as Lord. But he also argued that Christ cannot be born from David's seed:

> Therefore, when we say that Christ was David's son according to faith, we want to cancel with regard to Christ the natural way of the old fleshly birth (that Christ was not born from male seed) and to give an instruction that the word of God should be properly noted in which, yes with which, God promised to David a son as Saviour.[83]

Christ cannot be born from human, or more specifically, male seed. This was central to Schwenckfeld's whole understanding of what Incarnation means – that there has to be a radical separation between human physicality and Christ's origin. This separation was shown not by distancing Christ from physical existence, nor even from its symbolism, the female, but explicitly from *male seed*, that is, human male sexual and generative activity. This is an interesting and striking subversion of the normal symbolic location of humanity, especially in its weak and sinful aspects.

However, human physicality is not only represented by male seed – there is still the role of Mary, and that is to prove crucial. Christ had to have some connection with the patriarchs, or else the promise comes to nothing – there is no child of promise. And this connection is through the physical descent of Mary – she is the physical, human descendent of the Patriarchs, and as such she and she alone can be mother of the Saviour, the child of promise. It is important, as I have argued earlier that Mary's role in the Incarnation is not connected with any particular merit on her part. Here is the reason why Mary's is the body which conceives – she is the daughter of those who must be the Promised One's fathers, but who must not be physically connected with the

---

[82] *CS*, vol. 7, p. 298, ll. 5f.
[83] *CS*, vol. 7, p. 302, ll. 26f.

Promised One. This then suggests that physical descent cannot be passed on through the woman's body – or else these fathers of Mary would also be physical fathers of Christ. Thus, although her body is a product of their bodies, there is some disjunction which means that Christ's body, while being identified with hers, is distanced from theirs.

Since at least part of the reason why Christ must have no human father appears in Schwenckfeld's thinking to be connected to the ontological nature of sin, there must be a connection here between male embodiment and sin that is missing between female embodiment and sin. It is the identification with the male body as a generative force, indicated by the phrase *male seed* from which Christ must be separated, in order that his flesh can be sinless. His link with Mary's flesh however, does not give rise to such a necessity for separation.

The insistence on the purity of Mary's flesh discussed earlier is not a rejection of female flesh per se, but a rejection of the marks of creation. Creation is set in opposition to divine birth. The rejection here of male descent is linked more closely to the issue of sin.

Schwenckfeld was using language and concepts which emphasised not only Jesus' descent from no human man, but also the inappropriateness of Jesus being born as a result of human desire. There is nothing in the rest of his writing to suggest that he regarded the exercise of the sexual faculties within marriage as inappropriate for believers. But there is the hint here of a distrust, or even disgust with sexuality – it is not an aspect of human life that should be considered in the same context as the divine. If this is the case, then it is interesting that it is linked not with female sexuality, but with male desire. The paradigmatic assumption was that the female was the bearer of sexuality, and that divinity and sexuality were incompatible.

The connection that Schwenckfeld appeared to be making here was that male desire was the marker of the sexuality which was incompatible with divinity. In his insistence that Christ may not and could not have been born, as the Son of God, through any action of male desire, any expression of male sexuality carries the implication that what was normally predicated of female sexuality – a flaw that entered with the Fall, and a removal from God – was also, or perhaps all the more, to be predicated of male sexuality. In his insistence on the separation of Jesus from any possibility of earthly descent through male action, it may be that we are hearing an echo of Schwenckfeld's discomfort with his own sexuality, especially when taken together with his own unmarried state.[84]

To look at the ways in which Schwenckfeld's understanding of the Incarnation impinged on his anthropology especially in terms of women, it will be necessary to look further at the issue in broader terms, and to examine what the current understandings of *female* were, in the light of the scientific thought of the time.

---

[84] *CS*, vol. 7, p. 302, ll. ??????

The Meanings of *Female*

It has already been suggested that the general perception, which both created and was partly confirmed by the understanding of conception current at the time, was that women in their physical nature were inferior to men. Indeed, as we have seen above, it appears that the medical perception of the time was that women were *failed* men. This was an understanding which was based both on physical observation, insofar as that was possible, and the theory of humours. Physically, it was argued that the female genitalia were the mirror image of the male which had remained inside the body instead of achieving the perfection of the male. This in turn was based on the theory of the humours, which argued that that which was perfect became so because of its greater heat which drove it to fulfil its created purpose, and become complete. That which was imperfect and colder, did not achieve perfection, but stopped part way, unable to find the energy to be complete. Thus, men, by virtue of their greater heat, were perfect in their genitals, because the heat drove them to their *proper* place in the body. Women, who did not have enough heat for this, retained their genitals inside, an obvious example of lesser development. Thus the inferiority of women is both caused by and confirmed by their deficiency of heat, and is evidenced by the incomplete nature of their genitalia.

The theory of humours also had something to say about the various bodily fluids that were perceived to be important in healthy life. It was assumed that all bodily fluids were basically the same, blood, and that the different appearances and functions depended on the amount of heat or cold in a body. Women, being colder did not burn up all the blood that was produced, and so for the benefit of their health, the body evacuated the excess blood on a regular basis in menstruation. Men did not need to exercise this evacuation since their bodies being hotter, and therefore more active, used up the excess blood in other ways. Menstruation ceased during pregnancy because it was no longer necessary then. The extra blood was diverted to the building of the infant – it was from this excess that the mother provided the matter to give form to the generative seed of the father.

Lactation was also involved in this, since it was believed that milk was a refinement of blood, and that menstruation would be scanty during nursing. The excess blood was diverted to the breasts, where, by means of heat, it was transformed into milk. Semen too came into the understanding – like milk, this was seen as a refinement of blood, and its appearance was believed to demonstrate the heat and vigour of the male body, and the transformative power of male heat. For those who espoused the Galenic understanding that there was a female seed which was necessary, this was perceived to be less powerful because it was less hot and less far removed from the original blood. So, the fundamental fluid, in a theory that focused on fluids as the basis for all existence, was blood, and blood was common to male and female. The concept of blood in the thinking of a religion which has a death as part of its central salvific event must carry important meanings. In an exploration of the respective positions of male and female, as Bynum has argued, the fact that blood as fundamental is an element of common humanity between male and female means that certain boundaries turn out to be less fixed than might be assumed – and if female bodies can turn blood into other substances, so can male, at least in theory.[85] Given this permeability, issues of how male and female are to be determined, what it means to be male and female, and what the place and meaning of the Incarnation are, take on an additional layer of complexity, despite the seeming disjunction between male and female bodies in Aristotelian biology.

Patricia Crawford has discussed issues to do with beliefs about menstruation.[86] She divides the issues into those connected with physical existence, those with social and those with spiritual meanings. Physically, menstruation was understood as important for health, since it was the primary means of evacuation in the female body. In addition, the menstruum was the matter out of which the foetus, and after birth, the milk, were formed. Socially, menstruation itself also had repercussions. As Crawford has shown there was the perception that the menses were evidence of some level of malignancy, and might even be malign in themselves. It was believed that a menstruating woman ought not to churn butter or salt a pig, since both would turn sour. Spiritually and emotionally, the notions were of uncleanness – and uncleanness which was infectious. Thus, menstruation functioned symbolically both as a sign of profanity and as a boundary between sacred and profane. This in turn had its impact on the understanding of women and of their symbolic position.

The whole complex of notions of shame around sexuality and the physical expression of it became identified with the uncontrollable evacuations of the female body, both at menstruation and in childbirth and nursing. To put it bluntly, the female body was leaky, and therefore untrustworthy. Given this understanding, at one level, the perception was that inherently women were less close to God, especially when their physical experience was uppermost, since to draw near to God was to leave the physical behind, which entailed a control

---

[85] Thus, to a medieval writer, men's and women's bodies often did the same things. A medieval theologian, whose assumptions about the body were formed at least partly by this medical tradition, might therefore see the blood Christ shed in the circumcision and on the Cross as analogous to menstrual blood or to breast milk. Men and women had the same sex organs; men's were just better arranged. These assumptions made the boundary between the sexes seem extremely permeable. Bynum, *Fragmentation and Redemption*, p. 114. For example, all human exudings - menstruations, sweating, lactation emission of semen and so on - were seen as bleedings; and all bleedings - lactation, menstruation, nosebleeds, haemorrhoidal bleedings and so on - were taken to be analogous. Thus, it was not far-fetched for a medical writer to refer to a man menstruating, or to a woman emitting seed. Bynum, *Fragmentation and Redemption*, p. 220.

[86] Patricia Crawford, "Attitudes to Menstruation in Seventeenth Century England", *Past and Present,* vol 91, 1981, pp. 47ff.

of the body. But there are problems with such a belief in a faith centred on the Incarnation.

As Bynum as argued in her examinations of late medieval female spirituality, there was also a perception that, in their physicality, women were particularly close to God as seen in the Incarnate and suffering Christ.[87] The later medieval and early modern concentration on the physical reality of the body of Christ, seen in the mystical writings, in the rise of the festival of Corpus Christi and in the devotions which drew on the physical being of Christ all made this an important issue. The understanding of the blood of Christ as food for the believer, shaped by the Eucharistic theology of transubstantiation, but also drawing on humoral theory which identified breast milk as transmuted blood, meant that blood as a symbol was not straightforwardly linked to weakness and uncleanness. Thus, the menstrual cycle, as well as marking uncleanness, and functioning as a boundary marker, could also be a symbol of the physical reality of God in Christ, made present in the Eucharist. The complexity of blood as a symbol must surely be part of the reason why, in the discussions about the nature of the Eucharist, although, following the restoration of communion in both kinds, it is normally the bread which is the focus of the argument. It appears that the meaning of bread, and of body, was more clearly identifiable than that of wine and blood. Therefore, although we can see that the physical bleeding at menstruation had implications for physical sanctity, they are not always as clear as might be assumed.

The other symbolic impact of menstruation was the way in which it was used to *place* women: as pre-menarche/virgin/daughter; menstruating/mother/wife; menopausal/non-sexual/widow. As Reformation thinking developed, however, with its emphasis on the vocational nature of wife-and-motherhood, not to be married and fertile was to be in an anomalous position. For a woman, the physical paradigm of virgin-mother-post-menopausal was the parallel of the social one of daughter-wife-widow, and just as determinative.

Pollution and Purification

This connection between biology and perception makes it necessary to ask which was determinative – did the understanding of conception, and the perception of the physical body which that involved, entail the perception of women as dangerous, inferior and untrustworthy, or did the perception of women as dangerous, inferior and untrustworthy determine the understanding of conception and the picture of the body? The social and religious consequences of the image thus created are clear enough – women were God's secondary creation, created for the convenience of men, to bear children and keep home, to provide a remedy for the sinful (gloss – hysical) nature of men

---

[87] Bynum, *Fragmentation and Redemption*, p. 192; Bynum, *Holy Feast and Holy Fast*, pp. 246ff.

and requiring control and discipline at all times. That they received salvation in the same way as men was accepted – that they could demonstrate that salvation in the public involvement in religious life was not. Thus, a woman's nature, role and status were clearly defined and regulated, and were determined by and also served to emphasise her sexual and procreative role. For women it was clear that, not only socially, but also religiously, biology was destiny.

To this interpretation of *female* we can also add the biological one, that a woman was a less perfect man, that she was the receptacle for the seed of new life rather than playing any active part in its creation and that the fluids by which her physical life was dominated were a reflection of her inferiority. Mary Douglas has argued that female bodies, particularly in terms of their *leakiness*, were recognised "as inherently polluted and polluting"[88] – though this must be seen as being in relation to men, rather than in their own relationships to God. Given that, as Laqueur has put it: "There is one canonical body, and this body is male,"[89] and that which pollutes the male pollutes the world, the control of female bodies becomes not simply a social or political issue, though it was that, but also a religious one. If the pollution of a female body was, as Crawford has argued, *infectious*, then for the religious life of men to be continued without interruption, it is necessary that the polluting bodies be kept under discipline. This is obvious, for example, in the insistence on strict claustration of nuns, following the eleventh-century reforms: this was partly for their own protection, but also because their presence threatened the men around them. The reasons given for why monastic priests could not serve as priests to female communities was not because of the danger to the women, but that to the men. This was partly sexual but also reflected the notion that to be in the company of women in any way would unfit them to be in the company of God.

The control of the female body, then, was a religious issue. Susan Karant-Nunn has argued that the general control of bodies increased during the sixteenth century with the spread of the Reformation, and she has shown how the separation of men and women at the reception of bread and wine was perceived to be of importance, not simply by the church authorities, but by the laymen.[90]

The other area where the issue of pollution came to the fore in terms of the church community at this period was following childbirth. The medieval church

---

[88] According to Mary Douglas, bodily emissions are considered threatening because they are liminal, because they have traversed the boundary of the body and are thus of, but yet not of, the body and so do not fit the standard categories. An expansion of this would be to recognise that the reminder of death is because an uncontrolled body, male or female, is *losing* parts of itself, and therefore could be seen in terms of decay. See Douglas, *Purity and Danger: An Analysis of concepts of pollution and taboo*, London: Ark, 1984.

[89] Laqueur *Making Sex,* p. 63.

[90] Karant-Nunn, *The Reformation of Ritual*, p. 252, n. 162.

included in its rites the service of *churching* for a woman following the birth of a child. This drew on Levitical teaching,[91] and was reinforced by the account of Mary's purification in Luke 2: 22-38. Peter Rushton has suggested that while we cannot assign one single meaning to the rite, part of what was involved was a ritual of reincorporation into the community. He argues that this reincorporation was necessary because of a separation caused by pollution.[92] Susan Karant-Nunn, while accepting that it marked a sense of transition, points out that the official theological view was that women were not impure following childbirth and were not subject to the Jewish Law.[93] It is certainly clear that, although, with the Reformation of liturgy in the sixteenth century, there appeared to be little place for such a rite, it was kept and continued to be practised, in Lutheranism and in the Church of England, until the eighteenth century. Calvin, however, abandoned it altogether. Much of the impetus for its retention seems to have come from women, some of whom, whatever it was they understood by it, evidently believed it to be important, though others had to be compelled to take part.[94]

Luther was prepared to let it continue. In sermons on the Luke passage about Mary's purification, he argued that she did what the others around her did, not because it was necessary for her, but because it was the custom.[95] However, as Susan Karant-Nunn points out, Luther did retain a good many of the folk-beliefs of his community, and so may well have had some sense of impurity following childbirth. In his discussions of Mary, Schwenckfeld does not deal with this issue. The only place where he refers directly to the Luke passage, for example, is in a discussion about the nature of baptism. The document is one of a series of what he called *General Epistles* (*Sendbrieffe*), in which he was arguing that the Sacraments of the Christian church should not be compared with the Old Testament ceremonies. Part of his discussion was to show that: "Christian baptism is not a Jewish cleansing, much less has it sprung from the same."[96]

He outlined various forms of purification described in the Old Testament, and discussed the way in which baptism was different. Then he went on to

---

[91] Leviticus, 12:1-8.

[92] Peter Rushton, "Purification or Social Control? Ideologies of Reproduction and the Churching of Women after Childbirth", pp. 118-131, eds. Eva Gamarnikow, David H. J. Morgan, June Purvis and Daphne Taylorson, *The Public and the Private,* London: Heinemann, 1983.

[93] Karant-Nunn, *The Reformation of Ritual,* p. 76.

[94] Karant-Nunn, *The Reformation of Ritual,* pp. 79-80. Men seem to have been content to let the practice drop, seeing little need for it. See Miriam Chrisman Usher, "Haug Marschalk" p. 66. David Cressy has explored the mixed meanings of the ceremony in "Purification, Thanksgiving and the Churching of Women in Post-Reformation England", *Past and Present,* vol. 141, 1993, pp. 106-146.

[95] WA, vol. 9, 569: vol. 12, p. 422.

[96] *CS,* vol. 4, p. 158, ll. 25f

discuss the New Testament instances, and wrote:

> For the sake of the weak, Paul allowed himself to be purified with four men, before he went into the Temple in Jerusalem and kept the Day of Purification. (Acts 21:23-26). But what has this to do Christian Baptism? Without doubt nothing more than when Mary went in her day to purification with the Child Christ in the Temple. (Luke 2:22)[97]

So, it would appear that Schwenckfeld adopted a similar approach to Luther's; that purification was something that happened, as it were, socially, but had little religious meaning. He was not concerned with the purity or otherwise of Mary. This would suggest that this was not a major issue for him, and therefore that he did not have a perception of women's physical being as inherently problematic.

Since to be female was in terms of categories, to be in opposition to male – at is, female and male were defined in terms of each other – these beliefs and assumptions had their implications not only for women and their place in society and theology, but also for men. In discussing this area, Bynum uses the notion of *liminality* – the crossing of boundaries, which enables the norms to be understood.[98] Men use women to talk about themselves. She argues that:

> ...the dominant religious image of the self in the late middle ages was female; the soul was woman or bride[99]

Thus the understanding theologically and sociologically of women not only reflected on, but also helped to determine the understanding theologically and sociologically of *male*. So, if *female* is less than perfect, *male* is the image of perfection. If the female body is dangerous and leaky, to be male was to have the body under control, and to avoid any appearance of such weakness. Since bodies were not fixed – as we saw, women could become men – it was possible to think in terms of one *sort* becoming another. Thus men when considering themselves in a relation of weakness and humility before God could speak of themselves not as being like a woman, but as being female, while they could also speak of women being manly in the display of certain characteristics – and associate this with physical reality. However, because that which is male is nearer to perfection, such a position for a man in relation to God was one which was *chosen*, and in this respect, not at all parallel to a woman's experience.

Implications for Power Relationships

This also has implications in terms of power relationships. To have control over

---

[97] *CS*, vol. 4, p. 159, ll. 30f.

[98] Bynum, *Fragmentation and Redemption*, p. 33.

[99] Bynum, *Fragmentation and Redemption*, p. 165.

one's body is to have the authority to have power over other bodies, both individual and corporate – and indeed, such authority may have to be exercised in order to demonstrate the reality of maleness. As was argued above, there was a belief, so vehemently opposed by Giles of Rome, that there could be at least a theoretical possibility of parthenogenic conception, and this would undermine the whole of nature, since it would undermine the basis of order. Laqueur makes this point thus:

> [A belief in] The superior strength of the male sperm is necessary for the maintenance of hierarchy. The male is necessary for conception. It does not follow that the male contribution is thereby the more powerful one, and an immense amount of effort and anxiety had to go into proving that this was the case. [This is] testimony to the hierarchical ordering of the one sex.[100]

Whatever the strengths and weaknesses of this *One Sex* model, the point that biology was being used to explain and justify social reality is well made. Thus again, it is clear that the discussion of the mechanics of conception bears a much deeper significance in consideration of the perceptions of male, female and human. If to be female was to be defined in terms of a sexual role, to be defined over against that was also to be defined in sexual terms, albeit in a different way. To be a woman was to give birth, or at least to have the potentiality to do so. To be male was to have generative capacities, to be capable of reproduction. The theological and social implications of these biological assumptions are manifold.

For example it is impossible not to be anthropomorphic in considering God. If to be male is to be nearer to perfection, then that which is perfect must be seen as male. Therefore, *maleness* becomes included in the understanding of God. There is the basic axiom that God, if not male in gender, must reflect that which is perceived to be characteristic of maleness. In the same way, if maleness is defined in terms of generative capacity and in the exercise of authority, then a doctrine of God in terms of relationship with that which is not God must be predicated on the basis that part of the fundamental relationship is that of generation and authority. This type of perception, for example, underlies the tendency noted above, in the late Middle Ages to consider the self or soul female in relation to God. Such a relationship would reflect the social/political/biological perceptions of weakness, inferiority and submission modelled in human relationships. Thus, the images of male and female, drawn from social and theological categories, but bearing the mark of biological and specifically generative understanding, have their effect not only in the understanding of humanity in relation to God but also in the basic understanding of the nature of God.

So, in examining Schwenckfeld's understanding of the Incarnation in the

---

[100] Laqueur, *Making Sex*, p. 58.

context of the biology current at the time, and reflecting on its implications for his thinking, we can see that he is operating with an Aristotelian model of conception, which sees in the male activity the provision of the reality of the newborn, and recognises in the female only the supply of the material out of which the body is made. That this conception must be virginal is assumed in his understanding of how conception takes place – the initiative, and the nature of the infant must come from the father, in this case God, and therefore, given the necessary divine origin, no physical act can be recognised. However, the virginity of Mary is of no relevance, in this part of the discussion, other than as a necessary part of the reality of God's action. Her virginity has no importance in terms of her own being. This suggests that for Schwenckfeld, issues of female, and presumably therefore male, sexual purity are not of great religious significance. In his discussions of marriage, he was committed to a traditional understanding of fidelity and authority within the marriage relationship, but there is no suggestion there, or in the teaching about Jesus' conception, that sexuality carries with it a *particular* form of guilt and shame. However, given his absolute rejection of any form of human male action in the physical existence of Christ stretching back through generations, he is also betraying an unease with the notion of male desire, at least in relationship to the action of God. It appears that he could not make sense of the notion that male desire and sexual action have any place in the inheritance of the Son of God, although, in Mary, he is quite content to accept the experience of female sexuality as part of the process. Thus, it appears that he is more distrustful of male than of female sexuality, an unusual position, and one which raises interesting questions about the nature of his relationships.

It is clear that he is very affirmative of women – that so many adopted his teaching and were counted amongst his closest friends makes this unquestionable. There are obviously various social and religious reasons for this. This examination suggests that there may be deeper reasons present as well. In an atmosphere where, even if unspoken, there is a distrust of female sexuality, and where women are defined only or mainly in terms of their physical capacity for child-bearing, it is understandable that women would respond to one for whom their physical and therefore sexual nature appears to have been no theological, or even personal, threat, and whose arguments and teachings do not categorise them only in terms of their bodies. In a situation where male sexuality was thought of as only being an issue in the face of female provocation, the presence of one who treated male sexuality with suspicion must have created an area of safety for women who did not necessarily fit the social norm – and we know that many of Schwenckfeld's women followers were either widows or unmarried, and therefore did not *belong to* or were not *under the control* of a responsible male.

Nonetheless, for all his insistence that there was no human male activity in the conception of Christ, he still thinks of the conception within the normal categories. Thus, he speaks of Mary becoming pregnant not through anything in herself, but by the action of the Spirit, the power of God:

> Thus, Christ himself is not Mary's flesh, but the flesh of Christ is born in her and received from the Holy Spirit. [101]

The description that is often given of the Holy Spirit in this role is of *meyster* (master) or of exercising *meisterschafft* (mastery) and the words used frequently echo Matt 1:20, "that which is conceived in her is from the Holy Spirit" – *ist empfangen vom Heiligen Geist*. This may be a virginal conception in that no human man is involved, but that does not mean that there is no male activity, or that in this conception anything other than the normal male action of engendering is in process. All that is different is that the male is divine rather than human. Otherwise, the process is natural. The male action provides the being of the child and the female the material. What happens in the conception of Christ is very definitely to be thought of in parallel with the normal birth of a child. This is a point Schwenckfeld makes several times, both in speaking of Christ's mother and father and in the contrast he draws between God as Father and God as Creator. In his reference to God as Creator, *Schöpfer*, he is using language that is typically used of God. Indeed, the term *Schöpfer* and *schöpfung*, *creation*, to refer to humanity, are almost exclusively used in religious discourse. [102] His insistence on the separation of Creatorhood from Fatherhood is frequent:

> the fatherly role and the role of the creating of God must be properly distinguished [103]

> There is indeed a great distinction between the role or work of the creating of God and the role or work of his begetting. In the first, God is called a creator, in the other a father. [104]

It is this kind of distinction that suggests that in the discussion of the Incarnation, Schwenckfeld is operating with a model that is very definitely drawn from biology. Because we do not know where he studied, nor do we have a list of his library, it is impossible to prove conclusively which he model he adopted. However, the patterns of thought which show in the way in which he presents his material suggest that biology, and particularly Aristotelian biology, helped to shape his thinking.

That which is generative is male – and that includes God. It is from this fact that the name of Father is drawn – it is no courtesy title or metaphorical

---

[101] *CS*, vol. 7, p. 324, ll. 15.ff.
[102] See Fischer, *Schwäbisches Wörterbuch*, "schöpfung", vol V, column 1113.
[103] *CS*, vol. 8, p. 788, l. 27.
[104] *CS*, vol. 14, p. 320, ll. 21f.

description, but a definable and accurate explanation of what happened. If indeed Schwenckfeld's understanding of reproduction drew on the Aristotelian model, the notion of *father* would carry with it, almost as part of its definition, the sole creative and generative power. Thus, in his understanding of God as Father, the reference is not only or even primarily to an emotional relationship, perhaps characterised as loving, protecting, disciplining and so on, but to the one in whom there is origin, and from whom the possibility of life comes. This is what accounts for his paralleling and contrasting the roles of Creator and Father – in a basic way, there is a similarity of function, but the generative role of the father is to produce that which is like, while a Creator produces that which is other. Thus in his discussion of the nature of Christ, and his insistence that this nature was truly of God, truly divine, his insistence on the Fatherhood of God has as much to do with this *likeness*, reflected in the biological model which is available to him, as with any notions of emotional attachment. Since his understanding of the difference between the orders focused on precisely this issue of origin, the speaking of God as Father is both biologically and theologically fundamental. The separation of creative and generative capacities, for Schwenckfeld's model of the world is crucial. The theological implications of that separation have their impact, both in the understanding of the nature of Christ and in the perception of the nature of salvation.

If his rejection of Mary's virginity as having its own theological significance signals a particular attitude to women and to female sexuality, then the insistence that God is the literal father of the man Jesus also brings its implications for men. Fatherhood is a divine activity. Therefore to be a father is to reflect something of the divine nature – or so it would seem. But if there is little in his writing about women and their sexuality, there is nothing about men at all. On the rare occasions when he is writing about marriage and family life, he is either addressing women or a couple. He appears, unlike other writers, to have nothing to say directly to men about their relationships to the women around them – whether encouraging them to marry (or not to marry) or talking to them about the conduct of marriage. This absence may simply reflect the fact that Schwenckfeld wrote for occasions rather than systematically, and there happened to be no occasion when such a discussion was needed. Or it may be another echo of a discomfort with issues of male sexuality, and therefore its omission is as eloquent as anything that might have been said. That, in some sense, he images God in gendered terms is clear from the language used. That he does not follow this through into forming a model for male sexuality is also clear. Here, it is possible that again we are hearing the echoes of his discomfort with male sexuality expressed in human experience.

The duality of origins with which Schwenckfeld constructed his world took as its *philosophical* basis the Aristotelian understanding of the male generative capacity. Thus his theology is shaped by a particular construction of gender. However, he did not appear to draw the same conclusions from this basis as, for example, Aristotle himself did. He did not argue for the inherent inferiority of women, and his actions and expectations appear to contradict such a conclusion. Because his dualism focused not on the separation of flesh and spirit, but on the duality of origins, he was able to give a theological value to physical existence. This then meant that women, although identified with physical reality rather than spiritual, so far from being blamed or excluded, were in fact, valued and freed. Here, within the construction of the theology, and the theology's construction of the world-view, there is a reason for the response and the position of women in the movement. By giving a theological meaning to physical existence, those who, in Schwenckfeld's understanding as well as that of the wider community, symbolised that existence, were valued in it. Flesh is no longer that which must be left behind as inhibiting the spiritual life, but it is an integral part of the spiritual life, not only, as we saw in the previous chapter, because it is the place where the believer encounters God, but also because it is that which God takes for self-expression. The insistence that Christ's flesh was not brought from heaven, but given by his mother, the Aristotelian model, reinforces the position that flesh and God are not only not mutually exclusive, but are spiritually compatible.

The other important aspect of the theology which we see beginning to take shape as we explore Schwenckfeld's doctrine of the Incarnation is the continuing redefinition of gender placement in the divine-human relationship. In considering the Eucharist, we saw how Christ in the Sacrament functioned in both a male and a female role; he was both life-giver (male) and food (female). In this part of the theology, we find that the maleness of the First Person of the Trinity is not metaphorical but literal in its biological expression in relation to the Second Person. This raises an interesting theme which we will explore further in the fifth chapter on the relationship with the believer.

For Schwenckfeld, it is the Incarnation of Christ which is at the heart of a doctrine of salvation. His understanding of the Incarnation is strictly biological, and shaped by certain gender definitions. The impact of this gender understanding is not limited only to the scientific approach, but made itself felt throughout the theology and practice of the communities which adopted this teaching. For the women who became followers of Schwenckfeld, this teaching had very practical results in their self-perception, and in their roles in the circles of believers.

Chapter 4

Incarnation and Embodiment

Discussion of the mode of conception of Christ's flesh by no means exhausted Schwenckfeld's concern with the meaning of its existence. The accusations that he shared a Christology with Hoffman provoked him into discussing not simply the conception, but also the existence and meaning of the flesh during Christ's earthly ministry. Because of the importance he attached to this flesh as the way in which salvation happened, it was necessary for him to explore this as a theological category. As was made clear in the discussion of the eucharistic theology, it was the eating of the flesh and drinking of the blood which created the new life which was the experience of salvation. Schwenckfeld's perception of this, as his concentration on John chapter 6 makes clear, was that this was not to be understood symbolically, but there was something significantly physical in the meaning of flesh. Thus, it was not enough for him simply to explain his understanding of the conception and birth of Christ. He had also to explore the physical existence of the man, and the way in which such a physical existence could be said to continue, following the resurrection. It was in this continuation that this body was encountered through the Eucharist. As we have already seen in chapter two, it is possible to account for this body in terms of gender in a variety of categories. This therefore raises the question of just how Schwenckfeld conceptualised the physical existence of Christ.

McLaughlin, in his discussion of how Schwenckfeld developed his Christology, has demonstrated that at the heart of Schwenckfeld's thinking was a particular understanding about the being of the believer and the being of Christ.[1] The nature of Christ determined the nature into which the believer was understood to grow. McLaughlin's discussion indicates either that he, as biographer, is using "man" as a generic term, or that he believes Schwenckfeld to have understood the physical being of Christ as male to be an important salvific issue. I believe the former to be the case, especially in the light of this statement:

> The word had taken on human flesh not so much to stand in man's place and pay the price on the cross for man's sins, but rather, by assuming human flesh and undergoing pain and torment, the word had fashioned a new human flesh, which,

---

[1] All Christians become children of God through Christ, sharing the godly nature.*CS*, vol. 6, p. 241, ll. 4f.

given to Christians, made them a new race of spiritual men dwelling with God in heaven.[2]

It is clear that McLaughlin is using the words "human" and "man" interchangeably — but this raises the question about whether Schwenckfeld was doing the same thing. This is not simply an issue of linguistic style or political correctness, but a more fundamental question about the understanding of human existence and the nature of salvation, which is informed by the notion of gender. Thus, if the flesh of Christ was male rather than human in its intrinsic being, the relationship of women to salvation is centrally affected. We have already begun to look at this in the previous chapter in the discussion of Logos Christology, but it is now necessary to look at this in more detail.

Is Salvation for Humanity or Man?

In her discussion of what she calls the "patriarchalization of Christology", Rosemary Radford Ruether shows how Aristotelian biology combined with Logos Christology results in the Incarnation of the Second Person of the Trinity as male being an ontological necessity.[3] If this is so, then it raises the question about the salvation of women, if gender specificity is understood to be ontological. result. Gregory of Nazianzus, who represented what came to be accepted as orthodoxy following a crisis about the nature of Christ's humanity in the fourth century wrote: "The unassumed is the unhealed."[4] He then went on to argue that Christ had to assume a full humanity, or else only that part of humanity which was united with the Word of God in the Incarnation would be saved. In the light of this assertion, the suggestion that the maleness of Christ was an ontological necessity does raise the issue of the salvation of women at all as a problematic point.[5] If gender is an integral part of ontological existence, then the female was not assumed into the Incarnation, and that which is female comes into Gregory's category of the "unhealed."

There has been at least one strand of thinking in the soteriological debate that has insisted that salvation for a woman effectively meant becoming a man. In the earliest days, this was particularly strong amongst the Gnostic thinkers. The Gospel of Thomas records an incident in which Peter says to Jesus:

Let Mary [Magdalene] leave us, for women are not worthy of Life

Jesus answers:

---

[2] McLaughlin, *Reluctant Radical*, p. 87.
[3] Reuther, *Sexism and God-Talk*, pp. 125f.
[4] *Ep.CI*, 181C, Gregory of Nazianzus.
[5] Of course, it is to be understood that this was not part of the question when Gregory was writing. But it has become part of the discussion.

I myself shall lead her in order to make her male, so that she too may become a living spirit resembling you males.

He then adds:

For every woman who will make herself male will enter the Kingdom of Heaven.[6]

But it is also evident, despite Gregory's teaching, in some of the Patristic writings.[7] It is a type of thinking which brings us back again to the notion I explored in "Concepts of Conception" that to be female was to be a misformed male, and the achievement of perfection – salvation – meant the move to masculinity. It could also show itself by a disregard for hygiene, a refusal of clothes or an avoidance of food. The women who formed the circle around Jerome in the fourth century, for example, were famous, or notorious, for their disregard for their bodies (as were the male ascetics of the time).[8] Those who approved saw it as a proper attempt by these women to escape from the corporeality which prevented them from approaching the divine. The perception was that body, and in particular female bodies, interfered with the relationship with the divine. If this was the case, then the rejection of the body, especially of the female body in its female physical experience, was part of the search for salvation.

Is Christ Male or Human?

However, the question of gender and the nature of salvation is not limited to the gender of the believer. There is also the question of the gender of the body of Christ. The maleness that is expressed in the man Jesus of Nazareth is either a functional necessity – salvation can only be effected by a male body – or an accidental fact – the human being, Jesus of Nazareth had to be male or female, and was, in historical fact, male. Since, as I have indicated, for Schwenckfeld it was the flesh of Christ in and of itself which had saving power, this is a central question in considering his theology. That it does not appear to have been considered by other writers is evidence of the continuing assumption that the definitive body is male.

Did Schwenckfeld consider the flesh of Christ to be male or to be human – and, for Schwenckfeld, was there a difference? What was the relationship

---

[6] *The Gospel of Thomas, The Nag Hammadi Library*, ed. James M Robinson, Leiden, 1984, p. 130.

[7] Jerome wrote to a friend who had agreed with his wife to live in a celibate relationship "You have with you one who was once your partner in the flesh, but is now your partner in the spirit; once your wife, but now your sister, once a woman but now a man; once an inferior, but now an equal. Under the same yoke as you, she hastens towards the same heavenly kingdom." To Licinius, Jerome, *Letter LXXI*;3.

[8] See Elizabeth A. Clark, *Women in the Early Church: Message of the Fathers of the Church vol 13*, Wilmington, Delaware: Michael Glazier, 1983, pp. 133-140.

between the flesh of the believer and the flesh of Christ, and what were the gender implications of that relationship? Did Schwenckfeld understand the nature of existence within a male-gendered body to be ontologically different from that in a female gendered body, and did such a difference, if it existed, have a bearing on salvation and its operation?

In looking at what Schwenckfeld wrote about flesh, the material falls into several main parts. There is the early material, discussed in detail by both McLaughlin and Weigelt, in which, largely because of his developing Eucharistic theology, Schwenckfeld found himself having to examine and define his understanding of the Body of Christ as found in the sacrament. Weigelt suggests that the early developments can be understood in two stages – before 1528: and between 1528 and 1530.[9]

According to this scheme, in the first stage, Schwenckfeld and Crautwald were initially concerned to protect the importance of the humanity of Christ and to insist that it had been taken to heaven. Both Weigelt and McLaughlin argue that at this stage in his thinking, Schwenckfeld (deeply influenced by Crautwald according to Weigelt) presented an understanding of the flesh of Christ as being fully human in its initial existence,[10] and as deified in the resurrection and ascension.[11] Weigelt suggests that it was in 1528 that

---

[9] Weigelt, *The Schwenckfelders in Silesia*, p. 86.

[10] They cite, for example the statement; But when the Lord says "flesh avails nothing" he is speaking of his flesh in its first state [the state of humiliation] because it is still weak, mortal, corporeal or vulnerable.
CS, vol. 2, p. 555, ll. 1f.

[11] To exemplify this, Weigelt uses the passage which continues from the previous note. However, I am not convinced that the passage is exactly dealing with deification. The issue under discussion in the document is in what way the flesh of Christ is truly food, and the blood is truly drink. Schwenckfeld sets up the argument to show that, in its first, corporeal state, such flesh cannot save precisely because it is corporeal. That is the context of the statement cited in n 7. Schwenckfeld then goes on to argue that; Thus, the Lord Christ means nothing other through the statement 'The flesh avails nothing, but it is the Spirit which gives life' than to show them that he is rejecting the misunderstanding of those of Capernaum, who interpreted his words about eating his flesh and blood in a physical sense. Namely, that one will not eat his flesh and drink his blood as if it were physical or bodily, something one could see and touch, or weak, suffering and mortal; but he meant it in a different, divine, heavenly sense, as is appropriate and that is that bodily, fleshly, visible man Christ would not be good to eat or make us alive and blessed, but the Word of God in the physical Christ is able to do this alone.
So wil nu der Herr Christus durch den Spruch; Das fleisch ist nicht nütze/ sonder der geist ists/ das da lebendig macht/ nichts anders/ denn daß Er der Capernaiten unverstand/ die seine wort vom essen seines fleisches und trincken seines blüts fleischlich richteten/ damit wil abgeleinet haben/ Nemlich daß man sein fleisch nicht also/ wie es da fleischlich oder leiblich/ greifflich/ sichtig/ noch schwach/ leidlich und sterblich war/ würde essen und sein blüt trincken/ Sonder auff ein andre göttliche himmlische weise/ wie gehöret/ und ist eben so viel/ als daß der fleischliche/ leibliche sichtige mensch an Christo noch nicht nütz war zu essen/ und uns lebendig und selig zümachen/ Das Wort Gottes am leiblichen Christo

Schwenckfeld and Crautwald began to change their stance, and to argue that the divinisation of Christ's flesh actually began during his earthly life, through the action of the Holy Spirit. Weigelt points out that this became a necessary understanding because of the way in which the Eucharistic theology had developed.[12]

What McLaughlin understands to be the final stage in the development of Schwenckfeld's thinking has to do less with the spiritual existence of Christ's flesh and more with its relationship with other flesh, and specifically whether it can be referred to as "created" in the way that all else is created. McLaughlin dates the beginning of this change to 1531,[13] when Schwenckfeld came into controversy with the South German theologians, most notably Bucer and Frecht, as well as the discussions he had with Hoffmann. Weigelt appears to place this part of the development later, arguing that, although the denial of Christ's creaturehood, which was the position Schwenckfeld espoused with great vigour, was implicit from the earliest days of his spiritualism, he did not outline it until 1538.[14] Although they date it differently, both McLaughlin and Weigelt conclude that Schwenckfeld's final position was that Christ's flesh was inherently different from human, created flesh not only after the resurrection, but from its origin.[15] From that point on, they maintain, he was elaborating variations on a theme, and not moving off in any new directions.

As I have pointed out above, this means that over twenty years' worth of his thinking is left to one side, and the discussions into which he entered and the language he used during that period are not considered. That period is the time when most of the women who were important in the movement came to prominence. Thus, by finishing the discussion at 1538, a period in which the nature of body and the implications of embodiment were being worked out in

---

vermochte diß ganz alleine/ das fleisch solte aber darzü bereitet und außgefüret werden. *CS*, vol. 2, p. 555, ll. 15f.

The crucial phrase is "ein andere göttliche himmlische weise," which Weigelt appears to take as indicating that Schwenckfeld was working with two not only distinct but completely separated states. I am not convinced that the separation between the weak state of humility and the saving state of glorification can be so clearly drawn, even this early in Schwenckfeld's thinking.

[12] Weigelt, *The Schwenckfelders in Silesia*, p. 88.

[13] McLaughlin, *Reluctant Radical*, p. 207.

[14] Weigelt, *Schwenkfelders in Silesia*, p. 90.

[15] Both Weigelt and McLaughlin refer to a document from 1538 "Letter and Treatise to Martin Frecht concerning the Glory of Christ", *CS*, vol. 6, p. 119ff. There are several passages here which might be cited, including; And if nevertheless the man Jesus according to the physical birth of his flesh here on earth was included in the order of the earthly people (therefore he has been a true human in body and soul, as a human of our substance, flesh and blood suffering and mortal/ as he truly suffered and died) himself subject to all human chance (with the exception of sin): thus he does not belong in the old creaturely order of creation, but in the new order of the recreation or rebirth. *CS*, vol. 6, p. 136, ll. 27f.

Schwenckfeld's thinking in dialogue with these women is ignored. Since the understanding of body cannot be fully explored without the consideration of the issue of gender, this appears to be a weakness in the whole presentation. Whether explicitly or implicitly, gender was part of the context in which Schwenckfeld was discussing the nature both of Christ's body and of the body of the believer during this period. It had to be so, with the gender composition of the groups which adopted his teaching.

Also, neither Weigelt nor McLaughlin is concerned with the meaning of flesh in social and cultural terms or with how those who adopted this teaching understood it. Thus my discussion is not considering the development of Schwenckfeld's thought prior to 1538 – how he moved from the earliest beginnings through to working out the implications, – but the patterns which emerged from the fully-fledged thought and its implications for the questions I have outlined above. I am concerned with the ways in which he worked out the implications of this position in the particular context of a significant proportion of women followers after 1538. Therefore I will be concentrating on documents which relate to that period. These will be *"The Flesh of Christ"*, a substantial treatise dated 1540, although it was not published until after his death:[16] a letter to Johann Bader from 1544, which bears the heading *"On the Flesh of Christ from the Fathers and the Seed of David"*[17] and a letter to Sibilla Eisler which deals among other things with *"The Two States of Christ and The Origin of the Flesh of Christ and its Consequent glory on God"*,[18] which is dated 1549, and which allows exploration of the way Schwenckfeld wrote of this directly to his most frequent woman correspondent. There is also a letter which Schwenckfeld sent to Elizabeth Hecklin in 1553 (again allowing insight into the way he wrote specifically to women) in which he deals with certain question raised by Johann Marbach, about the origin of Christ's humanity and understanding of his flesh:[19] a treatise on *"The Origin of the Flesh of Christ"* from 1555 which was written to defend himself against charges of denying Christ's flesh:[20] and a letter of 1561 written to somebody unknown in Augsburg who evidently raised questions about previous statements Schwenckfeld had produced on the issue of flesh.[21] As well as these, there are some other shorter pieces, or short statements within longer works on different topics. This material therefore comes after the works considered by McLaughlin and Weigelt, and it is also written in a variety of styles and for various occasions. Thus we can see not only the theology with which Schwenckfeld was working, but also something of the ways in which he was working with it.

---

[16] *CS*, vol. 7, pp. 284ff.
[17] *CS*, vol. 8, pp. 852ff.
[18] *CS*, vol. 11, pp. 776 ff.
[19] *CS*, vol. 13, pp. 337 ff.
[20] *CS*, vol. 14, pp. 307ff.
[21] *CS*, vol. 17, pp. 829ff.

Theological Understandings of Flesh

To begin to approach these questions it is necessary to consider what the body or the concept of flesh meant theologically, and this is not a straightforward issue. Because of the doctrines of the Eucharist and the Incarnation, flesh was not simply that which was associated with humanity, but was also part of the understanding of the presence of God in the world, and, more particularly, in the experience of the believer. It is clear from his writings that Schwenckfeld had read in the Fathers significantly, and looked to them as authorities.[22] So, in trying to grasp where he was drawing his thinking from, it is appropriate to look at some patristic understandings of body and flesh. Despite the fact, as I have said above, that many aspects of normal physical life, such as the issue of sexuality, and particularly sexual activity was regarded with particular suspicion. Although such language is present from early in the past-apostolic period, the real, explicit and consequential link of sin and sexuality is in the writings of Augustine.[23] At the centre of his eating and sleeping, could be and were regarded as areas of potential sinfulness, it is clear that theology was the orthodox conviction about the nature of original sin, a theological position which he developed in detail, as I pointed out above, in the course of his controversy with Pelagius. Pelagius suggested that it was possible and necessary for an individual to co-operate with the grace of God in bringing about salvation. Augustine insisted that such a belief was to undermine the central Christian tenet of salvation depending on God's grace alone. In order, as it were, to "protect" the sufficiency of God's grace, he elaborated his theology of original sin, which insisted that every part of human nature was affected by sin, and therefore there was no potential to make an independent response to grace.

His elaboration of this theology led him to examine how such original sin was present even in a child which was too young to have independent action – and he located the passing on of sin in the lust accompanying the act of intercourse which led to conception. In "*On Marriage and Concupiscence*", he taught that marriage was a good, but that lust or desire, even within marriage

---

[22] Thus, for example, *The Flesh of Christ, CS*, vol. 7, pp. 284 ff, we find references to Ambrose, Athanasius,Augustine, Cyril, Hilary, and Tertullian. In *The Origin of the Flesh of Christ*, vol. 14, pp. 307 ff, he finishes his treatise with a string of quotations and citations which takes thirteen pages in the printed *Corpus Schwenckfeldianorum*. These quotations come from Ambrose, Augustine, Jerome, Hilary, Origen, Basil the Great, Cassiodorus, Chrysostom, Irenaeus, Tertullian, Athanasius, Gregory of Nazianzus and Epiphanius.

[23] Gregory of Nyssa, for example, argued that passion was not part of the original make-up of humanity, but became part of experience because of sin. He continued his argument, saying; Marriage, then, is the last stage of our separation from the life that was led in Paradise, marriage therefore, as our discourse has been suggesting, is the first thing to be left: it is the first station as it were for our departure to Christ. "On Virginity," chapter 12, Gregory of Nyssa, *Nicene and Post-Nicene Fathers of the Christian Church*, Second Series, vol 5, trans William Moore, London, 1893, p. 358.

was evil.[24] In his teaching therefore, original sin, sexuality and body became linked in a profound way. The stature of Augustine in shaping Christian thinking cannot be overestimated, and this link which he made was to be a basic assumption in Christian thinking for generations. In the previous chapter, I have examined Schwenckfeld's position on original sin, and the ways in which he agreed with Augustine and Luther, in believing that original sin was all pervasive, and left no room for merely human effort. However, even in the extended discussion which I quoted, there is nothing in Schwenckfeld's language to suggest that the "transmission" of this sin was linked to sexuality. Clearly, in accordance with the tradition of which he was a part, he would have understood sin as becoming part of a person at conception. Clearly also, with his insistence on Mary's purity as necessary for the sinlessness of Christ's flesh, he did understand original, or inherited sin as having at least a physical consequence, or reality.

However, he does not use the language of Augustine, nor the force of the Augustinian arguments to link original sin directly with sexual expression. It is an issue he does not discuss. The lack of discussion suggests that this was simply a question which did not arise, it was a link he did not consider. In the light of the context in which he was thinking and discussing this is in itself a suggestive omission. While it is dangerous to argue too much from silence, and to risk attributing to Schwenckfeld ideas which we cannot prove he held, the fact of the silence is to be taken into account. Not to discuss an issue, especially when others are discussing it, both contemporaneously and as part of the tradition within which one is self-consciously working, is surely to make a statement about it. In examining issues of gender and theology in Schwenckfeld's writing, what he did not write about must also be considered, especially when, as in this case, it was an unusual gap. By not making the link between sexual activity and the transmission of original sin, Schwenckfeld was creating a theological space in which women (and men) could confront issues of sin and salvation in a way which was different, and less gender-loaded than normal. The separation of the issues meant that women did not start the discussion already carrying a sin for which there was no cure, that of physical existence. This was significantly different from much of the traditional thinking, which had made a very close link between sexuality and original sin. Once more, it was not that Schwenckfeld was setting out to devise different answers to these questions, but rather that, because of the trajectory which his theology determined, different answers were inevitable.

When these traditional notions are added to the symbolic identification of female and flesh, this link becomes particularly important and potent in the

---

[24] Wherefore the devil holds as guilty even infants, who are born, not from what is good from the goodness of marriage, but of what is evil in concupiscence, which is used aright, indeed in marriage, but at which even marriage has occasion to feel shame...This is the carnal concupiscence, which, while it is no longer accounted sin in the regenerate, yet in no case happens to nature except from sin. *On Marriage and Concupiscence,* Augustine, chapter 27.

definition not only of sin but also of woman. That sexuality is ambiguous and that women were primarily defined in reproductive and therefore sexual terms meant inevitably that the place of women in terms of sinfulness was profoundly ambiguous. That women could be saved was, on the whole, not questioned.[25] But that women had more to be saved from was an assumption that was often voiced. What was clear from such discussions however was not simply that women were more prone to sin – Aquinas makes it quite clear, for example, that it is the soul which overrules the body, and there is no virtue in the body[26] – but also that a woman's physical existence was inherently further removed from the ideal of holiness than a man's. What was under review in such discussions was particularly menstruation, childbirth and lactation. The issue was not simply sexual activity as such, but the sexualisation of women's existence, understood only in terms of physical presence in the world.[27] In her body, woman was further removed from the presence of God than man was, let alone whatever she did with that body.

Women's bodies were in and of themselves a problem in terms of holiness from very early on.[28] Women's bodies in their physical being were regarded as dangerous, unclean, polluted and somehow particularly sinful. If the sinfulness of flesh was present in men, it was particularly present in women. Not only was such sinfulness present, it was as I have pointed out above, infectious. Thus, priests had to be celibate because if they had intercourse with women, the sanctity of the sacraments would be affected. The role of the Church in creating and recreating "purified" flesh was fundamental, and was a significant part of the theology of the sacraments. Transubstantiation was the "creation" of Christ's pure flesh in the bread. Baptism was the creation of purified human flesh.

Purification and Baptism

From the very earliest days of the faith, the church had practised the rite of baptism as a means of entry into the community of the faithful. Augustine taught that baptism was the means of removing the stain of original sin; the outer washing was indicative of the inner, and was the means by which it was

---

[25] There was a satirical debate about the nature of women, and whether they had souls during the fifteenth century. See Manfred P. Fleischer, "Are Women Human? The debate of 1595 Beween Valens Acidatius and Simon Gediccus", *Sixteenth Century Journal*, vol. 12, 1981.

[26] *Summa Theologica* II/II question 56, a 1.

[27] See Rublack, "Pregnancy, Childbirth and the Female Body, "Along with menstruation, lactation, and the menopuase, women's experience of birth defined identity. The conjunction of fertility and finality was part of their being." p. 92.

[28] Thus Dionysius of Alexandria could write; For it would never occur to pious devout women to touch the sacred Communion table or Lord's body and blood. *Epistolae* can. 2, Pg. 10, 1281A.

understood to happen.[29] Thus, the importance of baptism of infants was linked with the need for the purification of the body. With the reconceptualising of the sacraments which was part of the changes initiated by Luther, baptism came under scrutiny. In 1523, Luther produced the first of his "Reformed" orders of baptism which followed quite closely the existing traditional orders. Like previous patterns, it started with an exorcism to free the flesh from the grip of the devil.[30] This action was followed by various prayers, and in the prayers an interesting variation on the previous pattern emerged. Previously there had been separate prayers for male and female infants. Luther omitted the prayers for females, and, by implication, used the prayer for the boys for the girls as well. The service then continued, including prayers and actions to do with both exorcism and baptism. In the next year, Osiander brought out his own baptismal rite, and he included separate exorcisms for boys and girls, using the words of the old rite.[31] This was only in use until 1526, when Luther issued a second booklet on baptism which became the standard text.[32] This, a very much simplified form, made no distinction between boys and girls. Susan Karant-Nunn, in her discussion of the gender-determined prayers and exorcisms in the traditional baptismal formulae suggests that this was simply the first in a series of gender markers which were used throughout life both to define gender itself, and to demonstrate the relative positions of the genders in the hierarchy of the world.[33] If she is right, then the alterations which Luther made can be seen to be very significant. They are the assertion that, before God, and therefore in the scheme of salvation, gender is not an issue. Zwingli made this explicit with his identification of infant baptism with the rite of circumcision in the Old Testament. Baptism is seen to be superior to circumcision just as the new covenant is superior to the old by virtue of the fact that it is available to women as well as men.[34]

Zwingli became involved in defending infant baptism in Zurich because of the activities of the groups who would eventually call themselves the Swiss Brethren, and whom others would call Anabaptists: those who, because of their

---

[29] For example, in his argument against Pelagius, in the book *On Forgiveness of Sins and Baptism*, he said; Now, inasmuch as infants are not held bound by any sins of their own actual life, it is the guilt of original sin which is healed in them by the grace of Him who saves them by the laver of regeneration. Book 1, chapter 25.

[30] J.D.C Fisher, "Luther's First Taufbüchlein", *Christian Initiation: The Reformation Period. Some Early Reformed Rites of Baptism and Confirmation and Other Contemporary Documents*, London: SPCK, 1970, pp. 6-16. The new service imitates the previous one with the president blowing on the child three times and saying: "Come out, thou unclean spirit and give place to the Holy Spirit."

[31] Fisher, *Christian Initiation*, pp. 17-22.

[32] Fisher, *Christian Initiation*, pp. 23-25.

[33] Karant-Nunn, *The Reformation of Ritual*, p. 47.

[34] Zwingli, "In catabaptistarum strophas elenchus", *Huldreich Zwinglis sämtliche Werke*, ed. Emil Egli et al, 1905, VI/1, pp. 1-196, "Antwört über Balthasar Hubmaiers Taufbüchlein", *Sämtliche Werke*, ed. Emil Egli et al, pp. 577-642.

understanding of the nature of the church, rejected the baptism of uncomprehending infants, and looked instead for baptism as a voluntary act of believing adults. This was a significant shift in the understanding of baptism.[35] For the Anabaptists, the importance of the rite was focused on community membership, on identification with the suffering Christ and on repentance from sin, rather than any sense that baptism was effective in and of itself.[36] Baptism, an act undertaken as part of a conscious response was no longer linked explicitly with physical cleansing, but with community and identity, and with a spiritual, almost mystical identity between the believer and Christ.[37] The issue of cleansing was not at the forefront of the meaning, nor was there an explicit link to exorcism, either freeing the body from evil or rescuing the individual from the devil. So it is clear that among at least some of those who were identified by their commitment to limiting baptism to believers, a different model was operating.

Schwenckfeld frequently spoke of forgiveness in terms of *reinigung*, cleansing, which suggests a parallel idea of a stain or blemish in or on the body. Thus, he reflected some of the traditional thinking which was present in the understanding of baptism. However, he did not adopt the approach to baptism which understood it to be a physical washing. He wrote comparatively little about baptism, and what he did write was generally to explain his objection to the practice of infant baptism. In 1531, he wrote to Johann Bader:

---

[35] Edward Muir points out however that the Anabaptists did still associate baptism with birth, but they looked instead to the rebirth of the Christian as the decisive issue. Muir, *Ritual in Early Modern Europe*, p. 20.

[36] Timothy George argues that "baptism in the Radical Reformation stood in the place of the monastic vow as a solemn pledge of commitment to an ascetic community, signifying both a radical breach with one's prior life, and an intention to fulfill the 'counsels of perfection', not in the confines of a cloister but amid the conflicts of life in the world." Timothy George, "The Spirituality of the Radical Reformation", *The Study of Spirituality*, Eds. Cheslyn Jones, Geoffrey Wainwright, Edward Yarnold S.J., London: SPCK, 1986, pp. 334-371, p. 347.

[37] Thus, the Schleitheim Confession states: Baptism shall be given to all those who have learned repentance and amendment of life, and who believe truly that their sins are taken away by Christ, and to all those who walk in the Resurrection of Jesus Christ, and wish to be buried with him in death, so that they may be resurrected with him... Compare Luther's comments in the Epilogue to the First Taufbüchlein of 1523 about the intention of baptism: For here you hear in the words of these prayers how pitifully and earnestly the Christian church here treats the little child, and with sure undoubting words confesses before God that he is possessed by the devil and is a child of sin and disfavour, and carefully prays for help and grace through baptism that he may become a child of God.Weimar, vol. 19, pp. 531-541, p. 537.

Secondly, concerning infant baptism, believe it or not, it gives me little concern, and I have, for all of my life, never spoken of it to anybody without reason and never unfittingly[38]

and in 1556, he was saying much the same thing to Helena Streicher:

But on the question of infant baptism, which has come to us through the Fathers and which has been in use in the Christian church for hundreds of years, I let it be commended to God and let those who do it be responsible as to whether it is right or not. I say that it concerns me not. I will struggle with nobody over it.[39]

This approach of regarding the issue as one not to be struggled over was reflected among his followers. For example, in his confession of 1556, Bernhardt Unsinn, one of the known Schwenkfelders in Augsburg, said:

As regards the article about infant baptism I have little to say about it, except that I let it remain in the appointment of the Fathers of the Church. The church has, without doubt, set up this and other ceremonies with a good intention, therefore I let them remain.[40]

Schwenckfeld was however quite clear that ideally baptism as a church rite ought to be for adults or believers. In the same letter to Helena Streicher he wrote: "The order that Christ brings is clear, that the believer should be baptised."[41] He was equally clear that whatever form the rite took, of infant or adult, as in the Eucharist, the true baptism was "inner", and had little or nothing to do with the water:

To speak of it in short, the salvation of the soul and the cleansing of the heart are not in the transitory element nor in any outer water, but in the Word of God who for our sake has become flesh, that is our Lord Jesus Christ.[42]

The corollary of this was that salvation did not depend on baptism:

The young children were not thereby condemned, if at the time of the apostles they were not baptised.[43]

Salvation was always and only to be understood as coming through the encounter with Christ in the soul. In common with his understanding of the Supper, he argued for the primacy of the inner encounter over the outer

---

[38] *CS*, vol. 4, p. 242, ll. 36f.

[39] *CS*, vol. 14, p. 779, ll. 1f.

[40] Bernhardt Unsinn, *Bericht*, Staatsarchiv Augsburg, Schwenckfeldiana IV OA v 9, 1556.

[41] *CS*, vol. 14, p. 778, ll. 8f.

[42] *CS*, vol. 7, p. 431, l. 32.

[43] *CS*, vol. 14, p. 778, ll. 25f.

experience of water administered in the institutional church. Thus he wrote in a letter to Jacob Held von Tieffenau in 1535:

> The baptism of infants I can not hold as the baptism of Jesus Christ, for the baptism of Jesus Christ is grace, life, the Holy Spirit, and true, real strength of God in the baptizand's heart. [44]

Later, in 1552, he wrote to Sibilla Eisler:

> Secondly, that to Christian baptism belongs God's prevenient grace and an oral confession of the baptizand, Acts 8: 29-39, Rom 10, 9, 10, 13, 14.[45]

Outer baptism as reflective of this inner experience, therefore, was a rite for believers rather than infants. However Schwenckfeld was equally unwilling to be linked with the Anabaptists, writing:

> Therefore, in their teaching about this sacrament, they deal only in the letter, and must necessarily walk either to the left or to the right of the proper way, the spiritual understanding, example and knowledge of Christ.[46]

His theology of baptism therefore put him at odds both with the general understanding, which drew on a perception of the body as a place of sinfulness, with baptism as the sign and means of cleansing, and with the more symbolic Anabaptist view of baptism as the mark of belonging by choice to a new community and of identity with Christ. He did however, in one passage, appear to take account of some of the issues raised above about the need for some measure of purification, as well as considering the question of what happened to infants which died unbaptised. In the letter to Johann Bader he wrote:

> But I must also set this down, that by God's grace, one could deal well with new-born child Christianly through the witness of Holy Scripture in blessing, exorcism, the offering of the church and the introduction of the new mothers so that people are put at peace, especially the women who want from the physical love to help the child to heaven, though it is not necessary; for afterwards, when they should help, nobody is at home, and that one could well do, but one should leave Christ Jesus his holy baptism without stain, and leave his godly institution unaltered. [47]

Thus, Schwenckfeld, although he was not subscribing to a theology which downgraded the body and placed an emphasis on purification, was aware of it, and of its place in the lives of people in their self-perception. His insistence that the body had spiritual value had alongside it a recognition and a toleration of

---

[44] *CS*, vol. 5, p. 271, ll. 5f.
[45] *CS*, vol. 13, p. 51, ll. 32f.
[46] *CS*, vol. 7, p. 430, ll. 9f.
[47] *CS*, vol. 4, p. 253, ll. 5ff.

the values people already attached to the body. As the above quotation makes clear, he saw no difficulty in using ceremonies if they are helpful to people (a suggestion that he treated relationships and pastoral care as a priority) while at the same time maintaining that such ceremonies are always only ceremonies, and do nothing to affect the spiritual reality of the situation. He did seem, however, capable of drawing a distinction between spiritual reality and psychological need. He accepted the use of what looks like a traditional form of churching ("the introduction of the one giving birth…"), as a way of setting "people at peace", of meeting emotional need and giving reassurance, while preserving his theological position ("though it is not necessary"). He did separate this from baptism (one should leave Christ Jesus his holy baptism without stain), though, as we have seen above, he did not argue with great vehemence for a believers' baptism position. This attitude with regard to churching exemplifies the freedom with regard to the meaning of body which Schwenckfeld discovered as a possibility in his theology, and which may be another of the theological reasons why women found this an appealing teaching. In one way, despite his insistence on the reality of original sin present in the body considered as a theological concept, his attitude to the actuality of flesh was neutral. He allowed for the possibility of exorcism as a comfort, but suggested that it was not necessary. Although people in bodies were sinners and therefore sinned, sinfulness was not determined by the physical being of the body. However, the physical being of the body was to be taken into account in considering spiritual well-being, and therefore there is an openness to matters like churching. When we reflect that many women were distressed by the move of some Reformers to dispense with this ceremony for theological reasons, the freedom that Schwenckfeld's theology allowed for affirmation of bodily existence suggests that there was both a theological and a pastoral reason which drew women to this thinking.

Christ's Sinless Flesh

Whatever reinterpretations he may have been hinting at in his consideration of the bodies of the men and women around him, Schwenckfeld was nonetheless quite clear that Christ's flesh was sinless. This was the place of differentiation between Christ's flesh and that of other humans. He wrote frequently of Christ's flesh in terms such as "full of grace", "without sin, blemish or mark" and "new and spiritual".[48] It is clear that what in Schwenckfeld's understanding made Christ's flesh unique was its freedom not only from the action of sin – that is, Christ did not carry out anything which might be termed sinful – but also from the stain of sin, the physical presence of it within the body. He did not explore this in enough detail for us to establish whether his understanding of sinlessness meant that he believed Christ was not tempted, and therefore did not need to resist or whether, faced with temptation, he still maintained a

---

[48] "gnadenreich", "ohne sunde, mackel und Fluch", "new unnd geistlich".

sinless state. Although he frequently discussed the fact of sinlessness, he had little to say about its meaning in terms of Christ's own being. The meaning that Schwenckfeld was concerned with was the meaning in relation to saving fallen and alienated humanity.

Duality of Origins

Here we must examine again the issue of the duality of origins. The ontological distinction between the flesh of Christ and all else was that Christ's flesh was fathered by God, and everything else, including human flesh, was created. One of the arguments that Schwenckfeld produced to show that Christ's flesh could not be thought of as created like other people's was that of the Eucharist, and of God's action through the flesh and blood of Christ to feed the believer's soul. This could not be so, he argued, if this flesh were created:

> So it can clearly be seen that the flesh and blood of Christ is not like other human flesh and blood, as human reason invents of Christ, much less is it a creature, because eternal life comes from no creature, for God does not feed the soul with creatures, but with himself and with the flesh and blood of his son, Jesus Christ.[49]

However, although this was fundamental to Schwenckfeld, the issue of sinfulness was not one which he could ignore. In conventional theological terms, this was where the distinction between Christ and humanity was placed. As Incarnate Divinity, Christ was not sinful. He was understood both to be free from the "mark" of original sin and not to "do" anything which was accounted a sin. This was a significant part of the theological discussion of the nature of the virgin birth, as we saw in the previous chapter. Conventionally, as we have seen, human flesh was "marked" by original sin. That is the reason for the alienation between God and humanity. Salvation therefore involves forgiveness and cleansing. Reconciliation with the sinless God is effected through the death and resurrection of Christ. In such a theology, the Incarnation of the Second Person of the Trinity is necessary, but not sufficient for salvation.

For Schwenckfeld, the issue was to do with origins. That which was alienated from God was that which was created rather than fathered, was outer rather than inner. This leaves the question of where sin fitted into his understanding. This is one of the areas where his pragmatic rather than philosophical approach to issues of theology can be seen most clearly. He was aware that humans were sinful, and since to be human was to be embodied, human flesh was sinful. In his writing, he demonstrated nothing other than the conventional perception – that sin was part of human nature following the fall. There is, in his consideration, no exploration regarding what would have been the nature of the relationship between humanity and God had there been no Fall. The *fact* was what was important, and the fact was that human nature was sinful. He understood sin as a fundamental part of the alienation of humanity

---

[49] *CS*, vol. 13, p. 339, ll. 36f.

from God, though not the only cause.[50] However, as part of the cause, it had its effect on the being of humanity. The effect was identified with and in that part of human ontology which was most distinctive, the flesh. Thus, for Schwenckfeld, the flesh bore in its being the evidence of alienation in the stain or scar of sin.

As the Incarnate One, Christ was not alienated from God the Father. He was generated, not created. Therefore, he did not bear in his being the marks of alienation, including sin and sinful flesh. Christ was in his intrinsic being and in his actions, sinless. Thus, Schwenckfeld could still take a place in orthodox theology with regard to Christ's sinless being, while not compromising his theology of inner and outer, the duality of origins. Such a position also left him the theological space to argue for the transformation of the flesh of the believer which I will discuss in the next chapter. According to this understanding, flesh was not completely identified with sin, and so its transformation becomes a possibility. At the same time, the actual reality of alienation meant that flesh was sinful, and bore the spiritual "stain" of that sin. Despite this different direction of approach, we can see that Schwenckfeld still understood human flesh as sinful. He never suggested that human sin was unimportant or could be ignored. Salvation, the rescue from alienation, was signalled by and resulted in the forgiveness of sin and therefore the renewal or cleansing of the flesh. This had very practical consequences. This is to be expected in the light of the discussion earlier about the implication that the believer was female, the provider of "stuff" in relation to the male Saviour, the creator of "new life."

What is important in this discussion on the nature of Christ's flesh is the way in which Schwenckfeld understood flesh and sin, and the bearing of that understanding on his teaching about Christ's Incarnate body. Though he did not locate sin primarily in physical activity, he recognised sin as having a physical reality and consequence. He clearly saw that it was important for the Saviour's flesh to be free from the *taint* of sin – he spoke, as I have pointed out, about Christ's flesh as being without *sin, blemish or mark*. He also spoke, as I suggested above, about the experience of forgiveness in terms of "cleansing",[51] a term which clearly has echoes of a physical experience, but which I believe was deliberately chosen. Flesh which was sinful needed to be cleansed from its sin just as much as a dirty face needed to be washed. Clearly he believed that sin was not something which was extrinsic to the human experience, but intrinsic – that is, people did not become sinful by sinning, but sinned because they were sinful, just as Augustine and Luther taught, rather than the Pelagian thinking that by choosing to sin, an individual became sinful. Because flesh in its being was marked with the stain of sin – this was inherent in the nature of the being of flesh – there was no way of avoiding it.

We have seen that Schwenckfeld shared the Augustinian context in his understanding of the pervasiveness of sin through the person. The obvious connection in this context would be to identify sin with sexuality, and sinful

---

[50] Maier, *Caspar Schwenckfeld on the Person and Work of Christ*, p. 42.
[51] "reinigung".

action with the expression of sexuality. However, the link does not appear to have been made, at least consciously, in his thinking. Nevertheless, there are some hints in his discussion of the physical descent of Christ, which suggest that there is something going on in his understanding about sexuality, desire and sin. Two parts of his discussion exemplify this. Firstly there is the way he described the conception of Christ. He constantly linked it with the action of the Holy Spirit, and often referred to the conception as *newe, geistliche, ubernaturlich*. But sometimes he went even further in his description, as for example:

> But Christ's flesh is born in her [Mary] and conceived of the Holy Spirit. Therefore it must always have been in her and yet have been completely without sin, because it was not conceived in sinful desire.[52]

The sinlessness of Christ's flesh comes from its origin in God the Father through the action of the Spirit, who brings about conception without any lust or sinful desire. In the chapter "Concepts of Conception", I suggested that at various points in his writings we can hear echoes of Schwenkfeld's unease with male sexuality. I believe that this is another example of this unease. Within the biological model with which he appears to be working, the bringing into existence of the child is the action of the father – the expression of the father's will. Despite the impression that is sometimes given that sexuality as a problem was located in women, the sense of Schwenkfeld's argument here is that it is because Christ's conception is free from male sexuality that it is sinless. Therefore the origin of the celestial flesh in God is not only about the separation of the two orders of existence, but also because only God can act in a masculine manner – that is, give life (a sexual act), without it being sinful. As I argued in "Concepts of Conception", Schwenckfeld was unable to consider the conception of Christ as being in any way connected with male desire. On the other hand, however, he found himself unable to choose the path which Hoffman followed, of refusing to allow Mary any physical role in the conception and birth. The physical reality of the flesh of Christ and its identity with the material world was not a theological principle on which he was prepared to compromise.

However, with his presumed reliance on the Aristotelian model of conception, he was faced with yet another problem of descent. This model presupposed that each individual in some sense existed within the seed of his/her father before conception. And this therefore suggested that all existed within the seed of Adam, as the original father. Indeed, this is part of the argument for the existence of original or ontological sin in each person even before the consciousness necessary for actual sin to take place exists. "In Adam all sinned" is the way in which Paul phrases it. Schwenckfeld picked up this argument, coming to it through the writings of Augustine. He was commenting on Augustine's discussion of Hebrews 7, where the writer is arguing that the

---

[52] *CS*, vol. 7, p. 324, ll. 16f.

Son is a priest after the order of Melchizedek, and therefore greater than the Jewish priests, after the order of Levi. This argument is based on the story that Abraham, Levi's ancestor, presented tithes to Melchizedek, and therefore showed himself to be inferior to Melchizedek. By implication, since, as the writer argues, Levi was at this time existent "in the loins of Abraham", he also brought tithes (Heb 7:9-10). Schwenkfeld quoted Augustine's argument, developed from this, thus:

> [Augustine says] Just as in the case of Adam, all who were in his loins have sinned, so when he [Abraham] tithed, all who were in his loins have tithed. But this is not the case for Christ, says Augustine. Although he was in the loins of Adam and Abraham (understood as in his mother), he did not come according to the desire of the flesh.[53]

He went on to take the argument much further, but making much the same point, that is, that although Christ's physical body had to be within the loins of his male ancestors, because the nature of its birth was through Mary's body rather than through male impregnation, they cannot truly be said to be physical ancestors of Christ's physical flesh. Maier suggests that

> It is significant that "believing Abraham" but never "fallen Adam" is regarded by Schwenckfeld as the forefather of Christ. In Schwenckfeld's anthropology, Adam represented the quintessence of everything from which man had to be saved.[54]

In fact, as this quotation shows, Adam was cited as an ancestor, and in the context of his sinfulness. Surely what is important is not that Adam was not part of the chain, but that flesh born as part of this continuation was not inherently alienated. And the reason for this is that Christ's birth does not come about through "desire" – a notion which again and again appears to be associated in his thinking both with masculinity, and with the unease he seemed to feel over masculine sexuality.

The logic of his apparent understanding of biology at this point became a problem to him. With his emphasis on the male as the life-giver, descent should come through the male line. However, this was a position that he appears to have found untenable. Instead, he found himself forced to trace descent through Mary. There are several places in this argument in which Schwenckfeld's thinking appears to be inconsistent or incoherent – this is not the least of them![55] However, incoherence may not be a problem. Rather, it may be a place

---

[53] *CS*, vol. 7, p. 315, ll. 4f.

[54] Maier, *Caspar Schwenckfeld on the Person and Work of Christ*, p. 48, n.1.

[55] Of this whole discussion, Maier says "In tracing its [Christ's flesh] origin though Mary to the fathers, Schwenckfeld would not tolerate the thought that the flesh of Christ should have issued from a process of mere creaturely transmission. He rather posited an explanation of Jesus' physical ancestry which is easily the least clear and satisfying theologoumenon ever propounded by the Silesian reformer." Maier, *Caspar*

of creativity, and freedom, and it is possible that the apparently disjunctured theology here may have given a particular freedom with regard to gender which was to be fruitful. By refusing the common connection between female and sin, especially female flesh and sexuality and sin, Schwenckfeld provided a space for those who otherwise might have found themselves burdened by a guilt which they did not truly own.

However, since we cannot ask the women in question, and since our asking would probably have made no contemporary sense anyway, this must remain speculation – though speculation which can claim as its justification the fact that so many women did respond to Schwenckfeld's theology. What we do need to pursue is what in fact all this meant in Schwenckfeld's understanding of the flesh of Christ and of human flesh, as well as the connection between the two. It is clear that for Schwenckfeld it was the fact of the flesh of Christ that was the saving element in God's activity. This was not an issue purely of sacramental reality and reception. That the sacramental reception, with its salvific effect, was available and was dependent on the death and destruction of the physical body of Christ.

The Gender of Christ's Flesh and the Flesh of the Believer

If the biological model by which Schwenkfeld understood the mechanics of the Incarnation was also part of the model by which he constructed the whole of his world-view, then the same "division of labour" in birth might have applied to his understanding of the experience of the reception of body and blood. The body and blood which were given and received, could, because they were what provided life, be construed as male. He was certainly quite clear that the body and blood created life – that is his understanding of the verses in John 6. And so he could write

> Now it is clear and obvious from the sixth chapter of John that the flesh, the body and blood of Christ is not connected with condemnation or judgement for anybody, but only, for those who eat and drink it for life and eternal salvation; Who eats my flesh and drinks my blood, he remains in me and I in him (Jn. 6; 56). And regarding the heavenly bread (Jn. 6:54), Whoever will eat this bread will live in eternity. Thus therefore, the body of Christ is a body of grace in which the fullness of the Godhead dwells (Col. 2:9) as also his blood is full of strength and salvation.[56]

This comes from a document in 1549, which Schwenckfeld wrote for Hans Wilhelm von Laubenberg, in which he was detailing his objections to the Roman Mass. During the argument, he had shown the ways in which the

---

Schwenckfeld on the Person and Work of Christ, p. 48. Maier does however make the issue even more confusing for himself by not considering the gender and biological issues which are at stake for Schwenckfeld here.

[56] *CS,* vol. 11, p. 1049, ll. 12f.

Lutherans had continued much of the theology of the Roman Mass, and why he disagreed with their position. Thus, the writing was in the context of a broader discussion about the meaning of the bread and its connection with the body of Christ. What is interesting, in the light of the issue I am concerned with, is that Schwenckfeld did not take the position of suggesting that the eating, the bread and so on are "purely" symbolic. Rather, he emphasised the eating as a reality, and based its importance on the link between the eating and the having of eternal life – because that which is eaten is the body in which the fullness of divinity is present. He presented this case in a context of rejecting both the Roman doctrine of Transubstantiation and the Lutheran teaching of the Real Presence. Otherwise, such a statement could be read as presenting either of these positions. However, since he was so clear that he rejected them, another way of understanding what he believed to be the importance of such eating must be found. I believe that is found in understanding the body of Christ as an *inner* reality, that is, one with its origin in God's fathering rather than creating action, a reality which has a physical though not corporeal nature, and can thus be encountered by the body of the believer, and which brings the life of God to that believer's body. Thus, the body of Christ in the Supper directly parallels the action of God in the Spirit at the conception of Christ. In such a sense, the Body of Christ in the Supper can be said to be male in its activity.

It appears to be possible therefore to suggest that, for Schwenckfeld, the role of body and blood, conceived in universal terms, is male. If this is so, then it is important to examine what this means for his understanding of the one who is receiving the body and blood. If it is the property of the male to give life, then it is the property of the female to receive life, and to give matter to the male spirit of life – as Mary did in the Incarnation. If what is given in the Supper is the life, then what receives it, the hungry and believing heart, soul and body, must surely be the female part of the equation, that which gives physical reality to the impetus of life. It is true that Schwenckfeld never referred to the believer as female directly in this way, but that it was part of his understanding helps to make sense of the underlying pattern of his theology. Thus, if it is the role of the believer to give "stuff" to the life-giving activity of God, to "flesh it out", as it were, then we have a reason why Schwenckfeld believed so strongly that the true reception of the body and blood of Christ must have moral and practical implications. This was one of the reasons why he criticised the Lutheran Eucharist. Instead of provoking a new *way* of life, people were treating it like a new indulgence and looking to the reception of the sacrament as the receiving of forgiveness and the gift of new life. So, for example, he could write:

> How may we make repentance on the command of the Lord? how can the sinner repent as the prophet says? if he can be saved from his old sinful life through the use of the Sacraments, why should anyone crucify the old man with his lusts and desires?[57]

---

[57] *CS*, vol. 3, p. 144, ll. 13f.

If the believer's being is female, then the role of that being is to give physical reality to the eternal life of God – in other words, to live a life which is pleasing to and which exemplifies the desire of God, a life which is moral and upright. This was clearly an important part of Schwenckfeld's spirituality, and one which I will discuss further in "Men, Women and God". At this point in the discussion, I want to explore more of the implications of associating the being of the believer with the female role. We have established in the previous chapter that the biological pattern which Schwenckfeld brought to his notion of the conception of Christ appears to have been one which was driven by an Aristotelian understanding. The female role is to provide "stuff" and nothing else. It has also become clear in our consideration of Schwenckfeld's understanding of sin that he considered original sin to be a condition from which no person could move unaided – nobody could do anything which would create or enable his or her salvation. That must come from God alone. There are obvious parallels between these two positions, and it is surely justifiable to suggest that, in the way in which he constructed his teaching about the place of the Supper, the power of the flesh of Christ and its "generative" power in bringing new life, Schwenckfeld was working with a world view which was deeply shaped by this model. We can lay out the bare bones of his approach in this way:

- to generate life is to be male:
- to provide the stuff in which life takes shape is to be female:
- the flesh of Christ generates eternal life, which is lived out in the body and being of the believer:
- thus, in the procreative economy of salvation the flesh of Christ is male and the body and being of the believer female.

The thought that the soul is female in regard to the maleness of God is not an unusual approach in late medieval mysticism. Several men spoke of themselves as female in God's presence. But the important images normally being conveyed in such language were those of submission, weakness, humility and obedience. [58] This was an appropriate use of the image in a society where female virtue was shaped around such qualities. The definition of good female behaviour was to do with submissiveness, obedience and humility, and the definition of female included weakness as an assumption.

These are also qualities which were significant in the understanding of Christian living: the Christian before God was to be submissive, obedient and humble, and also acknowledged a profound weakness. It is not without its significance that the *representative* Christians in a community, the priests, were

---

[58] In *Holy Feast and Holy Fast*, Bynum picks up this theme. "Woman, in other words, was 'liminal' to men in the technical sense given the term by the anthropologist Victor Turner". p. 229 and then later: "Man became woman metaphorically to express renunciation". p. 284.

expected to represent at least part of this female persona. One of the issues about priests was the way in which, physically, they were marked as separate from the rest of the community. They broke the boundaries which identified gender identity. Hair and beard had long been associated with masculinity. The move that a boy made to the mature world of men away from the immature world of women was symbolised by the appearance of the beard. Monks and priests were shaven, not only on their faces, but, with the tonsure, also on their heads. In a world which depended on a whole series of gender markers, these monks and priests were anomalous figures. Indeed, this was part of their role – holy men who were signs of another reality, men who were on the edge and so could mediate. Their lack of sexual activity was part of this boundary-blurring.[59] The role of the priest as unequivocally male was not so straightforward as might at first appear. There was a way in which the priest, by not being immediately identifiable as male, also presented the female. The priest did not beget children (an action which, as we have seen, was constitutive of maleness), bear arms or present male political characteristics by heading a household. In presiding at the Mass, the holy meal, the priest carried out the female role of food-provider. A monk carried the pattern even further, with vows which included a vow of obedience, a giving up of autonomy and self-determination in a way which also put him in a *female* role. One parallel to the monastic vow would be the vow of marriage, in which a wife promised to obey her husband, a vow which like the monastic one was legally enforceable. Thus, within a community, the priest or monk could bear the "femininity" which signalled a good Christian in a representative manner, and which therefore allowed other men not to be thus compromised in their gender identity. This was a femininity of weakness and inferiority.

If Schwenckfeld was truly thinking of the believer as female, albeit not explicitly, but as part of fundamental assumptions about the nature of the world, then the expression of that femaleness was very different in nature. The issues concerning him were certainly to do with obedience, but not the obedience of an inferior to a superior – the normal model of female to male. What concerned him more was the embodiment of eternal life, which was the life of God. Just as the eternal Word took flesh or became flesh,[60] through the medium of Mary, so the eternal life, which is the nature and the gift of God given through the body and blood, takes or becomes flesh through the (female)

---

[59] Vern L. Bullough, "On Being a Male in the Middle Ages". Bullough sets out three ways in which masculinity was defined (p. 34): impregnating, protecting dependents, providing for the household. Celibate priests fulfil none of these criteria, and therefore are ambiguous characters. Bullough goes on to say of the danger of those who do not fulfil the criteria; it is almost as if the 'superiority of the male' has to be demonstrated continually or it is lost. p. 34.

[60] "So, to Christ Jesus, the eternal Word, (who for our sakes has become flesh and has taken that flesh with him to heaven for our comfort.) I ascribe alone the honour for salvation and justification, as is appropriate".
CS, vol. 2, p. 508, ll. 34f.

soul and body. Thus to receive the sacramental bread and wine, but not to show eternal life in the practice of living, was to demonstrate that the true receiving of the (male) body and blood had not taken place within the (female) soul and body of the believer, for there was no coming to life or embodiment. I will look in more detail at Schwenckfeld's understanding of the living of eternal life in "Men, Women and God". Here I want to examine in more detail what such an understanding demonstrated about the understanding of the nature of this bread and wine which fed the believer. It is unclear just what he believed was happening when bread and wine was received, but the appropriate consequences did not follow. Presumably, the inner feeding was not taking place. Indeed, this is what he said in the case of Judas, in the passage quoted in the second chapter: Judas ate the bread and drank the wine, but he did not receive the Eucharist.

The Results of Eating and Drinking

It was also possible to eat and drink in remembrance: this was presumably the experience of the faithful when they took part in the liturgical celebration. But, as we have seen, Schwenckfeld was quite clear that this was separate from the experience of feeding, which was the centre of new life. Just as the birth of the baby was the demonstration that conception had taken place, so the living of the new life, the life of eternity, was the demonstration that a true encounter had occurred. It is important not to understand Schwenckfeld's insistence on such signs as a limitation of the Christian life to one of a particular form of moral rigour, though that was clearly part of it. He seems to have been talking about a quality of spirituality, of experience and perhaps even of mystical awareness, which would then issue in morally appropriate behaviour. Again, we are on the borderlands of physical and spiritual, and again it is clear that for Schwenckfeld the "normal" boundaries separating spiritual and physical were not as firm as they might at first appear. What is clear is that there was a deeply important connection between receiving the body and blood of Christ in the inner encounter, and the experience of new, eternal – and morally visible – life. The link therefore between Christ's life-giving flesh as male, and the life-receiving being of the believer as female is, I suggest, one which it is not inappropriate to perceive in this language.

It is all the more persuasive an argument because it fits with an existing tradition, and we have already seen in various places the ways in which Schwenckfeld, although he was self-consciously shaped by and in reaction to Lutheran thinking, also bore the marks of an older perception of reality, particularly as it referred to the body. Christ, or God as male, and the believer as female was an existing pattern, and one which Schwenckfeld may have found it easy to be at home with. It would also have been one familiar, at least subliminally, to those who adopted his teaching. It is easily seen how women would easily adopt such theological symbolism, since it would run in an easy parallel with the place in which they already found themselves in the world.[61] Thus, a theology which presented the being of the believer as a persona which women would find it easy to identify and to identify with would, it could be argued, hold a particular appeal. However, in the language and the manipulation of concepts which mark Schwenckfeld's complex of ideas around the nature of the flesh of Christ there is also another pattern visible.

The Humiliated Flesh as the Place of Vulnerability

Bynum has argued that in the late medieval period it was the *vulnerability* of flesh that marked it as human.[62] This appears in Schwenckfeld's language when he spoke of Christ's body being *sterblich* and *leidlich* and it certainly seems that it was the vulnerability of this body which was a mark of its physical reality. Flesh was known to be real flesh because it could be hurt. It was here that the identity between the flesh of Christ and the flesh of created humans could be found. Thus, in his letter to an enquirer in Augsburg, when he was trying to explain just how he understood Christ's flesh to be human, Schwenckfeld could state:

> Thus one should notice this difference, that although Christ Jesus in the days of his flesh was a true human, of human substance, nature and being, *mortal and suffering*, subject to all neediness except for sin... [63]

It is a characteristic of Schwenckfeld's thinking that he understands Christ's bodily presence as being in two different forms or states:[64] one of humiliation and one of exaltation. The state of humiliation was the time of Christ's earthly ministry, and the exaltation started with the Resurrection and was understood to be the present state of Christ's body. He wrote about this in various places, as a theme through several of his works. One of the major works in which this appears was written in 1543, in both German and Latin, *Summarium von Zweierlay Stande*.[65] As is often the case with Schwenckfeld's major theological writings, this was written not as an exercise in theological reflection, but as an attempt to explain and defend his position against those who were attacking him. From his determination to defend the position, we can see that this was a

---

[61] We can find similar patterns from other periods in church history, when women's spirituality reflected the social norms of their community, sometimes even self-consciously. For example, some women hymn-writers of the nineteenth century explicitly use modes of "appropriate" female behaviour to describe the experience of a Christian. See, for instance, Frances van Alstyne's hymn "Blessed Assurance" (*Baptist Hymn Book,* 1962, No. 493), which is totally constructed around images of submission, obedience and a love in which the soul is completely passive.

[62] Bynum, *Fragmentation and Redemption*, p. 92.

[63] *CS*, vol. 17, p. 834, ll. 10f. My emphasis.

[64] He used the word *Stand.*

[65] "A Summary of the Two States".

central element in his thinking. After a very short introduction, he began the argument like this:

> Now we want truly to distinguish and to learn to understand the two states of the flesh of Christ through an orderly opposing of a personal unity; namely, the first here on earth and the second today in heaven. For, with Christ and his flesh, it was not always in only one way, but so that we might see clearly and understand what Christ has done for our sake in the humiliation, and what he has also now become in the glory of his Father with his flesh, body and blood. From that then, we might better know also the two knowledges of Christ in the grace of God; that according to the flesh and that according to the spirit.[66]

His discussion then proceeded with a series of comparisons between the two states, of humiliation and glory. Throughout the discussion, he made it very clear, as the above quotation suggests, that although the humiliation of the flesh was a significant part of the earthly being of Christ, this was not an inherent part of fleshliness per se. Thus, he argued quite explicitly that the current *spiritual* state of Christ was not non-fleshly:

> According to the first state, the Lord Christ Jesus was born as a true person from the Virgin Mary, with soul, body, flesh, blood, bone, and all human conditions, according to the outer truth of the physical human being. According to the second state, Christ is and remains even today after his exaltation and ascension, in eternity, a true person with a true body, soul, blood, flesh, bones, face, limbs and all the conditions of human nature, but a person not according to the quality of our temporal bodies and truth, but according to the eternal, heavenly, divine truth, a person in God, the spiritual, eternal being of God, his eyes are flames of fire, his face alight as the bright sun (Rev 1:14,16).[67]

It is important to note that it is not flesh itself which is the humiliation in Schwenckfeld's understanding. Rather, it is the vulnerability of the flesh. Thus he could argue

> Thus I believe that God the Son took to himself true human nature and united naturally with the same, and also truly in flesh as in human nature suffered and died.... He did not want only to be born human, but also in the assumed humanity had to and wanted to suffer and die.[68]

Humiliation consists not in having a physical body, for that can also be part of exaltation. It is vulnerability, suffering and death which are the mark of the depths to which God has stooped in Jesus. Vulnerability both consisted in and demonstrated a lack of self-determination, and it was that which signalled the loss that God endured. The weakness of humanity is its inability to determine

---

[66] *CS*, vol. 8 p. 735, ll. 23f.
[67] *CS*, vol. 8 p. 741, ll. 20f.
[68] *CS*, vol. 10, p. 140, ll. 4f

its own existence.

It is also suggestive that the weakness of the flesh could arguably be identified as a typically feminine characteristic – or rather, that one of the reasons for the symbolic link between female and flesh was focused on this notion of vulnerability. The link between female and flesh was (and is) profound and determinative, and there are all sorts of reasons for it, some of which I have explored above. In Schwenckfeld's time and earlier, the reasons for such an identification were not a matter for particular concern, because the assertion was so self-evident: it is bound up with the nature of patriarchy, and the need for definition over against the "other" – male: female, spirit: flesh. The realities of female existence – menstruation, childbirth and lactation – meant that for most women existence "in" the body could not be ignored or transcended. I want to argue that this is part of the reason for the identification of female and flesh: that for women, the embodied existence could not be ignored. This much is unexceptional. But I want to go further and to suggest that the imperiousness of such physical reality, the impossibility of ignoring it, brings with it the impossibility of ignoring the big issues of physical reality – vulnerability and mortality.

Thus I argue that women represented not simply *flesh* as opposed to spirit, but also the *vulnerability* of flesh – that which is part of the experience of being human, but which is most evident in the embodied existence of women. Women were those who experienced the implacability of physical existence in the greatest and most obvious measure, and they were also those who, by and large, had less freedom for self-determination. It is true that the death rates for men were higher than those for women, and that their propensity for injury in fights or in daily life was very high.

However, the fact that it was assumed it would on the whole be men who did the fighting is evidence of the assumption that physically men were stronger and less vulnerable. The notion that women were weak applied not only in the intellectual or moral consideration, but also physically – despite the fact that it was women whose lives were often physically the more demanding. However, the point is not so much the suffering of women, or the perceived suffering, but the implacability of women's physical existence. Her place in society, her activity in daily life and her identity as a person were to a large extent determined by the physical reality of her body; whether she was virgin, pregnant, nursing mother, sexually active wife, with the constant possibility of pregnancy, or widow. Her ability to travel, to leave the house, to take part in communal life was, to some extent dominated by her physical condition, in a way that was not the case for men, and her place in society was shaped by her biological identity. Since many of these conditions, for example, menstruation or pregnancy, were regarded as times of particular vulnerability, and could occur frequently and regularly, then both the experience and the perception of vulnerability was one which was associated with female existence.

Women were also especially weak in their lack of self-determination. Legally, a woman bore much the same position as a child. She was under the control of father, husband, brother or son. Her rights to determine her own life-pattern, to take her own decisions were severely restricted in comparison with men. Clearly, such an assertion must be modified in the light of other variables such as class, wealth and age, but compared with men of equivalent status, most women were legally minors, and therefore could not take decisions for themselves. Here again, a vulnerability which was a feature of human existence was true in an enhanced way for women, and therefore femaleness bore a particular mark of vulnerability.

I suggest that in the language which Schwenckfeld is using he is not only emphasising the *humanity* of Christ's flesh, but is also demonstrating a profound feminisation of that flesh. Christ was known to be human because in his flesh he was, like all humans, vulnerable. He was liable to injury and death and he gave up the right of self-determination. The vulnerability of the flesh was perceived most clearly in, and as a marker of, female bodily existence. It was the vulnerability of and the damage to the flesh of Christ which was the means of salvation. If I am right in my argument, then this associates Christ's flesh with female flesh. The Crucifixion, a death of pain, a destruction of life, and one inflicted at the hands of others, was, even with Schwenckfeld's particular emphasis on Incarnation rather than death as the centre of salvation, *the* significant feature of the story of Christ.

This has significant implications for the understanding not only of what it means to be female, but also for soteriology. If there is an identity between the saving flesh of Christ and female flesh, then the straightforward connection between female flesh and sinfulness that is often perceived is no longer as clear. In *Holy Feast and Holy Fast*, Bynum has presented a case that the extreme ascetic practices of certain women in the late Middle Ages were not an internalisation of body hatred and misogyny, as has often been asserted, but rather a deep assertion of identity between the saved believer and the suffering Christ who made salvation possible.[69] By his insistence that flesh continued to be part of the being of Christ following the exaltation and ascension Schwenckfeld refused the identification of flesh with sinfulness by its nature, and insisted that it was in and through the flesh that salvation was found. He also refused the idea that flesh was separate from God, and would be "lost" when God was found in final salvation. Because Christ continued in his "physical" existence following the ascension, flesh was taken into the being of the Godhead. This must clearly have had profound implications for the symbolic understanding of flesh – and therefore of those identified with flesh. The experience of body is now not one which separates, but which unites with

---

[69] Men and women might agree that female flesh was more fleshly than male flesh, but such an agreement led both sexes to see themselves as female-human. For it was human beings as *human* (not as symbol of divine) whom Christ saved in the Incarnation; it was body as flesh (not as spirit) that God became most graphically on the altar; it was human suffering (not human power) that Christ took on to redeem the world. Religious women in the later Middle Ages saw in their own female bodies not only a symbol of the humanness of both genders but also a symbol of - and a means of approach to - the humanity of God. Bynum, *Holy Feast and Holy Fast*, p. 296.

divinity. It is not a state to be saved from, but in. It does not define the nature of being, but is defined by the nature of being.

This latter point is particularly important when we are considering questions of gender. We have seen above how the alienation between God and humanity (and the rest of creation) was in part caused by an origin of creation rather than generation. The union between Christ and the father was dependent on the fact of Christ's generation by God the Father, his relation to him as son rather than creature. This extended to the flesh which was Christ's in the Incarnation. It was not that flesh separated Christ from God, but because the flesh was generated rather than created, there was a relationship. Thus, the nature of Christ's being defined the nature of his flesh. So, by extension, flesh is that which is defined by origin, rather than that which defines. The nature of being is not determined by being fleshly or otherwise. Flesh is determined by being created or fathered. This both puts a lower importance on the role of flesh, and allows for it, in its existence, to have a spiritual value. It is less important, because it does not, in and of itself, determine position before God. Rather, its value is determined by the position before God. It has spiritual value, because it can become, through salvation, that in which the encounter with God, and the embodying of the life of God is experienced. The symbolic feminisation of the flesh of Christ meant that real feminine flesh could be perceived differently. No longer did it have to be defined in terms of its fleshliness. Now there was the possibility that the position before God: that of believer, would actually determine the way the flesh was judged. In such a case, women were to be seen first as believers, then as women. This meant that roles and positions could be undertaken on the basis of ability, calling and activity rather than conventional gender roles.

The symbolic feminisation of the flesh of Christ in the state of humility which I am arguing is present on Schwenckfeld's theology may also have presented the same reversal of strength and weakness which Bynum suggests – and may therefore again have created another of these spaces which allowed women to find a theology to which they could respond. At the very least, the assertion that suffering flesh was also saving flesh controverted the other assertions that female flesh, by virtue of its suffering and weakness, was inherently inferior, and that suffering and sinfulness were intimately linked. The teaching that women's pains in childbirth – and all that went with that – were a direct result of the fall, and were God's punishment for that action, meant that the physical experience of women in that activity which was their defining feature was given a spiritual meaning. Pain in childbirth and lack of self-determination were because of sin.[70] Women's definitive experience therefore was focused on sin and guilt. That which was determinative of their being, childbearing, and subordination, was the sign of and result of the guilt which was peculiar to women by virtue of their sex. However, salvation comes

---

[70] Genesis 3:16; To the woman he said "I will greatly increase your pangs in childbearing: in pain you shall bring forth children, yet your desire shall be for your husband and he shall rule over you".

through a broken body, and one which has no self-determination, one which is feminised. If suffering was the means of salvation, then it could not also be, exclusively, a sign either of punishment or of weakness and distance from God.

Inherent or Contingent Maleness

The other area where such an emphasis on vulnerability as the means of salvation raises an interesting issue is the question of the maleness of the flesh of Christ. Despite my suggestion that there was a "feminisation" of the flesh of Christ, there was clearly no perception of the person, Jesus Christ, as anything other than a man. The body in which the Incarnation took place was, in its construction, (physical and social) male. At various points in Christian history, and perhaps especially in this century, as I have discussed above, there has been the question of whether the maleness of Jesus is inherent in the second person of the Trinity? Is the maleness of the Incarnate Jesus a functional necessity determined by the needs of a ministry in a patriarchal context or simply an accidental fact?

Such questions have implications both for soteriology and for ecclesiology. Soteriologically, the issue is whether, if the second person of the Trinity is to be understood as inherently male – and thus the maleness of Christ's flesh to be a fundamental expression of the nature of the divine being – women are saved in the way that men are. This debate centres on the understanding of salvation as rooted in the identity of Christ both with the divine and with the human. If the maleness is inherent, then the humanity with which the Saviour is identified is male. This puts in question the salvation of women *as* women. In the context of considering Schwenckfeld's theology, such a question is very sharply focused. Schwenckfeld clearly taught that in receiving the body and blood, and in the encounter which this mediated, the believer was taken into and identified with the divine being. If Schwenckfeld were working with an ontology which argued for the inherent maleness of the Second Person of the Trinity, then his theology would also demand that, for salvation to be complete, women would have to become male. And it is true that there he does appear to have held to a belief in the inherent maleness of the First Person of the Trinity. His understanding of the nature of fatherhood, and the need for a new origin as the means of salvation (fathered, not created) certainly argue that God the Father was, in Schwenckfeld's understanding, inherently male and not only metaphorically. However, there is nothing in his language, either explicit or implicit, about the nature of salvation and the way in which it is to be expressed which suggests that he expected women to become male either in order to be saved or as a consequence of salvation. Indeed, as we will see in the following chapter, it can be argued that he was quite clear that this was exactly what he was not saying.

However, there is still a soteriological issue here. We have seen that in terms of being life-creating, the flesh of Christ is symbolically male, while in its feeding and nurturing role, the flesh can be read as symbolically female. We have seen that there is at least a case for suggesting that, especially in its salvific activity, the vulnerable flesh of Christ also represents a female position. It does not seem, therefore, to be possible to be as definite about the inherent sexual identity of the Second Person of the Trinity as it is of the First. While the First Person of the Trinity is categorically male, because the only gender-defining characteristic which Schwenckfeld ascribes is that of fathering, with the Second Person there is this ambiguity. Once again, it is in the ambiguities that I suggest that space is found for women to interpret the gendering of the theology in ways which are freeing. I repeat what I said above, that there is no suggestion anywhere in Schwenckfeld's writing that the Incarnate Christ was anything other than male, or could have been anything other than male. However, the symbolic and the spiritual meaning of the flesh of Christ, the centre of salvation, is not so clearly defined. The ambiguity between male and female positioning is present, and this is enough to destabilise the categorisation. Once the link between physical attributes – that is, most fundamentally, the procreative role – and social gender position is severed, then other possibilities can be explored. That was precisely what Schwenckfeld's presentation of the flesh of Christ did. While physiologically male, this flesh played both male and female social roles. So, there was no reason why those who were physiologically female could not also explore a variety of social roles.

Nevertheless, before we come to a conclusion on this issue, there is another point to consider. This brings us to the ecclesiological issue. In many sacramental theologies, the Eucharistic celebrant is understood to be the presentation of the person of Jesus, re-presenting the sacrifice of Calvary. This has early roots in Christian thinking[71] and continues until the present. If the maleness of Christ is inherent, in the way discussed above, then the celebrant must be male. If Christ's maleness is contingent, then it is humanity which must be present at the altar, and the celebrant can be male or female. I have already discussed the issue of power which this involves in the chapter "Sexuality and Sacrament", but there is also the question of whether the physical and social gendering of Christ's body has soteriological significance. It certainly does not appear that Schwenckfeld had any notion that salvation applied to or was available to women and men in different ways. Indeed, if my argument about vulnerability is appropriate, then it might be claimed that women could have a particular sense of identity with the Saviour.

Nowhere does Schwenckfeld make any suggestion overtly of this sort, but the fact remains that there were so many women who responded to his theology. It is also suggestive that many of these women were, as I have also suggested above, "anomalous"; they did not fit the models which were

---

[71] For if Christ Jesus our Lord and God is himself the High Priest of God the Father and first offered himself as a sacrifice to the Father and ordered that this should be done in commemoration of him, then of course that priest functions rightly in the place of Christ who imitates what Christ did and offers in the church the true and full sacrifice, if so he begins to offer according to what he sees Christ himself to have offered. Cyprian of Carthage.

available for female existence under the new theologies, because they were single, widowed or childless. They did not, therefore, fit the physical role that their society was setting up for them at this point. What Schwenckfeld's model of embodiment seems to have provided was an alternative interpretation of what the body meant. It was neither an encumbrance which had to be discarded in order to permit a relationship with the divine, nor was it a snare and a trap. It was not, on the whole, either of these things for the other reformers. However, as we have seen, Schwenckfeld went further than simply to insist that having a body was not a spiritual handicap; his language, both about the being of Christ, and about the believer made it clear that it was by having, being and experiencing a body that salvation happened. Thus, once more, we find a theological reason for the response of women to his teaching.

The Glorified Flesh as the Place of Triumph

However, there is another area of discourse about the flesh of Christ, and that is in the second, the glorified state, which follows the Resurrection and Ascension. As I have already shown above, at some stage in the development of his theology Schwenckfeld began to explore that notion that the celestial flesh of Christ was a "physical" reality. It is the celestial flesh which the believer receives through inner feeding, and which creates new (saved) life. Celestial or glorified flesh is the presence of Christ in his "present" state. Most of the discussion about the nature of Christ's flesh was driven, as I have suggested above, by his Eucharistic theology. So we can find statements like:

> From all that has been said, about the origin, the conception and birth of Christ, and also about the completion and divinisation of the human in Christ, about the Transfiguration and Ascension of his flesh to God, we can see how necessary it is for Christian faith that one recognise the counsel and wisdom of God in the salvation of people, and to learn to judge the flesh of Christ properly according to its two states; then it will also be possible to understand why the Lord Christ said once "My flesh is a true food" and at another time "the flesh avails nothing."[72]

Following the Resurrection – by virtue of the Resurrection – all that is vulnerable is no longer part of the embodied existence of Christ. Schwenckfeld was not arguing that all that was *physical* was removed or destroyed. He insisted that Christ took that which was human in/of him to the heavenly realm. But it was not a straightforward loss of flesh. In his treatise on the flesh of Christ in 1540, he could state:

> In short and to speak of it in summary there are two births of the flesh of Christ to notice; one physical, according to which the flesh from God and Mary is born in a human being, come forth, grown and increased etc. According to this birth, Christ suffered, and submitted to death, the Cross all shame and neediness and all for the

---

[72] *CS*, vol. 7, p. 344, ll. 19f.

sake of human salvation; according to this birth his flesh also took flesh and was united with it to serve our holy salvation.[73]

He then contrasted this with the following

> The second birth of the flesh of Christ is completely spiritual, heavenly and divine, according to which the flesh in God is born to be God with God, because it is taken up into the divine essence, from death through the resurrection into life, from his human being through the renewing and transfiguring.[74]

However, he went on to insist:

> Not that it is extinguished in heaven, or destroyed through such a birth, and is no more a true flesh, but it is and remains even until today flesh, just so Christ remains today a true person, body and soul. [75]

Flesh is still present, but has a different meaning. Maier asks of this

> What, if anything, remains of the *human* qualities of the human nature of the glorified Christ? Here, obviously, is the weakest point in his entire Christological structure.

I believe that he has missed the point of Schwenckfeld's identification of *flesh* and *human*, and therefore does not realise that it is in the preservation of flesh that humanity is retained. Thus his suggestion two pages later (p.77) that "the human properties and attributes which are said to remain in the state of glory are mere tropes...little more than a concession to Chalcedonian orthodoxy", and the resultant explicit disagreement with what Schwenckfeld believed himself to be doing ("But the reformer would hasten to object.") is a recognition that Maier finds himself in the position of trying to explain a set of concepts while ignoring the central one. However, to adopt, as we have done here, the position that body is not a side but a central issue immediately allows a way of discussing this which is much more positive.

There is a difference between the two states of the flesh of Christ. But the difference was not that Christ gave up, left behind or was separated from that which marked him as human – having flesh – but rather that this flesh was no longer vulnerable and unable to determine its own being. The language Schwenckfeld used to speak of the post-Resurrection Christ is physical. Maier characterises it in this way:

> Far from surrendering his humanity, the glorified Christ had attained the very highest development which God had intended for man.[76]

---

[73] *CS*, vol. 7, p. 342, ll. 34f.
[74] *CS*, vol. 7, p. 343, ll. 19f.
[75] *CS*, vol. 7, p. 343, ll. 29 ff.

As with McLaughlin's language cited at the beginning of this chapter, we must ask in what way Maier is using the term man, and how he understands Schwenckfeld to be using it. Does Maier literally mean "man" as the sum of human being, or is it a generic term?[77] Does he believe Schwenckfeld is using it literally or generically, and what does Schwenckfeld's language suggest? The language which Schwenckfeld used is of glory, and of power. For example:

> ...Christ is now the ruler of the Kingdom of God, an eternal high priest mediator and king, also the head of his body and our complete Saviour.[78]

together with regular use of the words glory, majesty, power, strength and might.[79] These are words and images which, sociologically, carry with them an assumption of masculinity, and elite masculinity at that. In contemporary power structures, in theory if not always in practice, men and women functioned in an unequal way. Men, and elite men in particular were the ones who had the glory, power and strength and so on. Thus the descriptions of the post-Resurrection Christ exploit language which is significantly gendered, – indeed, as clearly marked as the language of vulnerability.

If, therefore, we can make a distinction between a *feminised* flesh in the state of humiliation and the *masculinized* glorified flesh, then we might justifiably claim that there is a way here of understanding something of what Schwenckfeld meant by celestial or glorified flesh – and the distinction that he drew was between male and female. The humiliated, suffering – and saving – Christ was in a feminised position, while the raised, glorified and reigning Christ was to be understood in masculine terms. This in itself would form a suggestive contrast – Christ as the dying Saviour presenting a feminised image: Christ as the glorious Victor, a masculine one. But I want to argue that something more was going on.

If in Schwenckfeld's thought there is a move in the conceptualising of Christ's flesh from feminine to masculine, it ought to be possible to suggest that this is part of the same pattern – a move from what is earthly and weak, as represented by the humiliated Christ who has feminised flesh, to that which is heavenly and strong, represented by the glorified Christ, a masculine figure. If that were so, we come back again to the position that the argument might continue that for women to be saved, particularly in the light of Schwenckfeld's assertion that salvation is becoming that which Christ is, would mean that women had to be gendered male.

Nevertheless, there are two factors which mean that we cannot make this assumption. Firstly as I have argued in various places, Schwenckfeld appeared to insist in several contexts that gender was irrelevant to salvation status. It is on this assertion that I have based the claim that women found a particularly

---

[76] Maier, *Caspar Schwenckfeld on the Person and Work of Christ*, p. 77.

[77] Maier, *Caspar Schwenckfeld on the Person and Work of Christ*, p. 75.

[78] *CS*, vol. 11, p. 778, ll. 24 f.

[79] Maier, *Caspar Schwenckfeld on the Person and Work of Christ*, p. 73.

sympathetic home in Schwenckfelder theology.

The Continuation of Christ's Flesh

Secondly, there is the language of flesh and body. The argument that women are saved by becoming men appears to be inseparable from the necessity for women to disregard or separate themselves from their physical existence – salvation involves being re-gendered male precisely because flesh is not part of salvation. However, in speaking of the glorified Christ in male terms, it is precisely of flesh or body that Schwenkfeld was speaking. He was using physical language of the reigning Christ – and of the believer's encounter, through which salvation is mediated. This is made explicit in the discussion of the two states to which I referred above. Having discussed the human reality of Christ's flesh in its state of humility, he contrasts this with the development, not of Christ's flesh in heaven, but of the believer's flesh in salvation:

> According to the first state, Christ was born of our flesh and bone in human physical life. (Heb 2:16)According to the second state, we will be reborn again out of his flesh and out of his bone in the divine spiritual life. (Eph 5:30) We are members of his body, from his flesh and from his bone.[80]

In discussing the development of this life, he spoke of food, drink and eating, insisting that it was a "true" food, drink, act of eating – the same language and the same insistence of Mary's motherhood of Christ. Schwenckfeld appears to have been adamantly refusing to allow the discourse to be cut off from some sort of physical reality.

So, although he speaks of the glorified Christ in male terms, that does not allow us to make the inference that salvation is to do with the abandonment of femaleness. Flesh is still part of the equation. To be saved did not mean to be separated from the body (and so by inference, symbolically, from the female) but to have the body and soul transformed together through an encounter (rebirth, eating and drinking) with a different kind of body.

It would be tremendously satisfying to assert that one of the reasons why so many women responded to Schwenckfeld's theology was because he overturned the assumption that to be saved meant to adopt a male persona – satisfying, but inappropriate. Clearly this was not what Schwenckfeld was saying. On the other hand, neither was he saying that it was necessary for women to cease to be women. Rather, we find evidence here as we have found elsewhere, firstly, that Schwenckfeld's assumptions about gender, and the effect of the assumptions on the shaping of the rest of his thought is profound and more subtle than might at first be assumed, and secondly, one of those assumptions is that gender is irrelevant to the status of the believer.

The consequence of the second of these assertions is that, while Schwenckfeld made no overt claims to equality of the sexes, nor did he

---

[80] *CS*, vol. 8, p. 739, ll. 21f.

challenge the social status quo, he did, as I have argued before, provide a theology within which women could find a place without becoming alienated from the basic cultural construction of their gender.

In a letter to the women in Isny, amongst his most frequent correspondents, we read:

> I see from your letter that some accuse or gossip of me as a woman's preacher, about which I am neither annoyed or complaining. Would to God in the grace of Christ I might only serve more devout women to their soul's salvation and the saving knowledge of Christ. [81]

He went on to speak of evidence from Christian history both about women as strong Christians and about men who were known for preaching to women in particular. Then he continued:

> So it is therefore nothing new or strange if some say also of me that I am a woman's preacher. The Lord Christ only wants to make me capable and worthy of it. But I hope that no woman is annoyed by my teaching, nor has become disobedient to her husband in godly fitting things. I also seek nothing other for women than for men; namely their salvation and to teach them in Christ our Lord to walk in all honour and fear of God. You might (if you will), give this as an answer to those who call me a woman's preacher, and I say that I am not at all annoyed by it.[82]

With his argument that women were to be taught and expected to respond in the same way as men, Schwenckfeld was side-stepping and discounting what had been a significant question in Christian thinking. While on the whole there had never been serious question that women needed and could gain salvation in parallel with men, there had frequently also been the additional question of their embodiment. Women, in symbolic terms, were so clearly identified with corporeality, and particularly with childbearing, that this became a particular factor in the question of their salvation. This direction to the women at Isny shows that Schwenckfeld simply laid that to one side. The shape of his theology, and the foundations on which it was built meant that it was possible for him to work with the assumption that gender was irrelevant before God. While, biologically, his understanding of male and female functions was clear and fixed, because of the ambiguity in his understanding of the function of the actual flesh of Christ: −male in giving life, female in feeding, female in weakness, male in triumph, − the identification of bodily reality and gender identity was not straightforward.

Since salvation was the identity of Christ and the believer, and the transformation of the believer into the likeness of Christ, the possibility of the separation of body and gender opened up for the believer. Schwenckfeld's

---

[81] *CS*, vol. 11, p. 930, ll. 12f.
[82] *CS*, vol. 11, p. 930, ll. 15f.

insistence that flesh was not the cause of alienation, nor to be abandoned at salvation, reshaped one of the most significant traditions in Christian theology, and one which had always been particularly limiting for women's activities. Without deliberately stating a desire to change the position of women, he still enabled them to explore new possibilities. More importantly, women found in his theology and the practices which it generated the opportunity to reshape their religious position. Perhaps because he did not explore this explicitly, it was not a case of a man telling women what was right and proper. Rather, what we seem to have is a pragmatic theologian who found himself brought to certain positions about bodies, gender and their meaning by the impetus of the argument. These positions were not what his main discussion was about. Therefore, he did not spend time dealing with the implications. Such a lack of interest in what his theology actually said about women, bodies and gender, especially when so many of his followers were women, is in itself indicative that he believed gender to be irrelevant in theological, especially salvation questions. Other reformers spent much more time considering these issues precisely because they could not make the assumption that before God, women and men were the same.

Those who adopted his theology likewise did not agonise over these questions. But the implications became clearer when the women found the psychic, spiritual and physical space to act in these new ways. In a world in which reality was profoundly shaped by the boundaries of body and gender, Schwenckfeld was making deeply subversive assertions and his followers were exploring dangerous possibilities.

Chapter 5

Men, Women and God

As we saw in the previous chapter, for Schwenckfeld, salvation was to be found in identity with Christ. This identity was not, as Luther argued, the giving of an alien righteousness, nor was it, as the Anabaptists suggested, entirely shaped by living a life modelled on the living of Christ. For Schwenckfeld, as might by now be expected, the identity was found in much more physical terms and explored through a biological image. The relationship between the First and the Second Persons of the Trinity was that of father and son. God the Father was – in a manner of speaking – the *biological* father of God the Son in Christ: it was from God's fathering, begetting, that Christ's Incarnate being took its existence. This was expressed in physical flesh and blood, and the flesh was not something which was shed or lost at the Ascension, but which was part of the Godhead, and was also that which gave life to the believer. In this chapter, I will consider firstly the way in which this new life came into being, and its pattern, and then, in the second part, the way in which Schwenckfeld understood the patterns of development in the new life. That will give us the opportunity to look at some of the images he used in his writings, the way in which he used them, and also some of the key concepts in his exploration of the nature of faith.

The New Life

For the believer, the new life, of faith and salvation, was parallel to that of Christ. In the state of alienation, people existed as creations of God. He was their origin as Creator. The move from alienation to salvation was the move from creature to being child. This is child not as infant (although that had its impact in the discussion), but child as offspring, as biological descendant. The Christian was saved by coming into the same relationship with God as Christ had; that of child to father rather than creature to creator.

> Thus God the almighty and Creator must take again newly the lost, ruined person, so that He is not only his Creator but also his Father, so that He bears him again and renews him; that is, so that he, for the sake of his beloved Son, Jesus Christ, (death, torment and spilling of blood) gives him all the various gracious gifts that

he lacks for salvation, which will set him up from the Fall, will clean him from sin and make him justified and pious before His sight.[1]

All of this perception was part of Schwenckfeld's fundamental separation of inner and outer. We have seen through the whole discussion how he insisted that that which was outer could not mediate that which was inner. We have also seen that in his understanding, inner and outer were not simply to be mapped onto spiritual and physical. The being of Christ, identified as it was with flesh, firstly in the Incarnation and continuing in the food which was the origin of life for the believer, was not to be understood as non-physical. What made it inner was not its separation from the physical world, but its origin in God's fathering activity, rather than his creative activity. Schwenckfeld was quite clear and explicit that there was a difference between the two, and it could be seen in the difference between Christ and the rest of humanity, figured by Adam:

> Just as the first old Adam had his origin from God the creator, who created his flesh from the clay of the earth; the earth has served the creator for such work and supplied its material in the figure; "This was a type of the future", Rom 5; 14. Thus the second Adam, Jesus Christ has his origin from God the father, who has, through a new working of his Spirit, generated and given birth to the flesh of Christ from the flesh of the holy Virgin (who in a new bearing work of God is set over against the created earth).[2]

The dualism which was the motive force for Schwenckfeld's theology, and from which it took all of its shape was a dualism of origins. He did not work with a model which suggested that there were equal and opposing forces of good and evil, and that created matter was a result of an evil will. He did not argue that matter in and of itself separated humanity from God. All matter had its origin in God. Some was created, and therefore did not have divine identity. It was alienated from God, and therefore subject to sin. The flesh which was Christ's body – and the flesh into which believers were called – was fathered by God. Its origin and identity was therefore divine and, in Schwenckfeld's categories, inner.

The centre of Schwenckfeld's soteriology, therefore, is the movement of the believer from the realm of outer createdness to that of inner biological descent. In this chapter, I will be particularly concerned with the consideration of how Schwenckfeld dealt with the nature of this movement, and the patterns he developed for discussing it.

Rebirth

The primary motif for explaining this movement in his writings was *rebirth,* the

---

[1] *CS*, vol. 17, p. 74, ll. 19f.

[2] *CS*, vol. 14, p. 321, ll. 15f.

consequence of which was a "new person".[3] Furcha has pointed out that this motif dominates Schwenckfeld's thought, and has also shown that this is clearly linked with a dependence on the Gospel of John.[4] This is not surprising, since it is only in that gospel that the teaching about rebirth or new birth appears in the teaching of Jesus.[5]

The image of rebirth is a common metaphor in Christian writing, and one of the intriguing things about the use of this language is the dominant place it has had in Christian thinking. It is by no means the most common type of language used either in gospels or epistles to describe or prescribe the experience of the encounter with Christ and the resultant life change. Paul used language around images of clothing and unclothing, dying and rising, and drawing on the law courts.[6] Jesus spoke more often about following and travelling, and also spoke of taking up the cross, with its implications of dying.[7] But this one use of the picture of new birth has exercised what appears to be an inordinate influence over Christian thought and description. It was certainly a deeply important image for Schwenckfeld, but he did not only use it within the type of context in which it appears in John's gospel, that is, exhortatory. His writing is not so much concerned with telling people that they must be born again, as exploring what it means to have been born again: to have started on this new life.

That it is fundamental is quite clear. There are statements like:

> May God the heavenly Father bear us again through Jesus Christ his beloved Son in our hearts, so that we are God's children, inheritors of his heavenly Kingdom and brothers in Christ.[8]

This is taken from the beginning of a letter to an enquirer who seems to have been involved in discussion with Lutherans, and was looking for clarification. In a document of 1558 in which Schwenckfeld was criticising a statement of faith, probably the Articles of the Frankfurter-Recess, an attempt to bring unity to Lutheranism, he wrote:

---

[3] "newe mensch"

[4] Furcha, *Caspar Schwenckfeld's Concept of the New Man*, pp. 42 and 54.

[5] John 3: 3 "Jesus answered him, "Very truly I tell you, no-one can enter the Kingdom of God without being born from above/again" *New Revised Standard Version*. The Greek text is ambiguous. The word can mean "from above" or "again", and either would appear to fit the discourse.

[6] See for example Rom 13:14, Gal 3:27, Eph 4:24 for clothing language; Rom 6:4, 8, Col 2:20 for death language; Rom chaps 4-5, Gal 3:11 passim for law-court language. Paul does not use the language of birth in his description of passing from one life to another. That language appears only in the Gospel and the Epistles of John. Given Schwenckfeld's marked preference for the Gospel of John as a source for Eucharistic thinking, it is not surprising that the other patterns of thought reflected in these writings are also important to him.

[7] For Jesus' language, see Matt 4:19, 16:24, John 10:27 as examples.

[8] *CS*, vol. 9, p. 221, ll. 5f.

Also, how can obedience to God begin in the old creature, in whom flesh resists the spirit? Yes, what is such new obedience of the old Adam other than the appearance without rebirth? Which is the beginning of God's work in the conversion of the sinner.[9]

There are also longer pieces such as his discussion of John 3:16, written between 1546 and 1550, when he wrote a series of devotional and exegetical expositions, almost model sermons. Within the postil on John 3, he wrote a four-page discussion on the meaning of the phrase "to be born again", and included such statements as:

Rebirth is such a work of God wherein the dead live, the stained are cleansed, the spoiled improved, the lost brought back, therein all the old godless being is in the name, that is in the strength of the Lord Christ and his Spirit, born from above before God (notice, before God) from heavenly water, which is God's word, Christ, the seed of all the children of God, and from the Spirit.[10]

Further:

Since then the Lord Jesus Christ said here "Unless a man is born from above, he cannot see the Kingdom of God", so it is necessary before all things that each person if he really wants to be saved and please the pure eyes of God, perceive clearly and eagerly the rebirth within himself, in his heart, soul and conscience.[11]

Language like this, and the ideas which cluster around the metaphor occur in many places in Schwenckfeld's writings, and this clearly functioned as an important category of thought for him. The move from creature to offspring, which was the move from damnation to salvation, was almost entirely expressed in this metaphor. However, one of the intriguing things about the way in which Schwenckfeld used the language is exactly this question of to what extent he treated this as a metaphor. I suggest that, for Schwenckfeld, this image of new birth and the systematic way in which he investigated and exploited it demonstrate that, for him, this functioned not *simply* as a conscious metaphor or a way of seeing, but as a construction of the world, and specifically of anthropology.

Schwenckfeld's Use of Metaphor

It will be useful at this point to consider the way in which metaphors work, and how Schwenckfeld and his contemporaries were using them in discussing the questions of the faith. Modern linguistic theory suggests that all language is metaphorical, in that it is a way of pointing to something beyond itself; the

---

[9] *CS*, vol. 16, p. 355, ll. 3f.
[10] *CS*, vol. 10, p. 294, ll. 22f.
[11] *CS*, vol. 10, p. 297, ll. 37f.

word is not the object, but indicates it. Religious language is metaphorical in a more restricted sense, for the reality to which it claims to point is never open to direct encounter except through language. The model of the sliding scale is a helpful way of conceptualising the relation of language to external reality.[12] The closer language is to the external reality to which it points, the less implicative and the more explicative statements it will contain. The more recognisably metaphorical language is, the more implicative and less explicative it is. Thus, the words of Jesus to Nicodemus, "no-one can see the Kingdom of God except he be born again,"[13] are clearly at the metaphorical end of the scale in this sense, because they contain little in the way of explicative sentences. By contrast, Schwenckfeld's use of the same metaphor was, in fact, strongly explicative, and indicates that he understood the language he was using as tending towards a literal statement. His language indicates that he understood himself not to be pointing towards something which could only be discussed in pictures and suggestions, but to a reality which could be defined and explored. Thus, however metaphorical his language may appear to the reader, the amount of explication which he used demonstrates his commitment to the notion that this was the way the world was to be understood.

One of the clearest places where this thinking is shown is in a document of Crautwald's which Schwenckfeld published in 1542: *Novus Homo*. Various Latin and German editions were produced, at least one of which Schwenckfeld was responsible for editing and publishing. The writing appeared in several collections of those known to be friends and followers of Schwenckfeld. The text starts with a discussion not of John 3:16, but of Jesus' description of the necessity to become like a little child in order to inherit the Kingdom.[14] Crautwald commented:

> With these words the Lord clearly indicates that all flesh, however old, however clever, however learned and skilful it may be, is not worthy or deserving of heaven. unless it be converted and become like a child, newborn, small and humble in Christ.[15]

From this starting point Crautwald went on to discuss the meaning of such birth and its consequences, focusing on birth itself, despite the fact that that is not the language in the passage he was discussing. This is another indication of the importance of this metaphor: that it was seen, or imported, in situations where it was not the controlling thrust of the original text. A central part of the discussion is taken up with enumerating the elements in the metaphor.

---

[12] For further discussion on this see Diane Blakemore, *Understanding Utterances: An Introduction to Pragmatics*, Massachusetts: Blackwell, 1992, pp. 50-52.

[13] John 3:3.

[14] See Mark 9:36, cf Luke 9:47. What makes the use of these words interesting in this context is that Jesus was not speaking of rebirth, but of a child-like approach, and he made it very clear that this was metaphorical language.

[15] *CS*, vol. 8, p. 47, ll. 14f.

Crautwald then goes on to outline questions he thinks people might ask, such as what is the seed, the womb, the mother and so on? He laid out very clearly his answers to these questions. Firstly, fatherhood resides firmly in God, and that is the essence of salvation:

> With Christ he has made us alive, risen with him, and made us heavenly in Christ Jesus to the praise of the splendour of his grace, through his kindness to us through Christ Jesus, so that now God is not only our creator, but has also become our father, though his beloved Son, Jesus Christ our Lord.[16]

This is distinct from the role of creator. The discussion continued:

> Now we want to say more of the conception of the new person and the birth and life of the same. The seed through which the birth of the new creature is formed in a person is the living word of God.[17]

This is followed by a string of biblical references to exemplify it, and then come the two paragraphs:

> The mother of this new heavenly child is the grace of God and the Spirit of Jesus, yes the bowels of Jesus Christ. Gal 4:6: The Jerusalem which is from above, which is the mother of us all. The womb or body wherein this child is carried is the lap of the heart and the flesh in which the new person is produced, grows and wherein he lives.[18]

Crautwald here was using physical language. The language is so strongly physical that it suggests that this is something more than the simple explanatory metaphor. The detail beyond the way in which such language is usually used as metaphor, and certainly beyond the way the metaphor is extended in either the gospels or the Epistles. This becomes even clearer when we examine the way in which Schwenckfeld used the concepts. As well as publishing Crautwald's discussion, and using it as a basis for his own description, Schwenckfeld worked through it in slightly different ways. He systematised the discussion, bringing it into connection with his understanding of the two orders, and the way in which they were or were not connected. He took the physical aspect of the whole language field into new realms, and worked with it in an even more concrete manner. In his theological understanding, the notion of rebirth was not one picture among many to describe the result of a saving encounter and the

---

[16] *CS*, vol. 8, p. 55, ll. 33f.

[17] *CS*, vol. 8, p. 65, ll. 16f.

[18] Die müter dises newen himlischen kinds/ ist die gnad Gottes/ und der gaist Christi/ Ja die inngewaid Jesu Christi/ Gala 4:26 Das Jerusalem das droben ist/ welches unnser aller müter ist.
Der bauch oder leib darinnen diß kind wird getragen/ ist die schoß des hertzens/ und das flaisch in welchem der new mensch wirt erzeuget/ wechßt/ darinnen er auch wonet. *CS*, vol. 8, p. 65, ll. 30f.

ongoing process of salvation. It was a physical-ontological reality which was the literal way of describing what it meant to be saved. Thus, for example, in the postil on John 3, he wrote:

> And in the same way that the first Eve was created by God as a mother of all natural people from the model of the first Adam, so the second Eve that is the Christian Church, is produced and born in truth from the second Adam, from his flesh and bone, by God the Father, through the Holy Spirit.[19]

So, in this development of the image, while God is still clearly the father, this time the mother is the church, and the "stuff" from which the new being is produced is the flesh and bone of Christ, rather than the physical being of the old person as Crautwald seemed to suggest.

Duality of Origins for the New Person

Again the roles of Father and Creator are carefully distinguished. This is part of the fundamental patterning of Schwenckfeld's thought, and we have seen how it was basic to his Christology – that which is created is not of the same order as the Divine. Here we see that it was also part of his anthropology. Christ is not created but is born of God. The believer, who is to be brought into relationship with God, must exist in the same way. That is the fundamental difference between the old and the new person -- the one is created and the other is born. To one God is Creator and to the other Father. God is the origin of both. There is no dualism here which suggests that creation is evil, or originates from outside God. But God has two means of originating; creating and fathering. While it is assumed, it is not required that creation is a male act. The giving of life, however, as I have discussed elsewhere, is part of the meaning of maleness, part of the way in which it is defined. Thus the constant insistence in any discussion of this model that God is Father is a reiteration of the maleness of God. This is not simply an inconsequential fact, but is fundamental to the being of God and therefore of the believer. It is by virtue of God's begetting, as male, that the believer is a new person.

Schwenckfeld clearly expects people to be asking for the kind of anatomical detail he is providing. In one set of discussions, he entitled a section "On the Father and Mother of a Christian Person" [20]and answered the question this way:

> About the Father of a Christian person there needs to be no further question, but look to the Scriptures. It is the almighty, merciful God who, through his only beloved son spiritually generates many children, as he also through one leads them all to the heavenly glory.[21]

---

[19] *CS*, vol. 10, p. 298, ll. 29f.
[20] "Vom vatter und mütter eines Christen menschens". *CS*, vol. 17, p. 383, l. 21.
[21] *CS*, vol. 17, p. 383, ll. 23f.

However, he was not content to leave the question there, nor did he expect his readers to. After discussing fatherhood in more detail, he then returned to the question of biology, and continued:

> But if you ask about the mother of the Christian person and the child of God, you should know that properly speaking, he has no physical mother, just as there is no physical father, for a Christian is not physically born, but spiritually reborn; his mother is the grace and mercy of God, the viscera or inner strength of Jesus Christ in the heart of the person.[22]

This is a complex passage, for on the one hand Schwenckfeld is insisting that there is no physical component to the birth, while on the other the metaphor which he uses, of *viscera* is strongly physical. We are reminded in this discussion again of Schwenckfeld's inability to consider a reality which does not have a physical presence. This is further reinforced when we consider this passage:

> Thus, he [Christ] produces them from himself, from his own innards, flesh and bones. Therefore I might now say He is father and mother, but because he himself is the grace of God, so it is fitting that we say the grace of God is our mother which is the mother of the Christian church, and say it freely also of the heavenly Jerusalem from which the water, out of which we are born from above, generously flows purifying and renewing us, which is also called the Holy Spirit.[23]

Again, there is a very physical image of the nature of this "motherhood". It is, of course, entirely in keeping with the biology we have already found reflected in Schwenckfeld's writing, which identifies the role of mother with the provision of the "stuff" of being. The presentation of Christ as the one from whom the "stuff" comes, and therefore in the "motherly" role also confirms the suggestions which I made in the consideration of the Eucharist. As the one from whom new life comes, and by whom the new person is nourished, Christ stands in relation to the believer as mother. In this kind of discussion, such a point was made explicit. It is worth noting in passing that Furcha comments on this passage in Schwenckfeld's writing that "God is both father and mother of the new-born creature".[24] This is, I believe, to misread the passage to some extent. While Schwenckfeld insisted that in Christ the fullness of the Divine

---

[22] *CS*, vol. 17, p. 384, ll. 14f.

[23] "Drumb so wirt sie auß ihm selbst erzeügt/ auß seinem eingeweide/ fliesch unnd gebeinen/ Da möcht ich nun sagen/ Er ist vatter und Muter/ Dieweil aber Er die gnade Gottes selbst ist/ so wills sich baß schicken/ daß wir sagen/ die gnade Gottes seÿ unser Muter/ daß ist der Christlichen kirchen Muter/ Unnd heist freilich auch daß himlische Jerusalem/ auß welchem die Wasser/ darauß wir/ von oben herab geboren werden/ mitiglich fleissen/ unns reinigen unnd ernewern/ Die sunst auch der H Geist heissen". *CS*, vol. 15, p. 188, ll. 8f.

[24] Furcha, *Caspar Schwenckfeld's Concept of the New Man*, p. 85.

was present, still, he made a very clear distinction between the roles of Father and of Son in the process of rebirth. It is clear in this passage that it is the Second Person of the Trinity to whom he is referring, and not God the Father. The fatherhood of God the Father is never compromised, because it is fundamental to his being. It is in the person of the Son that roles are less clearly defined and limited. This is another instance of Schwenckfeld's shifting of gender patterns and expectations. The notion of Christ as mother is, as we have seen, by no means unusual. What does seem to be new is the anatomical detail with which Schwenckfeld worked out this metaphor. He appears to have been quite clear that he was not saying Christ was *like* a mother. That was a much more common use of such an image: the idea that, metaphorically, in terms of nurturing and caring, Christ functioned in the way that a mother did. Rather, Schwenckfeld was arguing that, in spiritual biological terms, Christ was the mother of the believer; it was from the stuff of Christ that the new person took reality. Thus we find passages like this:

> Since, then, all Christian people have their descent, foundation and origin from this one man Jesus Christ, from his flesh and his bone (Eph 5:30), so they need to learn and to know whether the man, Christ is a natural creaturely person, as we are natural people, or a divine heavenly person.[25]

In this passage, we clearly find echoes of Mary's role in the being of Christ. The "stuff" from which the new believer is made is the "stuff" of Christ's being, his flesh and bone. Thus, in the Aristotelian model which we have seen Schwenckfeld use, Christ is the material, maternal partner in the birth of the believer. We must note however, that Schwenckfeld is very careful never to say that Christ is mother without qualifying it carefully – and even then, only uses such an image very occasionally.

The maternal role was not the only role that he presented Christ as playing in the process. He also regularly spoke of Christ as the seed, *samen*, through which the new believer came into being:

> The rebirth is a becoming alive before God…through our Lord, Jesus Christ, who is also the originator of the new birth as he is both the word and the seed through which God's children are born.[26]

I have discussed logos theology and its connection with biology in chapter three. In this statement, we see the connection laid out very clearly. It is obvious that Schwenckfeld was thinking of the rebirth of the children of God in strongly biological terms, and pursuing the biological implications of his theology as a way of making sense of it. The problem which his biology then posed for him is seen in the position he found it necessary to give to Christ: Christ is both female, in providing "stuff" and nourishment for the new person,

[25]*CS*, vol. 6, p. 513, ll. 20f.
[26]*CS*, vol. 17, p. 83, ll. 35f.

and male, as the seed which provokes the new birth.

It is this kind of ambiguity which underlies the destabilising approach to gender found in Schwenkfeld's writings. While never asserting that Jesus Christ in his bodily existence was female, in terms of role and presence, Schwenckfeld quite clearly, and at times explicitly, casts him in the female role. Many other writers, dealing with this aspect of theological discussion move into explicitly metaphorical language rather than becoming too closely entwined with the possibility of physical reality. Schwenckfeld, on the other hand, moves to a position which is even more insistently non-metaphorical. Thus, he demonstrated that physical reality and gender activity were not to be wholly identified. This then opened up the possibility that the physical reality of the believer did not entirely determine the gender position of that believer in the world. Such an assertion would have put him into direct opposition to the accepted assumptions of his age. Although, as we have seen, at one level, physical reality was held to be fluid, yet still there was a clear link between the reproductive reality of an individual and the social and gendered place which an individual held in a society.[27]

The Nature of Salvation

It was this rebirth through Christ and from Christ which made possible the position of being saved. To be in the natural state, that is, without Christ and the rebirth which comes through him, was to be separated from God and from the possibility of salvation. Salvation comes only through Christ, and sharing the identity which comes through the rebirth. Seguenny has argued that the difference between Christ's body and that of other humans is simply that of "moral properties".[28] The consequence of that could be that Schwenckfeld's theology led to a form of belief in auto-salvation. However, this is clearly not the case, and I believe that Seguenny is wrong in this assessment. It was not, or at least not *simply,* moral qualities which distinguished Christ's body from that of other humans: it was also the question of origins. Christ's body was one which was *fathered* by God, as I have demonstrated above, while the body and being of the "natural" person was *created* by God. Salvation was the move to being a child of God, which involved not simply a metaphorical rebirth, but a real one, which could be described in biological detail and which opened the way for growth in sanctification.

In one passage discussing the rebirth of the new person, Schwenckfeld made this parallel quite clear:

---

[27] See for example, Luther's notorious comment in his Tabletalk: "Men have broad and large chests, and small narrow hips and more understanding than the women, who have but small and narrow breasts and broad hips, to the end they should remain at home, sit still, keep house, and bear and bring up children". *Table Talk*, Martin Luther, translated by William Hazlitt, p. 334.

[28] Seguenny, *The Christology of Caspar Schwenckfeld*, p. 87.

As out of Mary the holy Virgin the Word of God has become flesh through the Holy Spirit in faith through new birth, so the flesh in the heart of a person is reborn in God for renewal.[29]

It was not that Schwenckfeld had no sense of sin, or of the need for salvation from it. Nowhere did he suggest that the rebirth and growth of the Christian is a natural process. He spoke powerfully about the reality of sin and its consequences. His starting point for considering human existence was the reality of sin in the life of each person, and the conviction that it could only lead to one end (though even here, he made the distinction between inner and outer):

Sin is a contradiction and disobedience of God, an evil, evil thing (Rom 7:11), inherited by us all from Adam, though which the whole human race is corrupted...There are two sins; the inner sin, which is the desire and law of the members and the outer sin, which is in dead works and evil living.[30]

He could write, in conventional Augustinian terms:

This evil sin has put the curse and judgement of God over us, so that the human heart is completely disturbed and made inappropriate for all good.[31]

Sin was not to be understood simply as the wrong deeds which an individual did in the course of his or her life, but was a state of existence inherent in the experience of being human. This sin, because it was inherent, was part of each faculty of a human. This was the meaning of total depravity: not that each individual was completely sinful, but that there was no aspect of a person's being which was not affected by the reality of sin:

Philosophy and the judgement of reason cannot, I say, understand the damage of sin. Philosophy cannot reach to the destruction of human nature (which has come in through disobedience and the Devil's poison) together with the inherited impurity of the heart, and that is why it calls sin only what is done with outer works against the goodness of the law and against God's will. Philosophy does not see that Adam with his fall has not just stained works, nor even emotions, desires or will, but has ruined and misdirected our whole human nature. [32]

The consequence of this sin is that humanity was separated from God, and from its own essential nature. In this Schwenckfeld was saying nothing new or unusual. But the separation as far as Schwenckfeld was concerned was not fully covered by such language, for there was also the inherent separation of orders, the created from the uncreated. This was not to be understood simply as a

---

[29] *CS*, vol. 17, p. 375, ll. 11f.
[30] *CS*, vol. 9, p. 159, ll. 37f.
[31] *CS*, vol. 7, p. 819, ll. 30f.
[32] *CS*, vol. 17, p. 68, ll. 17f.

matter of sinfulness. His language about the orders makes it clear that this was the nature of reality from the creation.[33]

He was also convinced that there is a moral requirement to live in the new life that comes from rebirth. His split from Luther had its origins in the distress he felt over the lack of moral improvement in the behaviour of those whose lives should be shaped by a new theology and experience. This was much deeper than simply a moral crusade. It involved his understanding of what it meant to be human. In the debate with Erasmus in 1524, Luther made it clear that he believed that free will was not an attribute of the human person. In *De Servo Arbitrio* he laid out his understanding of a will which must be under the power of either God or the Devil, but was certainly not under the control of the individual. This was at the heart of his argument about the doctrine of election and predestination. In 1546, Schwenckfeld printed a pamphlet called *Von Dreierlai Leben der Menschen*, in which, among other topics, he discussed the question of free will. This is a discussion which was central to the competing theologies of the Reformation, exploring, as it did, the understanding of human nature, and the relationship between the individual and God. It was also the thinking which showed in its clearest form the implications of belief in a doctrine of salvation only on the basis of faith. Because it is so complicated, I want to give the full flavour of his argument by quoting a long section. He outlined the issue like this:

> The third error is about free will with regard to good works, about which there are two parties, one turning the track to the right and the other to the left. Thus it is that one party admits and says of the will and potential of the natural human all too much; the person has also now after Adam's fall by nature a free will to do good works which please God to salvation, that they with natural strength may earn the highest grace of righteousness through fitting good works and also abstaining from sin.

> But the other party says the opposite, that the person, yes, even a Christ-believing person, has absolutely no free will, whether to do good or evil works, or to be obedient to God, nor to abstain from sin, but that all things happen from an unavoidable need according to the plan of God who works everything in all, as before Wycliff had taught and held.

> But now on such a point about free will we want to distinguish according to the witness of Scripture, thus namely that the natural person certainly has a free will, but only in outer works to do or to leave, and in the works which pertain to this

---

[33] See for example Maron, *Individualismus und Gemeinschaft*, p. 62, where he argues: "Nova vita ist für Schwenckfeld also keine irgendwie zu verstehende ethische Sache oder Neuformierung des menschlichen Willens, sondern ganz real die ontologische Anwesenheit des Novus homo in nobis".

life, be they good or evil. Such works each person can freely do or leave from the strength of his own will.

The will of the natural person, I say, stretches with its freedom, strength and possibility no further than to an outer human righteousness or piety (which likewise also God requires from all people and as said before the same is rewarded well temporally – as well as the unrighteousness and all evil according to its deserts here and eternally punishes.) But because the human heart, yes his whole nature, soul and conscience with all their strength through the sin of Adam's fall has been completely ruined, made crafty and nothing, so it is also impossible for his will to do the good works which serve for eternal life, not only to accomplish them, but also to inspire them, so that the person in this regard has no free will nor skill for good works: and just as little is he able to lay off or muffle his sinful emotion or inner evil desires from his own strength, before God or to know God and his Kingdom as is written in 1 Cor 2:14 "The natural person knows nothing of the Spirit of God. It is all foolishness to him". And Rom 8:6 "To think fleshly is enmity with God, since it is not subject to the law of God, for it can also accomplish nothing", says Paul.

But after a person is brought back to grace through Christ, new born, believing, and has become a Christian, so he overcomes and has a new and free will, to do all sorts of good works which please God, all through the service, grace and action of Christ our Lord, of whom the Lord himself spoke in the Gospel when he said, "When the Son makes you free, you are truly free," and Paul, "Where the Spirit of the Lord is, there is freedom. The law of the Spirit of life in Christ Jesus has made me free from the law of sin and death.[34]

It is important to see this argument in full, because he was carefully positioning himself between what he saw to be two errors, in order to explain not only his position with regard to the place of works and will, but also his understanding about the nature of the human being.

It is clear that for Schwenckfeld, there was meaning in speaking of the free will of a Christian, the freedom to do good and to please God: it was a freedom which was dependent on the action of God in grace through Christ bringing about new birth, but there was a responsibility which then properly belonged to the new person. In this, he was very close to the thinking of many Anabaptists, who also argued that those who were born again had a freedom of will to choose good.[35]

Thus, his notion of the new person combined the understanding of total dependence in terms of origin with a sense of appropriate growth and behaviour to be undertaken. Williams suggests that he derived this understanding from

---

[34] *CS*, vol. 9, p. 929. ll. 34f.
[35] C. M. Dent, "The Anabaptists", *The Study of Spirituality*, Eds Jones, Wainwright, Yarnold, p. 352.

Luther's early theology, but Luther came to change his mind about the place and value of free will.[36] Luther's theology of free will was worked out in confrontation with Erasmus in a famous controversy, and was, central to his understanding of the gospel. He insisted that an individual was not free to do anything which could be construed as a turning towards grace. That could only be effected by the sovereign grace of God. For Luther, such a position was necessary to protect the centrality of God's saving action over against any possibility of a works-based salvation. However, it did leave him open to the accusation of antinomianism, and indeed, it was the lack of moral improvement in those who were shaped by his theology which led Schwenckfeld to question the validity of that theology in the first place.[37]

This is, I believe, a further demonstration of my argument that, for Schwenckfeld, the "metaphor" of rebirth was far more than picture language to illustrate a point. Rather, it was a description of the reality of the situation, and could be used as a tool both for describing and prescribing the way in which that situation was worked out. I will return to the ideas of growth and development below.

The other point which I believe Schwenckfeld's exposition of free will demonstrates is, once more, his commitment to the notion that meaningful reality has a physical as well as a spiritual content. The "good works" which are the potential and the expression of the new person's free will are to be carried out in the body. They are part of the "fleshly life" or physical reality which is the concomitant of the spiritual.

It is worth noting, as a side issue here, that in his understanding of "good works" Schwenckfeld did not distinguish between men and women in what should be done. Nor did he argue that true Christian living would somehow distinguish a person from "good living" within society as it was then constituted – that is, there was nothing of the social revolutionary about him. In "Of Three Kinds of Human Life", one of the writings in which he discussed the nature of good works and right living at some length, he wrote that it was right to love one's neighbour, because we were all created by the same God and therefore:

> In the same way, he requires of the magistrate to promote and encourage civil righteousness and peace in the city's life in that which belongs to him, because he will be required by God in his time.[38]

Part of what is significant about this remark is that Schwenckfeld clearly assumed that it was possible to lead a good life as a magistrate, taking part in normal civil life, or at least, the normal part for a member of the elite. He does not argue for any of the separation or rejection of wider society which was part

---

[36]Williams, *The Radical Reformation*, p. 203.

[37] For further discussion of this controversy, see Bornkamm, *Luther in Mid-career*, pp. 337-354, 417-458, Brecht, *Martin Luther*, pp.213-238,

[38] *CS*, vol 9, p. 836, ll. 2ff.

of the position of other radicals, such as the Anabaptists. Thus men who adopted his teaching found themselves still enabled to share in their expected way in the wider community. It is clear that they did. In the essay "Schwenckfeld and the South German Schwenkfelders", Emmet McLaughlin demonstrates that there were individuals highly placed in the magistracy and the Councils who were followers of Schwenckfeld's teaching. A "good life" therefore, for a man, involved undertaking social responsibility.

By the same token, a "good life" for a woman was not socially radical, at least within the understanding of marriage. As we saw in his discussion of himself as "weiber predige" (see page 263), he was insistent that his teaching should not lead to any "disobedience" by a wife towards her husband. Although he did not spend any time considering what such disobedience might be, or alternatively, what the content of appropriate obedience was, it seems justifiable to assume that he held a fairly traditional understanding of the marriage relationship.

Thus in two of the major social experiences of the lives of people around him, marriage for the women and civic society for the men, Schwenckfeld's definition of a good – and by extension, God-pleasing – life was closely identified with the social norms of his time. To become a Schwenkfelder was to remain within the boundaries of acceptable behaviour. McLaughlin argues that this was one of the reasons why people of the elite responded as they did:

> He was able to offer a warm personal piety and a sense of commitment and rigor without requiring a break from the world in a political or social sense...Schwenckfeld offered a religious dissidence shorn of its political and social corollaries.[39]

We might suggest that this was even more appealing to men than to women, since they might be argued to have had more to lose, socially and politically, from a more radical religious position.

In the light of this, however, it is also worth reiterating, the difference he does seem to have made in the definition of "good living" for women. As was pointed out above, by moving the focus away from defining female existence in terms of marriage and motherhood, he did challenge something of the social perception of how women should live. Although he did not challenge the wider social norms and preconceptions, his assumptions about the meaning of the physical nature of women did undermine part of the foundation on which those social norms were built.

This left him with the question of how that substance was to take shape. I have suggested throughout this thesis that this was one of the major problems with which Schwenckfeld found he had to wrestle. Thus, although he insisted that the rebirth in Christ which was the origin of new life was an "inner" experience, that is, it was not brought about by any outer medium, such as the sacraments, he could also argue:

---

[39] McLaughlin "Schwenckfeld and the South German Schwenkfelders", p. 166.

That Christ, the incarnate Word, must also become flesh in us, is always true but spiritual. And it is nothing other than that Christ is born, formed and planted in us through faith, so that he dwells in our hearts. So must Christ come into our flesh (1 Jn 4:2). He must make it the same as his, give birth to it again, which is to say, taking on our flesh and making a new one out of the old. What is the new person in us other than Christ? So Christ takes us into himself, in the majesty of God. (Rom 15:7). It is, in short, the putting on in us of the secret of the birth and incarnation of Christ. For outside of us (that is, outside of our flesh) Christ avails nothing for us.[40]

This is a very confused passage, since we have here both the suggestion that the new flesh is made from the old – that there is a continuation of physical existence – and that it is Christ who gives birth, plays the role of mother. Part of the confusion here is a reflection of the fact that Schwenckfeld was neither trained as nor functioned as a systematic theologian. He was a theological pragmatist.

What is clear is that there must be a "physical" presence for there to be an ontological reality. He insisted that "There must be a new Christian flesh created in us".[41] It was this insight which helped to shape Schwenckfeld's rejection of Luther's teaching, not simply in his understanding of the sacraments, but also in the result of these sacraments. He had become distressed at the lack of moral improvement among those who adopted Lutheran teaching, and he traced this back to a misunderstanding of the Eucharist. But it is here in his theology of new birth and the new being that the root of the unease can be seen. The new being, brought to birth by the action of God in Christ and nourished by the true Body and Blood, must have its "physical" reality, because it is the presence of Christ in the believer. This was not understood as an instantaneous experience, but one of growth and development, which fits with his controlling language of birth.

Spiritual Growth

The understanding of spiritual development in terms of growth and gradual change again raises some interesting echoes from late medieval female spirituality. Bynum has suggested that, for many women, their vocation to a spiritual life began in early childhood, while for men, there was more likely to be an episode of conversion, which marked a disjuncture in life.[42] Drawing on work by Donald Weinstein and Rudolph Bell, she brings forward evidence of the developing nature of women's spirituality, and argues that women's lives were marked "by continuity rather than by change".[43] This certainly appears to be the model with which Schwenckfeld worked. With the emphasis which it is

---

[40] *CS*, vol. 5, p. 425, ll. 23f.
[41] *CS*, vol. 4, p. 699, ll. 13f.
[42] Bynum, *Holy Feast and Holy Fast*, pp. 24f.
[43] Bynum, *Holy Feast and Holy Fast*, p. 25.

clear he placed on the ongoing growth, development and struggle, he seems to have had a clear sense of the life of the believer as one in which, while it might be marked by significant incidents, was also one which was never finished until glory was reached in heaven. At several points he outlined his *ordo salutis*, in particular in "The Steps of Regeneration"[44] written in 1529, and "The mystery of the Growth of Christ in the Christian",[45] which is undated.

In the first, he outlined ten stages: a sense of remorse provoked by the action of the Father, rebirth "through the strength of the resurrection of Christ",[46] a developing understanding through the enlightening of God and a recognition of the true nature of Christ which leads to a reform of life. The fifth step is a certainty of the Christian faith, the sixth baptism in the Holy Spirit, the seventh feeding with the true body and blood of Christ in the Supper. Then comes a confirmation in the faith, a recognition of the continuing struggle and of persecution, and finally the experience of the likeness of Christ which will continue for eternity. The outline is very clear about the sense of progression, and that all of it is dependent on God's activity. This journey leads in the end to the full likeness of Christ which is the completion of salvation. This outline of the process makes it clear that Schwenckfeld understood salvation as something which was not complete until the believer was in glory.

"The Mystery of the Growth of the Christian" examines the progression from another angle. In this one, Schwenckfeld is concerned to display the growth of Christ in the flesh of the believer, and to do this, he explained the believer's experience in terms of the story of Christ as given in the gospels. Thus, he covered seven steps, and they are:

Christ conceived and born in the believer, developing in and teaching the believer, crucified in the believer, buried in the believer, raised to life in the believer, ascended through the believer, sitting in the believer at God's right hand. This recapitulation not only in the spiritual experience (a pattern which others had also developed), but also in the body of the believer underlines just how seriously he took the notion of the physical expression of the life of Christ in a Christian – this was not a metaphor, or a colourful way of speaking, but a literal, physical-spiritual description. This seemingly nonsensical formulation is the nearest he can get to making sense of holding spiritual and physical together. As such, it is important not just for what it shows about Schwenckfeld's understanding of the life of faith as growth and progression, but also because it reinforces the identification between the believer and Jesus, not simply in moral terms, but also in physical terms. This is part of the pattern that says salvation is not just about the forgiveness of sins, but the receiving of a new origin.

---

[44] *CS*, vol. 3, pp. 571ff.
[45] *CS*, vol. 18, pp. 478 ff.
[46] *CS*, vol. 3, p. 572, l. 23f.

Heimsuchungen

However, as well as a sense of progress, Schwenckfeld did acknowledge and depend on significant events or encounters which he called *Heimsuchungen,* visitations. The word itself can be translated simply as "visit". But, depending on its context, it can bear various connotations. It is the word used of Gabriel's visit to Mary at the time of the Annunciation. There was therefore a history of its use to mean an encounter with the divine which was life-changing. It was also the term which was used of the "visitation" of an epidemic of plague or a severe storm. So, it was not necessarily a benign word. Rather, it was a word which carried implications of suddenness, unexpectedness and uncontrollability. It certainly had the sense of an event which broke in from outside. When used of God, it did not always imply a comforting or comfortable encounter.

Schwenckfeld did not use the word often, and when he did, it was usually in one of two ways. He sometimes used it to refer to a cataclysmic event in history, such as the Reformation. Thus in his open letter "A General Epistle, The Ground and Cause of the Error and Controversy Concerning the Lord's Supper" in 1527, describing the changes of the last decade he wrote this:

> For although he [God] before this time had overlooked the lack of knowledge, according to Acts 17, now another time began to enter, which is the time of the revelation and the visitation of God.[47]

His other area of use was to refer to significant events in his own faith-journey, normally his conversion. There has been significant debate about how many *Heimsuchungen* Schwenckfeld actually referred to in his writings, and when they happened. It is generally agreed that the first was in 1519, and refers to his spiritual awakening. The question is whether there were one or two others. McLaughlin summarises the discussion and the conclusions.[48] I agree with his arguments with regard to the number (that there were three in total), and the dates and events (the second in 1525, when Schwenckfeld abandoned a belief in the Real Presence in the Eucharist, and the third in 1527, when he committed himself fully to the spiritualist outlook). However, I suggest that there is more to be said about the meaning of such events, and of Schwenckfeld's description of them.

One of the significant places where he used the term was in a letter he sent in 1534 to Phillip of Hesse to explain his position. In the letter he said:

> Although since the gracious visitation of God until now I have not totally joined with any party or church over the use of the Sacrament and other things, nor allowed anybody to rule over or subjugate my belief, neither have I despised any church or any person, leader or teacher, desiring to serve each person in God, to

---

[47] *CS*, vol. 2, p. 465, ll. 1f.
[48] McLaughlin, *Reluctant Radical*, p. 95, n.23.

be friend and brother to every person who is eager for God, who loves Christ from his heart, follows his truth and is dedicated to his blessedness.[49]

It was the *Heimsuchung* which gave him the confidence, the impetus and the authority to separate from the wider community. He did not describe the experience except as something which happened – there is no exploration of the sensations involved, for example. But that it was radical and not to be denied is clear from the consequences he attributed to it. This was a perception which remained throughout his life. In the summary of his Confession which appeared in 1555, he closed his discussion in this way:

> From all of this, I hope, it should now be obvious and announced what I believe, hold, speak and know with the witness of the holy Scriptures about Christ Jesus, which I have always, praise God, for some years constantly believed and held in my heart, since the time of the gracious visiting of God in my heart.[50]

His whole sense of who he was, and the ground of his faith was rooted in this experience of *Heimsuchung,* a shattering inbreaking from outside, beyond his control. Although he never went into detail about the actual experience itself, he clearly looked to it, or them, as the formative bases of his whole theology. It was the *Heimsuchungen* which gave him the possibility of moving away from the accepted theological line. This "visitation" which came from God, and which was so much an inbreaking of the Other was a concept which fitted well with his perception that rebirth and all that followed from it came not from human will, but from the activity of God. This perception allowed a great degree of freedom in terms of existing structures, both the visible and the assumed. With the authority which such direct experience allowed to him, he was in an ideal position to challenge contemporary assumptions in both his thinking and his practice.

There is a repeating pattern in church history of a charismatic authority standing over against the official and recognised power base. It can be seen in the Montanists of the second century, in the roles of the Confessors in readmitting the lapsed after persecution in the third century against the decision of the bishops, among the mystics of the twelfth and thirteenth century, in the life and practice of Francis of Assisi, Teresa of Avila, and others, whose direct encounter with the divine had given them an unassailable sense of their ability to speak, especially to speak in criticism and judgement – and which left those around them with a very difficult task in contradicting what was spoken.

One of the interesting aspects in the light of this thesis about this pattern is how often women exploited it. Denied an official voice in the community, they spoke to it from outside, but standing on the certainty of their own, unmediated

---

[49] *CS*, vol. 5, p. 100, ll. 21f. He makes a very similar argument in "Christian Warfare and the Knighthood of God", vol. 4, p. 677, ll. 3f. in which he explained why he was no part of any of the contemporary Christian communities.
[50] *CS*, vol. 14, p. 400, ll. 18f.

experience of God. This can be seen as very close to the pattern which Schwenckfeld adopted. Although he was socially privileged, ecclesiastically, laymen and all women were in the same position, under the authority and teaching guidance of the clergy. One of the challenges which the Reformation in general offered to the status quo was to question the nature of such authority, and, by providing the Bible in the vernacular, opening the possibility of people reading outside of official interpretation. One of the reasons many leaders of Reform wrote such quantities of Scriptural commentaries was to guide thinking and keep it under official control.

By speaking and writing on the basis, not of an ecclesiastical authority, but his *Heimsuchungen*, Schwenckfeld was claiming for himself a similar position to the charismatics I have listed. A movement which has such a pattern at its foundation at least has the possibility of providing a space for others to act with authority in their own and others lives, which may not be officially recognised or sanctioned. Once again, a reflection on the theology and the way in which he worked it out helps to shape an account of the reasons why women may have accepted this with such enthusiasm.

The New Person

Nevertheless, Schwenckfeld did not stop at describing the conception and birth of the new person. He also discussed the nature and being of this reborn individual. In these discussions again, we see clearly his refusal to consider being without physical reality. He did not allow any description of the new person to be located entirely spiritually. Seguenny discusses it in these terms:

> Basing his position on Genesis 1.26 "Let us make man in our own image", Schwenckfeld develops an interpretation different from that of traditional exegesis, emphasising a dynamic conversion of the individual who is not created in the image of God, but is developing towards it.... the carnal individual and the natural world constitute the only unique point of departure for the process of deification...The spiritual is not a chimera. It exists in a real way. One might indeed say that it exists in a material way, although matter is not its principle...Caspar Schwenckfeld's intent is not to enunciate the dualism, but to overcome it; for him the individual is whole, body and spirit.[51]

It is certainly clear that the new person had in Schwenckfeld's view a physical reality as well as a physical origin, where physical is defined in the spiritual way which was so central to him. In 1547, he wrote this:

> The reborn person is called new, because of the Spirit of God in Christ who renews all things, who sanctifies people and embellishes and ornaments with heavenly newness, so that he is not engendered and born in the previous fleshly way as the first old Adam, but in a new spiritual way in the flesh, yes in the heart

---

[51] Seguenny, *The Christology of Caspar Schwenckfeld*, pp. 3-5.

of the old person, out of a new heavenly seed, through the Holy Spirit. He is a person of two natures, spirit and flesh, nature and grace. He who is born from God (that is, the new person) is also washed, fed, taught in and from God and to this all external things, all symbols and church services point and bear witness.[52]

This was evidently a really important formulation for him, since he repeated almost word for word in 1560, in a "Deutsche Theologia",[53] a document in which he attempted to explain his theology systematically. The final sentence does not appear in that text, but is worth commenting on, for the insight it gives into Schwenckfeld's understanding of the position of the new person. Again, it is clear that he takes the image of rebirth more than metaphorically. His description of what God does for the new person – washing, feeding and teaching – is strongly reminiscent of the language used of a parent (more particularly a mother) in relation to a child or infant. The emphasis is both on dependence and growth. Schwenckfeld was convinced that nobody can do anything for themselves in the realm of spiritual regeneration; that rebirth comes only and always from God.[54]

One of the oddities about the use of "body" language in Schwenckfeld's writing, and particularly the mother image, is that he did not use it in the most expected way, to reflect the nature of the church. The image of the church as the body of Christ is, like rebirth, a biblical picture, and again, one which has been very important in Christian writing. The notion of the church as the mother of believers is very common, both in patristic writings and in medieval theology. However, for Schwenckfeld, it was clearly not a helpful or straightforward concept.

> And in the same way that the first Eve was created by God from Adam, a mother of all natural people as a model, so the second Eve, that is the Christian Church, is produced and born in truth from the second Adam, from his flesh and bone, by God the Father, through the Holy Spirit.[55]

So, in this development of the image, while God is still clearly the father, this time the mother is the church, and the "stuff" from which the new being is produced is the flesh and bone of Christ. Again the roles of Father and Creator

---

[52] *CS*, vol. 10, p. 307, ll. 40f.

[53] *CS*, vol. 17, pp. 54f

[54] Although he did not draw the parallel explicitly, it is interesting to note that among the references to washing in the gospels is the occasion when Jesus washed the disciple's feet at the Last Supper, a time when Peter tried not to let this happen. Jesus insisted that it must be done if Peter was "to have a part in him". The symbolism of the story as the evangelist tells it is clearly linked with baptism and with rebirth: and the emphasis is on the need to allow Christ to do that which cannot be done alone. This would further reinforce Schwenckfeld's insistence on the life of the new person as that which cannot be achieved in the individual's own strength.

[55] *CS*, vol. 10, p. 298, ll. 29f.

are carefully distinguished. In the discussions of the church as the second Eve, in parallel to Christ the second Adam, we are well within normal language for this kind of discussion. The story of Eve created from Adam's rib and then coming to him as his wife also provides a powerful typology. Eve's being is derived from and dependent on Adam's just as the believer's is on Christ. The relationship between the now existing Eve and Adam then takes on a particular shape, as Eve functions no longer as a derivative of Adam, but as his partner in the creative activity of making life. Now possessing "stuff", she supplies that in the birth of the children whom Adam fathers. In the same way, the church derives its being from Christ, and, once in existence, is the means by which the life which Christ supplies takes shape in the world through the believers.

The Nature of the Church

The Church as the female agent in the coming into being of the new believer would fit into a long-existing pattern of Christian teaching which argued, in the words of Cyprian: "He cannot have God as his father who has not the Church as his mother".[56] In adopting this kind of thinking about the church, Schwenckfeld was very close to Luther who wrote: "The Christian Church is your mother, who gives birth to you and bears you through the word".[57]

This statement, however, worked with the notion of the institutional and visible church, which was not central to Schwenckfeld's thinking. Luther focused the marks of the Church around preaching and the sacraments. For Schwenckfeld the understanding of the church was much more spiritualised. In his great "Confession" of 1547, he wrote:

> Of the Christian Church, I hold and believe that there is one holy Christian church on the earth, of which it may be said, as well as about faith, gospel, sacraments and a couple of other points, there are two ways of speaking; firstly according to the ground of truth as it stands before God, as the Church from Christ is built and generated here in his Kingdom of grace through the Spirit, as he cares for her, maintains her, spiritually nourishes and reigns, as she is his spouse and holy body.[58]

He went on to demonstrate how others have spoken of the church in this way, in Scripture, Creed and among the Fathers, and then he continued

> But the second way in which the Holy Scriptures speak of the church is according to her outer gathering in the service of the Apostles and other servants of the Holy Spirit, the true under-shepherds, prelates, teachers, soul-carers, and overseers, which have been ordained above all by the heavenly King to serve his people and

---

[56] Cyprian, *De unit eccl* 6.
[57] Luther, *WA*, p. 51. "Predigt auf das Fest der Opferung Christ im Tempel, in Eisleben gehalten", 2 Feb, 1546.
[58] *CS*, vol. 11, p. 96, ll. 27f.

in the building of his body which is the congregation, according to their condition of service, for then each particular Christian gathering is called a church or a congregation of God, as we read in the Holy Scriptures of the New Testament.[59]

The Church exists because it is the body of Christ. It may conduct the functions of preaching and sacrament, but these do not make it a church; they are the activities of the church. The Church is the body of Christ, and consists of the people of God, who gather together.

The notion of Church as body, and more particularly as the body of Christ, was fundamental for Schwenckfeld. So, for example, to go again to the postil on John 3, there he wrote:

From this now also follows the proper understanding of the Christian church, which is the holy community of the living God, the body and bride of Jesus Christ and the crowd of all new people, all holy chosen children of God, which has its beginning, origin, being and independence nowhere other than from, in and with the God-raised person Jesus Christ *ex verbo incarnato*, through the new birth.[60]

This identification of the Church not as institution but as body is very strong throughout his writings. This then had implications for how he understood the "mother" and the "body" images. In his "Criticism on the Augsburg Confession", in particular the Article on the Church, he wrote:

Therefore the Church of Christ is not to be directed towards the circumcised people of the Law, but according to Christ the head, according to his Spirit and new spiritual being. It is not the band of baptised Christians, nor those who are named Christian and who boast of the Gospel of Christ, or take it on externals alone; but the pious, repentant new people and true children of God who through faith truly know Christ, who have the Spirit of Christ and according to the Spirit act and behave in a Christian fashion, regardless of where they may be externally.[61]

The church cannot be identified by outer signs, but is formed of those who have experienced this spiritual-biological transformation which was at the centre of Schwenckfeld's understanding.

He was also not consistent in his use of language of church as mother. Thus he could write in a letter to Sibilla Eisler of John's language in the Apocalypse describing the New Jerusalem coming down out of heaven like a bride prepared for her husband. He continued the discussion in this way:

And I, John, saw the Holy City, the new Jerusalem come from God, from heaven above, prepared as a bride for her husband. This means the congregation as it stands before us, and as she is built here in the Holy Spirit and by the service of

---

[59] *CS*, vol. 11, p. 98, ll. 15f.
[60] *CS*, vol. 10, p. 298, ll. 21f.
[61] *CS*, vol. 3, p. 916, ll. 4f.

her servants. They [the opponents against whom he is writing] will then prove from that that such a congregation is herself a mother, and one Christian is born from another. They should judge it much higher, that is, as it stands before God in eternity, and that the heavenly Jerusalem or the grace of God is mother of the Christian congregation; not that the congregation is its own mother, as is often said; "The mother, the Christian churches", by which the papists mean Rome. But thus such a mother is in heaven, as well as her father and the seed through which she is born.[62]

He is concerned to argue that the Christian is not born through or of the church, although this was a traditional view. It does, however, imply that the church is prior to and somehow separate from the community of believers. Such a position did not accord with Schwenckfeld's understanding of the church. According to his theology, the church *was* the community of believers, and therefore logically the existence of the believers was prior to that of the church.[63]

We have seen above how there were times when he did write of the church as mother. There were other occasions when he understood Christ in a maternal role, especially as the provider of "stuff". The grace of God could also be spoken of as mother, in particular when present in Christ. Here, the mother of the believer is in heaven, but is not more clearly defined, although a careful separation of mother, father and seed is maintained. In all of his arguments, the father of the believer, as of Christ, is always the First Person of the Trinity. The only definition of seed he gives in any of his discussions is either Christ or Word-as-Christ. Thus, since Seed is referred to in the passage, we can infer that Schwenckfeld was not meaning to imply that Christ was mother of the Christian when he wrote this. In Trinitarian terms, that leaves the Spirit to fill the role, but he pointedly did not say that. However, he was also not able simply to leave the role of mother uncommented on. Since the idea of rebirth as the origin of a Christian was not, for Schwenckfeld, simply a metaphor, but a biological reality, all the participants have to be identified and named. Other people working with these images, acknowledging them as metaphorical, were prepared to live with logical inconsistencies in the discussion, because it was not so important that the father and mother be understood in relation to each other. Such freedom was not a possibility for Schwenckfeld. Hence the confusion that appears in his writings on this topic. While being utterly convinced of God the Father's spiritual and biological paternal role, he seems to have been unable to locate the role of the believer's mother to his satisfaction. Therefore, in different contexts he produced a different actor. His pattern of gender was defined entirely by function, rather than the more normal approach of locating certain functions within one or other gender. That meant that, in certain contexts, considering certain aspects, Christ, although

---

[62] *CS*, vol. 15, p. 188, ll. 19f.

[63] For more on Schwenckfeld's understanding of the nature of the church, see Maron, *Individualismus und Gemeinschaft*.

physiologically male, could be considered female. This was not the result of some imaginative leap or spiritual or poetic license, but because of function. In using body language of the church, he was more frequently drawn to the conception of the church both as body and as bride of Christ, notions which carry with them specific gender implications. Part of the nature of a body is to bear sexed characteristics. During his earthly ministry, the body of Christ was male. If the church is the body of Christ, what kind of body is it? As we have seen, although the temporal body of Christ was male, there were other patterns going on in Schwenckfeld's thinking when he discussed the nature of Christ's body in its salvific mode: namely, providing stuff and feeding. Thus, the identification of the body of Christ as the being of the believer is not easily fixed in terms of gender. Similarly, language of bride is strongly gendered, a gendering which casts Christ unequivocally as male and the church as female. However, his rejection of the mother role as part of the nature of the church does not allow for what appears to be the natural progression, from bride to wife to mother. Both of these ways of speaking about the church, although they are important to Schwenckfeld, were not followed through in anything like the same detail as his language of rebirth and body. Maron has suggested that for Schwenckfeld the church is purely individualistic; this examination of Schwenckfeld's use of language appears to suggest that Maron's interpretation is justified

Public and Private, Sacred and Secular

It is partly through this reinterpretation of the nature of the church that McLaughlin finds the roots of his explanation for the numbers of women in the movement. This shift away from an institutional understanding of the church moves the focus more to informal gatherings in the home, and this is clearly what happened among the Schwenkfelders. McLaughlin argues that the move to homes as the centres of the religious life of the groups allowed the women to take a greater part because it was a withdrawal into the private world where women were less restricted. I have insisted that this is an anachronistic understanding of the meaning of "home" in early modern Europe, and that home would be better understood as the smallest of the public institutions, since it was the "building block" of all other aspects of community. Muir has shown how the home became more of a centre for what he refers to as social interaction during this period, and in that way was recognised as a "public" place.[64] However, McLaughlin is right in pointing out that there is a significant difference between gatherings in a church and gatherings in a home. The

---

[64] Muir, *Ritual in Early Modern Europe*, p. 130; see also Natalie Zemon Davis' comments "Sexual symbolism, of course, is always available to make statements about social experience and to reflect (or conceal) contradictions within it…In the little world of the family, with its conspircuous tension between intimacy and power, the larger matters of political and social order could find ready symbolism", Davis, "Women on Top", *Society and Culture in Early Modern France*, p. 127.

difference is not so much between public and private[65] or even domestic and civic, as between sacred and for want of a better word, secular, although that is an anachronistic term. He suggests that the change in ideas about the nature of the church, which he understands to be centred in the change in belief about sacrament and Scripture,

> was to displace the focus of religious activity from the public arena dominated by the clergy to the private sphere of the home, where the supper table replaced the pulpit as the focus. Here, fathers and mothers ruled. Here was truly a priesthood of all believers. And here women could take responsibility for themselves and teach and "minister" to others.[66]

He is right that the shift to the home was both a result of and symbolic of a significantly different theology, but I do not believe he has pursued the matter far enough. Not only is the question of a public/private distinction between home and church anachronistic, he has not dealt with the real shift which Schwenckfeld made, which is in terms of the body.

Scribner has suggested that one of the major effects of the development of Reformation spirituality was to create "a firm break between the sacred and the secular worlds",[67] and that this was something significantly different from the previous position. The spirituality of the late middle ages, as Scribner and others have shown, was centred as much in the home and the rituals involved in daily living, such as keeping feasts and fasts, as it was in the public services of the church. It was in this aspect of religious life that women were particularly involved, as the providers of a household's meals, as those who were especially concerned with the rituals of birth and death, and those with significant care of the young or ill. The move which occurred with the development of a reformed spirituality, while it still had its household aspect, located much more of the expression of faith in the domain of the church and in the physical church building.[68] As Wiesner and others have argued, this was a significant "defeminisation" of religion. The centre of faith was now less in ritual and everyday practice and more in intellectual belief and culture.[69] However, as McLaughlin has suggested, Schwenckfeld did keep or reintroduce a focus on the home rather than the public space of the church. It is interesting to note that, according to Fritz, when the Schwenkfelders in Ulm were challenged to

---

[65] See Wiesner's discussion of the distinctions of public, private and personal in "Nuns, Wives and Mothers: Women and the Reformation in Germany", Marshall, *Women in Reformation and Counter-Reformation Europe*, pp. 8-9.

[66] McLaughlin, "Caspar Schwenckfeld and the Schwenkfelders" in *The Freedom of the Spirit*, p. 28.

[67] Scribner, *Popular Culture and Popular Movements in Reformation Germany*, p. 15.

[68] Thomas Brady Jr., "You Hate Us Priests, p. 185.

[69] Virginia Reinburg, "Hearing Lay People's Prayer", *Culture and Identity in Early Modern Europe 1500-1800: Essays in Honor of Natalie Zemon Davis*, Eds. Barbara B. Diefendorf and Carla Hesse, Ann Arbor: Michigan University Press, 1993, pp. 29, 31.

account for their absence from public worship, the women gave theological reasons for it, and the reasons they gave, at least in the case of the confessions of faith which are quoted, focus on the nature of Christ. Thus, Fritz quotes Katherina Streicher, for example, as stating:

> The preachers preached one thing today and another tomorrow. They wanted to make Christ a creature and to bind salvation to outer things and ceremonies. Therefore she remained with her friends at home and relied upon Christ alone according to biblical and evangelical writings.[70]

She, and the others to whom Fritz also refers, is quite clear that there are theological reasons for her actions, and her remaining in the home is a result, not a cause, of her theological position.

A New Body

As I have argued above, Schwenckfeld's understanding of the new person was closely identified with his understanding of physical existence. He was quite clearly convinced that the new person was body and soul, brought to birth by God and given substance and nourishment through Christ. The inner spiritual change had a physical reality. Part of the result of this was the shift which McLaughlin outlines, but it is not simply from church to home. It is from ceremony and activity to being. It was not so much that Schwenckfeld shifted the emphasis from the public to the private. Rather, he made sacred what had previously been non-sacred – and therefore made sacred what it represented, including the domestic role of women. Kieckhefer points out that this is in fact a normal role of "devotional" spirituality, a spirituality which can "breed either a sense of attachment to the church or a feeling of detachment from it".[71] It was not coincidental to his Eucharistic theology that Schwenckfeld shifted the focus from the church to the home. It was the consequence of the same thinking. And the theological meanings of both moves are the same. It was the making spiritual of what had previously been considered unspiritual, with all that that meant for the theological as well as the social position of women. In doing this, Schwenckfeld was not necessarily doing something new. It may be that, as we have seen in other aspects of his theology, he was continuing an existing tradition, but in a novel way, and, because it was in a different context, with a new meaning.

What we also see in this is the driving of a wedge between form and content. The content, the spiritual experience, is now no longer dependent on the form, the ritual of worship. This type of separation is one of the constants in

---

[70] D. F. Fritz, *Ulmische Kirchengeschichte vom Interim bis zum dreißigjährigen Krieg 1548-1612,* Stuttgart, nd, p. 186.

[71] Richard Kieckhefer, "Major Currents in Late Medieval Devotion", *Christian Spirituality Volume II; The High Middle Ages and the Reformation.* ed.J. Raitt, Bernard McGinn amd John Meyendorff, London, SCM, 1989 p. 100.

Schwenckfeld's thinking. We have already seen how he could separate the physical earthly body of Jesus, which was clearly gendered male, from its activity and meaning in the relationship of rebirth and nurture. Here we see the meaning of the sacrament being separated from the physical reality with which, throughout most of church history, it has been associated. The meaning of the sacrament involves the taking of that which is profane and rendering it holy in the context of a liturgy in a public, or at least potentially public space. The now-sanctified elements serve to bring the holy to the profane, the congregation, and to enable them to encounter the Divine in a (relatively) unmediated way. Clearly, there is mediation through the elements, but they are now part of the divine world, through the consecration, and so in that sense, the encounter is unmediated. However, their sanctification also emphasises the non-sanctification of bread, wine, water and oil which have not been consecrated. In a similar way, the practice of these sacramental acts in a particular space both defines that space as sacred and, in consequence, all other spaces as profane. The other major consequence is that those who enable the consecration, the priests, are identified with the holy, which desacralises the rest of the people.

What Schwenckfeld did with his separation of form and content was to destroy all of these distinctions. I have suggested in chapter two that Schwenckfeld's theology led him to the position of regarding the body of the believer, rather than the bread and wine of the Eucharist, as the site of divine activity, and therefore as the sacramental element. It is in the body, the physical being of the believer, that God is present in and to the world. We have seen how this was further underlined in his understanding of the nature of the "saved" body, and its physical existence. The destabilisation which this offers to a theology of sacrament is second only to the destabilisation it offers to an understanding of body. If sacrament is no longer that which happens within the confines of a sacralising context, whether physically (a church), temporally (during the service) or socially (conducted by a priest and offered to the faithful), then the meaning which the sacrament confers on any of these elements is altered, or even destroyed. By moving the encounter which is the meaning of the sacrament away from the physical bread and wine, Schwenckfeld inevitably also robbed the previously assumed contexts of their meaning. The physical, social and temporal patterns which had hitherto been an integral part of the sacramental experience may now be divorced from it.

Likewise, the understanding of body is destabilised. In this new pattern, rather than being the representation of the profane which is sanctified through encounter with the consecrated elements, it becomes itself that which is holy. Schwenckfeld's insistence that the new person is a *person*, and therefore embodied, was shaped by his belief discussed above, that the new person came into being in and through the flesh of the believer as it encountered the flesh of Christ. This sense that the body of the believer had a positive spiritual meaning was a significant shift of focus. No longer were the sacralising effects of consecrated elements necessary to enable the encounter with God; this could now happen directly in the believer's flesh. It is this shift, I believe, which is the true reason why women were capable of taking the roles which they did. The cause which McLaughlin cites is rather a symptom of the profound destabilisation which Schwenckfeld's separation of form and content brought about. It was not because the focus moved from public church to private home that women could "minister". It was possible both for women to minister and for the focus to be in the home because it was now in the physical existence of the believer, the reborn one, now existing as a child of God and whose flesh was now part of the inner order, that the presence of the divine was located.

Thus, we see again that there is a theological principle which was shaping the reaction of people to Schwenckfeld, and particularly women. However, the radical nature of this principle, and in particular the far-reaching consequences in anthropology and soteriology, can only be truly appreciated when the question of gender is taken seriously in examining what Schwenckfeld said. Those who have written about his theology have disregarded the whole question of gender, and those who acknowledged that there is an issue of gender to be considered have failed to consider it from a theological position. To bring the two together enables us to see that the theology which Schwenckfeld presented created the possibility for thinking about body, about being human and about the relationship of humanity and divinity in a new way.

Patterns of Growth

As I argued in the first part of this chapter, Schwenckfeld was not content to consider only the birth and immediate coming into being of the new person. As I have said, he took seriously the idea that the new person was an infant, and therefore much of his teaching concerned the growth and development of the new person into a mature Christian. He spoke of this in several ways, and I want to examine several of them at this point. The ways of speaking I am going to concentrate on fall into two groups, and between them exemplify the different patterns of teaching which he developed. Firstly, there are the extended metaphors concerned with growth and maturing which he used, and of which I will examine the three most frequent and most developed. Secondly, there is a group of words which he used to speak of Christian experience and progress, again the most common of which I will consider, and which help us to explore the underlying metaphors which he used. In both these examinations, we will see that, just as with the metaphor of birth, Schwenckfeld did not use metaphorical language simply to illuminate an otherwise dark abstract principle or to present his notions in a more accessible way. For him the metaphors were a significant construction of the reality he was expressing.

There are three main treatises in which he wrote extended discussions or meditations on three particular ideas: *Christian Warfare and the Knighthood of God*, which was written in 1533,[72] *The Heavenly Balm and the Divine*

---

[72] *CS*, vol. 4, pp. 658ff.

Physician, written in 1545,[73] and *The School of Christ*, which dates from 1558.[74]

Christian Warfare and the Knighthood of God

The first metaphor which I want to discuss here appears in its most developed form in *Christian Warfare and the Knighthood of God*,[75] and in this discussion, there is the presentation of a contrast between condemned flesh and the saved life. Here, although the Christocentrism is the main focus of the spirituality, the emphasis is on the responsibility of the believer in the light of the action of God, and the need for the new life to have an "embodiment" if it was to be understood as real. The reality of the new life is defined by its demonstration in the new flesh. The development which he outlined in this writing looked to the creation of a new person, identified emphatically as flesh, albeit of the new type. This flesh must grow, and undertake the battle against evil. However, he also spoke of the remaining strength of the old flesh, and of its continuing reality, fighting on the side of evil and threatening to pull the believer down. This metaphor provides perhaps the clearest example of his conviction that the Christian life was a matter of development and growth, not a finished state. It is in this discussion that we get what is perhaps the only instance of Schwenckfeld using the language in the way in which it was commonly used, that is, associating Eve with sin, and in particular, lasciviousness:

> For our flesh is in the likeness of Eve, whose eyes daily view the desirable snake with the excitement of the lusts. If the snake is not resisted initially through the struggle from the beginning, Eve will cause Adam to fall too, so that the whole person leaves God, and follows the word of the Devil. [76]

Here quite clearly flesh is presented as metaphorically and symbolically female, warring against the rational – and perhaps saved? – male spirit. The other uses of Eve metaphorically are normally either in the context of the Incarnation or, more usually, as we have seen as the image of the Church, where Eve represents the Church created out of the side of the Second Adam, as the first woman was created from the first man.

Here, however, Schwenckfeld was using a different metaphorical field, and picking up on a long tradition of seeing flesh as female in contrast to spirit or reason as male. Normally, his ontology does not seem to indicate the belief that the soul was gendered, and if that was his habitual approach, then we are not reading here a suggestion that women were more likely to sin than men – the consequence which was often drawn from such symbolism. Rather what we have is an assertion that each person carries male and female, Adam and Eve,

---

[73] *CS*, vol. 9, pp. 512ff.
[74] *CS*, vol. 16, pp. 484ff.
[75] *CS*, vol. 4, p. 658.
[76] *CS*, vol. 4, p. 709, ll. 1f.

in their symbolic beings, within their own person. This would be in line with the assumption that there was no sexing of the soul. It also reinforces the sense that there is a separation between form and content: that the way in which the "body" is presented to the world, bearing a gender, is not determinative of the reality of that flesh when understood spiritually.

The discussion of the warfare of the Christian continues with its placing within a wider context, that of the cosmic struggle between good and evil, Christ and the Satan, and the place of the individual as part of it:

> This is also the struggle which is raised in heaven, when Michael and his angels struggle with the Dragon; Heaven is the Christian Church, Michael and all his angels are the Lord Christ and all his faithful, but the Dragon and his angels are Satan with all the evil spirits, who struggle with and tempt the world.[77]

Schwenckfeld never suggested either that this struggle would be easy or that it was only to do with major or grave sins. He emphasised that sin is not to do with outer actions, but with an inner disposition inherent in unredeemed humanity. Having examined this in some detail, and discussed Romans 7 as an example of the point he was trying to make, he then went on to speak of the reward that would come to the one who succeeded in the fight. This reward was the meal, the heavenly banquet. Then he argued that since this is a spiritual and not a physical fight, women as well as men will gain this reward.

> Since, then, the Christian struggle is not to do with strength of body nor with the power of the old person, but consists in the strength of the reborn soul and the power of the inner new person in Christ Jesus, so it is shared by women, yes and even young virgins, just as much as youths and men together with its reward. As it often happens that a weak women or even a young girl has been stronger in the struggle of faith, which is to say to overcome death, sin and the world for the sake of Christ, than many men were and still are; therefore all people are called Christian knights.[78]

This is in some ways an odd comment. There has been nothing in his discussion to suggest that there is any difference between men and women in the Christian life, and so the question arises as to why he should say it. Part of the answer is surely that this is a very male-orientated metaphor, focusing as it does on battles, soldiers and armour, a part of the world from which women were more or less totally excluded. Throughout his writings, Schwenckfeld made it clear that he considered women to have the same religious rights and responsibilities of response and salvation as men – not always as obvious in his context as it might at first appear. That is clearly part of what he was doing

---

[77] *CS*, vol. 4, p. 713, ll. 6f.

[78] *CS*, vol. 4, p. 728, ll. 36f.

here.[79]

However, I believe he was also saying something else, linked to the argument I have suggested above. He deliberately specifies women and virgins, as well as men and youths. There was long a tradition that chastity in a woman made her more acceptable to God, surer of salvation. The virgin was a mighty spiritual warrior because she had conquered the flesh in her own flesh. What is happening here is not simply his expansion of a metaphor into "literal" language to show that women can also take part in the struggle he was outlining. It is also his assertion that sanctity was not related to inviolability of the body – that is, virgins did not have a particular advantage. Just as a woman did not have to "become" male in order to participate fully in salvation, so a woman did not have to separate herself from the reality of her physical existence to achieve sanctity.

Luther was insistent that very few women were called to celibacy, as were very few men, and there was no particular religious merit deriving from it. Indeed, in Luther's scheme, the proper place for a woman was as the mother of children – that was the point of her existence. This could be read as suggesting that those who were not mothers were in a worse state than those who were – a reversal of the previous pattern. Luther may be coming up with a different answer, but is actually asking the same question as had been asked throughout Christian history – how is a woman's sexuality, or rather, her existence as a child-bearer to be integrated into a scheme of salvation? The traditional and medieval scheme had argued that to be safe, she should deny it, and remain *as a fountain sealed*. Luther argued that it was the point of her existence and there

---

[79] Compare Basil of Caesarea: "We will speak not only of the [ascetic life of] men, for women too are fighting for Christ, being enrolled for the campaign because of the courage of their souls, not rejected because of the weakness of their bodies. Many women have excelled no less than men; some have even become more renowned. Among these are those who make up the choir of virgins, those who shine in the contests of the confessors and the victories of martyrdom". Basil of Caeserea, "Outline of the Ascetic Life", *Patrologia Graeca*, ed. J.P. Migne, Paris, 1857-1866, vol 31, columns 624C-5A, cited by Graham Gould; "Women and the Fathers", W.J. Sheils and Diana Wood, *Women in the Church*,Oxford, Basil Blackwell, 1990, p. 2. We know that Schwenckfeld read Basil, and quotes him with approval on various issues. What is interesting here is the differences that appear in the discussion. Basil appears, by implication at least, to limit his "victorious women" to virgins and martyrs, and he also makes the point that they are defined by the weakness of their bodies. Neither of these issues appear in Schwenckfeld's comment. Nor is he using the examples of the women to shame the men into greater effort, as sometimes happened in the Patristic writings. Jerome was asked to write to a man who, having made a vow of continence with his wife, broke it. She went on pilgrimage to Palestine in penance, but he failed to follow as he had promised. Jerome wrote to urge him to do so: "Therefore, lest you may be snatched away before you have fulfilled your promise, imitate her whose teacher you ought to have been. For shame! the weaker vessel overcomes the world, and yet the stronger is overcome by it!" Jerome, *Letter 122*, pt 4, To Rusticus.

was no other place for her.

Schwenckfeld appears to have rejected both of these approaches. Women, by which he presumably means those who live within the normal social role of wife, mother and so on, and virgins, either those as yet too young or those who were not married for whatever reason, were warriors. They were equally deserving of reward as those who were assumed to be the normal saved souls, the men. Souls are not gendered, each person carries both Adam and Eve, and now their sexual, maternal position is irrelevant. In presenting each of these assertions or assumptions Schwenckfeld was challenging both what had gone before and the wider theology of his time. Without arguing for social revolution – indeed, arguing against social revolution, – Schwenckfeld nonetheless managed to exhibit and invite others to share a spirituality which was deeply subversive of the notion of God and of what it meant to be human. Within this, there was a radical understanding of what it meant to be female. This was clearly something which struck Schwenckfeld's own contemporaries. Therefore he was put in the position of explaining his position in this way:

It is strange to people that the virgins all remain unmarried, which the world, which is full of all kinds of indiscipline outside of marriage, can scarcely suffer. We want however still to experience that many pious virgins and women will offer and surrender themselves to the Lord. Now Lutheranism has spoiled everything as Luther has recently interpreted the seventh chapter of Corinthians quite against the mind of the Holy Spirit, and through that has wounded many hearts and consciences; Whoever marries does not sin, but who remains the same does better. The preachers want to insist upon the promise of Gen 1:28; Grow and increase for the people of the New Testament, and to make a command of God from it.[80]

Werner Packull, in his article "Commentary on the Apocalypse",[81] discusses a significant Commentary on the Book of Revelation which, he argues, was

---

[80] *CS*, vol. 11, p. 13, ll 9f. This is in a letter to Sibilla Eisler. McLaughlin's comment is; "Schwenckfeld himself seems to have been aware of the special liberative effects of his teaching for women. He was rare among Protestant reformers in praising the unmarried state for his women followers, either as celibates or widows, because it left them unencumbered to pursue Christ more freely". *The Freedom of Spirit*, p. 28.

He has approached this argument in the way in which he does similar comments in *Reluctant Radical*, with the suggestion that the reason women responded so favourably to Schwenckfeld's teaching was focused on the move from church to home as the main arena of religious practice. I still want to argue that this is both to misunderstand the nature of home as a "private sphere" in Early Modern Europe, and to miss the importance of the theology itself, and the symbolism which it constructs. The notion of home as "private sphere" appears to me to owe more to the nineteenth century doctrine of separate spheres than it does to the early modern understanding of the home as the microcosm and pattern of society.

[81] Werner O. Packull, "The Schwenkfeldian Commentary on the Apocalypse", Peter C. Erb *Schwenckfeld and Early Schwenkfeldianism*, pp. 47-87.

written by Schwenckfeld and Crautwald together. He examines the origins of their thinking and draws attention to what he understands to be their possible pre-Reformation commitment to celibacy. He writes

> Adultery with Jezebel, the mother of all false prophets, practised at Thyatira, allegedly referred to all those "wives of preachers, who mislead their husbands to avarice, unchastity and idolatry". Not clear is whether this statement was directed against the practice of pre-Reformation concubinage or to Reformation marriages. Whatever the case, the statement seems to indicate continued attachment [on the part of Schwenckfeld and Crautwald] to the traditional ideal of celibacy.[82]

Packull therefore understands Schwenckfeld to have argued *for* celibacy as the ideal. I suggest, however, that he permitted celibacy and marriage, and believed that neither had the spiritual advantage. In Schwenckfeld's edition of Crautwald's *Novus Homo* of 1542, we find as part of the description of the practice of the new person:

> The new person, since he exists and moves in the flesh, takes a wife in the Lord should he want.[83]

Marriage was not incompatible with the life of a new person. However, what is clear is that he did not limit the position of women to that of wife and mother. If we are looking for the type of sociological reason that McLaughlin attempts to describe for the response of women to Schwenckfeld's teaching, then this is surely it. There were a significant number of widows and single women among the Schwenckfelder circles. Sibilla Eisler, that very significant female presence, although married, does not appear to have had any children of her own. For the mainstream Reformers, the most obvious category in which to think of women was that of wife and mother. Women who were not in this category did not fit easily into the models such theologians developed for the world. With what was effectively an insistence that the social estate, either of marriage or of non-marriage, was irrelevant to the spiritual position, Schwenckfeld was providing the possibility of an alternative model of Christian living.

It is worth reflecting on the rise of celibacy among women in the early church. This was probably as much to do with the increasing sense of autonomy and a desire to assert that as it was with a development of a deeply ascetic spirituality. Society at the time, in a similar way to that of Reformation Europe, understood women best as wives and mothers. Celibacy was a means by which women could find a certain degree of independence.

The position Schwenckfeld seems to have begun to outline, and which is implicit in so much of his writings, was that before God there was no one way

---

[82] Packull, "Commentary on Apocalypse", Erb, *Schwenckfeld and Early Schwenkfeldianism*, p. 65.

[83] *CS*, vol. 8, p. 74, ll. 34f.

of living which was particularly appropriate for women purely in term of their gender. He did not argue for any form of social revolution, as did many of those who shared his radical approach to theology. He could write:

> But this freedom is not a freedom of the flesh but of the spirit and the conscience, not such a freedom which wants to withdraw from the authorities their appropriate honour and fitting obedience...[84]

He could maintain this separation because of the dichotomy between inner and outer. He used the division to argue that outer forms should be preserved, partly at least to ensure social cohesion. But, because the true spiritual life was inner, the outer forms in themselves had no life or meaning.[85] Thus, although he did not want to destroy them, he emptied them of virtually all their life and power.

Heavenly Balm and the Divine Physician

However, such a focus on the ongoing struggle and the final defeat of sin did not mean that Schwenckfeld ignored the present experience of sin. In *Heavenly Balm and the Divine Physician,* he made the reality of sin very clear, employing the language of decay and corruption to do it. In this treatise, he was concerned to show how Christ as both the *warer Artzt* (true physician) and the *gottlich Artzney* (divine medicine) came to restore those whose souls were sick to death, were corrupt and rotting, were suffering and condemned. The contrast of images in this piece, of corruption and beauty, condemnation and renewal, is extremely striking. Although, as we have seen, the body in and of itself was not the cause, nor even a symptom, of alienation from God in Schwenckfeld's understanding, yet the fact that he uses such strongly physical and physically distressing images suggests that body still carried even for him an ambiguous message. The contrast he appears to have been concerned with is the separation between the body as a created existence, and the renewed body, which was being transformed into the likeness of Christ's flesh. Certainly, if the language of these passages is anything to go by, his notion of that body which was no longer to be the believer's was as full of loathing as can be found in any of the patristic writings.

In *Heavenly Balm*, he also spoke of the church, not as an institution to be condemned, or even as useful outwardly, but as he understood it to be seen by God: the church as body.

---

[84] *CS*, vol. 3, p. 874, ll. 4f.

[85] For example; What does not feed eternal life is a food which is of no use to salvation. Sacramental eating does not feed for eternal life. *CS*, vol. 3, p. 880, ll. 11f; and Whether then such outer things as preaching, the Holy Scriptures, Sacraments, Church orders, prayers and the like through which grace comes? may serve and enhance that the person is reborn and renewed in heart, so may no outer thing or element give rebirth... *CS*, vol. 17, p. 85, ll. 9f.

In short, seen in God, the limbs of the body of Christ, the body which is the congregation or the church, are without spot, stain or scar.[86]

This is language which he used elsewhere, but it is particularly important here precisely because of the metaphor. Sickness and healing are bodily images, and so speaking of the church as body carries a particular connotation. Once more Schwenckfeld's metaphors are not, for him, simply pictures to help us to see, but ways of explaining and defining the truth for which he was grasping. To say that the church is a body is not simply to draw a picture, or set up a simile. It is, for Schwenckfeld, to state a truth, which can be worked out through a series of explications. This means that we must take seriously his understanding of body in understanding the nature of his vision of the church.

To look at the actual words used is to be struck by the power of the images. He used very physical words both for the discussion of the sickness and for the healing, and, as with the church as body, in the context these carry great weight. Presumably, it was at least partly the actual metaphor itself that led him to use such body-orientated words, but they are none the less striking for that. The horror with which he presented the corruption of damnation of the sick soul, while it may have been unremarkable in some other writers, reads quite strangely in one whose writing is often very restrained. It echoes some of the horror with which he wrote of the suggestion that the reception of the physical bread and wine was the physical reception of the body of Christ. Words such as *der tode faul / stinckende sünder* [87] are not restrained or dispassionate. He spoke of the soul-sickness as "unspeakably harmful illness"[88] and described such a soul as "dead in sin".[89] By contrast, the healthy, healed soul is described as being cleaned from all *befleckingen*,[90] stain, as altogether whole in God's sight[91] and anointed with the pleasant, joyful oil of rejoicing.[92] The one who heals is also described in almost sensuous terms, with words like, salve, balm, sweet-smelling, joyous oil, fragrance.[93]

The images here speak again of someone who was struggling to hold together opposing perceptions of reality. There is a reaction of horror and

---

[86] *CS*, vol. 9, p. 607, ll. 3f.

[87] "dead, rotten, stinking sinner", *CS*, vol. 9, p. 546, l. 19.

[88] "unaußprechenliche schädliche krankheit" *CS*, vol. 9, p. 544, l. 36

[89] "in sünden todt..." *CS*, vol. 9, p. 533, l. 10.

[90] *CS*, vol. 9, p. 530, l. 27. Interestingly, in the light of some of the suggestions I have made above about the themes of sexuality in this discussion, this is a term which can carry sexual overtones: sich befleckung means masturbation, a practice which was, at the time, considered an extremely serious sin.

[91] *CS*, vol. 9, p. 562, l. 28.

[92] "das senfften freüdenöl" *CS*, vol. 9, p. 593, l. 3.

[93] See chapter 21 of *Heavenly Balm* p. 581f, which uses words like der *gesalbte gottes*, the anointed of god: *mit dem freüdenöl des H gaists erfüllet*, filled with the oil of the joy of the Holy Spirit: *der süsse liebliche namme Jhesus*, the sweet lovely name of Jesus: *der salbung Christam*, the salve of Christ.

disgust to physical reality, especially as found in human bodies. But there is also delight in the senses and a willingness to acknowledge that, albeit only within an appreciation of the divine. It is almost as if all that is good and pure and beautiful – and physically delighting and enticing – can only be admitted if it is projected onto God. The predominant language in which human bodies can be spoken of is of disgust, decay and damnation. And yet, he was unwilling to reject body as an expression of being. As has been made clear throughout this argument, without "body" there was no meaning in the term "being". Thus, his horror at the realities of the human body in its corruption and decay had to be kept separate from the spiritual reality of flesh as the place where the divine is encountered. Therefore, there is this straining to hold together two sets of language, both describing one (physical) reality. The only way in which they could be united was to keep very separate the categories of divine and not-divine, and to project horror onto one, and delight onto the other.

In this, Schwenckfeld would not have been so very different from many of his contemporaries, especially if viewed not simply in a Reformation context. There was a horror of bodies, particularly, as explored elsewhere, female bodies, not only as sinful in themselves, but as the cause of sin in men. However, nowhere in this discussion does he suggest that it is bodies themselves, not even female ones, that are the problem. Rather he was using bodily language to show the corruption of the soul – and also its restoration. The distinctions he drew were between physical categories, not between physical and non-physical.

Clearly, in his discussion of soul-sickness in terms of bodily decay, Schwenkfeld was by no means advocating the mortification of the flesh. That was not a category which received much consideration in his writing. But I suggest that there is something of the same significance going on here. It has been normal through much of Christian thinking to speak of sin in terms which bear at least a family relationship to the language Schwenkfeld used. The whole notion of sickness and healing is one which, as he demonstrated, goes back to Jesus' own language, and indeed beyond that to the Old Testament. The idea of sin as corruption appears in much Christian writing. I suggest that what is important in the language which he used is the holding together of bodily images of corruption and bodily images of delight. He was certainly not advocating sin for sin's sake, so that grace may abound, but there is a hint at least of felix culpa in the way that he wrote. In "Incarnation and Embodiment", I suggested that one of the distinctive things about Schwenckfeld was his refusal to make the identification between sin and flesh. Instead, the way in which he used language and the images that he used argue, as we have seen, for a perception that it is in and through the body that the believer finds salvation. However, he clearly did share the perception that sinful flesh was a horror. But because of the other ways in which he speaks of flesh, we can perceive that this is a horror precisely because it is not the way that things are supposed to be. This is exactly the horror of what should be good turned rotten. Salvation, spoken of with such delight, and in such sensuous terms, is the recovery and rediscovery of something even better than that which might have been expected. Again we recognise that salvation, in Schwenckfeld's thinking, is not about the loss of body, but its rediscovery within the being of God.

Schwenckfeld was not arguing for a move back to felicity of Eden, but a move forward to something new. He was looking for a bringing together of that which was ontologically separate, the two orders. This is the new thing which appears: the bringing of the outer into relationship with the inner, as the believer is reborn with God now as Father and no longer only as Creator. Rebirth is not out of the body, but is in a body. So the life to which it leads, the life of salvation, can be discussed in such bodily terms, and, in particular in these terms of delight and joy. The body, which is now to be given to the believer, is one to rejoice in.

The School of Christ

The final metaphor to be discussed is that of the school. Part of the interest in his use of the image of school is the light which it sheds on the education among the elite, an education which Schwenckfeld himself would have received, an education which was very gender-specific. In the *School of Christ*, the discussion was laid out along these lines:

> Firstly, the School of Christ is in heaven, as is proved by the saying of the Lord (Matt 23:8-10) "You have one Master in Heaven". The Schoolmaster is God the Father, through his Word in the Holy Spirit. The lesson is the knowledge of God in Christ.[94]

There follows a discussion of the nature of the pupil, which reads like a list of school rules in any day school:

> Let him be patient, obedient, eager and willing for his schoolmaster[...]It does not depend on his Schoolmaster, he is always ready, gets up early in the mornings, knocks at the door of the school to be let in, and hears his lesson. He keeps to his own and is encouraging. Let him protect himself from other teachers and lessons, otherwise it would go with him, like his father Adam and all the others who have moved from the proper Teacher to those who do not walk straight, and have fallen into the school of Satan, the AntiChrist and false scribes...Let him avoid the Fencing-school and philosophical squabbles over words and useless matters, which do not take things further.[95]

Then there is a discussion of the curriculum:

> Now in this school the School master leads him to a living spiritual discovery/apprehension/knowledge, which is hidden in Christ alone, which is the sealed book which is sealed with seven seals, that is, the gifts of the Holy Spirit,

---

[94] *CS*, vol. 16, p. 485, ll. 5f.
[95] *CS*, vol. 16, p. 487, ll. 8f and *CS*, vol. 16, p. 488, l. 1.

which nobody can undo and read, or look within, except a new person, born from
God, one who understands the very first judgement of the mystery of the
Kingdom of God, hearing the word of the Schoolmaster, though which word he
previously received the sense of hearing.[96]

Then Schwenckfeld examined the aim of such an education:

> In this school, the Schoolmaster causes him [the pupil] to share in his [God's] own
> nature through Jesus Christ in the Holy Spirit, takes him as a child, a brother of
> Christ and an heir of heaven.[97]

and:

> In this school the pupil is also clothed with the Son of the Schoolmaster, he is not
> allowed to stand naked.[98]

Both of these passages give us glimpses into the system of education which
Schwenckfeld probably grew up with, and which, in his period as tutor to the
von Thumb family, he used. The pupil lived as a member of the tutor's family,
and shared in that life. This then puts a particularly intimate gloss on this
metaphor. It is also a very male metaphor: it was boys who were tutored and
men who were tutors in this system. However, Schwenckfeld did not appear to
be using it as a means of excluding the women from the life and the learning.
The description was not entirely individualistic, since Schwenckfeld also
discussed the role of other teachers:

> He also even has other undermasters and teachers whom he uses externally for his
> outer, old, lazy, forgetful and poor man, so that they should also externally follow
> him, learn, nourish, wash, feed and clothe him.[99]

Although he wrote of the School of *Christ*, he made it very clear that the
Schoolmaster, the one who teaches and is ultimately responsible, was God the
Father. This reads rather oddly in a theology, and particularly in a series of
metaphors, which is profoundly and overwhelmingly Christocentric. It would
have appeared natural for the Schoolmaster to be identified with Christ, for
although there is little suggestion in the Bible of the life of faith being
considered a school, still there are many references in the Gospels to Jesus as
teacher. Paul even uses the word pedagogue of the Law in Gal 3:24. However,
it is very clear in the discussion that Schwenckfeld understands the
Schoolmaster in his image to be the Father – "You have one Master who is
heaven".

---

[96]*CS*, vol. 16, p. 488, ll. 12f.
[97]*CS*, vol. 16, p. 489 , ll. 30f.
[98]*CS*, vol. 16, p. 490, ll. 1f.
[99] *CS*, vol. 16, p. 490, ll. 28f.

By insisting on this identification, Schwenckfeld has opened up for himself an interesting series of explorations within the metaphor that would otherwise have been closed. This is another example of explication which suggests that the metaphor is more than simply a helpful tool in description. So, for example, he could make the assertion that the aim of the school is to make the pupils children of the Master, an image which softens the rather harsh picture of the Christian life as entirely about learning and discipline. He can speak too, of our brotherhood with the Master's Son, an image of identity which was to prove very important in many of his metaphorical explorations. The Christocentrism which is so important in his thinking is in fact located here in this metaphor – the aim of the education is to enable the pupils to become like the Son, to share in the life of Christ. He worked with a clear distinction between God the Father and Christ the Son, the one to whom the believer was to be conformed. Thus, it was appropriate that the Schoolmaster should be understood as God. This left Christ "free", as it were, to be the model.

Another recurrent motif, which is illustrated well in this discussion of the Schül Christi, is the distinction between good and bad teaching, learning and living. In Schwenckfeld's thinking, there was a profound discontinuity between the things of God and the things which are not of God. In this, he was in agreement with the other Reformers of his time – and indeed, with many of the theological thinkers who had gone before him. The opposition between God and the world has been very deeply rooted in Christian thinking from early days, and in the Reformation period this was, on the whole, a non-negotiable assumption. However, different thinkers drew the lines of demarcation in different places. By different metaphors, Schwenckfeld drew the lines in different ways. Here, in the discussion of the school, the line is drawn around proper teaching, and this is one of the most significant markers for him. The contrast between *recht Leerer* (proper teaching) or *warer Leerer* (true teaching) and *falsche Leerer*(false teaching) or *Leerer von irrung*(teaching of error) was for him obvious and dangerous. The natural inclination as far as he saw it was to follow the *falsche Leerer*, and only extreme vigilance and trust in God could ensure that this did not happen. Part of the issue, which does not come out here, but appears for example very clearly in *Deutsche Theologica*,[100] is the distinction between *vernunnft* (reason) or *Philosophia* (philosophy) and *seligmachende geistlich erkandtnis* (saving spiritual knowledge), the one marked entirely by the Fall and unable to grasp the things of God, the other a gift of God in the Spirit and necessary not only for understanding but for salvation itself. This distinction arises in various forms in all the metaphorical discussions, and also very importantly in the other literature.

It is clear that for Schwenckfeld there can be no self-taught Christian. The teaching comes from God. This is part of his conviction that the Christian life depends, in its entirety, on the action and initiative of God. It is not possible for an individual to create their own Christian birth, to promote their own Christian growth or to attain to the aim of Christian existence through their own actions

---

[100] *CS*, vol. 17, pp. 54 ff.

or attitudes. In all of these things, it is God who acts and has the power.

Secondly, there is the importance of the progressive nature of Christian growth. [101] By using the metaphor of School, Schwenckfeld was able to suggest that Christian maturity was not something which was achieved or arrived at quickly and easily. Rather, he could point to a developmental model, within which he could outline various stages, each of which had its appropriate exercises and expectations. In line with the editors of the Corpus, I suggest that in this we can see evidence of his pastoral concern for those with whom he was involved. Although he could make what seem like difficult demands, he also allowed that not all could be achieved at once, and thus allowed room for people to develop some sense of individuality.

Gleichförmigkeit and Erkenntnis

As I mentioned above, Schwenckfeld was clear that he did not accept the theology of the Anabaptists, especially their understanding of discipleship. Furcha suggests that the area of disagreement focused on the question of immediate or gradual life change. While I agree this is part of the difference, I want to suggest another that is visible in this discussion. The Anabaptists argued that Christ could not be known unless he was followed:

> But the medium is Christ, whom no one can truly known unless he follow him in his life and no one may follow him unless he has first known him. [102].

They insisted that the whole of Scripture should be read though the lens of the gospel as pointing to Christ. This approach focused on an imitation of Christ in earthly living. Such an approach entailed a self-conscious identification with the persecuted and crucified Lord. Timothy George suggests that "following" rather then "faith" was the great word of the radical Reformation, and that far from being vicarious, as Luther taught, the Passion of Christ was a contemporary process in which they shared. [103] This was not the approach which Schwenckfeld adopted, and is another of the areas in which he differed from the Anabaptists. The Christ as the centre of his spirituality was not the humiliated and dying One, but the glorified and ascended One. The means of following was different too. Schwenckfeld spoke of identification (*Gleichförmigkeit*), but it was identification with this exalted Lord brought about by the action of God in the believer, not by literal imitation of hardship. It was to do with participation in the divine nature. This brings us on to the

---

[101] Furcha lists several passages where he believes Schwenckfeld was laying out what was almost a programatic "ordo salutis". I want to consider the issue particularly in the context of the discussion of the School.

[102] Hans Denck. "The Contention that Scripture Says", 1526, *Hans Denk Schriften 2 Teil Religiöse Schrifften*, Walter Fellmann, Gütersloh, 1956, pp. 45, 50.

[103] Timothy George, "The Spirituality of the Radical Reformers", *Christian Spirituality II,* ed. Raitt, pp. 338f.

second part of the discussion, the terms which Schwenckfeld used to speak of the life of the new person.

An important element in this discussion is the notion of *Erkenntnis*,[104] which is effective for the healing of all spiritual ills. He was concerned to demonstrate the uselessness in an ultimate sense of external ceremonies or historical knowledge, speaking for example of the Scriptures and services of the church as useful, but not sufficient, for nobody gives life but Jesus. The encounter with Jesus, which is the essence of *Erkenntnis*, was not simply knowing *about* but *knowing* Jesus. In 1560, in "Deutsche Theologia", he defined it in this way:

> The spiritual apprehension of Christ is a knowledge of Christ as the Holy Spirit knows, preaches, praises, glorifies him, and with his heavenly reign and gifts through the gospel, which is the strength of God, brings into the believing heart, therein makes glorious and well-known. It is an apprehension of faith.[105]

The immediacy of this contact formed the central element in the spirituality which was the counterpart of Schwenckfeld's theology. Schwenckfeld came to his theological conclusions, not primarily through intellectual consideration, but through what he understood as a spiritual process. What was known about God and of God's activity was known, not through intellectual effort, but through the action of God. In any consideration of Schwenckfeld's theology and spirituality it is as important to understand this method as it is to understand the conclusion itself. In his discussion of Schwenckfeld's epistemology, Russell H. Hvolbek raises this point.[106] Although he suggest that Schwenckfeld divided reality into physical and non-physical, a conclusion I do not believe to be warranted in the light of Schwenckfeld's actual language, he does argue that this cosmology brings with it a particular epistemology, one in which

---

[104] The translation of the term *erkenntnis* is not straightforward. In many of those who write about Schwenckfeld, the English term "apprehension" is used, and I will follow this practice. However, it is not the full translation, as it misses some of the sense of immediacy and encounter, which is involved in the German expression. Grimms Worterbuch gives several references. There is a link with physical reality: nhd "Adam erkandte seine weib Heva": to recognise something through the senses, 1 Sam 26:17: to know through something, "gott wirt erkandt aus seinen werken". In her essay "Did Mystics Have Sex?", in *Desire and Discipline: Sex and Sexuality in the Premodern West,* eds. Jacqueline Murray and Konrad Eisbechler, Toronto, 1996, pp 296-311, Nancy F. Partner shows how the encounter with God which is the experience of the mystic was often spoken of in sexual terms, and the language of "knowing" becomes significantly eroticised. It also carried implications of "spirituality". Fischer records this usage: "as you free my spirit from desire, you adorn me with the hidden jewels of knowledge", Fischer, *Schwäbisches Wörterbuch,* "erkennen", vol II, columns 802-809.

[105] *CS*, vol. 17, p. 75, ll. 19f.

[106] Russell H. Hvolbeck, "Being and Knowing: Spiritual Epistemology and Anthropology from Caspar Schwenckfeld to Böhme", *Sixteenth Century Journal,* vol 22. Spring 1991, pp. 97-110.

...a deep personal understanding of Christ necessarily preceded full participation in the Christian message: and this understanding had to be given to the individual by the Holy Spirit.[107]

This insistence on *Erkenntnis* was part of Schwenckfeld's experience and teaching from the very beginning. How truth is to be known was an important part of what the truth that was known was conceived to be. I have already discussed how, in the letter of 1556 in which he discussed the way in which he reached his conclusions on eucharistic theology, he described the whole process in terms of a spiritual rather than an intellectual exploration. Thus he could argue that his consideration of the case of Judas was at the leading of God,[108] and also that the solution to his dilemma was given to him by God.[109] This process in itself is an example of the precedence of inner over outer: what Schwenckfeld came to was an inner grasp of an inner truth, which he was later to distinguish from "outer" truth, which might be just as concerned with "spiritual" realities, but which was taught by human beings and not directly by God. Therefore, it was outer, and as such, could not mediate the being of God. So the theology of Schwenckfeld was shaped not only by a formal separation between categories of inner and outer, but also by a differentiation of experience. *Erkenntnis* is not knowledge but experience. It is the experience that is central to the reality which the theology proclaims and explores.

> This is repentance; that we, through the apprehension of sin, turn round and have regret and sorrow over them.[110]

This apprehension is at the centre of the ongoing life of the believer:

> What is God? Does not Peter also say (2 Pet 1:3-4) of a great, great, magnificent promise that we, through the apprehension of Christ, will take part in the divine nature, providing we flee the lusts of this world?[111]

Proper knowledge, *Erkenntnis* was not just a grasp of the facts, but of the essence of salvation. Maier argues that in Schwenckfeld's thinking, there were four aspects to *Erkenntnis*. He defines them as: the promise, the pre-existent Word: the accomplishment, Christ in humiliation: the glorification: Christ in exaltation and the participation: the encounter with Christ, and becoming like him. He suggests that all four elements were present in Schwenckfeld's

---

[107] Hvolbeck, "Being and Knowing", p. 100.
[108] "he threw Judas before me and made me think about what kind of fellow he was" *CS*, vol. 14, p. 802, ll. 19f.
[109] "until the Spirit of the Lord came to help me with his teaching in the sixth chapter of John", *CS*, vol. 14, p. 802, l. 25.
[110] *CS*, vol. 17, p. 91, l. 11.
[111] *CS*, vol. 8, p. 405, ll. 3f.

discussion and in his expectation of the development of the believer.[112] Maier also argues that *"Erkenntnis Christi* [is] a soteriological necessity for the Christian also because the Lord's glorified humanity constituted the nexus between his person and work and the believer".[113] It is through *Erkenntnis* that the encounter with Christ which is the eating and drinking takes place. This is what leads to the new life. It is not primarily a learning, but an experience. But the notion of encounter goes beyond that contained within the notion of the Supper. He described the *Erkenntnis Christi* as a *Herzleere*, and insisted that it is only through this that salvation can be found. It was not entirely removed from intellectual knowledge, and he warned of the dangers of not understanding the doctrines that were involved in it. But it was much more than this intellectual knowledge, and he issued much stronger warnings about depending only on historical or literal faith.

The *Erkenntnis* appears to have been to do with encounter, experience and personal commitment to the perceived living and glorified presence of Christ, and might almost be spoken of in mystical terms. In fact, Schwenkfeld was not given to using mystical language, but the occasions when he did are very instructive. His description of his *Heimsuchungen* suggests that such an experience of the overwhelming and undeniable presence of Christ can be taken as the ultimate in *Erkenntnis*. Such an experience brings with it a sense of certainty which cannot be challenged by anybody else.

As Maier points out, the question of whether Schwenckfeld was a mystic has been asked over and over again.[114] Maier discusses the different ways in which Schwenckfeld might be understood to be, or not to be a mystic, but he includes the following important statement:

> With all the important mystics, both Christian and non-Christian, Schwenckfeld shared a basic conviction; the external was to be subordinate to the internal, the flesh to the spirit, the objective to the subjective.[115]

and he goes on to point that, however else the discussion is shaped, it must focus on his soteriology.

It will be clear that I do not agree with the dichotomies suggested by Maier, but his basic thesis seems to me to be sound; that Schwenckfeld was committed to a dualism which valued one side above the other, and that the heart of this is found in his soteriology. Whether this is best understood as mysticism lies outside the scope of this discussion. But what it points us towards is the intensely interior and personal heart of the spirituality which Schwenckfeld invited others to share. This was a spirituality which was not shaped mainly by liturgical prayer, by the sacraments of the church or even by the experience of the community, but by the direct encounter between the risen and ascended

---

[112] Maier, *Caspar Schwenckfeld on the Person and Work of Christ*, p. 47.

[113] Maier, *Caspar Schwenckfeld on the Person and Work of Christ*, pp. 38-39.

[114] Maier, *Caspar Schwenckfeld on the Person and Work of Christ*, pp. 95ff.

[115] Maier, *Caspar Schwenckfeld on the Person and Work of Christ*, p. 100.

Christ and the believer. This intimate encounter, although it draws on images of knowledge, goes far beyond "knowing about", or that which can be taught. This relationship is much closer to that which exists between friends or even lovers. It is an encounter which is as much to do with emotion as with intellect. Werner Packull, in his discussion of mysticism amongst Anabaptists, demonstrates how Meister Eckhardt's use of the notion of Erkenntnis showed it to be "a saving knowledge of the divine", which presupposed some sort of identity, and he argues:

> To achieve saving knowledge of the Divine, therefore, implied divinity on man's part and humanity on God's.[116]

It is clear that a similar approach can be distinguished in Schwenckfeld's thought. Out of the encounter comes the *Gleichförmigkeit*, the identification of the believer with Christ. Maier presents it this way:

> The ultimate object of soteriology according to Schwenckfeld – man's salvation from sin and creaturity[sic], and the realisation of his true humanity through participation in the divine nature – was achieved by means of a process which the reformer summarised as "the participation" in Christ, the sharing of the Christian in the glorified body of his Lord.[117]

The education we have examined above is to enable *Gleichförmigkeit Christi*. True teaching could be judged because it led to *Gleichförmigkeit*. This is another of the terms which Schwenckfeld used to explain and explore his understanding of the nature of the life to which the believer was reborn. As a term, it meant quite simply "making one thing like another". However, it is clear that it could carry particular theological weight, especially in terms of the will. One definition speaks of "How we should make our will like the will of God". [118] In *The Threefold Life*, he spoke of it in this way:

> The third good work of the Christian life and faith go and are directed at us and are the works of proper penitence, repentance and sorrow for sins; the killing of the evil desires of the flesh and the complete death of our old person in the following of Christ to his likeness, as an entry into the Kingdom of God.[119]

The *Gleichförmigkeit* or likeness to Christ is the way Schwenckfeld spoke of the experience of the new identity which developed through rebirth. It was much more than simply an imitation, or a set of actions. It appears to have carried for him the connotations of identity, and almost merging. Thus, in a

---

[116]Werner O.Packull, *Mysticism and the Early South German-Austrian Anabaptist Movement,* Scottdale, Pennsylvania: Herald Press, 1977, p. 22.

[117] Maier, *Caspar Schwenckfeld on the Person and Work of Christ*, p. 83.

[118] "Wie wir unsern Willen gleich söllen machen dem Willen Gottes", Fischer, *Schwäbisches Wörterbuch*, "gleich", vol III, columns 683-689.

[119] *CS*, vol. 9, p. 864, ll.13f.

letter to Dr Johann Keller in 1542, he wrote:

> Such a holy Christian church is called and is truly a body of Christ Jesus, because he has given himself for her, so that he has generated the same from his flesh and blood in the Holy Spirit (for God has come in flesh, so that the flesh should come back to God). So now he judges our flesh through his divine flesh, so that the same might become a likeness to eternal life.[120]

This statement expresses again the strongly physical way in which he understood the nature of the Incarnation, and the encounter between the believer and God; it is through the *flesh* of the divine that judgement takes place, and it is in the flesh of the believer that the *Gleichförmigkeit* happens. It is the flesh which is "made like". This is of a piece with his insistence that rebirth has a physical element and the new person a physical being.

What is also clear from this quotation is that *Gleichförmigkeit* happens not by the exercise of the will, but through the activity of the Spirit. This sets this notion apart from, for example, the Anabaptist expectation of "walking the way of Christ", which looked to the individual to do this by effort and commitment. There was an understanding of the necessity for various activities and actions which would be a consequence of this *Gleichförmigkeit*. In "The Life and Mind of a Christian"[121] in 1560 he wrote:

> But read Eph 1:5 about the election, calling and foreseenness of the Christian child. For all whom God the Father had foreseen in terms of childhood and inheritance of his Kingdom according to the plan, those he also ordained that they should be like the image of Christ his Son.[122]

The passage that Schwenckfeld is referring to here goes on to speak of the deeds which Christians are called to: that is, there is a behavioural element. However, it was not what Schwenckfeld takes from the passage. Instead he led it back to his own novel concerns. Therefore, after reiterating his language about predestination he continued:

> Thus God the Father acts in the conception and birth of a Christian person, the bones, skin, even to say hair, flesh, veins, blood and all that a Christian needs for his spiritual humanity from the inner strength of the Spirit of God and which the strength of the firstborn son of God, Jesus Christ, who became flesh and blood for his benefit, who also lives in his heart, for the Christian becomes one flesh with Christ, one bone and one spirit.[123]

---

[120] *CS*, vol. 8, p. 254, ll. 33f.
[121] "Vom Christen Menschen/ Bericht auß h. Schrifft/ von seinem Wesen/ Geburt/ Ursprung unnd Heerkommen und von der Ordnung Christliche Leere und Lebens". *CS*, vol. 17, pp. 355 ff.
[122] *CS*, vol. 17, p. 383, ll. 28f.
[123] *CS*, vol. 17, p. 384, ll. 7f.

Once more, the emphasis of his argument was the identity of the believer with Christ, and the physical expression of that identity. The image of Christ which Paul was talking about was to be understood not as actions, or as a form of spirituality, but as an identity of body, flesh, blood, skin hair and bones.

The likeness which Schwenckfeld represented as the end and fullness of salvation was not a moral likeness, or one of activity. It was understood as one of identification and eternal nature. Salvation was, as I have suggested above, moving into the relationship of child to father which was the identity of Jesus. It was experienced and expressed in "physical" terms, and therefore was something to do with flesh.

When this is examined, using the categories of gender, some interesting points emerge. We have already explored the ways in which Schwenckfeld is happy to blur gender identity in his description of the roles and functions of Jesus, in particular his inner-physical meaning. The suggestion contained in the assertion that the flesh of the believer will be conformed to that of Christ's or will share in its identity is surely that the gender identity of the believer's physical being is also less than rigid. Once more, we see the destabilisation of the notion of gender, when the theology is examined.

It is clear that, for Schwenckfeld, enabling and guarding the relationship between the believer and God was the aim and end of theological exploration. He also demonstrated the conviction that such a relationship was open to and required of both men and women. In all of this, he was doing nothing exceptional. Where it did become exceptional was his implication that, before God and in relationship to the divine, the categories were not only equal but were meaningless. With separation of bodily sexuality and socially functional gender, seen first in Jesus and then offered to believers, he was presenting a radically altered understanding of the meaning of physical existence. Such existence was not, in Schwenckfeld's theology, a temporary phase which would pass away with the attainment of complete salvation. Rather, transformed physicality was an inherent part of salvation, and as such began in current experience, through rebirth and Christian growth.

However, a fundamental part of determining the meaning of physical existence, and the way it was worked out, reproductive sexuality, was reshaped. With the multiplicity of gender roles which the flesh of Christ played, and the identification of that flesh with the means and the meaning of salvation, the bodily reality of male and female no longer determined the social and spiritual position of the believer. The causes which others have suggested for women's response to this teaching are in fact symptoms of this theological cause. By destabilising the notions of gender and the links between gender and bodily meaning, Schwenckfeld created the possibility for new types of relationships, communal activities and roles.

Chapter 6

Schwenckfeld, Women and Theology

Contemporary discussions about women in the reformation, while dealing with the social and cultural forces which helped to shape the position of women, also point out that women were not simply victims of or passive reactors to forces beyond themselves. Investigations have helped us to see that women felt themselves to be able to come to conclusions on religious and theological issues in their own competence, and to act on these. However, as we have seen, there has not been a great deal of work done yet on exactly why some women chose particular theologies, and what questions they found answered within them. Apart from the work of Nancy Roelker, Peter Matheson, Elsie Anne McKee and Marion Kobelt-Groch, the exploration of women as theological agents, with intellectual as well as social reasons for responding is as yet a largely ignored field.

In the study of Schwenckfeld's own thinking this is also an area in which exploration has been limited. Although a great deal of work has been done both to trace the influences on his thinking, and to explore what is its heart and controlling principle, several gaps still remain. Little has been done to examine the reasons why people, men and women, responded to a teaching that was not presented publicly, and which opened its devotees to suspicion and pressure. Nor has there been any extended discussion about the theology itself in terms of the claims it makes about the place and destination of the human body, despite the fact that the notion of the body is clearly central to Schwenckfeld's own thinking. Such examination as has been made of this aspect of his thinking has assumed that body is an undifferentiated category, with no symbolic or spiritual meaning attached to it. This type of approach has not taken into account the recent discussions about the perceptions of body and the impact of gender studies in helping us to examine in a more effective way the patterns of thought inherent in certain ways of talking about body and its place.

While, for most of those who have written about Schenckfeld and about the community which was shaped by his thelogy, the presence of women both in significant numbers and in significant roles has been acknoweldged, there has been little attempt to explore what these two facts mean. It has been suggested, most clearly by Schulz, and by implication by others, that the courtesy and attention which Schwenckfeld undoubtedly showed was the primary reason for the response. The adoption of an unorthodox theology and the role of leadership within the groups resulted from the depth of relationships which Schwenckfeld developed with the women he called friends.

Others, in particular McLaughlin, have argued that the move away from formal and public religion created more opportunity for women to take part in the movement. In the private sphere, women were more visible anyway, and therefore there was a greater freedom for women to exercise roles of leadership and teaching.

It is the argument of this thesis that these two accounts are inadequate, both in the light of an investigation of Schwenckfeld's theology, and the contemporary examinations which are being made into the place and activities of women in the reformation period. Any account of women's roles which does not take women's own power of choice and theological awareness into consideration must be regarded as seriously flawed. To account for the women's response in the ways that have been outlined above is to suggest that they had no theological interest as such, and that their reaction to theological debate and discovery was entirely shaped by social realities or emotional reactions.

In this thesis, I have been concerned to show that by assuming that there were theological reasons for the response of those women who identified themselves with Schwenckfeld, it is possible to construct an account of such women which takes seriously their own testimony regarding their position. As part of this argument, I have questioned the theology in terms of gender, in order to explain why some women found this, rather than other theologies, something to which they responded.

It has also been part of my concern to show that asking these questions of Schwenckfeld's thought has provided the tools which allow us to discover a coherent system of thought in his work. Working from the assumption that he was essentially a pragmatic rather than a theoretical theologian, I have suggested that gender, especially the scientific and functional aspects of gender, were never far below the surface in shaping the way he thought about God and the activity of God.

Schwenckfeld's theology was driven by his understanding of the eucharist, and when this theology is examined in terms of its gender content, it becomes clear that, for Schwenckfeld, the central ideas were less to do with the relationship between body and bread and more with the relationship between believer and Christ. He presented a position in which the sacramental encounter took place not in the transformation of the bread, nor in the receiving of the bread, but in the body of the believer. This became the site of spiritual reality. Central to this notion was his understanding of a spiritual physicality, an ontology which he referred to as inner. The flesh of Christ, which is the origin of the Christian's life was understood as having this inner being, and was encountered in an inner way. However, the emphasis on physical language and the recognition of the need for a physical expression of the Christian life demonstrate that although a dualism operated in Schwenckfeld's thought, it was not one which separated body and spirit. Rather, it was one which, in certain contexts gave spiritual meaning and value to physical being.

I have argued that in traditional social and theological thinking a symbolic link had developed between female and physical, a link which in general denied spiritual meaning to physical expression. The status, therefore, of that which was female was lowered. Schwenckfeld's position, on the other hand, affirmed the spiritual worth of the physical, and by extension, those who symbolically and physically represented it.

In addition to this, I have also considered the patterns of thought demonstrated by his language about the eating and drinking which were at the heart of this experience. These show an identification of Christ with the female functions both of preparing food in the kitchen and of being food in lactation. Since he made no suggestion that physiologically Christ was female, such a position offered the possibility of a less than rigid insistence on gender definition, especially in terms of function. Thus, theologically, it became possible for those whose physiological gender might have been expected to rule them out of certain positions in fact to undertake them. Physiological gender and social function could be separated.

This argument depends entirely on the understanding which Schwenckfeld developed with regard to the nature of Christ's flesh, and in this thesis I have examined this under two aspects; Mary's conception of the flesh and the continuing being of the flesh.

In examining Mary's conception, it became clear that underlying much of Schwenckfeld's thinking was an Aristotelian view of biology, and in particular of conception. Aristotle taught that the giving of the being of life was the function of the father, and the mother's contribution was simply that of providing the stuff or material within which life was expressed. Schwenckfeld's explanation of the place of Mary in the divine economy quite clearly demonstrates this position. With that insight into his understanding of the world, it also becomes clear that he applied this not only to Christ's birth, but to the being of the Christian believer.

By locating the origin of Christ's being, including his flesh, in the fatherly activity of God, Schwenckfeld demonstrated that flesh and spirit need not be opposed categories, and that divinity could be present in and include flesh. He also insisted that Mary's role in the Incarnation could be limited to that of "stuff-giver", and therefore, she was not in any particular way, especially that of her virginity, a model for women. He removed any sense that virginity as physical integrity had a spiritual value. However, he did not, in consequence, suggest that marriage in itself was a higher spiritual state, a position which separated him from the majority of other reformers. His discussion of marriage focused on it as a social estate, which was effectively theologically neutral. This appears to have been because, like other sacramental activities of the church, marriage came under the heading of outer, and so had no spiritual vitality per se. By avoiding, on theological grounds, the suggestion that marriage and motherhood were the only calling of God on a woman's life, he provided another theological reason why those women who were anomalous – unmarried, widowed or childless – found a spiritual and intellectual home with his thinking, and it is striking that, as we have seen, several of the most prominent women in the movement were in these categories. His position on marriage and virginity, positions he adopted from theological convictions, meant that he was not suspicious of or wary of women as sexual beings.

The suggestion that women warmed to his teaching because he treated them with courtesy and respect has merit in this context, but it is important to notice that, while this position may have been perceived in a particular way because of his courtly background, it was driven and shaped by a definite theological position.

In examining the continuing flesh of Christ, the relationship between a male saviour and both male and female believers has been considered. Because of the position which he adopted about the value of body, Schwenckfeld had effectively created theological space for saying that physiological gender was irrelevant in the consideration of salvation. Thus, there were no differences in the salvation of men and women, nor was the working out of that salvation in appropriate Christian living different. In this way, on the basis of his theology, he discounted one of the ways in which gender had been used to determine religious position and behaviour.

As we have seen, role and function had long been determined by gender, and by particular beliefs about gender, shaped by theology and science. Theologically, the belief that woman was responsible for sin had led to the conviction that women were more in danger of sinning, and therefore had to be more closely controlled, and also that women were more likely to be occasions for sin, and thus men had to be protected from them. Scientifically, the belief about women's inherent weakness and imperfection had led to the conviction that women were not capable of certain roles or tasks, and that their life was to be shaped by the biological requirements of child-bearing and rearing. Since science and religion were both understood to be ways of defining truth, they reinforced each other, and as a result, the place of women in society, and the roles which were open to women were clearly defined on the basis of scientific and religious foundations. By raising the possibility that physiological gender was not the only defining feature in activity or in position before God, Schwenckfeld challenged these assumptions.

His consideration of the nature of Christ's flesh in its continuing existence, as well as reinforcing the spiritual nature and value of flesh which had been fathered by God, also allowed him the freedom to differentiate physiological from symbolic and functional gender. That Christ's flesh, while physiologically male, also functioned in a female way, was extremely important in the theology which he was expounding. He was not saying that here was a man *acting* as a woman, in the sense of pretending, or adopting a role which was unexpected, but rather that the actual being of the flesh which was Christ's functioned in the world as female flesh, in feeding, giving form to life and in its weakness and lack of self-determination. He presented an understanding of the flesh of Christ, as weak and yet redeeming, thus removing the stigma of weakness as a punishment. He also showed flesh not only as that which gives life, in the sacramental experience, but as that in which divine life was expressed. This insistence that flesh was not removed from divinity, but in fact was central to it was a very important theological statement. With these assertions, he refused any suggestion that in order to be saved women must give up their femaleness, with its connotations of physicality. Theologically, he claimed the opposite; that it was in and through physicality – in the believer's body and through the body of Christ, both understood as having spiritual-physical reality – that salvation happened.

This position had its consequences in the way in which that theology was worked out in a spirituality. His understanding of the nature of the believer was shaped by a literal concept of rebirth. Although this involved him in some incoherence of ideas, particularly about the being of the mother of the Christian, it did allow him to reinforce the place of physicality in spirituality, and the role of biology in theology. The duality of origins, of God's fathering activity and God's creative activity lies at the heart of his understanding of soteriology. This can only be understood if the notion of God as a father in the Aristotelian model is perceived. There are several models by which Schwenckfeld explores the physical origins of redeemed flesh. One of the ways in which he used the language suggests that the redeemed flesh takes it form from the existing flesh of the believer. The existing physical being becomes the "stuff" out of which the new person is created. This therefore feminises the flesh of the believer, including that of male believers.

In another mode of discussion, Christ is the stuff, and so it is his body which functions in the female role. In both of these ways of discussing the new person, as a result of theological convictions, the separation of physiological and functional or social gender is once more asserted.

The discussions, therefore, of Mary's conception of Christ, and of the continuing flesh which is Christ's and which becomes the believers, raise the possibilities firstly, of the separation of function and physiology, and secondly, of the spiritual value of physical existence. In both of these possibilities lie the opportunities for women to be affirmed in their bodily presence, and to undertake different roles within a community. Since it is clear from the court and other records that women represented themselves as responding to Schwenckfeld's teaching because of its theological content, and particularly because of his teaching about the nature and being of Christ, it is an appropriate conclusion that the possibilities which the teachings presented were ones which some women exploited.

His consideration of the developmental patterns of the believer, explored in a series of metaphors, while reinforcing the idea of a growing individual, also opens up the meanings of his central themes of *Erkenntnis* and *Gleichförmigkeit*. In the notion of *Gleichförmigkeit*, we find again that the spiritual value of flesh is reaffirmed. *Gleichförmigkeit*, as Schwenckfeld used it, referred not simply to a moral or even spiritual identification, but one of origin and being. In Schwenckfeld's thinking, being had to be expressed in physical form. This is the pattern I have called physical spirituality. It was in the spiritual physicality that progress towards *Gleichförmigkeit* was to be made by the believer; there was to be an identity between the flesh of the believer and the flesh of Christ. Thus, flesh is that in which divinity was encountered and in which the divine life of faith was to be expressed.

The emphasis on *Erkenntnis*, leads to a freedom from external authority which validates the voice of each individual's experience. This was consciously a position of freedom, and a rejection of any need for hierarchical approval. Such a position has historically been the one adopted by women, denied a voice within the structures of the church. In both of these affirmations, Schwenckfeld was again leaving to one side the current gender issues about the nature of authority and the expression of spirituality. Once more, these positions, with all that they meant for women speaking with their own voice and acting in their own right, emerge from a particular set of theological convictions. These convictions were deeply shaped by biological presuppositions, and carried with them significant conclusions about the nature and expression of gender.

Caspar Schwenckfeld did not set out to write a theology which would undermine or even challenge the gender understanding of his community. In fact, he did not set out to write a theology at all. Rather, impelled by a desire both to live himself and to enable others to live lives which were shaped by the calling of God in Christ, he started from a position of pragmatism and ended with a fully-shaped, though not always completely coherent world-view. This view contained within it a profound destabilisation of the gender constructions of his day. He did not make this explicit, nor did those who adopted his teaching cite this as a reason for their commitment. However, by their practices, they demonstrated that gender expectations were changed, and the implications of sexed bodies were perceived in a different way.

Those who have written on Schwenckfeld previously have separated the theology from the widely acknowledged fact that women played a significant and unusual role in his movement. This thesis maintains that bringing these two together provides a fresh insight both into the theology and into the reasons why so many women responded in such a powerful way. With Schwenckfeld's own insistence that the reality of faith was worked out in a life of growing Christlikeness, it seems appropriate that one of the most radical elements of the life of the community should be credited to the power of the theology. Schwenckfeld gloried in the title *weiber prediger*. I suggest that we need to take the meaning of that seriously, and recognise that the women who responded did so on theological as well as social grounds.This theology offered these women the possibility of a space to call their own. In limiting their response to social or emotional reaction we do a disservice both to them, and to the man whose theology helped to shape them. Instead, in their stories, we hear again the response of individuals to a call of truth, which affirmed their humanity and called them to divinity.

Bibliography

Primary Sources

Aristotle *Generation of Animals*, trans A. L. Peck, Harvard, 1943.
Aquinas *Summa Theologica*
Augustine *Confessions*
Cyprian *Epistles*
Erasmus *Twenty Select Colloquies*, trans Sir Roger L'Estrange, London, 1680.
Galen *Oeuvres de Galen*, trans Dr Ch Darembourg, Paris, 1854.
Gregory of Nazianzus *Epistles*
Chester David Hartranft, Otto Berhardt Schlutter, Elmer Ellsworth
Schultz Johnson, Selina Gerhardt Schulz, Eds. *Corpus
Schwenckfeldianorum*, 19 vols,Pennsburg, Pennsylvania: The Board of
Publication of the Schwenkfelder Church, 1907-1961.
Irenaeus *Against the Heretics*
Jerome *Letters*.
Martin Luther *Table Talk*, trans William Hazlitt, London, 1995.

Secondary Sources

Abray, Lorna Jane, *The People's Reformation, Magistrates, Clergy and
Commons in Strasbourg, 1590-1598*. Oxford: Blackwell, 1985.
Aston, Margaret. *Faith and Fire: popular and unpopular religion, 1350-1600*.
London: Hambledon, 1993.
Atkinson, Clarissa W., *The Oldest Vocation: Christian Motherhood in the
Middle Ages*, Ithaca and London: Cornell University Press, 1991.
Bainton, Roland, *Women of the Reformation*, 3 vols, Minneapolis: Augsburg
Publishing House, 1971-1977.
Becker-Cantarino, Barbara, *Die Frau von der Reformation zur Romantik: Die
Situation der Frau vor dem Hintergrund der Literatur- und
Sozialgeschichte*, Bonn, Bouvier, 1980.
Bielfeldt, Dennis, "Deification as a Motif in Luther's Dictata super psalterium",
in *Sixteenth Century Journal*, vol 28, 1997, pp. 401-420.
Blakemore, Diane. *Understanding Utterances: An Introduction to Pragmatics*,
Mass: Blackwell, 1992.
Brady, Thomas A. Jr., *Ruling Class, Regime and Reformation at Strassburg*,
Studies in Medieval and Reformation Thought, vol XXII, Leiden: Brill,
1978.
- *Communities, Politics and Reformation in Early Modern Europe*, Leiden:

Brill, 1998.
- "In Search of the Godly City: The Domestication of Religion in the German Urban Reformation" in Hsia R. Po-chia ed. *The German People and the Reformation*, Ithaca: Cornell University Press, 1988, pp.14-31.
- "Architect of Persecution: Jacob Sturm and the Fall of the Sects at Strasbourg" *Archiv für Reformationsgeschichte*, 79, 1988, pp. 262-281.
- "You hate us priests: Anticlericalism, communalism and the control of women at Strasbourg in the age of the Reformation",in Peter A. Dykema, and Heiko A Oberman,. *Anticlericalism in Late medieval and Early Modern Europe*, Leiden: Brill, 1993.
Bornkamm, Heinrich, *Luther in Mid-Career, 1521-1530*, trans E. Theodore Bachmann, London: Darton, Longman and Todd, 1983.
Børresen, Kari Elisabeth, (ed.) *Image of God and Gender Models in Judaeo-Christian Tradition*, Oslo: Solum Forlag, 1991.
Bossy, John, *Christianity in the West, 1400-1700*, Oxford: Oxford University Press, 1985.
Boxer, Marilyn J., and Quaetart, Jean H., (eds.), *Connecting Spheres: Women in the Western World 1500 to the Present*, Oxford, New York: Oxford University Press, 1987.
Brecht, Martin, *Martin Luther: Shaping and Defining the Reformation, 1521-1532*, (trans James L. Schaff) Minneapolis: Fortress Press, 1990.
Bridenthal, Renathe, and Koonz, Claudia, (eds.) *Becoming Visible: Women in European History*, Boston: Houghton Mifflin, 1977.
Brink, Jean R., Coudert, Allison P., and Horowitz Maryanne, (eds.) *The Politics of Gender in Early Modern Europe*, London: Kirkville, Mo. Sixteenth Century Journal Publishers, 1989.
Brown, Peter, *The Body and Society, Men, Women and Sexual Renunciation in Early Christianity*, London: Faber, 1989.
Brundage, James A, *Law, Sex and Christian Society in Medieval Europe*, Chicago: University of Chicago Press, 1987.
- *Sex, Law and Marriage in the Middle Ages*, Aldershot:Variorum, 1993.
Bullough, Vern L., "On Being a Male in the Middle Ages", in Clare A. Lees, Thelma Fenster, and Jo Ann McNamara (eds) *Medieval Masculinities: Regarding Men in the Middle Ages*, Minneapolis and London: University of Minnesota Press, 1992.
Bullough, Vern L. and Brundage, James A., *Sexual Practices and the Medieval Church*, New York: Prometheus Books, 1982.
Büsser, Fritz, "The Spirituality of Zwingli and Bullinger", in Jill Raitt, Bernard McGinn, and John Meyendorff, (eds.) *Christian Spirituality, Vol 2, High Middle Ages and Reformation*, London: SCM 1989.
Butler, Judith, *Bodies that Matter: In the Discursive Limits of "Sex"*, London and New York: Routledge, 1993.
Bynum, Caroline Walker, *Jesus as Mother: Studies in the Spirituality of the High Middle Ages*, Berkeley and London: University of California Press,

1982.

-*Holy Feast and Holy Fast: The Religious Significance of Food to Medieval Women*, Berkeley and London: University of California Press, 1987.

- *Fragmentation and Redemption: Essays on Gender and the Human Body in Medieval Religion*, New York: Zone Books, 1991.

- "...And Woman His Humanity", in Caroline Walker Bynum, Steven Harrell and Paula Richman, *Gender and Religion: On the Complexity of Symbols*, Boston, Massachusetts: Beacon, 1985.

- "The Body of Christ in the Later Middle Ages: An Answer to Leo Steinberg", Bynum, *Fragmentation and Redemption: Essays on Gender and the Human Body in Medieval Religion*, New York, 1991.

Bynum, Caroline Walker, Harrell Stevan and Richman Paula, *Gender and Religion: On the Complexity of Symbols*, Boston, Mass, Beacon, 1985.

Cadden, Joan, *Meanings of Sex Difference in the Middle Ages: Medicine, Science and Culture*, Cambridge; Cambridge University Press, 1993.

Cameron, Euan, *The European Reformation*, Oxford: Clarendon, 1991.

Chrisman, Miriam Usher, "Women and the Reformation in Strasbourg, 1490-1530", *Archiv für Reformationsgeschichte* 63-63, 1972-73, pp. 143-168.

- "*Lay Culture, Learned Culture: books and social change in Strasbourg 1480-1599*, London and New Haven: Yale University Press, 1982.

- "Haug Marschalck: Lay Supporter of the Reform", in Andrew C. Fix and Susan C. Karant-Nunn, (eds.) *Germania Illustrata: Essays on Early Modern Germany, Presented to Gerard Strauss*, Kirksville, Mo: Sixteenth Century Journal Publishers, 1992

Chrisman, Miriam Usher and Gründler Otto, *Social Groups and Religious Ideas in the Sixteenth Century*, Kalamazoo: Western Michigan University, 1978.

Clark Elizabeth A., *Women in the Early Church: Message of the Fathers to the Church*, vol 13, Wilmington, Delaware: Michael Glazier, 1983.

Clasen, Claus-Peter, *Anabaptism: A Social History, 1525-1618. Switzerland, Austria, Moravia, South and Central Germany*, Ithaca and London: Cornell University Press, 1972.

Cohn, Norman, *The Pursuit of the Millennium: Revolutionary Millenarians and Mystical Anarchists of the Middle Ages*, London: Pimlico, 1993.

Crawford, Patricia, (ed) *Women and Religion in England, 1500-1720*, London: Routledge, 1993.

- "Attitudes to Menstruation in Seventeenth Century England", *Past and Present*, vol 91, 1981, pp. 47-73.

Crawford, Patricia and Mendelson Sara, "Sexual Identities in Early Modern England: The Marriage of Two Women in 1680", *Gender and History*, vol 7, 1995, pp. 362-377.

Cressy, David, "Purification, Thanksgiving and the Churching of Women in Post-Reformation England", *Past and Present*, vol 141, 1993, pp. 106-146.

Davis, Natalie Zemon, *Society and Culture in Early Modern France: Eight*

Essays, Cambridge: Polity, 1987.

-"Boundaries and the Sense of Self in Sixteenth-century France", in Thomas C. Heller, Morton Sonsa and David E. Wellberg, (eds) *Reconstructing Individualism: Autonomy, Individuality and the Self in Western Thought*, Stamford, Calif: Stanford University Press, 1986.

Davis, Natalie Zemon and Farge, Arlette, (eds) *A History of Women, Vol 3,Renaissance and Enlightenment Paradoxes*, Cambridge, Massachusetts and London: Belknap, 1993

Dent, C. M., "Zwingli",in Cheslyn Jones, Geoffrey Wainwright and Edward Yarnold SJ.,(eds) *The Study of Spirituality*, London: SPCK, 1986.

- "The Anabaptists" Cheslyn Jones, Geoffrey Wainwright and Edward Yarnold SJ.,(eds) *The Study of Spirituality*, London: SPCK, 1986.

Deppermann, Klaus, *Melchior Hoffman: Social Unrest and Apocalyptic Visions in the Age of Reformation*, trans Malcom Wren, ed. Benjamin Drewery, Edinburgh: T&T Clark, 1987.

Diefendorf, Barbara B. and Hesse, Carla, *Culture and Identity in Early Modern Europe 1500-1800: Essays in Honor of Natalie Zemon Davis*, Ann Arbor: Michigan University Press, 1993.

Douglass, Jane Dempsey, "Christian Freedom: What Calvin Learnt at the School of Women", *Church History*, 53, 1984, pp. 155-173.

-"The Image of God in Woman as seen by Luther and Calvin", in Kari Elisabeth Børresen, (ed.) *Image of God and Gender Models in Judaeo-Christian Tradition*, Oslo: Solum Forlag, 1991.

-*Women, Freedom and Calvin*, Philadelphia, Pa: Westminster Press, 1985.

Douglas, Mary, *Purity and Danger: An analysis of concepts of pollution and taboo*, London: Ark, 1984.

Duffy, Eamonn, "Holy Maydens, Holy Wyfes: The Cult of Women Saints in fifteenth and sixteenth century England.", in W.J. Shiels, and Diana Wood, (eds) *Women in the Church*, Oxford: Basil Blackwell, 1990.

Dunn, James D.G,. *Christology in the Making: An Inquiry into the Origins of the Doctrine of the Incarnation*, London: SCM, 1989.

Dykema, Peter A. and Oberman, Heiko A., *Anticlericalism in Late medieval and Early Modern Europe*, Leiden: Brill, 1993.

Ecke, Karl, *Kaspar Schwenckfeld: Ungelöste Geistesfragen der Reformationszeit*, Ulm, 1965.

Edwards, Mark U. Jr., *Printing, Propaganda and Martin Luther*, London and Berkley: University of California Press, 1994.

Egli, Emil et al., *Huldrych Zwingli sämtliche Werke*, Zurich, 1905.

Eltis, D.A., "Tensions Between Clergy and Laity in some Western German Cities in the Later Middle Ages", *Journal of Ecclesiastical History*, vol 43, 1992, pp. 231-248.

Epstein, Cynthia Fuchs, *Deceptive Distinctions: Sex, Gender and the Social Order*, New Haven and New York: Yale University Press, 1988.

Epstein, Julia and Straub Kristina, (eds) *Body Guards: The Cultural Politics of*

Gender Ambiguity, London: Routledge, 1991.

Erb, Peter C., *Schwenckfeld in his Reformation Setting*, Valley Forge, 1978.

- *Schwenckfeld and Early Schwenkfeldianism: Papers Presented at the Colloquium on Schwenckfeld and the Schwenkfelders, September 17-22, 1984*, Pennsburg, Pa: The Schwenckfelder Library, 1986.

Estep, William R., *The Anabaptist Story: An Introduction to Sixteenth Century Anabaptism*, Third Edition, Michigan and Cambridge: Eerdmans, 1996.

Fellmann, Walter, *Hans Denk Schrfiten 2 teil Religiöse Schrifften*, Gütersloh, 1956.

Fildes, Valerie, (ed) *Women as Mothers in Pre-industrial England: Essays in Memory of Dorothy McLaren*, London: Routledge, 1990.

Finch, A. J., "Sexual Relations and Marriage in Later Medieval Normandy", *Journal of Ecclesiastical History*, vol 47, 1996, pp. 236-266.

Fissell, Mary, "Gender and Generation: Representing Reproduction in Early Modern England", *Gender and History*, vol 7, No 3, 1995, pp. 433-456.

Fisher, J.D.C., *Christian Initiation: The Reformation Period. Some Early Reformed Rites of Baptism and Confirmation and Other Contemporary Documents*, London: SPCK, 1970.

Fix, Andrew C. and Karant-Nunn, Susan C., *Germania Illustrata: Essays on Early Modern Germany, Presented to Gerald Strauss*, Kirksville, Mo: Sixteenth Century Journal Publishers, 1992.

Fletcher, Anthony, *Gender, Sex and Subordination in England 1500-1800*, London and New Haven: Yale University Press, 1995.

Fleischer, Manfred P., "Are Women Human? The debate of 1595 Between Valens Acidatius and Simon Gediccus", *Sixteenth Century Journal*, vol 12, 1981, pp. 107-120.

Fritz, D.F., *Ulmische Kirchengeschichte vom Interim bis zum dreißigjährigen Krieg, 1548-1612*, Stuttgart, 1934.

Furcha, Edward J., *Caspar Schwenckfeld's Concept of the New Man: A Study in the Anthropology of Caspar Schwenckfeld von Ossig as Set Forth in His Major Writings*, Pennsburg, Pa, The Schwenkfelder Library 1970.

Gäbler, Ulrich, *Huldrych Zwingli, His Life and Work*, trans. Ruth C.L. Gritsch, Edinburgh, T&T Clark, 1986.

Gamarnikow, Eva, Morhan, David H.J., Purvis, June and Taylorson, Daphne, *The Public and the Private*, London: Heinemann, 1983.

George, Timothy, *The Theology of the Reformers*, Nashville, Tenn: Broadman 1998.

- "The Spirituality of the Radical Reformation", in Cheslyn Jones, Geoffrey Wainwright, Edward Yarnold S.J. (eds) *The Study of Spirituality*, London: SPCK, 1986.

Goertz, Hans-Jürgen, *Thomas Müntzer: Apocalyptic Mystic and Revolutionary*, trans. Jocelyn Jacquiery, ed Peter Matheson, Edinburgh: T&T Clark, 1993.

Gould, Graham, "Women and the Fathers", in W.J. Shiels, W.J. and Diana Wood, *Women in the Church*, Oxford: Basil Blackwell, 1990. pp. 1-14.

Graham, Elaine, *Making the Difference: Gender, Personhood and Theology*,London: Mowbray, 1995.

Graef, Hilda, *Mary: A History of Doctrine and Devotion*, London and NewYork: Sheed and Ward, 1963.

Greenblatt, Stephen, "Fiction and Friction", in Thomas C. Heller, Morton Sosna, and David E. Wellberg., *Reconstructing Individualism: Autonomy, Individuality and the Self in Western Thought*, Stanford, Calif: Stanford University Press, 1986.

Haliczer, S., *Inquisition and Society in Early Modern Europe*, London, Croom Helm, 1987.

Hamilton, Bernard *Religion in the Medieval West*, London: Edward Arnold, 1986.

Hanley, Sarah, "Family and State in Early Modern France: The Marriage Pact.", in Marilyn J. Boxer, and Jean H. Quaetart, (eds.), *Connecting Spheres: Women in the Western World 1500 to the Present*, Oxford, New York: Oxford University Press, 1987.

Harrington, Joel F., *Reordering Marriage and Society in Reformation Germany*, Cambridge: Cambridge University Press, 1995.

- "Hausväter and Landesväter, Paternalism and Marriage Reform in Sixteenth Century Germany", *Central European History*, vol 25, 1994, pp. 52-75.

Harrison, Wes, "The Role of Women in Anabaptist Thought and Practice: The Hutterite Experience of the Sixteenth and Seventeenth Centuries", *Sixteenth Century Journal*, 23, 1992, pp. 49-69.

Haskins, Susan *Mary Magdalene: Myth and Metaphor*, London, 1993.

Heller, Thomas C., Sonsa Morton and Wellberg David E., *Reconstructing Individualism: Autonomy, Individuality and the Self in Western Thought*, Stanford, Calif: Stanford University Press, 1986.

Hsia, R. Po-chia,(ed.) *Social Discipline in the Reformation: Central Europe 1550- 1780*, London: Routledge, 1989.

- "Münster and the Anabaptists", in Hsia. R. Po-chia, *The German People and the Reformation,* Ithaca: Cornell University Press, 1988.

Hsia, R. Po-chia ,(ed.) *The German People and the Reformation*, Ithaca: Cornell University Press, 1988.

Horowitz, Maryanne Cline, "The Science of Embryology Before the Discovery of the Ovum" in Marilyn J. Boxer, and Jean H. Quaetart, (eds.), *Connecting Spheres: Women in the Western World 1500 to the Present*, Oxford, New York: Oxford University Press, 1987, pp. 86-94.

Hufton, Olwen, *The Prospect Before Her: A History of Women in Western Europe, Vol 1, 1500-1800*, London: Harper Collins, 1995.

Hvolbeck, Russell H., "Being and Knowing: Spiritual Epistemology fromSchwenckfeld to Böhme", *Sixteenth Century Journal*, 22, 1991, pp. 77-110.

Irwin, Joyce, *Womanhood in Radical Reformation 1525-1675*, New York, 1979.

Jacobsen, Grethe, "Women, Marriage and the Magisterial Reformation: the case of Malmø, Denmark", in Kyle C. Sessions and Phillip N. Bebb, *Pietas et Societas: New Trends in Reformation Social History. Essays in Honour of Harold J. Grimm*, Kirksville Mo.: Sixteenth Century Journal Publishers, 1985.

Jones Cheslyn, Wainwright Geoffrey, Yarnold Edward S.J., *The Study of Spirituality*, London: SPCK, 1986.

Kamen, Henry, *European Society, 1500-1700*, London: Hutchinson, 1984.

Karant-Nunn , Susan, *The Reformation of Ritual: An Interpretation of Early Modern Germany*, London: Routledge, 1997.

-"Continuity and Change: Some Effects of the Reformation On the Women in Zwickau", *Sixteenth Century Journal*, vol 13/2, 1982, pp. 17-42.

-"Kinder, Küche, Kirche: Social Ideology in the Sermons of Johannes Mattheius", in Andrew C. Fix and Susan C. Karant-Nunn, (eds.) *Germania Illustrata: Essays on Early Modern Germany, Presented to Gerard Strauss*, Kirksville, Mo: Sixteenth Century Journal Publishers, 1992. pp. 121-144.

Kay, Sarah and Rubin, Miri, (ed), *Framing Medieval Bodies*, Manchester: Manchester University Press, 1994.

Kelly, Joan, *Women, History and Theory*, Chicago and London: University of Chicago Press, 1984.

Kieckheffer, Richard, "Major Currents in Late Medieval Devotion", in Jill Raitt, Bernard McGinn, and John Meyendorff, *Christian Spirituality, Vol 2, The High Middle Ages and the Reformation*, London: SCM 1989.

Klaassen, Walter, "The Abomination of Desolation: Schwenckfeld's Christological Apocalyptic" Peter Erb, (ed) *Schwenckfeld and Early Schwenkfeldianism: Papers Presented at the Colloquium on Schwenckfeld and the Schwenkfelders, September 17-22, 1984*, Pennsburg, Pa. 1986.

Klassen, John, "Women and Family Among the Dutch Anabaptist Martyrs", *Mennonite Quarterly Review*, 60, 1986, pp. 548-571.

Kobelt-Groch, Marion, *Aufsässige Tochters Gottes: Frauen im Bauernkrieg ndin der Taüferbewegungen*, Frankfurt am Main, Campus, 1993.

- "Von "armen frowen" und "bösen wibern", Frauen Im Bauernkrieg zwischen Anpassung und Auflehnung", *Archiv für Reformationsgeshcichte*, 79, 1988, pp. 103-137.

Laqueur, Thomas, *Making Sex: Body and Gender from the Greeks to Freud*, Cambridge, Mass. and London: Harvard University Press, 1990.

Lerner, Gerda, *The Creation of Patriarchy*, Oxford and New York: Oxford University Press, 1986.

Leinhardt, Marc, "Luther and the Beginnings of the Reformation", in Jill Raitt, Bernard McGinn, and John Meyendorff, *Christian Spirituality, Vol 2,High Middle Ages and Reformation*, London: SCM, 1989. pp. 168-300.

Lorenz, Dagmar, "Vom Kloster zur Küche: Die frau vor und nach der reformation Dr Martin Luthers." in Barbara Becker-Cantarino, (ed) *Die Frau von der Reformation zur Romantik: Die Situation der Frau vor dem*

Hintergrund der Literatur- und Sozialgeschichte, Bonn, Bouvier, 1980.

Lumpkin, William L., *Baptist Confessions of Faith*, Valley Forge: Judson Press 1969.

MacCormack, Carol and Strathern, Marilyn (eds.), *Nature Culture and Gender*, Cambridge: Cambridge University Press, 1980.

McGinn, Bernard "The Changing Shape of Late Medieval Mysticism", *Church History*, vol 65, 1996, pp. 197-219.

McLaughlin, R. Emmet *Caspar Schwenckfeld,Reluctant Radical: his Life to 1540*, New Haven and London: Yale University Press, 1986.

- *The Freedom of the Spirit: Social Privilege and Religious Dissent, Caspar Schwenckfeld and the Schwenkfelders*, Bibliotheca Dissidentium, Scripta et studia, No. 6, Baden-Baden: v. Koerner, 1996.

McKee, Elsie Anne *Reforming Popular Piety in Sixteenth century Strasbourg: Katherina Schütz Zell and Her Hymnbook*, Studies in Reformed Theology, vol 2, Number 4, 1994.

- *The Writings of Katherina Schutz Zell*, Leiden: Brill, 1999.

Maclean, Ian, *The Renaissance Notion of Women*, Cambridge: Cambridge University Press, 1981.

McNamara, JoAnn and Wemple, Suzanne F., "Sanctity and Power: The Dual Pursuit of Medieval Women", in Renathe Bridenthal and Claudia Koonz, (eds) *Becoming Visible: Women in European History*, Boston: Houghton Mifflin, 1977.

Macy, Gary, "The Dogma of Transubstantiation in the Middle Ages", *Journal of Ecclesiastical History*, vol 45, 1995, pp. 11-41.

Maier, Paul, *Caspar Schwenckfeld on the Person and Work of Christ: A Study of Schwenckfeldian Theology at its Core*, Assen: Royal van Gorcum, 1959.

Maron ,Gottfried, *Individualismus und Gemeinschaft bei Caspar von Schwenckfeld: Seine Theologie dargestellt mit besonderer Ausrichtung auf seinem Kirchenbegriff*, Stuttgart: Evangelisches Verlagswerk, 1961.

Marr, Lucille M., "Anabaptist Women in the North: Peers in the Faith, Subordinate in Marriage", *Mennonite Quarterly Review*, 60, 1986, pp. 347-358.

Marshall, Sherrin, *Women in Reformation and Counter-Reformation Europe: Private and Public Worlds*, Bloomington: Indiana University Press, 1989.

Matheson, Peter, *Argula von Grumbach: A Woman's Voice in the Reformation*, Edinburgh: T&T Clark, 1995.

Moxey, Keith, *Peasants, Warriors and Wives: Popular Imagery in the Reformation*, Chicago and London: University of Chicago Press, 1989.

Müller, Max and Uhland Robert *Lebensbilder aus Schwaben und Franken, im Auftrag der Kommission fur geschichtliche Landeskunde in Baden-Wurrtemburg*, Stuttgart, 1960.

Murray, Jacqueline and Eisbenechler, Conrad, (eds) *Desire and Discipline: Sexand Sexuality in the Premodern West*, Toronto: University of Toronto

Press, 1996.

Muir, Edward, *Ritual in Early Modern Europe*, Cambridge: CambridgeUniversity Press, 1997.

Nowicki-Patuschka, Angelicka, *Frauen in der Reformation, Untersuchungenzum Verhalten von Frauen in der Reichstädten Augsburg und Nürnberg zur Reformatorischen Bewegung zwischen 1517 und 1537*, Bamberg, Pfaffenweiler Centaurus Verlagsgesellschaft, 1990.

Obelkevich, Jim, Roper, Lyndal, and Samuel, Raphael (eds.), *Disciplines of Faith: Studies in Religion, Politics and Patriarchy*, London: Routledge and Kegan Paul, 1987.

Oberman, Heiko A., *Luther, Man between God and the Devil*, translated Eileen Walliser-Schwarzbart, New Haven: Yale University Press 1989.

- "Teufelsdreck: Eschatology and Scatology in the "Old" Luther", *Sixteenth Century Journal*, vol 29, 1988, pp. pp. 435-450.

O'Neil, Mary, "Magical Healing, Love Magic and the Inquisition in Late Sixteenth Century Modena", in S.Haliczer, *Inquisition and Society in Early Modern Europe*, London, Croom Helm, 1987.

Oestreich, Gerhard, *Neostoicism and the Early Modern State*, trans. David McLintock, Cambridge: Cambridge University Press, 1982.

Ortner, Sherry B., "Is Female to Male as Nature is to Culture", in Michelle Z. Rosaldo, and Louise Lamphere, *Women, Culture and Society*, Stanford: Calif, Stanford University Press, 1976.

Ozment, Steven *Homo Spiritualis: A Comparative Study of the Anthropology of Johanner Tauler, Jean Gerson and Martin Luther (1509-1516) in the Context of the Their Theological Thought*, Leiden: E.J. Brill, 1969.

- *The Reformation in the Cities: The Appeal of Protestantism to 16ᵗʰ Century Germany and Switzerland*. New Haven and London: Yale University Press, 1975.

- *When Fathers Ruled: Family Life in Reformation Europe*, Cambridge, Mass and London: Harvard University Press, 1983.

Packull, Werner O., *Mysticism and the Early South German-Austrian Anabaptist Movement*, Scottdale, Pa: Herald Press, 1977.

- "The Schwenkfeldian Commentary on the Apocalypse", Peter Erb, (ed) *Schwenckfeld and Early Schwenkfeldianism: Papers Presented at the Colloquium on Schwenckfeld and the Schwenkfelders, September 17-22, 1984*, Pennsburg, Pa: The Schwenkfelder Library, 1986.

- "Anna Jansz of Rotterdam, a Historical Investigation of an early Anabaptist Heroine.", *Archiv Für Reformationsgeschichte*, vol 78, 1987, pp. 147-172.

Partner, Nancy F., "Did Mystics Have Sex?", in Jacqueline Murray and Conrad Eisbenechler, , (eds) *Desire and Discipline: Sex and Sexuality in the Premodern West*, Toronto: University of Toronto Press, 1996.

Pietz, Reinhold, *Der Mensch Ohne Christus (Eine Untersuchung zur Anthropologie Schwenckfelds)* Theolg Diss, Tubingern, 1956.

Pollock, Linda A., "Embarking on a rough passage: the experience of pregnancy in early modern society", in Valerie Fildes *Women as Mothers in Pre-industrial England: Essays in Memory of Dorothy McLaren,* London: Routledge, 1990.

Prior, Mary, *Women in English Society 1500-1800,* London: Methuen, 1986.

- "Reviled and Crucified Marriages: the position of Tudor Bishops' wives", in Mary Prior, *Women in English Society 1500-1800,* London: Methuen, 1986, pp 118-148.

Ranke-Heinemann, Uta, *Eunuchs for Heaven: The Catholic Church and Sexuality,* translated by John Brownjohn, London: Penguin, 1991.

Raitt, Jill, McGinn, Bernard and Meyendorff, John. *Christian Spirituality, Vol 2, High Middle Ages and Reformation,* London: SCM 1989.

Raitt, Jill, "Saints and Sinners: Roman Catholic and Protestant Spirituality in the Sixteenth century", in Jill Raitt,, Bernard McGinn, and John Meyendorff, *Christian Spirituality, Vol 2, High Middle Ages and Reformation,* London: SCM 1989.

Reinburg, Victoria, "Hearing Lay People's Prayer", in Barbara B Diefendorf, and Carla Hesse, *Culture and Identity in Early Modern Europe 1500-1800: Essays in Honor of Natalie Zemon Davis,* Ann Arbor: Michigan University Press, 1993.

Reinhard, Wolfgang, *Augsburger Eliten des 16 Jahrhunderts: Prosopgraphie wirschaftlicher und politischer Fuhrungsgruppen 1500-1620,* Berlin, Akademie, 1996.

Rempel, John D., *The Lord's Supper in Anabaptism: A Study in the Christology of Balthasar Hubmaier, Pilgram Marpeck and Dirk Philips.* Waterloo, Ont: University of Toronto 1993.

Ruether ,Rosemary Radford, *Sexism and God-Talk: Towards a Feminist Theology,* London: SCM, 1983.

Robinson, James M., *The Gospel of Thomas,* Leiden: Brill, 1984.

Roelker, Nancy L., "The Appeal of Calvinism to French Noblewomen of the Sixteenth-Century", *Journal of Interdisciplinary History,* volume II, 1972, pp. 391-418.

Roper, Lyndal, *The Holy Household: Women and Morals in Reformation Augsburg,* Oxford: Clarendon, 1989.

-*Oedipus and the Devil: Witchcraft, Sex and Religion in Early Modern Europe,* London: Routledge, 1994.

-"Sexual Utopianism in the German Reformation", *Journal of Ecclesiastical History,* 42, 191, pp. 394-418.

- "'The common man', 'the common good', 'common women': gender and meaning in the German Reformation Commune." *Social History,* 12 1987, pp. 1-21.

Rosaldo, Michelle Zimbalist and Lamphere, Louise, *Women, Culture and Society,* Stanford, Calif: Stanford University Press, 1976

Rubin, Miri, *Corpus Christi: The Eucharist in Late Medieval Culture,* Cambridge: Cambridge University Press, 1991.

- "The Person in the Form: medieval challenges to bodily order" in Sarah Kay, and Miri Rubin, *Framing Medieval Bodies*, Manchester: Manchester University Press, 1994.

Rublack, Ulinka, "Pregnancy, Childbirth and the Female Body in Early Modern Germany", *Past and Present*, vol 150, pp. 84-110.

Rushton, Peter, "Purification or Social Control? Ideologies of Reproduction and the Churching of Women after Childbirth", in Eva Gamarnikow, David H.J. Morhan., June Purvis and Daphne Taylorson, *The Public and the Private*, London: Heinemann, 1983.

Russell, Paul, A *Lay Theology in the Reformation:Popular Pamphleteers in South-west Germany, 1521-1525*, Cambridge: Cambridge University Press, 1986.

Sabean, David Warren, *Power in the Blood: Popular Culture and Village Discourse in Early Modern Germany*, Cambridge: Cambridge University Press, 1984.

Safley, Thomas M., "Civic Morality and the Domestic Economy", R. Po-Chia Hsia, *The German People and the Reformation*, Ithaca: Cornell University Press, 1988.

Schantz, Douglas H., "The Role of Valentine Crautwald in the Growth of Sixteenth Century Schwenkfeldian Reform: A New Look at the Crautwald-Schwenckfeld Relationship", *Mennonite Quarterly Review*, vol 65, 1991, pp. 287-307.

Schiess, Traugott, *Briefwechsel der Brüder Ambrosius und Thomas Blaurer 1509-1567*, Freiburg: 3Bd, 1908-1912.

Schulz, Selina Gerhardt, *Caspar Schwenckfeld von Ossig, (1489-1561) Spiritual Interpreter of Christianity, Apostle of the Middle Way, Pioneer of Modern Religious Thought*, Pennsburg, Pa, 1977.

Schüssler Fiorenza Elisabeth, *Jesus: Miriam's Child, Sophia's Prophet: Critical Issues in Feminist Theology*, London: SCM, 1995

Scribner, R., *Popular Culture and Popular Movements in ReformationGermany*, London: Hambledon, 1987.

Scott, Joan Wallach, *Gender and the Politics of History*, New York, Columbia University Press, 1988.

- *Feminism and History*, Oxford and New York: Oxford University Press, 1996.

- "Gender: A Useful Category of Historical Analysis", Scott, *Feminism and History*, Oxford and London: Oxford University Press, 1996.

Scott, Tom, *Thomas Müntzer: Theology and Revolution in the GermanReformation*, London: Macmillan, 1989.

Séguenny, Christopher, *The Christology of Caspar Schwenckfeld: Spirit andFlesh in the Process of Life Transformation*, trans Peter C. Erb and Simone Neiuwolt, New York: E Mellen, 1987.

Sessions, Kyle C. and Bebb, Phillip N., *Pietas et Societas: New Trends in Reformation Social History. Essays in Honour of Harold J. Grimm,*

Kirksville, Mo.: Sixteenth Century Journal Publishers, 1985.

Shiels, W.J. and Wood, Diana, *Women in the Church*, Oxford: Basil Blackwell, 1990.

Shorter, Edward, *A History of Women's Bodies*, London: Allen Lane, 1983.

Sieh-Burens, Katarina, *Oligarchie, Konfession und Politik Politik im Jarhundert zur sozialenVerflechtung der Ausburger Burgermeister und Stadtpfleger 1518-1618,* Munchen: Vogel

Snyder ,C Arnold and Huebert Hecht, Linda A., *Profiles of Anabaptist Women: Sixteenth Century Reforming Pioneers*, Waterloo, Ont: Wilfrid Laurier University Press, 1996.

Sporhan-Krempel, Lore, "Agathe Streicher", Max Müller and Robert Uhland, *Lebensbilder aus Schwaben und Franken,im Auftrag der Kommission fur geschichtkliche Landeskunde in baden-Wurrtemberg* Stuttgart, 1960.

Steinberg, Leo, *The Sexuality of Christ in Renaissance Art and Modern Oblivion*, London: Faber, 1984.

Stephens, W.P., *The Theology of Huldrych Zwingli*, Oxford: Clarendon, 1986.

Stone, Lawrence, *The Family, Sex and Marriage in England, 1500-1800*, London: Penguin, 1990.

Strauss, Gerald, *Luther's House of Learning: Indoctrination of the Young in Reformation Germany*, Baltimore and London: John Hopkins University Press, 1978.

Stratton, Suzanne L., *The Immaculate Conception in Spanish Art*, Cambridge: Cambridge University Press, 1994

Strehle, Stephen, "Fides aut Foedus: Wittenberg and Zurich in conflict over the Gospel." *Sixteenth Century Journal*, vol 23, 1992, pp. 3-20.

Tentler, Thomas N., *Sin and Confession on the Eve of the Reformation,* Princeton, Guildford: Princeton University Press, 1977.

Thelwell, Rev S. *Ante-Nicene Fathers*, n.d.

Thomas, Keith, *Religion and the Decline of Magic*, London: Wiedenfeld and Nicolson, 1991.

Thompson, John L., *John Calvin and the Daughters of Sarah: Women in Regular and Exceptional Roles in the Exegesis of Calvin; His Predecessors and His Contemporaries*, Geneva: Librarie Droz S.A. 1992.

Tripp, D.H., "The Protestant Reformation", in Cheslyn Jones, Geoffrey Wainwright and Edward Yarnold S.J., *The Study of Spirituality*, London: SPCK, 1986.

- "Luther" in Cheslyn Jones, Geoffrey Wainwright and Edward Yarnold S.J., *The Study of Spirituality*, London: SPCK, 1986.

Turner, James Gratham, (ed) *Sexuality and Gender in Early Modern Europe: institutions, texts, images*, Cambridge: Cambridge University Press, 1993.

Umble, Jennifer Hiett, "Women and Choice: An Examination of the Martyrs' Mirror", *Mennonite Quarterly Review*, 64, April 1990, pp. 135-145.

Walsh, Walter, *Women Martyrs of the Reformation*, London: Religious Tract Society, n.d.

Webb, Diana M., "Woman and Home: The Domestic Setting of Late Medieval Spirituality", in W.J. Shiels and Diana Wood (eds) *Women in the Church*, Oxford: Basil Blackwell, 1990.

Weber, Franz Michael, *Kaspar Schwenckfeld und Seine Anhänger in den freybergischen Herrschaften Justingen und Öpfingen*, Stuttgart, 1962.

Weigelt, Horst, *The Schwenckfelders in Silesia*, Pennsburg, Pa, The Schwenkfelder Library, 1985.

Wiesner, Merry E., *Women and Gender in Early Modern Europe*. Cambridge: Cambridge University Press, 1993.

- *Gender, Church and State in Early Modern Germany*, London: Longman, 1998

Wiesner , Merry, "Beyond Women and the Family: Towards a Gender Analysis of the Reformation", *Sixteenth Century Journal*, XVIII, 1987, pp. 311-322.

- "The Death of the Two Marys", Jim Obelkevich, Lyndal Roper, and Raphael Samuel, (eds) *Disciplines of Faith: Studies in Religion , Politics and Patriarchy*, London: Routledge and Kegan Paul, 1987.

- "Women's response to the Reformation", in R. Po-chia Hsia, ed. *The German People and the Reformation*, Ithaca: Cornell University Press, 1988, pp. 148-171.

- "Nuns, Wives, Mothers: Women and the Reformation in Germany", in Sherrin Marshall, (ed) *Women in Reformation and Counter-Reformation Europe:Private and Public Worlds*, Bloomington: Indiana University Press, 1989.

Wiethaus, Ulrike, "Sexuality, Gender and the Body in Late Medieval Women's Spirituality: Cases from Germany and the Netherlands", *Journal of Feminist Studies in Religion*, vol 7, pp. 35-52.

Williams, G. H., *The Radical Reformation*, Third Edition, Kirkville, Mo.: Sixteenth Century Journal Publishers, 1992.

Wilson, Adrian, "The ceremony of childbirth and its interpretation.", Valerie Fildes, *Women as Mothers in Pre-industrial England: Essays in Memory of Dorothy McLaren,* London: Routledge, 1990.

Wiltenburg, Joy, *Disorderly Women and Female Power in the Street Literature of Early Modern England and Germany*, Charlottesville and London: University Press of Virginia, 1992.

Wogan-Browne, Jocelyn, "Chaste Bodies: Frames and Experiences", in Sarah Kay, and Miri Rubin, *Framing Medieval Bodies*, Manchester: Manchester University Press, 1994.

Wolfson, Harry Austryn, *The Philosophy of the Church Fathers: Faith, Trinity and Incarnation*, Cambridge, Massachusetts and London: Harvard University Press, 1976.

Wunder, Heide, *'He is the Sun, She is the Moon': women in early modern Germany*, translated by Thomas Dunlap, Cambridge, Mass and London, Harvard University Press, 1998.

Wyntjes, Sherrin Marshall, "Women in the Reformation Era", in Renathe

Bridenthal, and Claudia Koonz,. *Becoming Visible: Women in European History*, Boston: Houghton Mifflin, 1977.

- "Women and Religious Choice in Sixteenth Century Netherlands", *Archiv für Reformationsgeschichte*, 75, 1984, pp. 276-289.

Yost, John K., "The Reformation Defense of Clerical Marriage in the Reigns of Henry VIII and EdwardVI", *Church History*, vol 50, 1981, pp. 152-165.

Zagorin, Perez, *Rebels and Rulers, 1500-1660*, Cambridge: Cambridge University Press, 1982.

Zika, Charles, "Hosts, Processions and Pilgrimages: Controlling the Sacred in Fifteenth Century Germany", *Past and Present*, 1988, pp. 25-64.

Zophy, Jonathan W., "We must have the Dear Ladies: Martin Luther and Women" ,in Sessions, Kyle C. and Bebb, Phillip N. *Pietas et Societas: New Trends in Reformation Social History. Essays in Honour of Harold J. Grimm*, Kirksville, Mo.: Sixteenth Century journal Publishers, 1985.

Index

Studies in Christian History and Thought
(All titles uniform with this volume)
Dates in bold are of projected publication

David Bebbington
Holiness in Nineteenth-Century England
David Bebbington stresses the relationship of movements of spirituality to changes in their cultural setting, especially the legacies of the Enlightenment and Romanticism. He shows that these broad shifts in ideological mood had a profound effect on the ways in which piety was conceptualized and practised. Holiness was intimately bound up with the spirit of the age.
2000 / 0-85364-981-2 / viii + 98pp

J. William Black
Reformation Pastors
Richard Baxter and the Ideal of the Reformed Pastor
This work examines Richard Baxter's *Gildas Salvianus, The Reformed Pastor* (1656) and explores each aspect of his pastoral strategy in light of his own concern for 'reformation' and in the broader context of Edwardian, Elizabethan and early Stuart pastoral ideals and practice.
2003 / 1-84227-190-3 / xxii + 308pp

James Bruce
Prophecy, Miracles, Angels, *and* Heavenly Light?
The Eschatology, Pneumatology and Missiology of Adomnán's Life of Columba
This book surveys approaches to the marvellous in hagiography, providing the first critique of Plummer's hypothesis of Irish saga origin. It then analyses the uniquely systematized phenomena in the *Life of Columba* from Adomnán's seventh-century theological perspective, identifying the coming of the eschatological Kingdom as the key to understanding.
2004 / 1-84227-227-6 / xviii + 286pp

Colin J. Bulley
The Priesthood of Some Believers
Developments from the General to the Special Priesthood in the Christian Literature of the First Three Centuries
The first in-depth treatment of early Christian texts on the priesthood of all believers shows that the developing priesthood of the ordained related closely to the division between laity and clergy and had deleterious effects on the practice of the general priesthood.
2000 / 1-84227-034-6 / xii + 336pp

Anthony R. Cross (ed.)
Ecumenism and History
Studies in Honour of John H.Y. Briggs
This collection of essays examines the inter-relationships between the two fields in which Professor Briggs has contributed so much: history—particularly Baptist and Nonconformist—and the ecumenical movement. With contributions from colleagues and former research students from Britain, Europe and North America, *Ecumenism and History* provides wide-ranging studies in important aspects of Christian history, theology and ecumenical studies.
2002 / 1-84227-135-0 / xx + 362pp

Maggi Dawn
Confessions of an Inquiring Spirit
Form as Constitutive of Meaning in S.T. Coleridge's Theological Writing
This study of Coleridge's *Confessions* focuses on its confessional, epistolary and fragmentary form, suggesting that attention to these features significantly affects its interpretation. Bringing a close study of these three literary forms, the author suggests ways in which they nuance the text with particular understandings of the Trinity, and of a kenotic christology. Some parallels are drawn between Romantic and postmodern dilemmas concerning the authority of the biblical text.
2006 / 1-84227-255-1 / approx. 224 pp

Ruth Gouldbourne
The Flesh and the Feminine
Gender and Theology in the Writings of Caspar Schwenckfeld
Caspar Schwenckfeld and his movement exemplify one of the radical communities of the sixteenth century. Challenging theological and liturgical norms, they also found themselves challenging social and particularly gender assumptions. In this book, the issues of the relationship between radical theology and the understanding of gender are considered.
2005 / 1-84227-048-6 / approx. 304pp

Crawford Gribben
Puritan Millennialism
Literature and Theology, 1550–1682
Puritan Millennialism surveys the growth, impact and eventual decline of puritan millennialism throughout England, Scotland and Ireland, arguing that it was much more diverse than has frequently been suggested. This Paternoster edition is revised and extended from the original 2000 text.
2007 / 1-84227-372-8 / approx. 320pp

Galen K. Johnson
Prisoner of Conscience
John Bunyan on Self, Community and Christian Faith
This is an interdisciplinary study of John Bunyan's understanding of conscience across his autobiographical, theological and fictional writings, investigating whether conscience always deserves fidelity, and how Bunyan's view of conscience affects his relationship both to modern Western individualism and historic Christianity.

2003 / 1-84227-223-3 / xvi + 236pp

R.T. Kendall
Calvin and English Calvinism to 1649
The author's thesis is that those who formed the Westminster Confession of Faith, which is regarded as Calvinism, in fact departed from John Calvin on two points: (1) the extent of the atonement and (2) the ground of assurance of salvation.

1997 / 0-85364-827-1 / xii + 264pp

Timothy Larsen
Friends of Religious Equality
Nonconformist Politics in Mid-Victorian England
During the middle decades of the nineteenth century the English Nonconformist community developed a coherent political philosophy of its own, of which a central tenet was the principle of religious equality (in contrast to the stereotype of Evangelical Dissenters). The Dissenting community fought for the civil rights of Roman Catholics, non-Christians and even atheists on an issue of principle which had its flowering in the enthusiastic and undivided support which Nonconformity gave to the campaign for Jewish emancipation. This reissued study examines the political efforts and ideas of English Nonconformists during the period, covering the whole range of national issues raised, from state education to the Crimean War. It offers a case study of a theologically conservative group defending religious pluralism in the civic sphere, showing that the concept of religious equality was a grand vision at the centre of the political philosophy of the Dissenters.

2007 / 1-84227-402-3 / x + 300pp

Byung-Ho Moon
Christ the Mediator of the Law
Calvin's Christological Understanding of the Law as the Rule of Living and Life-Giving
This book explores the coherence between Christology and soteriology in Calvin's theology of the law, examining its intellectual origins and his position on the concept and extent of Christ's mediation of the law. A comparative study between Calvin and contemporary Reformers—Luther, Bucer, Melancthon and Bullinger—and his opponent Michael Servetus is made for the purpose of pointing out the unique feature of Calvin's Christological understanding of the law.
2005 / 1-84227-318-3 / approx. 370pp

John Eifion Morgan-Wynne
Holy Spirit and Religious Experience in Christian Writings, c.AD 90–200
This study examines how far Christians in the third to fifth generations (c.AD 90–200) attributed their sense of encounter with the divine presence, their sense of illumination in the truth or guidance in decision-making, and their sense of ethical empowerment to the activity of the Holy Spirit in their lives.
2005 / 1-84227-319-1 / approx. 350pp

James I. Packer
The Redemption and Restoration of Man in the Thought of Richard Baxter
James I. Packer provides a full and sympathetic exposition of Richard Baxter's doctrine of humanity, created and fallen; its redemption by Christ Jesus; and its restoration in the image of God through the obedience of faith by the power of the Holy Spirit.
2002 / 1-84227-147-4 / 432pp

Andrew Partington,
Church and State
The Contribution of the Church of England Bishops to the House of Lords
during the Thatcher Years
In *Church and State*, Andrew Partington argues that the contribution of the
Church of England bishops to the House of Lords during the Thatcher years was
overwhelmingly critical of the government; failed to have a significant influence
in the public realm; was inefficient, being undertaken by a minority of those
eligible to sit on the Bench of Bishops; and was insufficiently moral and
spiritual in its content to be distinctive. On the basis of this, and the likely
reduction of the number of places available for Church of England bishops in a
fully reformed Second Chamber, the author argues for an evolution in the
Church of England's approach to the service of its bishops in the House of
Lords. He proposes the Church of England works to overcome the genuine
obstacles which hinder busy diocesan bishops from contributing to the debates
of the House of Lords and to its life more informally.
2005 / 1-84227-334-5 / approx. 324pp

Michael Pasquarello III
God's Ploughman
Hugh Latimer: A 'Preaching Life' (1490–1555)
This construction of a 'preaching life' situates Hugh Latimer within the larger
religious, political and intellectual world of late medieval England. Neither
biography, intellectual history, nor analysis of discrete sermon texts, this book is
a work of homiletic history which draws from the details of Latimer's milieu to
construct an interpretive framework for the preaching performances that formed
the core of his identity as a religious reformer. Its goal is to illumine the
practical wisdom embodied in the content, form and style of Latimer's
preaching, and to recapture a sense of its overarching purpose, movement, and
transforming force during the reform of sixteenth-century England.
2006 / 1-84227-336-1 / approx. 250pp

Alan P.F. Sell
Enlightenment, Ecumenism, Evangel
Theological Themes and Thinkers 1550–2000
This book consists of papers in which such interlocking topics as the
Enlightenment, the problem of authority, the development of doctrine,
spirituality, ecumenism, theological method and the heart of the gospel are
discussed. Issues of significance to the church at large are explored with special
reference to writers from the Reformed and Dissenting traditions.
2005 / 1-84227-330-2 / xviii + 422pp

Alan P.F. Sell
Hinterland Theology
Some Reformed and Dissenting Adjustments
Many books have been written on theology's 'giants' and significant trends, but what of those lesser-known writers who adjusted to them? In this book some hinterland theologians of the British Reformed and Dissenting traditions, who followed in the wake of toleration, the Evangelical Revival, the rise of modern biblical criticism and Karl Barth, are allowed to have their say. They include Thomas Ridgley, Ralph Wardlaw, T.V. Tymms and N.H.G. Robinson.
2006 / 1-84227-331-0 / approx. 350pp

Alan P.F. Sell and Anthony R. Cross (eds)
Protestant Nonconformity in the Twentieth Century
In this collection of essays scholars representative of a number of Nonconformist traditions reflect thematically on Nonconformists' life and witness during the twentieth century. Among the subjects reviewed are biblical studies, theology, worship, evangelism and spirituality, and ecumenism. Over and above its immediate interest, this collection provides a marker to future scholars and others wishing to know how some of their forebears assessed Nonconformity's contribution to a variety of fields during the century leading up to Christianity's third millennium.
2003 / 1-84227-221-7 / x + 398pp

Mark Smith
Religion in Industrial Society
Oldham and Saddleworth 1740–1865
This book analyses the way British churches sought to meet the challenge of industrialization and urbanization during the period 1740–1865. Working from a case-study of Oldham and Saddleworth, Mark Smith challenges the received view that the Anglican Church in the eighteenth century was characterized by complacency and inertia, and reveals Anglicanism's vigorous and creative response to the new conditions. He reassesses the significance of the centrally directed church reforms of the mid-nineteenth century, and emphasizes the importance of local energy and enthusiasm. Charting the growth of denominational pluralism in Oldham and Saddleworth, Dr Smith compares the strengths and weaknesses of the various Anglican and Nonconformist approaches to promoting church growth. He also demonstrates the extent to which all the churches participated in a common culture shaped by the influence of evangelicalism, and shows that active co-operation between the churches rather than denominational conflict dominated. This revised and updated edition of Dr Smith's challenging and original study makes an important contribution both to the social history of religion and to urban studies.
2006 / 1-84227-335-3 / approx. 300pp

July 2005

Martin Sutherland
Peace, Toleration and Decay
The Ecclesiology of Later Stuart Dissent
This fresh analysis brings to light the complexity and fragility of the later Stuart Nonconformist consensus. Recent findings on wider seventeenth-century thought are incorporated into a new picture of the dynamics of Dissent and the roots of evangelicalism.
2003 / 1-84227-152-0 / xxii + 216pp

G. Michael Thomas
The Extent of the Atonement
A Dilemma for Reformed Theology from Calvin to the Consensus
A study of the way Reformed theology addressed the question, 'Did Christ die for all, or for the elect only?', commencing with John Calvin, and including debates with Lutheranism, the Synod of Dort and the teaching of Moïse Amyraut.
1997 / 0-85364-828-X / x + 278pp

David M. Thompson
Baptism, Church and Society in Britain from the Evangelical Revival to
Baptism, Eucharist and Ministry
The theology and practice of baptism have not received the attention they deserve. How important is faith? What does baptismal regeneration mean? Is baptism a bond of unity between Christians? This book discusses the theology of baptism and popular belief and practice in England and Wales from the Evangelical Revival to the publication of the World Council of Churches' consensus statement on *Baptism, Eucharist and Ministry* (1982).
2005 / 1-84227-393-0 / approx. 224pp

Mark D. Thompson
A Sure Ground on Which to Stand
The Relation of Authority and Interpretive Method of Luther's Approach to Scripture
The best interpreter of Luther is Luther himself. Unfortunately many modern studies have superimposed contemporary agendas upon this sixteenth-century Reformer's writings. This fresh study examines Luther's own words to find an explanation for his robust confidence in the Scriptures, a confidence that generated the famous 'stand' at Worms in 1521.
2004 / 1-84227-145-8 / xvi + 322pp

Carl R. Trueman and R.S. Clark (eds)
Protestant Scholasticism
Essays in Reassessment
Traditionally Protestant theology, between Luther's early reforming career and
the dawn of the Enlightenment, has been seen in terms of decline and fall into
the wastelands of rationalism and scholastic speculation. In this volume a
number of scholars question such an interpretation. The editors argue that the
development of post-Reformation Protestantism can only be understood when a
proper historical model of doctrinal change is adopted. This historical concern
underlies the subsequent studies of theologians such as Calvin, Beza, Olevian,
Baxter, and the two Turrentini. The result is a significantly different reading of
the development of Protestant Orthodoxy, one which both challenges the older
scholarly interpretations and clichés about the relationship of Protestantism to,
among other things, scholasticism and rationalism, and which demonstrates the
fruitfulness of the new, historical approach.
1999 / 0-85364-853-0 / xx + 344pp

Shawn D. Wright
Our Sovereign Refuge
The Pastoral Theology of Theodore Beza
Our Sovereign Refuge is a study of the pastoral theology of the Protestant
reformer who inherited the mantle of leadership in the Reformed church from
John Calvin. Countering a common view of Beza as supremely a 'scholastic'
theologian who deviated from Calvin's biblical focus, Wright uncovers a new
portrait. He was not a cold and rigid academic theologian obsessed with probing
the eternal decrees of God. Rather, by placing him in his pastoral context and by
noting his concerns in his pastoral and biblical treatises, Wright shows that Beza
was fundamentally a committed Christian who was troubled by the vicissitudes
of life in the second half of the sixteenth century. He believed that the biblical
truth of the supreme sovereignty of God alone could support Christians on their
earthly pilgrimage to heaven. This pastoral and personal portrait forms the heart
of Wright's argument. *2004 / 1-84227-252-7 / xviii + 308pp*

Paternoster
9 Holdom Avenue,
Bletchley,
Milton Keynes MK1 1QR,
United Kingdom
Web: www.authenticmedia.co.uk/paternoster